THE VICTORIANS

# The Victorians

## *An Age in Retrospect*

John Gardiner

Hambledon and London

London and New York

Hambledon and London
102 Gloucester Avenue
London, NW1 8HX

838 Broadway
New York
NY 10003–4812

First Published 2002

ISBN 1 85285 385 9

A description of this book is available from the
British Library and from the Library of Congress.

Typeset by Carnegie Publishing, Lancaster

Printed on woodfree paper and bound in
Great Britain by Bath Press, Bath

# Contents

# Illustrations

# *Preface*

One evening in the spring of 1916 a willowy man with large brown eyes, slightly bulbous nose and long reddish-brown beard, a tartan travel rug clutched beneath his arm, slowly made his way into the council chamber of Hampstead Town Hall. He was Giles Lytton Strachey, a thirty-six-year-old minor man of letters, homosexual, and habitual frequenter of Bloomsbury. He was attending a tribunal convened to pass judgement on his refusal to join the army after the introduction of military conscription several months earlier.[1]

Strachey's behaviour at this tribunal proved to be eccentric in the extreme. The magistrates were obliged to wait while he inflated an air cushion to place on the wooden bench of the council chamber (he was, admittedly, a martyr to his posterior). Later, asked what he would do if a German soldier tried to rape his sister, he replied that he would try to put himself between them. Strachey, for all his nerves, had decided to play quite literally to his friends and supporters in the gallery – and in a way to posterity, too. For in mocking the assembled dignitaries and all that they stood for – patriotism, duty, respectability, authority – Strachey was taking issue with the accumulated weight of Victorian tradition.

In slyly deriding these pompous old men, Strachey had been obliged to take time away from his current literary project. This was a book which would appear two years later with the title *Eminent Victorians*. It was to have a huge impact not only upon Strachey's celebrity and the art of biography, but upon the very way in which the Victorians were seen. The style and theme of this irreverent book were to resonate throughout the twentieth century, often chiming with or informing fashionable views of who the Victorians had been. Back in the bloodbath of the First World War, his 'teeth chattering with fury' as he once put it, Strachey announced a view of the Victorians with which we have become familiar. It was a view which he was to elaborate in many subsequent writings. Take, for example, this haunting, surreal vision of mid-Victorian bourgeois existence, from Strachey's 1928 review of the letters of Thomas Carlyle:

[Mrs Carlyle's] tragedy may be traced in those inimitable letters, whose intoxi-
cating merriment flashes like lightning about the central figure, as it moves in
sinister desolation against the background of a most peculiar age: an age of
barbarism and prudery, of nobility and cheapness, of satisfaction and desperation;
an age in which all the outlines were tremendous and all the details sordid; when
gas-jets struggled feebly through the circumambient fog, when the hour of dinner
might be at any moment between two and six, when the doses of rhubarb were
periodic and gigantic, when pet dogs threw themselves out of upper storey
windows, when cooks reeled drunk in areas, when one sat for hours with one's
feet in dirty straw dragged along the street by horses, when an antimacassar was
on every chair, and the baths were minute tin circles, and the beds were full of
bugs and disasters.[2]

Strachey was not the first critic of the Victorians, nor would he be the
last. But, by the end of the twetieth century, criticism of this sort had become
highly influential in generating a negative view of the Victorian age. This
book is about how far such a view seized the imaginations of contemporaries
and descendants, and about how it was rivalled by other views of the past.
In short, it is a study of the changing reputation of the Victorians in the
twentieth century.

# Acknowledgements

The shade of Matthew Arnold hovers over this book in a number of places. There are not a great many Arnoldian institutions still in existence, but I wish to signal my debt to two of them. For many years I have profited from the resources and professionalism of Sittingbourne Public Library. I owe an even greater debt to that Arnoldian place across the road, Borden Grammar School.

I have had a most rewarding time trying out some of my ideas about the impact of the Victorians on the twentieth century while teaching a course at Queen Mary, University of London. For particular kindnesses at Queen Mary I wish to thank David Brooks, Virginia Davis, Peter Hennessy and John Ramsden. Hugh Cunningham has offered invaluable encouragement and expertise since I began working on the Victorians about five years ago. Stephen Bann and David Cannadine have also made useful suggestions as to how my work might be developed. I have benefited from a studentship from the Humanities Research Board of the British Academy. Parts of this book have already appeared in articles in *Historical Research* and *History Workshop Journal*, and I am grateful to the editors of those journals for permission to reuse material.

The authors and publishers are grateful to the following for permission to reproduce illustrations: the BBC, pl. 14; the Imperial War Museum, pl. 13; A. F. Kersting, pl. 16; King's College, Cambridge, pl. 11; Michael Holroyd and the Estate of Lytton Strachey, pl. 9; the National Portrait Gallery, pls 5, 7, 8, 10, 12; Royal Holloway, University of London, pl. 4; Samuelson Productions, pl. 15.

Affectionate thanks go to friends who have continued to offer help and support: David Allinson, Chris Baker, Lee Byrne, Richard and Jean Carter, David Dagnall, Alun Davies, Neil and Julie Simons, John Threadgold, Peter Ward, Matt Whitehead and David Winspur.

At Hambledon and London I have benefited from the enthusiasm and skill of Tony Morris and Martin Sheppard. They have helped to make working on this book a great pleasure, and I hope that some of that pleasure communicates itself.

My greatest debt, however, is to my relatives. I thank my grandparents and my brother, Jamie, for their encouragement across the years. Above all, I thank my parents, John and Glenis, without whose moral and material support this book – and much else – would not have been possible.

PART ONE

*Themes*

# 1

## The Victorians

Who were these people that Lytton Strachey took such sly pleasure in deriding? This is not at all an easy question to answer. Fools and satirists rush in where angels (and historians) fear to tread. It was this very sense of slaphappy generalisation that imparted to Strachey's barbs much of their lethal edge. The notion that an age teeming with incidents and personalities could be reduced to a few glib formulae was a profound insult both to the Victorians and to history itself. (It had added effrontery because the Victorians had seen history as a kind of divine commentary on their own achievements.) One of Strachey's sternest critics, himself recognisably a Victorian who had laid eyes on Queen Victoria and William Gladstone, was G. M. Young. His *Portrait of an Age: Victorian England* (1936), a work of enormous erudition and dense with classical allusions, claimed to be no more than that – a 'portrait' that was impressionistic in places, reflecting as much as anything else the temperament of the artist.

The charges made by Strachey and his intellectual descendants against the Victorians will surely stand unless we try to make some sense of the crinoline and antimacassars, the gilt-clasped Bibles and bristling whiskers, the smoking factories and Neo-Gothic spires. We can all readily identify one or two characteristics popularly associated with the Victorian age. Prudish, we might suggest, or old-fashioned, the 'Victorian' a synonym for people who led lives as tightly-corseted in the mind as they were in the flesh. In fact, these are the very terms – 'prudish, strict; old-fashioned, out-dated' – which the Supplement to the *Oxford English Dictionary* cites as a standard definition of 'Victorian' from as early as 1934.[1] That, of course, says more about the changing fortunes of an age in retrospect than it does about the Victorians.

Contemporaries themselves first used the adjective 'Victorian' in 1839, two years after the accession of the eponymous queen.[2] Then the word had all the appeal of novelty, and had yet to be filled out and find its own set of resonances. Many such new-minted historical terms fail to do this: the 'New Elizabethanism' of the early 1950s did not sustain itself, partly because Britain at that point was still in thrall to its past. The Victorian age had a remarkable

afterlife. Winston Churchill, born when Queen Elizabeth II's great-grandfather was a mere boy, dotingly trailed after the new monarch as Lord
Melbourne to her young Victoria. The libretto of Benjamin Britten's coronation opera, *Gloriana*, ironically came straight from the pages of Strachey's
*Elizabeth and Essex*. (Nobody thought to blame the opera's underwhelming
premiere on that most disaffected of Victorians.) [3]

In 1837, when Queen Victoria came to the throne, the only emotional
baggage left behind was that of her dreadful uncles, and this was unequi-
vocally set to be thrown out. George IV – more pantomime dame, perhaps,
in his bewigged and berouged corpulence – died of the uniquely Georgian-
sounding ailment of 'obesity of the heart', an overdose of laudanum
notwithstanding. He had already scandalised the nation by marrying to clear
his debts with Parliament and subsequently abandoning his bride; she turned
up some years later at his coronation, hammering in vain on the doors of
Westminster Abbey for access. His successor, another uncle of Victoria,
was William IV, a sailor who found himself run aground on the throne of
Britain. 'His Majesty has an easy and natural way', Washington Irving
observed, 'of wiping his nose with the back of his forefinger which, I fancy,
is a relic of his middy habits.' [4]

When William died there was a palpable feeling of excitement at the
prospect of a fresh start. Whether the eighteen-year-old Victoria really did
proclaim, on hearing of the fall of the curtain on the Georgian age, 'I will
be good', later Victorians wove it into the fabric of the tale they liked fondly
to recount of their own era. And, in the case of Victoria, fortune conspired
with the years to make this tale one of epic proportions, and to give the
adjective derived from her name lasting power. She lived sufficiently long
to impart to an age of unprecedented change and complexity the epithet
'Victorian'. This became an adjective filled out, stretched, over-stretched
and continually re-invented to describe all manner of things that occurred
in the space of sixty-four eventful years.

The Victorians themselves tried to make sense of this teeming complexity
by dividing the age up into 'early', 'mid-' and (by implication) 'late' Victorian
phases. (One recent commentator, sensibly trying to indicate the different
connotations of the term, is wrong to suggest that the Victorians did not
think of themselves as 'Victorian'.) [5] Historians in the twentieth century
followed suit, seeing the early Victorian period (1837 to around 1850) as a
rather turbulent time of adapting to industrial life; the mid-Victorian period
(around 1851 to 1870) as a time of relative peace and prosperity; and the late
Victorian period (after around 1870) as a time in which all was subject again
to challenge and change. Still, the general adjective retained much of its
resonance. By the time of Victoria's death on 22 January 1901, almost exactly

on cue for the new century, the term 'Victorian' sat like some awesome monolith, staring modernity in the face with a sphinx-like countenance. Only those who got closer could see this inscrutability for what it was – a mass of contradictory impressions and details. But few at the time were able to achieve such objectivity, and the long search for independent perspectives and real meanings, whether to reject or to rehabilitate, is the subject of this book.

Writers like Lytton Strachey and Virginia Woolf described the beginning of the Victorian age as the descent of some dismal cloud over Britain. For them, the outlines of Victorianism soon became apparent. 'Duty, industry, morality and domesticity triumphed', Strachey reflected of Prince Albert's rearrangement of the royal household. 'Even the very chairs and tables had assumed, with a higher responsiveness, the forms of prim solidity. The Victorian Age was in full swing.'[6] For more favourable commentators, too, 1837 was a watershed in history. When Queen Victoria died there were few newspapers that did not comment on the end of an era which had opened sixty-four years earlier – or, as many pointed out with even greater precision, sixty-three years, seven months and two days before. 'Epochs sometimes find names that do not very accurately fit them,' commented The Times on 23 January 1901, 'but we can speak with singular accuracy of the Victorian age.'[7]

Victorianism was not, however, simply a reaction against the more dissolute aspects of the Georgian period: the gin-swilling, cranium-cracking, bed-hopping rake's progress depicted by Hogarth. The Victorian middle classes did come to worship the home with almost religious fervour, sanctifying it as a retreat from the modern world and barricading themselves behind heavy furniture and an army of ornaments and knick-knacks. Here the bourgeois couple par excellence was Victoria and Albert, no doubt mindful of the less than exemplary domestic record of some of their forebears. Prince Albert brought the Christmas tree to Britain; and Charles Dickens provided the sentiment and fireside cosiness – at least one way of reading his work, consumed voraciously by Victorian readers in serial form, is as a prolonged exhortation to domestic-mindedness.

Yet it is worth bearing in mind that Victoria and Dickens, born respectively in 1819 and 1812, were both Regency figures: the school for Victorianism had opened its doors long before 1837. Britain in the eighteenth century had come to enjoy an international reputation for its polite and commercial people. The origins of Victorian decorum and gentility are to be found in the drive towards 'politeness' after the bloodshed and bitterness of the seventeenth century.[8] Artistic networks developed in the eighteenth century, speeded along by technological innovation and mounting prosperity. The very idea of 'culture' as a matter of breeding and high

art, passionately taken up by Victorians like Matthew Arnold, owed itself
in large part to an earlier age increasingly divorced from the countryside,
conscious of a need for national 'heritage', and with new middle-class
consumers to pay for it. Romanticism, wild-haired and impetuous, was
waiting in the wings; sensibility – the powerful, spontaneous reaction to
impressions – became ever more marked, so that Jane Austen felt compelled
in 1811 to contrast it (not altogether favourably) with sense. The Victorians,
with their animal paintings and perfumed poetry, turned sentimentality
into an art form, but they inherited much from the late eighteenth-century
softening of Enlightenment rationality.

Nor did they invent, more importantly, the profound religious sense that
underpinned almost the entire Victorian age. 'No one will ever understand
Victorian England', wrote the historian R. C. K. Ensor, 'who does not appreciate that among highly civilized ... countries it was one of the most
religious that the world has known.'[9] Faith began to crumble in the later
nineteenth century under the impact of evolutionary theory and agnosticism,
but even its very absence could generate a powerful atmosphere. In William
Dyce's painting *Pegwell Bay* (1859–60) the human figures seem very small
and lonely against the backdrop of the ancient cliffs, their craggy profile full
of the fossil evidence that would bring the faith of many individuals crashing
down. And in Matthew Arnold's majestic poem *Dover Beach* (1867) it is
again the shore that is the most appropriate setting for the 'melancholy,
long, withdrawing roar' of the Sea of Faith. The crisis of faith showed many
Victorians at their most Victorian: or at least, we might say, grappling so
earnestly with issues as to imbue their work with a lasting existence they
were not sure of in their own lives. Agnostics, in an age where agnosticism
was an ethical choice rather than a matter of simple indifference, often
displayed an earnestness and delicate appreciation of the human predica-
ment. George Eliot, for example, concluded *Middlemarch* (1872) with words
about 'the growing good of the world' being 'dependent on unhistoric acts'
from those 'who lived faithfully a hidden life, and rest in unvisited tombs'.[10]
Whatever the state of their spiritual affairs, few educated Victorians could
escape the prevailing mood of moral earnestness.

Much of this moral impulse owed itself to the evangelical revival of the
eighteenth century, most famously symbolised by John Wesley and the
Methodist movement. Evangelicals of various persuasions felt themselves
personally accountable to God: in the driven quality of Lord Shaftesbury's
campaign to improve factory and mine conditions, or in Gladstone's painstaking diary account of nearly every waking moment of his life, we can see
something of its legacy. The missionary impulse remained very strong
throughout the Victorian age and long into the twentieth century, as an

organisation like the Salvation Army shows. This developed from a mission settlement by William and Catherine Booth, both Methodists, to the East End in the 1860s. Missionaries were by no means restricted to far-flung parts of the empire: just as many could be found in Britain, working earnestly to bring the gospel to those who had not seen the light. Religious folk had, after all, been appalled by a census in 1851 showing that a 'mere' 40 per cent of adults attended church.[11] Many of those who did not attend were working-class, and so they became the natural target of bright-eyed missionary workers. Those who inhabited the narrow, dark East End streets prowled in the late 1880s by Jack the Ripper stood a better chance (and better fortune) in encountering future politicians, and in one case a future Prime Minister in the shape of the young Clement Attlee.

Not, of course, that the Victorians were uniform in their religious beliefs. Faith was a varied, lively and often passionately debated topic, interacting with everyday life in the most vibrant ways. Evangelicalism could generate protest as well as conformity – in the so-called Celtic fringe, and in the mining villages of Wales and crofts of Scotland, the connection between religious non-conformity and support for the Liberals was a marked feature of political life long into the nineteenth century; David Lloyd George and Aneurin Bevan were both fiery products of this culture. In the Church of England, evangelical strains led in one direction to the Oxford Movement of the 1830s and 1840s, an attempt by clerical dons of the university to reassert the spiritual serious-ness and worldly independence of Anglicanism through a rediscovery of its catholic inheritance. Some, like John Henry Newman, took a logical step and converted to Catholicism – for many of his aghast followers the retreat into incense and idolatry was an unforgivable betrayal. Religion was something over which friendships could be broken and lifelong rifts made. Catholic Eman-cipation, allowing Catholics to become MPs and hold public office, effectively brought down the Duke of Wellington's government in 1830: there was to be no sentimental loyalty to the victor of Waterloo after such an egregious blunder. At the time there were more rabid anti-Catholic protests to Parliament than there were petitions for long-overdue electoral reform.[12]

Although the Victorians technically lived in a united kingdom, there was often tension between its constituent parts. It was not simply that the political establishment was Anglocentric: after all, in a still largely decen-tralised England, people from one county often failed to understand the dialect of another not far away. But it did help when there were 'foreign' bodies like Catholics. When Friedrich Engels visited Manchester in 1844, he found that Irish immigrants were considered animals. 'The southern facile character of the Irishman,' he wrote, falling in with opinion, 'his crudity, which places him but little above the savage, his contempt for all humane enjoyments, in which his very crudeness makes him incapable of sharing, his filth and poverty, all favour drunkenness.'[13] In later years any abating of this sinister anti-Irishness was offset by reactions against the Home Rule movement. Gladstone may have disestablished the Irish Church (a Protestant institution) and framed two Home Rule bills in 1886 and 1893, but the Liberal Party came to grief on them. By the time that Queen Victoria died, the United Kingdom seemed less united than ever before, with the Conservatives holding the trump card in politics: a heady mix of virulent Protestantism and noisy imperialism.

The Victorians believed, not for the first time in British history, that they were 'God's elect'. This infused them with both the right and the duty to spread civilisation throughout the world. The Victorians were, famously, an imperial people. By 1901, they possessed an empire on which the sun never set – somewhere amongst their possessions there would always be daylight. The great jewel in the crown was India, the most lucrative holding of all (for the empire was about money as much as it was about its civilising mission). British foreign policy, and not a little imperial manoeuvring, was designed to safeguard the link with India: whether in Disraeli's purchase of the Suez Canal shares, or in the virulent Russophobia that marked attitudes until the end of the nineteenth century. France and Russia, not Germany, were deemed by Victorian politicians to be the biggest strategic threats: France for its Napoleonic and revolutionary associations, Russia for its potential encroachment on India.

Imperial culture was, we are often reminded, exploitative and fundamentally racist. At home Britain was far from being the multi-cultural nation it would become after the collapse of empire, and such attitudes are therefore perhaps hardly surprising. But the most notorious phase of Victorian imperialism, that associated with aggressive chauvinism, only really opened in the late 1870s with the coming of 'jingoism'. Before that point there had been interaction with indigenous cultures and a general emphasis upon the trade benefits of empire. Later these attitudes hardened, as blood accrued on native spears and international rivalry inaugurated the helter-skelter scramble for possessions. Relatively few people in Victorian Britain knew anything about the dynamics or even the geography of empire, but they knew about martyrs like General Gordon and responded enthusiastically to the imperial flavour of Victoria's jubilees. For them, the empire was hazily exotic but no less a matter of real pride.

The Victorians knew that they were living in an age of dramatic change. Here, again, the past bequeathed two epoch-shaping influences: population growth and the Industrial Revolution. Both profoundly affected the way the Victorians lived and saw their world, changing their attitudes towards government action, politics, class, wealth, city life, the ever-expanding empire, and even history. It is difficult to think of any area of life that was not touched, or, as G. M. Young once said of the Victorians, of any beliefs (beyond the family and representative institutions) which were not at some time challenged and debated.[14] Indeed, it was the vigorousness and variety of the Victorian response to their own age that was the crucible of modernity, the reason for their huge impact on the twentieth century, and the explanation for many of the profound difficulties that young intellectuals then had in casting off the emotional legacies of the past.

The population of Britain had reached unprecedented levels by the 1780s, and it continued to grow throughout the nineteenth century, even though the rate of expansion slowed towards the end of the era. This was mainly, it seems, through choice rather than any revolution created by cheap contraceptives. The consumer society offered more attractive outlets for disposable income than yet more babies' bonnets: Selfridges, Army and Navy and countless shops selling fresh fruit and manufactured clothes were all creations of the late Victorian period. Women also increasingly tended to marry at a later age, and the archetypical large Victorian family, especially amongst professional people, began to fade away. Even so, Britain must sometimes have seemed, in the light of the past, to be overflowing with people – in 1831 the population stood at about 24,000,000; seventy years later it had galloped ahead to 41,000,000.[15]

There was alarm at this veritable explosion of humankind. Early Victorians here tended to follow the thinking of the Reverend Thomas Malthus, whose 1798 essay on population posited the theory that people and resources act in natural, if occasionally catastrophic, balance. As population increases, Malthus argued, the pressure on resources intensifies, and will continue to do so until starvation, war or some other calamity eases it by removing the 'surplus' population. It is a measure of how far Malthusian theory permeated social attitudes that Dickens included a scene in *A Christmas Carol* (1843) in which two charity-collectors ask for a donation from Scrooge:

> 'What shall I put you down for?'
> 'Nothing!' Scrooge replied.
> 'You wish to be anonymous?'
> 'I wish to be left alone,' said Scrooge. 'Since you ask me what I wish, gentlemen, that is my answer. I don't make merry myself at Christmas, and I can't afford to make idle people merry. I help to support the establishments I have mentioned: they cost enough: and those who are badly off must go there.'
> 'Many can't go there; and many would rather die.'

'If they would rather die,' said Scrooge, 'they had better do it, and decrease the surplus population.' [16]

Here is an insight into the early Victorian mind – as much, of course, for Dickens's generous indignation (shared by many contemporary observers) as for its reflection of orthodox opinion. The 'establishments' to which Scrooge refers are the workhouses set up under the New Poor Law of 1834 – the 'old' one of Elizabethan days having been deemed too soft and inadequate to meet the demands of an ever-sprawling populace. To be a 'pauper' in the Victorian age, at least until the last few decades, was a grave matter indeed. Paupers, those dependent upon the Poor Law, were considered moral failures who were dependent upon charity because they were lazy, feckless and unrespectable. Not until social surveys in the 1880s and 1890s would this attitude begin to change, when investigators like Charles Booth and Seebohm Rowntree developed the startling notion that many paupers were indigent because they had been born into an almost inescapable life-cycle of poverty.

The stigma of pauperism nevertheless retained its bite into the twentieth century: when old age pensions were introduced in 1908, many beneficiaries – though doubtless grateful – were slightly suspicious of the scheme. Asquith's government, sensitive to this unease, took care to administer it from post offices rather than from the shame-associated workhouses. And this stigma was not one simply handed down from above, from those who had the ease and comfort to pass judgement on their less fortunate fellow humans. Nowhere was the hankering after respectability more pronounced, and more fraught with anxiety, than amongst the working classes. Given that they constituted about four-fifths of the population of Victorian Britain, their own division into skilled and unskilled workers may have been the most pronounced class 'fact' of the age.

Class mattered a very great deal to the Victorians. Slum-dwellers probably did not have the time, energy or disposition to reflect on their lot, but elsewhere the perceptions and nuances of class suffused society at every level.[17] For those at the very top of the tree – monarch, peers and landed gentry – society was a seamless hierarchical web: a vision brilliantly staged on occasions like Queen Victoria's Diamond Jubilee (and, it is worth adding, cheered to the echo by those who lined the streets). For the working classes, it was sometimes a disaffected case of 'them' and 'us', but more often a case of striving to move up in the world, epitomised most influentially by Samuel Smiles's *Self-Help* (1859). For the middle classes, society was often envisaged as a pyramid divided into upper, middle and lower segments. Their own segment, however, was far from fixed in character; and indeed it is the

minefield of middle-class mores that we most often have in mind when
thinking of the Victorians as class-obsessed – this is the territory of the
Grossmiths' Mr Pooter. An enormous gulf separated humble clerks, com-
muting from the suburbs every day to toil at menial office jobs, from rich
plutocrats, reinventing themselves as country gentlemen or buying their way
into Parliament. This gulf became, if anything, wider towards the end of
the nineteenth century, as the middle classes expanded with mass education
and suburban growth, while the businessmen and financiers became even
richer from the proceeds of trade and empire.

Although the Victorians worshipped wealth, they were also suspicious of
it. It was not simply that social campaigners in the 1830s and 1840s, urging
more humane conditions in factories and mines, saw the hypocrisy behind
employers supposedly motivated by the honest commitment to hard work.
(Thomas Carlyle, a prophet of this kind of secular evangelicalism, proclaimed
in 1843: 'There is a perennial nobleness, and even sacredness, in Work.') [18]
There was the sense, too, that social standing could not necessarily be bought.
Although the traditional landed orders had lost much of their political power
by the late Victorian period, they retained much of their influence in other
areas of public life. For a people so concerned with self-help and social
advancement, the Victorians were remarkably deferential. There was certain
vulgarity in being *nouveau riche.*

This was closely related to a characteristic mid- and late Victorian preoccupation, once industrial wealth had fully feathered many *arriviste* beds:
what it was to be a 'gentleman'. The real question was this: was a gentleman
bred or born? Did growing up in genteel surroundings confer gentlemanliness, or was it – as Smiles earnestly reassured his readers – an innate quality
with which an individual was born? Victorian novels, especially those by
male writers who had known straitened or precarious financial circumstances (including Thackeray, Trollope and Dickens) were often greatly
exercised by the dilemma. William Makepeace Thackeray, who worked
himself to an early grave in order to keep his family financially afloat,
continually mused on the nature of gentlemanliness. The author of *The
Snobs of England* ('by one of themselves') felt that it took three generations
of genteel living to make a gentleman. With a few distant gentrified ancestors,
one contemporary wryly noted that Thackeray was 'not at all disposed to
under-value his own rather slender title to be ranked with persons of
ancestral dignity'. [19]

Dignity, standing and resourcefulness were important in a society in
which there were few safety nets. There was private charity and philanthropy, but government itself was reluctant to intervene in the daily lives
of individuals. Partly this was by mutual agreement, for the forces of

regional identity were often very strong and fiercely protective of their
relative autonomy. Law and politics were administered (and very often
manipulated) by local landowners at a time when many only had eyes for
the potential intrusiveness of central government, alien and grasping in its
metropolitan sophistication. Flora Thompson, growing up in an Oxford-
shire village at the end of the Victorian era, recalled that the road to it
brought 'No motors, no buses, and only one of the old penny-farthing
bicycles at rare intervals. People still rushed to their cottage doors to see
one of the latter come past.' [20] All this was eventually to change, as com-
munications, transport links and national politics brought local
communities into an overarching national framework. At a surprisingly
late stage in Queen Victoria's reign, though, local politics and society could
often be found going their own (usually traditional) ways.

This arrangement suited the Victorian political establishment which,
generally speaking, favoured non-intervention on ideological and practical
grounds. Sir Robert Peel's repeal of the Corn Laws in 1846 (taxes imposed
on imported corn to protect the home market) marked the final ascent of
*laissez-faire* in British politics. Free trade, felt politicians like John Bright
and Richard Cobden, might promote world peace: never again should
national interests be allowed to foster conflict as they had done in the
horrendously expensive Napoleonic Wars. Peace favoured the Victorians'
own view of themselves as moderate beneficiaries of the bloodless Glorious
Revolution, just as it lined their pockets from untrammelled trade as the
world's leading industrial nation. Small wonder that its ascendancy was
never again questioned until after Victoria's death, or that governments
believed in running a tight ship in domestic affairs too. Pressure mounted
for more paternal care in the late Victorian period, when economic trends
no longer seemed so certain, or Britain's wonderful vistas entirely cloudless,
but even here reform was frequently patchy.

In the early Victorian period governments had been swayed by the logic
of utilitarianism, Jeremy Bentham's doctrine about promoting the greatest
happiness of the greatest number of people. Calibrated against a 'happiness'
quotient, reforms and institutions had to be seen to work – there was no
place for unnecessary expenditure or sympathy for individual cases, never
mind what depth of personal unhappiness they might present. Something
of this mindset lingered long afterwards in an age which preached the
virtues of individual accountability, hard work and government economy.
State-provided education from 1870, although beneficial, was rudimentary
and in the first instance discretionary.[21] By the same token, the Artisans'
Dwellings Act of 1875, empowering local authorities to clear away slums,
was to be employed only at their will. In the hands of someone like Joseph

Chamberlain, radical mayor of Birmingham, it could make a tremendous difference; elsewhere the fetid tenements remained gloomily standing.

If peace and free trade abroad were two of the key concerns of Victorian politicians, the consequences of industrialisation at home were its natural corollary – the powerhouse of Britain's place in the world, after all, was essentially industrial. To the Industrial Revolution has been attributed all manner of evil effects: bourgeois complacency, greed and exploitation, the sprawl of towns and desecration of the countryside. There is a degree of truth in all of this, but many of the charges made against the Victorians tell us more about our post-industrial culture than they do about the past. There were, of course, industrial cities like Dickens's Coketown, churning out sun-obliterating smog and reducing workers to mere cogs in a wheel. Manchester in the 1840s was the great shock-city of the age. 'The town is abominably filthy, the Steam Engine is pestiferous, the Dyehouses noisome and offensive, and the water of the river as black as ink or the Stygian lake', one visitor wrote in 1808 of Manchester, where the average age expectancy of a mechanic thirty-four years later was still a mere seventeen.[22] In Benjamin Disraeli's *Sybil* (1845), Elizabeth Gaskell's *Mary Barton* (1848) and Dickens's *Hard Times* (1854), such circumstances spawned the Condition of England novel. Elsewhere, it should be added, the Industrial Revolution took its time transforming practices: far into the nineteenth century, many mills employed a modest number of workers and continued to draw upon traditional handcraft techniques. Such continuity may help to account for the lack of enthusiasm that British workers felt for socialism, as foreign to their sensibilities (however downtrodden) as a plate of frogs' legs.[23]

Industrialisation helped to change the political geography of Britain. Only about 13 per cent of men had the vote in England and Wales before 1832, and these were located largely in the south, reflecting the old distribution of Elizabethan days.[24] By the early nineteenth century many of these constituencies had fallen into less than constitutional ways. Some were 'pocket' boroughs, in which almost everyone was a tenant of the local landowner, and where his choice of MPs was returned with unfailing consistency. In the constituency of Old Sarum, a thriving city in the thirteenth century, the only things to be found by the early nineteenth century were a handful of yokels, some old buildings and one or two sheep. By contrast the ever-expanding industrial cities – Birmingham, Manchester, Leeds and Sheffield (with a combined population of over 500,000) – boasted not a single MP between them. Unsurprisingly, pressure was growing for political representation of this new wealth.

Queen Victoria came to the throne five years after the passing of the Great Reform Act. It was 'great' not because it redrew the landscape of politics in

Britain but on account of its symbolic resonance. The Act underlined the viability of agitation for political reform and encouraged radicals to campaign for change. Though boasting some radical reformers, the government itself had acted under duress, and it was only on the third attempt that the Bill had been passed. Outside Parliament, tensions ran high: on the rejection of the second Bill in October 1831 rioters had terrorised Bristol for three days, the Duke of Newcastle's residence in Nottingham was torched, and in Derby several people lost their lives in mob violence. Lord Melbourne, the Home Secretary, was said to be 'frightened to death' by the happenings in Bristol. Lord Grey, the Prime Minister, declared dramatically that 'The principle of my reform is to prevent the necessity for revolution'.[25]

There is little need to question his sincerity. In order to understand both this alarm and the ultimate caution of the reform, we need to look at politics through the eyes of what would soon become the early Victorian establishment. Virtually all MPs, in an age when they were not paid, came from the landed gentry or had aristocratic patrons. Most had little direct experience of the working classes, and it was easy, when parliamentary authority seemed endangered, to think of them as 'the mob'. It is difficult to exaggerate the impact of the French Revolution on Victorian establishment minds. It cast a long and uneasy shadow over British politics: as late as 1867, during the passing of the Second Reform Act (bringing the vote to 36 per cent of men), politicians prowled the corridors of Westminster muttering ominously about it being a 'leap in the dark' and about opening the floodgates of revolution. The albino MP Robert Lowe, his white brows furrowed in consternation, blinked in the light of what was about to be unleashed. Would electoral reform, he argued, not put Britain at the mercy of the trade unions, and jeopardise all that had been achieved:

> If [the law] can be enforced, society will have freed itself from a great peril; dangers to our manufactures and commerce, the amount of which no man can measure, will have been arrested, and a demoralization which threatens to lower the character of the English operative to the level of the Thug of India will have been stayed; if not, we must be prepared to see our prosperity wither and perish under the ruinous influence of persons as ignorant of their own true interests as they are careless of the feelings and reckless of the interests of others.[26]

Lowe became a figure of hatred amongst the reformers, but he was as myopic about the death-threats as he was about democracy. His stance was not entirely uncharacteristic. The revolution had unleashed the mob in France – a destructive, all-consuming power that may have given Mary Shelley part of the idea for Frankenstein's monster. British politicians, brought up to believe in parliamentary progress and Edmund Burke's theory of the state as a slowly-evolving organism, wanted no truck with arcane experiments in unfettered democracy.[27]

It is easy to be cynical about such anxious stewardship of politics, attributing it to a rearguard defence of property and privilege by a small interested elite. That, admittedly, was how Victorian radicals outside Parliament saw it, whether they were Chartists in the 1840s or fledgling members of the Labour Party in the 1890s. Yet, for an establishment which only became committed to modern party politics and mass electioneering in the 1870s, it took itself and its parliamentary traditions very seriously. There was corruption and careerism, naturally; Disraeli famously remarked of his premiership that it was a climb to the top of the greasy pole. But beneath the curls and purple velvet and ingenious words he, too, was sober about the responsibilities of power.

It will have been noticed that women did not figure largely in the Victorian establishment's view of politics. Throughout the nineteenth century, women were not able to vote in general elections, even though John Stuart Mill campaigned in vain – for an appropriate amendment to the 1867 Reform Act. Admittedly, women were able to serve on school boards from the 1870s, and on county councils after 1888; and in many unseen ways they could find ways to influence politics through their husbands. But they were seen late into the Victorian period as the property of their husbands. Until 1882, women forfeited their own property and any earnings made since marriage in the event of divorce. And where marital infidelity was concerned, there were dual standards: a man's indiscretions, it was felt, would not endanger the integrity of the home, whereas a woman's indiscretions would make the very foundations of domestic morality totter and quake.

Victorian women were elevated – largely by men, but also often with their own complicity – to the position of the 'Angel in the House'. They were supposed to be meek, dutiful and supportive, the linchpin of the place that was a retreat from the hustle and bustle of the outside world. As John Ruskin wrote in *Sesame and Lilies* (1865):

> The man's power is active, progressive, defensive. He is eminently the doer, the creator, the discoverer, the defender ... But the woman's power is for rule, not for battle – and her intellect is not for invention or creation, but for sweet ordering, arrangement, and decision ... Within his house, as ruled by her, unless she herself has sought it, need enter no danger, no temptation, no cause of error or offence. This is the true nature of the home – it is the place of Peace; the shelter, not only from all injury, but from all terror, doubt, and division.[28]

The Victorian age witnessed a sharper division between 'public' (work, politics) and 'private' (home) spheres as industrialisation and urbanisation replaced traditional working methods. Previously work had often been carried out in the home, on a family basis; the coming of new technologies and markets inevitably took many men away from that setting. Their absence helped to underpin the theory (supported by Charles Darwin, of all people) that women were simply not capable of dealing with life beyond domestic and motherly duties. They were too given to irrationality and hysteria, and – so biology showed – were of inferior cranial capacity to men; clearly such people could not be entrusted with the vote. Young working-class girls might make for efficient housemaids, but married middle-class women really had no business leaving the family nest when there were husbands to care for and children to raise.

If Victorian women were victims, as many of them clearly were, then it is also true to say that the whole age was struggling to come to terms with modernity. Some of the most notorious features of the age – hypocrisy, the sanctification of women, cloying sentimentality – might also be seen as examples of psychological over-compensation amongst people deeply uncertain of their surroundings. This was an age, after all, that had been fearful of inventions like the railway train. Somehow the politician William Huskisson, at the opening of the Liverpool to Manchester railway line in September 1830, found himself on the track: transfixed by the steam and slowly shunting machinery, 'like a man bewildered' as one eye-witness put it, he was crushed to death beneath the *Rocket*. And Dickens, although an enthusiast for the order and progress brought by the railway, had a good eye for the *Inferno*-like chaos its building could create. 'There were a hundred thousand shapes and substances of incompleteness, wildly mingled out of their places, upside down, burrowing in the earth, aspiring in the air, mouldering in the water, and unintelligible as any dream', he wrote in *Dombey and Son* (1848), piling word upon word to convey the bewildering materiality of progress. 'Hot springs and fiery eruptions, the usual attendants upon earthquakes, lent their contributions of confusion to the scene.'[29]

Gothic revivalists idolised the past as a better and more certain place than the present, with its clanking factories, population-swollen society and danger of revolution. Old ways of life, old certainties had been lost. For the first time in history, the census of 1851 showed, more people lived in towns and cities than in the countryside; its evacuation allowed the country-side to be colonised in the imagination with much of the whimsy with which we are familiar today. From the Pre-Raphaelites with their iridescent landscapes, to A. E. Housman with his bitter-sweet poems of lost love, to the young Ralph Vaughan Williams exploring bramble-laden lanes in search of authentic folksong, the Victorians could be profoundly nostalgic and touchingly vulnerable.

What is remarkable is the extent to which this atavism managed to coexist alongside a belief in progress without pulling Victorian Britain apart. Sometimes these contradictions went unresolved: there was, of course, no single 'Victorian' way of looking at the world. Sometimes they worked themselves out in self-criticism and debate, hugely energetic affairs for which the next generation gave the Victorians insufficient credit. And sometimes they worked themselves out in escapism, repression or outlets for which, again, a more psychologically sophisticated generation would have very little time. Confidence and uncertainty jostled with one another at every turn. That uncertainty would increase throughout the nineteenth century, so that by the 1890s Britain had an almost split personality: a jangling and colourful jingoism abroad, and a soft, effete decadence at home – the age of bristle-moustached Kitchener was also the age of long-haired Wilde. In a way both were signals, in their excess, that Victorian self-doubt was beginning to surmount Victorian self-confidence. The twentieth century began not with a clean sheet but with the reaction against the Victorians already underway.

2

# Anti-Victorianism

In May 1918 the man who had inflated the rubber balloon and made risqué quips about German soldiers finally published his book on the Victorians. *Eminent Victorians*, as it was called, was a study of the lives of Cardinal Manning, Florence Nightingale, Thomas Arnold and General Gordon. There was nothing especially remarkable in this – after all, people had been producing worthy biographies of eminent figures since time immemorial. But Strachey's book had a sting in its tail. In method and tone *Eminent Victorians* was quite revolutionary, and contemporaries knew it. The adjective 'eminent', part of the verbal fabric of Victorianism itself, here was twisted into a sneer. Religion, public schools, philanthropy, the empire – all the pillars of the Victorian establishment were undermined by the insidious mockery which seeps through the pages of this book.

To understand why Strachey sneered so much we need to bear in mind the backdrop against which *Eminent Victorians* was written. The final sentence of the book, discussing the resolution of the rebellion in the Sudan which had cost General Gordon his life, runs: 'At any rate, it had all ended very happily – in a glorious slaughter of 20,000 Arabs, a vast addition to the British Empire, and a step in the peerage for Sir Evelyn Baring.'[1] First readers encountered these words, brimful with sarcasm, in May 1918. At that stage the killing fields of the Western Front were still claiming the lives of young British men by the thousand. This was not, of course, a coincidence. Strachey wrote once about his teeth 'chattering with fury' at the war and its effects, and for one so unblinkingly committed to a rational perspective on life, we should take heed. Not that the link in Strachey's mind between the complacencies of the nineteenth century and the outbreak of the First World War is difficult for us to comprehend.

The war has become for us a site of fascination, pity and myth – the quintessential twentieth-century tragedy. We have tended to see it as the great dividing-line in modern experience: beyond the chasm lies sunlight and certainty, the Edwardian garden party in easeful repose and perpetual summer; on our side, darkness and unease, the world of angry recriminations and disorientating modernity.[2] Perhaps the most compelling reason for our having made the war such a repository of myth is the sense of lost innocence – never such innocence again, as Philip Larkin put it. It is a feeling of betrayed innocence which makes sense of the yawning gaps in photographs of pals' battalions taken before and after active service. What we feel looking at these photographs, or reading Rupert Brooke ('If I should die, think only this of me ...'), or listening to that folksong threnody which closes George Butterworth's *The Banks of Green Willow* (its composer another casualty of the Somme), is merely an echo of what intelligent observers – helpless to stop the bloodbath in their midst – felt ninety years ago.

Thoughtful contemporaries fumbled for words to make sense of the war. For Henry James, it was 'the leap of some awful monster out of his lair – he is *upon* us, he is upon *all* of us here, before we had time to turn round':

> It fills me with anguish and dismay and makes me ask myself if *this* is what I have grown old for, if this is what all the ostensibly or comparatively serene, all the supposedly *bettering* past, of our century, has meant and led up to. It gives away everything one has believed in and lived for – and I envy those of our generation who haven't lived on for it.[3]

(One of James's fondest memories was of being punted on the Cam by Rupert Brooke; when Brooke died in April 1915 James was almost inconsolable at 'the stupid extinction of so exquisite an instrument and so exquisite a being'.)[4] For some younger observers without the luxurious prospect of an imminent natural death (James was to die in February 1916), the war was also a disaster for civilisation; but it was also, and sometimes invigoratingly so, an indictment of history. This is where it had all led, the bourgeois morality and the complacent materialism and the jingoistic patriotism – straight to Flanders and Gallipoli.

The writing, in any case, had been on the wall for some time. When Wyndham Lewis's journal *Blast* was launched in June 1914 it trumpeted: 'BLAST years 1837 to 1900'. Robert Graves told Edward Marsh, the man to whom James had lamented the loss of Brooke, that when the war was over he and his generation would 'try to root out ... the obnoxious survivals of Victorianism'. Wilfred Owen told his mother in 1917 that he did not covet the Victoria Cross on account of its title and the values for which it might be taken to stand ('Is it not *Victorian*? yah! pah!').[5] Ezra Pound spoke for the younger generation with one of the most shocking images of the day. The botched civilisation, he declared contemptuously in 1920, was 'an old bitch gone in the teeth'. And, like James, even older commentators had to admit that Victorianism was one of the lights that had failed. 'If any question why we died, / Tell them, because our fathers lied', penned a guilt-stricken Rudyard Kipling, whose son went missing at Loos. 'That England of the

Victorian old men,' wrote H. G. Wells in 1918, 'and its empire and its honours and its court and precedences, it is all a dead body now.'[6] The obsequies were intoned by Elgar's Cello Concerto of 1919, a work pervaded even more than usual for this composer by sadness and regret – its closing pages a pained recollection of lost happiness which even a moustache-bristling harrumph cannot efface.

Anger, bitterness and resentment became the keynotes of fashionable intellectual talk by the end of the war. 'For a considerable time past', wrote the critic Edmund Gosse in 1918, 'everybody must have noticed, especially in private conversation, a growing tendency to disparagement and even ridicule of all men and things, which can be defined as "Victorian".'[7] The First World War was the final catalyst in distilling that mood of listlessness, escapism and satire which wells up from the pages of Evelyn Waugh and Lytton Strachey, D. H. Lawrence and Aldous Huxley. In its wake, the 1920s became the zenith of what we might call anti-Victorianism, that series of attacks on the values by which the Victorians had lived and died. But these attacks, in fact, predated the disillusioning carnage of the war, having their roots in a range of interconnected anxieties at the end of the nineteenth century. And so, ironically, the case for the prosecution began with the Victorians themselves.

With its bunting and flags, jingling harnesses and cheering crowds, Queen Victoria's Diamond Jubilee on 22 June 1897 was a splendid veneer on a nation not entirely sure of itself. There is something oddly symbolic about the figure of Queen Victoria, a little old lady with a black bonnet and white parasol, perched in the carriage before hundreds of expectant dignitaries gathered outside St Paul's Cathedral for a service of thanksgiving.[8] Here was a nation in thrall to its icons and traditions, and never more so than now; for what this little old lady seemed almost to defy was the passage of time.

Time, they knew, was not on their side. In the years leading up to the Diamond Jubilee it had become clear that Germany and the United States would soon challenge Britain's place in the world. At least in industrial terms, Britannia would soon no longer rule the waves. In any case, faith in economic progress, underscored by a protracted agricultural depression in the 1870s, had itself begun to wane. This was reflected by a renewed awareness of poverty, diffusing itself through late Victorian society sometimes like a dull ache, sometimes with all the power of sudden revelation. Seebohm Rowntree, a confectioner with a social conscience, found that in York some 62 per cent of working-class families lived in houses with 'an average frontage of about 12 feet 6 inches':

> Many houses ... are jerry built, with thin walls of porous and damp-absorbing bricks, put together with inferior mortar, and with wood so 'green' that after a short time floors, window-frames, and doors shrink, and admit draughts and dust. Such houses will soon tend to degenerate into slums.

A labourer in such a house would eat virtually no vegetables or fruit, and have meat of any substance only once a week; the rest of the time he would subsist on low-grade bread, bacon, butter, tea and the occasional treat like an egg or a piece of shortcake.[9] And he was one of the lucky ones, in regular employment.

Rowntree estimated that about a third of the inhabitants of York lived below the poverty line at the turn of the twentieth century, and a very similar statistic was reached for the people of London by Charles Booth. These revelations generated a more sympathetic climate for the pessimistic readings of the Industrial Revolution to be found in the pages of Arnold Toynbee and of the famous Fabian duo Sidney and Beatrice Webb.[10] In the Edwardian years these revelations were also to encourage both government intervention into basic living and working conditions, moving away from conventional *laissez-faire* principles, and a wave of industrial action which threatened to cripple Britain on the eve of the war.

Such misgivings about the state of the people accentuated worries about the empire. Educated Victorians knew their Gibbon, and feared that their empire might go the way of ancient Rome. Indeed, in 1897, that strange and unsettling bard of empire Kipling had written 'Recessional', a poem prophesying decline and fall if care were not taken. The poem struck an oddly minor-key note amidst the triumphant strains of the jubilee celebrations. (Its insistent refrain, 'Lest we forget', of course attained another, sadder, resonance after the First World War. A superstitious man, Kipling later wrote that he had intended 'Recessional' as a *nuzzur-wattu*, 'an averter of the Evil Eye' in the context of 'a certain optimism that scared me'.)[11] Just a couple of years later, the poor physical condition of volunteers for the Boer War seemed to confirm that there was a terrible flaw at the heart of the empire. Others, like the economist J. A. Hobson, were in any case wholly critical of the jingoistic posturings of late Victorian imperialism. For liberal intellectuals the carnage of the First World War would seem an inevitable outcome of these shameful excesses. Joseph Conrad already pointed the way in *Heart of Darkness* (1902), a work which was later to achieve iconic status.

Acute uncertainty abroad mirrored acute anxiety at home: the last generations faced an identity crisis of unparalleled gravity. At least earlier Victorians, for all their dizziness amidst the whirl of modernity, had drawn consolation from religion and settled gender relations. Both were challenged in the late Victorian period. Evolutionary theory burrowed its way into conventional faith for intellectuals, even if a rearguard action was fought by conservative scientists and liberal theologians to reconcile science with religion.[12] So, too, did growing state welfare and the nascent leisure industry sap church attendance for ordinary people – why keep on the vicar's good side when charity could be procured elsewhere? Why go on church trips when Blackpool beckoned?[13] Earnestness became a quality widely mocked: a small essay might be written on the uses (or rather abuses) of the term in late Victorian culture, from Oscar Wilde's *The Importance of Being Earnest* to Samuel Butler's naming of his hero, Ernest Pontifex, in *The Way of All Flesh*. Also increasingly stigmatised as a relic of the past was the convention of separate spheres for men and women. The polite conception of the 'Angel in the House' was disagreeably challenged by the recognition of female sexual pleasure, and never really recovered from the revelation that women had brains.

So by the 1890s – that decade dizzy with the contradictory impulses to aestheticism and jingoism – there was much that was self-consciously 'new': new women, new unionism, new journalism, and so on. Fashionable circles made a fetish of the experimental: the seeds of modernism were being sown.[14] Under these various influences, the early and mid-Victorian periods emerged as targets for the severest criticism, almost as if those descriptive tags 'early' and 'mid' reflected something half-formed, a primitive experiment in human existence.[15] Many of those who were young or who grew up at the time remembered this denigration. As the former Prime Minister H. H. Asquith (born in 1852) put it in a lecture he gave at Oxford in June 1918: 'That which we roughly call the Victorian was over some time – a decade at least – before the end of the great Queen's reign.'[16] The historian G. M. Young (born in 1882) concurred, noting that 'early Victorian had become a term of reproach when Victoria still had ten years to reign'.[17]

Confidence in the trajectory of her reign had been rattled even as Queen Victoria, the little old lady with the black bonnet and white parasol, was driven up to the steps of St Paul's Cathedral in June 1897. Much subsequent anti-Victorianism grew out of this unease and irreverence, becoming bolder and generating its own momentum as the years passed. The diversity of the phenomenon makes generalisation difficult, but let us now try to take in some of its scope.

The grim economic mood down to the Second World War continued to nurture resentment against Victorian industrialism. These were, after all, the years of the first Labour governments, of the General Strike, and of the Jarrow Hunger March – that column of ragged but dignified men who walked the 300 miles from Tyneside to London to show the plight of 'the town that was murdered'. In such a climate, economic and social history flourished under concerned historians like G. D. H. Cole, R. H. Tawney, Eileen Power and the husband and wife team of John and Barbara Hammond. Cole and Tawney were old-world sages, scholars who saw no tension between their deep-rooted socialist commitments and their didactic responsibilities. Power, one of the first women dons, used her sharp intellect and feminine sensibilities in probing beneath the public history of kings and battles to unearth the private reality of ordinary people. The Hammonds were perhaps the most influential of all: well-heeled social democrats who, with austere and indomitable energy, produced a series of works denouncing the industrialists. The thrust of their argument – pursued from *The Village Labourer* (1911) to *The Age of the Chartists* (1930) – was that the Industrial Revolution had happened much too quickly, and that the poor had been brutalised and many of the cherished attitudes and traditions of the past needlessly lost.

Chartism was discovered anew in the years after the First World War, drawing scholarly attention from labour historians like Mark Hovell and Julius West.[18] The reasons for this are not difficult to see. War, the Russian Revolution and the volatile international situation all seemed to confirm that early Victorian radicals had been right about the political establishment. Even Hugh Gaitskell, a future leader of the Labour Party, felt moved to write a celebratory tract once universal suffrage had been achieved in 1928.[19] For others, this was not enough. 'The struggle for the People's Charter is the most glorious chapter in the history of the people of England', wrote one pamphleteer on the centenary of the movement in 1938. 'Enriched by their experience, the march of the people towards freedom continues.'[20] Sober, sophisticated scholars like J. H. Clapham were certainly at work in these years, but even he had to admit in 1929 that 'It has been burned in on us these last ten years that nothing makes history ... like changes in the value of money.'[21] The generations slipped away with the Hammonds' publication in 1934 of a shorter version of *The Age of the Chartists*, pointedly retitled *The Bleak Age*. And for many, with the subsequent rise of fascism, the writing of the past became a political act in itself – one in which Victorian industrialists were almost invariably cast as the stooges (and scrooges).

The links between material possession and imperialism had long been known, and often frowned upon, by intellectuals. After the blunders and bloodshed of the war, they subjected late Victorian imperialism to even more barbed comments. We have already encountered what Strachey had to say about certain Victorian imperialists, and these comments were highly influential in shaping works like J. M. Keynes's *The Economic Consequences of the Peace* (1919) and E. M. Forster's *A Passage to India* (1924).[22] It was Forster's great novel, together with George Orwell's fictional account of his experiences in the Indian Imperial Police in *Burmese Days* (1934), that did most to establish an attitude of unease and misgiving amongst literary people between the wars. And although maps of the world were coloured as pink-red as ever, some of these feelings were shared by other prominent individuals. J. B. Priestley and Stanley Baldwin both forged careers as Little Englanders, Priestley in literature and Baldwin in politics. Not for Baldwin, who eulogised the sights and sounds of the English countryside, the expansive imperial rhetoric of many of his Conservative predecessors. Public tastes had shifted, and with them the style required by canny politicians.

With traumatic memories of one world war behind them and the mounting prospects of another to come, it is striking how Victorian diplomatic history could be reassessed in these years. Benjamin Disraeli, that brilliantly charismatic premier who had created the title of Empress of India for Queen Victoria in 1876, came in for particular criticism over his treatment of the so-called Eastern Question. In hindsight it seemed that Disraeli had been one of the chief architects of the tragedy of 1914. By propping up the corrupt Turkish regime so as to protect British imperial interests in the Balkans against Russia, critics claimed, Disraeli had fuelled that nationalism which was to provide the flashpoint nearly forty years later. 'To the clear-sighted in 1878', lamented the historian R. W. Seton-Watson, Balkan nationalism 'was bound to end as we in 1934 see that it has ended.' 23 By contrast, and as we shall later see, the posthumous reputation of Gladstone benefited from his principled stance over the Eastern Question. Still, this was hardly sufficient in the eyes of a critic like Strachey, for whom Gladstone provided rich comic material in *Eminent Victorians*. For some, the whole business of Victorian imperialism was beyond redemption.

Many of the old arguments about society and social expectations also deepened in the early decades of the twentieth century. What particularly critics had in mind in the Edwardian period was a sense of the prudery, repressiveness and double standards within Victorian morality: it was the human side of things that witnessed the great backlash. Here the sense of an imaginative watershed brought about by the death of Queen Victoria and the passing of the nineteenth century was clearly important. The novelist T. H. White, who was born in the Edwardian period, recalled from the perspective of 1933:

> She died on 22 January, and the first blow was struck. After a decent interval, after an interval of sincere regret, the audience breathed again, began to talk. The lights shone; the curtain rose upon the Harlequinade, leaving nothing but disjointed memories. The old conventions were dubbed oppressive ... the old scandals and order and family feeling (the result of the Victorian home) were

relegated to the past … Edwardianism rose in their place. It came, like the Harlequinade, with a crash. The King tootled on his horn, the motors rushed the stage.[24]

The poop-pooping of this royal Toad of Toad's Hall was but the least of advances. At the Grafton Gallery in November 1910 Roger Fry unleashed the first Post-Impressionist exhibition on a public used to Victorian realism and sentiment. Fashionable ladies who strolled through the gallery tittering at what they saw were, by comparison with other reactions, paragons of progressive opinion. One man began to hyperventilate in reaction to Cézanne's portrait of his wife. Others fulminated at the mad Matisse and talentless Van Gogh. 'These are not works of art at all,' stormed the poet Wilfrid Blunt, 'unless throwing a handful of mud against a wall may be called one. They are the works of idleness and impotent stupidity, a pornographic show.' [25]

Sex was indeed often the issue. In the mind of Virginia Woolf, a new era of frankness was inaugurated by Lytton Strachey's one-word question on noticing a stain on her sister Vanessa's dress: 'Semen?' [26] Sex was intricately bound up with artistic expression, as Blunt recognised. (Woolf also famously saw the Post-Impressionist exhibition as a watershed, suggesting that 'on or about December 1910, human character changed'.) [27] At Covent Garden, audiences in 1913 did not riot as had Parisian ballet-goers in response to Stravinsky's *The Rite of Spring*, but after the virgin had danced herself to death and the work had pounded and shrieked to its conclusion, the applause, as the *Times* put it with exquisite understatement, was 'measured'.[28] On the theatrical stage, the works of George Bernard Shaw also continued to challenge conventional attitudes to politics and morality. In *Pygmalion* (1912) he was to sum it up in a line: 'Such nonsense all this early Victorian prudery.' [29] H. G. Wells, that incorrigible frequenter of young ladies' bedrooms, had his say too. 'What is the use of keeping up this note of indignation, Ann Veronica?', he wrote in one novel. 'Don't frown me off now. Don't go back into Victorian respectability and pretend you don't and can't think and all the rest of it.' [30]

This theme of a deliberate pretence at chaste morality was amplified by critics after the First World War. Church attendance, already in decline since the late nineteenth century, had been temporarily stimulated during the conflict by stretched nerves and metaphysical ponderings. The stance of the Anglican church – exemplified by A. F. Winnington-Ingram, the Bishop of London, who told congregations that the war was a 'crusade' to kill Germans and save the world – did not, however, stand it in good stead in the years ahead. Many left their faith behind on the barbed wire of Flanders. Many of those who were bereaved – and few were untouched by loss – also turned to seances and other forms of spiritual succour. Britain was still nominally a Christian nation in the inter-war years, but the proportion of the population who went to church continued to plummet, and the place of religion in society became subject to unprecedented mockery and disregard. People like Lytton Strachey led the way in satirising the great religious debates of the Victorian age, seeing issues like Tractarianism as little more than a symptom of disordered brains and muddled hearts. Victorian morality, such observers felt, had acted as a suffocating corset around the human spirit.

In the area of personal relations hypocrisy was soon identified and attacked. Middle-class women were no longer expected to collude in a pretence at sexual innocence. This was not of course the same thing as sexual liberation, as Virginia Woolf would have been the first to point out. But even if men after 1918 were slow to accord women equality of regard, the past could act as a gauge against which to measure progress. And at least, many held, the truth about the Victorians could begin to be told. 'I have no reason to believe that the Victorian woman was more reticent than the modern girl', wrote one commentator in 1933. 'Not to put too fine a point on it, the Victorians were the world's greatest humbugs.'[31] The novelist E. F. Benson, although admittedly hampered by misogyny and a Victorian reserve about his own ambiguous sexuality, was equally scornful of past mores:

> There is a great deal to be said for any besom that sweeps away the cobwebs of Victorian conventionalism, which harboured such dusty rubbish as the axiom that no nice girl knew anything about anything till she was married, and that if she remained a spinster she continued to believe that babies were found under the gooseberry bushes of the kitchen-gardens of married couples, or that the chance of exposure of her calves to the lascivious gaze of men was a shock to her modesty which could only be correctly expressed by a timely swoon.[32]

Meanwhile, a 1940 farce by Barbara Shaw called *A Mid-Victorian Trifle* focused upon the 'scandal' of the daughter of a respectable family marrying a man without her parents' permission (and, to add insult to injury, apparently a foreigner to boot). In the production notes Shaw gives a description of the mother as 'the acknowledged "delicate wife", the tremulous, fluttering "little woman" so beloved of Victorian fiction, who, behind all her hysterics, was as hard and self-centred a creature as one could wish to avoid'.[33] Those repeated inverted commas speak volumes about the emotional distance opened up since the nineteenth century. This was a different age, both less naive and less innocent; in the era of Freud and votes for women, commentators were keenly sensitive to any trace of psychological ambiguity or inconsistency.

It hardly comes as a surprise that Victorian artistic taste also continued to be widely attacked. It was not necessarily that critics failed to see the diversity at the heart of Victorian aesthetics, or to acknowledge that the Victorians themselves had never agreed on what art should express. The more general failing was in being unable to find within its different expressions much that was 'relevant' to the modern age. For historical 'relevance' people tended to look back beyond the Victorians, though not so far back as the ancient Greek, Gothic and medieval eras to which the Victorians themselves had looked. Many aesthetes in the early twentieth century preferred the design of the Georgian period, not least because its clean restrained style complemented avant-garde tastes in interior and exterior decoration.[34] The art critic John Steegman wrote in 1936 about the collapse of the Georgian 'rule of taste' as a result of Victorian material wealth being too quickly gained and ostentatiously displayed.

Not all Victorian interiors were dark and dingy: that was a phenomenon largely of the late nineteenth century.[35] But even the exuberant gaudiness of some earlier Victorian rooms was seen to carry the stigma of new wealth vulgarly on show. Thoughtful contemporaries had already alighted on the problem. William Morris urged peers to 'have nothing in your houses that you do not know to be useful, or believe to be beautiful'. The Victorian *nouveaux riches*, however, rarely paid heed to such advice. The result was interiors like that described in Wilkie Collins's *Basil* (1852):

> Everything was oppressively new. The brilliantly-varnished door cracked with a report like a pistol when it was opened; the paper on the walls, with its gaudy pattern of birds, trellis-work, and flowers, in gold, red, and green on a white ground, looked hardly dry yet; the showy window-curtains of white and sky-blue, and the still showier carpet of red and yellow, seemed as if they had come out of the shop yesterday; the round rosewood table was in a painfully high state of polish; the morocco-bound picture books that lay on it, looked as if they had never been moved or opened since they had been bought; not one leaf even of the music on the piano was dogs-eared [*sic*] or worn. Never was a richly furnished room more thoroughly comfortless than this – the eye ached at looking round it.[36]

Collins's great friend Charles Dickens reached a similar conclusion about new wealth when describing the home of the Veneerings in *Our Mutual Friend* (1865). They are 'bran-new people in a bran-new house in a bran-new quarter of London': 'what was observable in the furniture, was observable in the Veneerings – the surface smelt a little too much of the workshop and was a trifle stickey [*sic*]'.[37] For Victorian commentators like Oscar Wilde obsessed with 'the house beautiful', the problem was not so much the acquisition of wealth itself but the absence of any guiding tradition of taste to inform how it was spent.

Twentieth-century artistic commentators felt that the clock needed to be both set back and wound on from the Victorian period. The search for 'relevance' in Victorian art continued, but here disappointment and prejudice fed off one another. Victorian painting was widely criticised as being inferior both by eighteenth- and emerging twentieth-century standards. Early and mid-Victorian art, dominated as it was by realism, historical settings and the moral-sentimental vignette, was widely disparaged for what one commentator in 1934 called its 'complete predominance of subject over treatment, and of the intellectual and moral elements over the sensory and aesthetic'.[38] 'Reputations, in the cases of ages no less than of individuals, depend, in the long run, upon the judgments of artists; and artists will never be fair to the Victorian age', Strachey had written twenty years before. 'To them its incoherence, its pretentiousness, and its incurable lack of detachment will always outweigh its genuine qualities of solidity and force.'[39] Lack of detachment was one of the charges raised against other strands of Victorian art. The Pre-Raphaelites were often seen as pedlars of the lurid and the indulgent: among the items found by Lady Chatterley in a lumber room at Wragby are 'pathetic William Henry Hunt birds' nests'.[40] Not until the psychedelic 1960s would the stock of such artists rise again.

Equally, while the Arts and Crafts movement found renewed popularity at the close of the twentieth century, it was not so popular amongst aesthetes at the beginning. Having turned its back on the ugliness of industrial life, the Arts and Crafts movement was in many respects anti-Victorian in itself; but it fell prey to a later brand of anti-Victorianism which derided its retreat into blind rural nostalgia. Evelyn Waugh wrote in 1930 of 'The detestation of "quaintness" and "picturesque bits" which is felt by every decently constituted Englishman'. Like Waugh before his descent into unbridled *Brideshead* nostalgia, the young John Betjeman also had an axe to grind, producing an attack in 1933 on 'quaint old-world artiness' called *Ghastly Good Taste*.[41] As Humphrey Carpenter has noted, 'He and his friends hated "tea-shop Tudor" not just because it was false, but because it was a symbol of the bad taste of their parents' generation, a *kitsch* offshoot of the Arts and Crafts movement, rather than a serious expression of either art or history.'[42]

Waugh and Betjeman, like many other aesthetes of the early twentieth century, began by deploring Victorian architecture. Denigrating the attempts of William Morris and others to return to a pre-industrial idyll, critics of the Victorians also found fault with other widespread forms of revivalism in the nineteenth century. Many Victorian buildings in the Gothic style were considered heavy and over-ornate, like George Gilbert Scott's design for the front of St Pancras Station and hotel. William Butterfield, who designed amongst other things the chapel of Keble College, Oxford, was attacked by early twentieth-century observers for his aesthetic 'sadism' and 'deliberate ugliness'.[43] (In 1906 Rupert Brooke, then a pupil at Rugby, blamed a bout of conjunctivitis on 'gazing too often on Butterfield's architecture'.) [44] More modest Victorian brickwork, meanwhile, was doomed to denigration until at least the 1960s. 'Whatever may be said in favour of the Victorians,' quipped P. G. Wodehouse in a 1937 novel, 'it is pretty generally admitted that few of them were to be trusted within reach of a trowel and a pile of bricks.' [45]

Victorian buildings were often smothered with ivy, and reactions to that plant provide us with an intriguing footnote in the history of anti-Victorianism. Like the interiors it encased, ivy was a potent symbol of Victorian clutter and restriction. For the architectural critic A. E. Richardson there was a clear link between interior and exterior, writing in 1934 that 'Victorian decoration, in its tenacity, resembles the smother of ivy on ancient walls'.[46] But it was Virginia Woolf who furnished the most extraordinary treatment of ivy as an emblem of suffocating Victorianism. As if in anticipation of nature films in which the life-cycles of plants are dramatically compressed into a minute or less, Woolf wrote in *Orlando* (1928) of the descent of Victorianism on England as a damp chill bringing florid growth:

> Outside the house – it was another effect of the damp – ivy grew in unparalleled profusion. Houses that had been of bare stone were smothered in greenery. No garden, however formal its design, lacked a shrubbery, a wilderness, a maze. What light penetrated to the bedrooms where children were born came naturally of an obfusc green, and what light penetrated to the drawing-rooms where grown men and women lived came through curtains of brown and purple plush. But the change did not stop at outward things. The damp struck within. Men felt the chill in their hearts; the damp in their minds.[47]

Florid ornamentation and emotional claustrophobia were often felt to be rife in Victorian literature. The literary critic Douglas Bush wrote in 1932 that it tended to consist of 'pink pills for pale people, a tissue of hypocritical compromises and evasions; it was smugly materialistic, smugly optimistic, mawkish, sentimental, timid, prudish, untrue to life'.[48] The work of Dickens, as we shall later see, was widely denigrated before the Second World War on many of these grounds. Dickens was one of the writers dealt with in Lord David Cecil's *Early Victorian Novelists* (1934), together with Thackeray ('involves more trouble than you and I, dear reader, like often to take'), the Brontës, Mrs Gaskell and Trollope ('his superiority to his contemporaries is mainly negative; he did not make their mistakes').[49] Although by no means unresponsive to Victorian novels, and evidently not enamoured of much modern writing, Cecil reflected many of the new aesthetic priorities of the twentieth century. Writers and critics were more interested in matters of form and language. One of the great clarion calls here was Virginia Woolf's essay 'Mr Bennett and Mrs Brown' (1924), ostensibly a critique of the novelist Arnold Bennett, but in its wider resonance a call for fiction to come out of the post-Victorian vestibule of realism.[50]

Poetry, too, felt the cold winds of change. The cultural politics of canon-isation are instructive. Subsequent editors of *Oxford Books* of verse, themselves of differing levels of sympathy towards the Victorians, faced the dilemma of selection. Sir Arthur Quiller-Couch, an eminent man of letters and critic of the old school, was robust in his 1912 selection for an *Oxford Book of Victorian Verse*, arguing that anti-Victorianism was a mere 'flippancy of fashion'. But it proved to be longer-lived than that, not least as the threshold of the modern age passed the Edwardian years. In 1936 W. B. Yeats in his *Oxford Book of Modern Verse* included only Victorian poetry which seemed to run counter to the general tendencies of nineteenth-century verse, thereby implying that the 'Victorian' and the 'modern' were some-how irreconcilable.[51] The elderly Thomas Hardy, whose verse eschewed sentimentality in favour of tough realism, enjoyed a certain celebrity in the 1920s as what Siegfried Sassoon called 'The Wessex Wizard'; but Rudyard Kipling, another survivor into the post-war world, received fewer visitors at Bateman's in Sussex. He was too much associated with late Victorian imperialism for that – T. S. Eliot referred to him in 1919 as 'a laureate without laurels'.[52]

The culture of anti-Victorianism was clearly very wide-ranging, and could rise to pitches of tremendous emotional intensity. Sometimes this was because critics felt passionately about issues like imperialism, or social standards, or about what art should be and do. But it must also be remem-bered that these critics had their roots in the Victorian age: they were either Victorians by birth, or had grown up in Victorian homes. From Queen Victoria downwards, one of the great priorities in Victorian society had been the sanctification of the middle-class home. Much anti-Victorianism was the response of sensitive, articulate, usually middle-class observers who had grown up in such a climate and found reasons for disliking it. This would eventually become almost a cliché in itself. As L. P. Hartley (born in 1895) wrote to Lord David Cecil in 1971 of his childhood home, with a curious mixture of revulsion and humour:

Fletton, for some reason, is inimical to me. Whether my father was more severe than other Victorian parents I don't know – he certainly didn't mean to be – but I always felt at Fletton I had done something *wrong* – especially in the North Wing! [53]

Seen in this light, anti-Victorianism was a particular version of that universal phenomenon of inter-generational tension. But this version was more intense and historically specific, because Queen Victoria had lived sufficiently long to create the impression that the age to which she gave her name had a timeless authority. It is something of a commonplace that grandchildren can appeal more readily to the uncritical sympathy of their grandparents; but those who were born in the late Victorian period, and who would become amongst the most vociferous critics of the past, could hardly look to their grandparents for inspiration: for they, too, were likely to be earnest early Victorians. There was of course the colourful Regency period before that; but again, this was largely beyond living connection by 1901, and had become the province of antiquarians, aesthetes and historical specialists. Starved of such sources of support and consolation in youth, it is not surprising that much was made in adulthood of the suffocating nature of middle-class Victorian homes. All happy families are alike, but each unhappy family is unhappy in its own way, wrote Tolstoy. Critics of the Victorians in the early twentieth century would doubtless have agreed. Still, they might have added, it did not much help if your family happened to be steeped in Victorian values.

The trend towards attacks on the Victorian home began early. In 1903 Samuel Butler's novel *The Way of All Flesh* was published posthumously – a time bomb that had been ticking away since its completion nearly twenty years before. Butler, born into a clerical family, had been destined to follow in his father's footsteps into the church. These plans were unsettled by religious doubts and an interest in painting, leading Butler at one stage to flee England for New Zealand and life as a sheep-farmer. On his return he took up various literary pursuits and developed an idiosyncratic neo-Darwinian theory which would feed into *The Way of All Flesh*. In his satire, which became a crucial reference point for Edwardian critics of the past, Butler wrote feelingly about the oppressive climate in which he had grown up. At certain points of high emotion he seems almost to merge the narrator (a version of himself?) with his ostensible hero (another version?). The memory of childhood lessons is noteworthy here:

Of all the rooms in the home [Ernest] hated the dining-room worst. It was here that he had had to do his Latin and Greek lessons with his father. It had the smell of some particular kind of varnish which was used in polishing the furniture, and neither I nor Ernest can even now come within range of the smell of this kind of varnish without our hearts failing us.[54]

Edmund Gosse was another writer in this vein, publishing his memoir *Father and Son* in 1907. Gosse was a distinguished man of letters, and had an equally distinguished father, the zoologist Philip Gosse. Like Butler, Gosse had an intense evangelical upbringing: his father was a prominent member of the Plymouth Brethren, and after painful adjustment managed to reconcile his scientific calling with his religious convictions. This was a crisis which had occurred in Edmund Gosse's youth (it is portrayed in the book); and while the father might have kept his religion, the son did not. A rift ensued, and left a troubling emotional legacy which stamps itself on nearly every page of *Father and Son*. Gosse promises to make it an objective memoir; yet, of course, such things are difficult to achieve even without memories of childhood unhappiness. The pressure is clear enough when Gosse describes the point at which he regretfully asserted a 'human being's privilege to fashion his inner life for himself'. Gosse as a young adult had moved to London, where his father pursued him with letters asking after his spiritual welfare, little knowing that his son's faith had waned. On a visit home, Gosse's patience with what he called this 'police-inspection' finally snapped, and in 'the hot-house at home' he gave 'violent and hysterical' replies to a further round of questions. 'He made no answer', Gosse quietly comments; but a liberation had been won. 'I broke from the odorous furnace of the conservatory, and buried my face in the cold grass upon the lawn.' [55]

In later years, memories of the Victorian home would continue to haunt many people. Nowhere was this more the case than with the Bloomsbury Group, who invested such faith in intimate but open-minded domesticity. No doubt much of the incentive here was an attempt to relive and rewrite childhoods which they felt had been stifled by their Victorian parents.[56] Virginia Woolf was born (literally and metaphorically) in a cul-de-sac in Kensington, an area recently developed as part of Prince Albert's vision of a new suburb for the arts and sciences. In a diary entry made in 1918, she remarked of reading another Kensington-based writer's work:

> The breath of South Kensington lives in her pages ... where they would not speak of copulation or wcs ... She makes me consider that the gulf which we crossed between Kensington and Bloomsbury was the gulf between respectable mummified humbug and life, crude and impatient perhaps, but *living*.[57]

It was not only the location that mattered. Her father was Sir Leslie Stephen, editor of the *Dictionary of National Biography* and as eminent a Victorian as any. Woolf adored her father, but he was a temperamental man who often made life at home bleak and constricting. Most of Woolf's novels contain families in which domineering parents and domestic unhappiness are never far away. Most autobiographical is *To the Lighthouse* (1927), in which Stephen appears as Mr Ramsay, brilliant but irredeemably self-centred, tapping others' emotional resources with 'a beak of brass, barren and bare'. The following year Woolf reflected again in her diary: 'Father's birthday. He could have been ... ninety-six ... but mercifully was not. I used to think of him and mother daily; but writing *The Lighthouse* laid them in my mind.'[58] But the memories were not entirely exorcised. Significantly enough, when Woolf wrote in 1929 about women's rights (and by implication her own liberation) it was the metaphor of domestic space that she used: a room of one's own. And the Victorian family was back, with its hypocrisies and tensions, in the domestic saga *The Years* (1937).

Lytton Strachey grew up in Kensington at the same time as Woolf, having been born in 1880 into a well-connected upper middle-class family. His father, General Sir Richard Strachey, was sixty-three when Lytton appeared on the scene, and had spent an active career in India as an imperial administrator. (The 'Lytton' of Giles Lytton Strachey, ironically enough for this arch-debunker of empire, came from his godfather the Earl of Lytton, Viceroy of India.) The general was to prove, in Michael Holroyd's words, a paragon of 'benevolent remoteness', perpetually with open novel in hand, even at the dinner table.[59] Lady Strachey was literary, absent-minded and devoted to her children, but like many Victorian wives modestly allowed her husband to set the tone within family life. In 1884 they moved to 69 Lancaster Gate, Kensington: a large, gloomy, ramshackle house furnished in the mid-Victorian style. Strachey never forgot his life there, and once commented that his profoundly mixed feelings about the hideously furnished drawing-room represented for him 'the riddle of the Victorian Age'.[60]

E. M. Forster was another writer deeply preoccupied with upbringings and habitats. He wrote continually about the repressed lifestyle of the suburban inhabitants of Sawston, a fictional town based upon the Tonbridge of his youth. He had moved there with his mother at the age of fourteen from an idyllic country house near Stevenage called Rooksnest, which became the Howards End of his 1910 novel. Forster's years in Tonbridge, by contrast, were a deeply unhappy time, and he satirised the town and its public school in *Where Angels Fear to Tread* (1905) and *The Longest Journey* (1907). His self-confidence was not greatly improved by a loving but powerfully over-bearing mother. Much too sceptical and intelligent to take any crudely anti-domestic stance, Forster wrote in *Where Angels Fear to Tread*, at the age of twenty-six:

A wonderful physical tie binds the parents to the children; and – by some sad, strange irony – it does not bind us children to our parents. For if it did, if we could answer their love not with gratitude but with equal love, life would lose much of its pathos and much of its squalor, and we might be wonderfully happy.[61]

He later incorporated Butler's *The Way of All Flesh* into *A Room with a View* (1908): it is one of the books owned by the free-thinking Emersons, perhaps significantly making its appearance shortly before the homoerotic frolickings around the Sacred Lake.[62]

Perhaps though it was Henry James, that penetratingly shrewd commentator on late nineteenth-century England, who demonstrates better than anyone else the powerful emotional resonances which Victorian domestic interiors might hold. In *The Wings of the Dove*, published only a year after the death of Queen Victoria, there is a scene in which Merton Densher, a young and impoverished journalist, goes to visit Mrs Lowder, the formidable aunt of the woman he secretly hopes to marry. Awaiting her arrival, ill at ease and trying to prepare himself mentally for a confrontation, Merton Densher considers his surroundings:

> He read more vividly, more critically ... the appearances about him; and they did nothing so much as to make him wonder at his aesthetic reaction ... It was the language of the house itself that spoke to him, writing out for him with surpassing breadth and freedom the associations and conceptions, the ideals and possibilities of the mistress. Never, he felt sure, had he seen so many things so unanimously ugly – operatively, ominously so cruel ... He would write about the heavy horrors that could still flourish, that lifted their undiminished head, in an age so proud of its short way with false gods; and it would be funny if what he should have got from Mrs Lowder were to prove after all but a small amount of copy. Yet the great thing, really the dark thing, was that, even while he thought of the quick column he might add up, he felt it less easy to laugh at the heavy horrors than to quail before them. He couldn't describe and dismiss them collectively, call them either Mid-Victorian or Early – not being certain they were rangeable under one rubric ... He had never dreamed of anything so fringed and scalloped, so buttoned and corded, drawn everywhere so tight and curled everywhere so thick. He had never dreamed of so much gilt and glass, so much satin and plush, so much rosewood and marble and malachite. But it was above all the solid forms, the wasted finish, the misguided cost, the general attestation of morality and money, a good conscience and a big balance. These things finally represented for him a portentous negation of his own world of thought – of which, for that matter, in presence of them, he became as for the first time hopelessly aware. They revealed it to him by their merciless difference.[63]

The sweep of James's prose here, in all its elaborate circumlocutions and relentless detail, conveys just how resonant, strange and oppressive the domestic trappings of Victorianism could seem at the turn of the twentieth century. And just as Mrs Lowder's home represents a negation of Merton

Densher's whole 'world of thought', we should not forget that this domestic form of anti-Victorianism often intermeshed with the varieties of criticism considered earlier. For many, the first experience of attitudes to the outside world, and the first encounters with Victorian painting or books, occurred within a family setting. The reaction against the Victorians began at home. As we shall see in the next chapter, this had important consequences.

# 3

## Survivals

*Eminent Victorians* was one of the clarion calls that martialled the reaction against the past at the end of the First World War. By that point anti-Victorianism had a definite momentum. In the generation that followed critics were able to draw upon a tradition of denigration which had been developing for a number of years, and which had been emphatically endorsed by the senseless carnage of the war. Lord Annan recalled that young public school teachers in the 1920s encouraged pupils to read Lytton Strachey, Robert Graves and Aldous Huxley.[1] And Virginia Woolf in 1939 traced a tradition of debunking memoirs and biographies back through Strachey to Edmund Gosse and earlier – a lineage of which she, in novelistic form, was part.[2]

Here, however, we need to begin making some serious qualifications. Although the multi-generational nature of anti-Victorianism encouraged greater range and explicitness of criticism, it also led to fragmentation of an already diffuse movement. There was never any 'programme' to anti-Victorianism: individuals attacked elements of the past according to personal inclination. Some attacked Victorian art, others Victorian imperialism; some associated the age with dark satanic mills, others with the clutters and constraints of childhood. Not surprisingly, then, generations of critics did not always see eye to eye. Oscar Wilde, who led the reaction against propriety in his own day, was often characterised a generation later as a faded emblem of late Victorian decadence. Modernists agreed that art should be different after the Victorians, but disagreed about *how* it should differ: neither E. M. Forster nor Virginia Woolf thought much of James Joyce's *Ulysses* (Woolf, writing to Strachey, called it 'the scratching of pimples on the body of the bootboy at Claridges').

Earlier critics of the Victorians tended to be more cautious. We should remember that *The Way of All Flesh* sat for nearly twenty years in a drawer, to be published at Samuel Butler's own insistence only after his death. Edmund Gosse first published *Father and Son* anonymously, revealing his name only after a positive reaction and good sales. Gosse, who lived on until 1928, nevertheless remained a careful critic of the past. When he reviewed *Eminent Victorians* in 1918 he found it wanting in 'imaginative insight' and 'sympathy', qualities which had both abounded in his own seminal work. Strachey, for his part, admired *Father and Son*, but thought Gosse the man unnecessarily repressed. Gosse found Strachey's 1921 biography of Queen Victoria more congenial, and the following year invited its author to join the Royal Society of Literature; Strachey declined. This did not stop Strachey from sending Gosse a copy of his collection *Books and Characters*, eliciting from the older writer the compliment that he was 'the best writer under fifty'. An elaborate comedy of manners – *autre temps, autre moeurs*, even for two key figures within the post-Victorian biographical tradition.[3]

It was not only the diffuseness and multi-generational tensions of the anti-Victorian tradition that limited its impact. There was also the fact that critics in the early twentieth century were Victorians themselves, or had grown up in Victorian homes. To take just members of the Bloomsbury Group: Forster was born in 1879, Strachey in 1880 and Woolf in 1882. However disaffected they may have been, they were all effectively Victorians. And strikingly enough, all showed a profound ambivalence in their criticism of the past. Forster once described himself as belonging to 'the fag-end of Victorian liberalism', and in old age had the late Victorian furniture of his childhood home moved into his rooms in King's College, Cambridge. 'Still with me . . . are writing table, mantelpiece with four long dishes etc, fender, carpet', he wrote in 1962 on the back of a photograph depicting a prim Rooksnest drawing-room in 1885.[4] He was the most decorous of debunkers. Like Rickie Elliot, his most autobiographical hero, Forster remained highly sensitive to human nuance and the dilemmas that such awareness brought: he 'suffered from the Primal Curse, which is not – as the Authorized Version suggests – the knowledge of good and evil, but the knowledge of good-and-evil'.[5]

Strachey's angry irreverence towards the Victorians is also best seen as an emotional engagement with the past rather than a flippant rejection of it. Such a response would, in any case, have been almost impossible. When he read a paper in 1922 to Bloomsbury's Memoir Club, Strachey reflected on the way that his adult dreams were haunted by childhood memories:

> We are in a drawing-room, among the old furniture, arranged in the old way, and it is understood that we are to go on there indefinitely, as if we had never left it. The strange thing is that, when I realize that this has come about, that our successive wanderings have been a mere interlude, that we are once more per-manently established at number 69 [Lancaster Gate], a feeling of intimate satisfaction comes over me. I am positively delighted. And this is strange because, in my waking life, I have never for a moment, so far as I am aware, regretted our departure from that house, and if, in actuality, we *were* to return to it, I can imagine nothing which would disgust me more.[6]

He conceded of the drawing-room which had been his formative encounter with Victorianism: 'it is almost impossible for me to come to an impartial judgement on it. I know it far too well.'[7] Strachey, the master of sly subversion and the subtle snub, was in fact a deeply ambiguous critic of the Victorians.

When it came to property, Strachey was a thoroughly Victorian figure. He intended to leave Ham Spray House to Dora Partridge (née Carrington), and yet in 1924 made the freehold out in his will to Ralph Partridge, even though the law had long since been changed to enable married women to own property.[8] His inconsistency on matters of sexual propriety was shared by many of his intimates. When Michael Holroyd was about to publish the first volume of his biography of Strachey in 1967, the year coincidentally of legal changes concerning homosexual practices, there was opposition to public revelations of Strachey's private life from people like David Garnett. He felt that it would shock friends of his, including a retired colonel and his wife. Duncan Grant and Frances Partridge also had some reservations, but the latter was able to comment in her diary: 'There was always that foot fumblingly advanced by Bloomsbury towards the conventional and aristocratic enclave, their Victorian childhoods perhaps coming to the surface in a way totally inconsistent with their defiance of *idées reçues.*'[9]

As we have seen, Virginia Woolf harboured profoundly mixed feelings about her father. These seeped through her novels. In *Night and Day* (1919) a heroine struggles to write a biography of her grandfather, a great Victorian poet, while trying to live her own life in a confusing, uncertain present. 'The glorious past, in which men and women grew to unexampled size, intruded too much upon the present, and dwarfed it too consistently', laments Woolf, 'to be altogether encouraging to one forced to make her experiment in living when the great age was dead.'[10] Life, for Woolf, was an experiment in living; and it was one carried out under the shadow of the past. She, too, gave papers to the Memoir Club, and wrote recollections of her parents and sketches of the past. 'The reason why Virginia Woolf could never have a Room of her Own', one psycho-analyst has observed, was because 'her father was always in there with her.'[11]

It seems clear enough that anger and ambivalence, as opposed to indifference and flippancy, were the keynotes of the early reaction against the Victorians. Given the tendency later in the twentieth century for some to treat the Victorians with casual dismissiveness, this is a most important point to make. Butler, Gosse, Forster, Strachey and Woolf were anything but casual in their criticism of history. For them it was not so much distant history as personal memory. This is only one way in which we have mischaracterised the anti-Victorianism of the early twentieth century. We have also tended to exaggerate the extent of anti-Victorianism up to the Second World War, relying as we have done on Bloomsbury and the 'Bright Young Things' for guidance as to the mood of Britain in these years. But, as we need to remind ourselves, childhood memories were not the only survivals from the past; in more direct and tangible ways, society kept much of its Victorian character after 1918.

If we look beyond Bloomsbury and the 'Bright Young Things' what we find in 1918 is a world shocked and saddened by war, but one not severed from its past. Traditional habits and outlooks survived the war, and in some respects may even have been intensified by them. Women who had been 'liberated' by work amongst the shells and gun parts were rudely sent packing when their husbands came home. Those men remained markedly conservative. The general election of 1918, rather than witnessing a backlash against the 'Old Men', saw a significant swing to the right; inter-war politics remained dominated by the Conservatives, and committed to deference, quietism and respectability. As Robert Graves and Alan Hodge recalled, 'The average man thought fondly of stepping back into civvies and resuming his old job, with the sole difference that he would no longer be b———d about by people in authority'.[12] It is difficult to say with absolute certainty how conscious ordinary people were of the Victorianism of their attitudes. Working-class people, unlike the garrulous Bloomsberries, did not spend much time committing their thoughts to posterity. Even then it is not clear that they would have been conscious of any specifically Victorian habits on their part.

This is not to say that such habits did not permeate working-class culture. As the historian W. L. Burn remarked of the working classes in the inter-war years, 'the mid-Victorian period was not really "history" at all ... they retained and used without self-consciousness their direct, personal links with the past'.[13] Richard Hoggart, who grew up in a very poor district of Leeds in the 1920s, concurs:

> Working-class people have virtually no sense of their own history except the oral and that is usually scrappy, confused and soon lost as they reach back to those unrecorded years ... Such historical memory as my grandmother had would have been mediated through sensationalist news-sheets at second or third hand until she learned to read herself, or through the very prescriptive frames of reference deployed from the pulpit, or simply from gossip. The relief of Mafeking was one of the great remembered moments of her life, Kruger one of the great villains. Kaiser Bill followed him. Dramatically, it was a sub-Kiplingesque world.[14]

Not until 1937, and the sense of a rift between establishment and ordinary opinion over the Abdication Crisis, would social investigators begin probing what working-class people thought of the world around them. The findings of Mass-Observation, as it was called, largely corroborate the thoughts of Burn and Hoggart. There were few comments about historical awareness, but the underlining conservatism of most people shines through: one woman from Marlow was determined to escape from the class into which she had been born ('crude, dirty and irresponsible') by marriage to 'a decent man'; men professed that they would not 'take advantage' of women; in Bolton in the late 1930s *Victoria the Great* was the most popular film amongst patrons of three cinemas.[15]

There is evidence, too, of continuity with the past outside Mass-Observation. Popular statuettes, engravings, plates, jugs and cartoons depicting Gladstone could still be found in many homes during the inter-war years, and the young Asa Briggs experienced at first hand the lingering glow of excitement from his grandfather, who had heard him speak.[16] John Drummond remembers Aunt Laura's slightly more genteel but equally atavistic home in the 1930s, a place 'absolutely of its time: chiming clocks, chenille tablecloths with bobbles, antimacassars on the arms of chairs, a piano with a candelabra, and a huge steel engraving of *The Monarch of the Glen*. There was nothing there I particularly liked, but I respected it as a rather sombre time capsule.'[17] When the Crystal Palace, the emblem of the Great Exhibition, went up in flames in 1936, observers mourned the passing of 'a link with the Victorian era' and 'a monumental relic of the Victorian "golden age"'.[18]

Modernism simply did not touch most people. Working-class literary culture in the first half of the twentieth century lagged a generation behind 'advanced' taste, partly because of the high cost of new books. While a university-educated minority might have revelled in Lytton Strachey and Virginia Woolf, the vast majority thought Arnold Bennett and H. G. Wells the height of progressiveness. (This may have been part of the spur for Woolf's dismissive 1924 essay 'Mr Bennett and Mrs Brown'.) In a survey of borrowing trends from the library of the workmen's institute at Tylorstown, a Welsh mining village, it was found that 7783 loans were made throughout 1941. Most frequently borrowed were popular romances and crime stories, though P. G. Wodehouse's *Right-Ho Jeeves* (incongruous reading for Welsh miners, one would have thought) was taken out seventeen times, and Jane Austen's *Pride and Prejudice* twenty-five times. E. M. Forster's *A Passage to India* was borrowed just once, Robert Graves's *Goodbye to All That* twice, and Virginia Woolf's *The Years* only five times.[19]

Such a trend was partly because cheap and highly influential imprints like the Dent Everyman series, inaugurated in 1906, did not cover the Modernists until the late 1930s. But more importantly, within working-class culture there was an inherent conservatism and preference for realism. A survey of favourite authors amongst the London branch of the Workers' Educational Association in 1936 gave John Galsworthy over 29 per cent, H. G. Wells over 11 per cent, Charles Dickens nearly 10 per cent, Thomas Hardy over 7 per cent, and J. B. Priestley over 5 per cent. Woolf languished with just over 1 per cent, and Forster with less than that.[20] A WEA instructor in Yorkshire six years before had already discovered that students had little time for feminism or the finer points of stream-of-consciousness. 'The women in one of my classes were not in the least impressed by Mrs Ramsay in *To the Lighthouse*', he commented. 'That she should allow her mind to wander while trying on the stocking that she was knitting for her little son, seemed inept, and their sympathy was for the little boy with so introspective a mother!'[21] D. H. Lawrence was widely considered 'smut'.

Working-class readers preferred Dickens, Ruskin and Morris – authors with clear, respectable, exalting voices. These were the writers who appealed most to those looking to educate themselves through scholarship exams and WEA classes. It was a headmaster's querying of his comment 'Thomas Hardy was a truly cultured man' that set Richard Hoggart thinking more deeply about abstract matters in the early 1930s; scholarship boys identified more easily with Jude Fawley than Stephen Dedalus.[22] Howard Spring, the working-class autodidact who rose to succeed Arnold Bennett and J. B. Priestley as book reviewer for the *Evening Standard*, went further: 'I think that in the immortality stakes *Ulysses* hasn't a dog's chance with *Kipps*, or *Orlando* with *The Old Wives' Tale*.' In 1941 he added that much of the blame for this appalling Modernist literature might be placed at Strachey's door. 'Look at the celebrated portrait of him by Henry Lamb', he sighed, 'the dry, desiccated, juiceless, cynical man whose very contact is enough to freeze all generous emotion and immobilise all noble endeavour.'[23] So much for suggestions that the Victorians had been rendered obsolete by 1918.

Unbroken continuity with the past amongst working-class people was matched by those who took up pens in the inter-war years to proclaim their Victorianism. Many described themselves explicitly as 'Victorians', and more specifically still, as 'mid-Victorians'. Even taking account for a certain novelty value on the part of publishers, it was clearly still tenable for individuals to identify themselves as Victorians after 1918. Their motives for doing so, admittedly, are not always clear. Perhaps it was in reaction against fashionable anti-Victorianism: as one literary critic observed in 1937, the very stigmatisation of the word 'Victorian' led to some older people gamely 'outing' themselves.[24] Or perhaps, after the long road travelled since the nineteenth century, some of these older writers felt the need to commit their thoughts to paper before it was too late. It may have been a combination of such motives.

Many of these works underlined the happiness of Victorian children. Dora Montefiore, for example, penned a memoir in 1927 called *From a Victorian to a Modern*.[25] The title might at first glance suggest a transition away from her upbringing. But Montefiore had enjoyed a contented childhood, and was particularly close to her father, Francis Fuller, who had been a key figure in the organisation of the Great Exhibition. It soon becomes clear that her title describes not liberation but natural development, and a healthy awareness of the temporal distance of the Victorian period by 1927. The tone of Montefiore's memoir was echoed by Molly Hughes, who in the 1930s wrote recollections of 'just an ordinary, suburban, Victorian family'. 'Expressions of jollity and enjoyment of life are understatements rather than overstatements', she warned the reader at the outset. 'It occurred to me to record our doings only because, on looking back, and comparing our lot with that of the children of to-day, we seemed to have been so *lucky*.'[26] William Kent was another memoir writer who offered a salutary example of how responses to youth were dependent upon the idiosyncrasies of character.[27] Kent praised Gosse's *Father and Son* as an exemplary model for autobiography, and revealed that he too had been given a very religious upbringing, subsequently losing his faith during the First World War. We might well expect ambivalence of the kind that Gosse showed towards his father; but Kent was not as thin-skinned, and, because he had lost his faith without trauma, there was none of that pained disaffection which Gosse had experienced.

Others, meanwhile, were exuberantly and pugnaciously in love with the past. The artist James Thorpe felt moved in 1933 'voluntarily [to] plead guilty, as a proud, obstinate and unrepentant Victorian'.[28] And Arthur Baumann, a former Conservative MP and editor of the *Saturday Review*, referred to himself in 1927 as 'a Victorian Tory, naked and unashamed'.[29] As the social historian Alan Bott noted in 1931: 'The second half of the nineteenth century has become a "period" admitted by its fondest survivors, the praisers of bygone days, to be quaint as well as golden.'[30] Amidst all of these efforts to establish a link between past and present, it was the mid-Victorian period which emerged as a sort of essence of Victorianism.[31] For in addition to works by Montefiore, Hughes, Kent, Thorpe and Baumann, there appeared in the early 1920s a number of memoirs by those who had grown up even earlier in the Victorian age, in the 1850s or 1860s.

Evelyn Hopkinson, for example, in 1928 identified herself as a 'Mid-Victorian Girl'. Hopkinson writes that she had been born in 'that austere and fine air' when Queen Victoria was 'at her commanding mid-career'.[32]

The memoirs of the popular middle-class novelist Matilda Betham-Edwards (born in 1837) offer another example. Introducing this posthumously published work, Sarah Grand wrote that Betham-Edwards was a mid-Victorian on account of 'the high sense of the dignity of her calling, and of its moral responsibility common to the choicer spirits of her day'.[33] Betham-Edwards would doubtless have approved of such a definition. After all, her memoirs must have reinforced many negative stereotypes of the mid-Victorian period, appearing as it did just a year after *Eminent Victorians* and the extension of the vote to women over thirty. On that subject she had to say: 'in advancing years I am more and more struck with the littleness and self-seeking of my sex, and less and less desirous of seeing them either in Parliament or holding any public office of responsibility whatever'.[34]

Mid-Victorian writers were sometimes more canny than this. The barrister and novelist R. E. Francillon, for instance, defined his mid-Victorianness in the usual qualitative terms; yet his memoirs also contain an element of irony lacking in Betham-Edwards. 'Mine, then,' he asserts, 'are the eyes, the spectacles, and the point of view of a mid-Victorian who has not cared to move with the times: who dislikes all change, and is hard to convince that any given case of it can be for the better.'[35] Francillon's work was published slightly earlier than the others discussed above, and also anticipated *Eminent Victorians*. Had Francillon been writing a decade later he might possibly have adopted a more cautious style; but, as it is, the work seems deliberately and attractively to parody its own reactionary tone. Francillon does in fact pay tribute to the technological advances of the twentieth century; and in another piece of mock exasperation concedes that, while not to his approval, Cambridge seemed just about to have survived the admission of female undergraduates.

Some, though, recalled memories of their mid-Victorian youth with ambiguity – and here we are reminded of the disaffection which underpinned so much anti-Victorianism. The socialist thinker and historian Ernest Belfort Bax (born in 1854), who published his memoirs in 1918, had very mixed attitudes towards history.[36] Belfort Bax passed his childhood in what he describes as a claustrophobic religious home. 'It was my lot to grow up under no very favourable conditions for intellectual development', he observed. 'A severe censorship in the matter of literature that was allowed into the house was maintained ... The most cruel of all the results of mid-Victorian religion was perhaps the rigid enforcement of the most drastic Sabbatarianism.'[37] In consequence, Belfort Bax's recollections of youth were tarnished:

Though my youthful days were passed towards the end of the period in question,

I experienced quite enough for it to have left an enduringly unpleasant reminiscence behind it. This is the more to be regretted as it affects one's memories of persons long since dead, whom one cannot altogether dissociate in one's mind from the at once morally repulsive and intellectually foolish beliefs they held, or professed to hold, and expected other people to hold. In themselves doubtless excellent, good-hearted people, their characters were poisoned and warped by the foulness and follies of their creed.[38]

This is an intelligent and touching passage, though it is an exception which proves the rule amongst those who explicitly identified themselves as Victorians in the early twentieth century. Most were keen to attest to their happiness with history. And if there may have been a certain element of curiosity value on the part of publishers and readers, then at least it was still possible for ordinary people in the inter-war years, consciously or otherwise, to belong emotionally to the past.

Such continuity of attitude was partly made possible by the character of an establishment which very much clung to its Victorian roots. From the monarch downwards, the political and social elite was steeped in the values of the past.[39] George V, who had come to the throne in 1910, was, in the words of A. J. P. Taylor, 'a model of constitutional rectitude and a model of conservative respectability also in his private life'.[40] The lavish public ceremonials which had been created to rehabilitate the monarchy in the last days of Queen Victoria continued to flourish in the reign of her grandson. The marriages of Princess Mary and the Duke of York in 1922–23 were held not in royal seclusion but in the public grandeur of Westminster Abbey, and were the culminations of regal processions through the streets of London. George V inaugurated the tradition of Christmas broadcasts on the BBC in 1932, the intimacy of the medium underlining his role as a Victorian father figure to each individual household. Three years later, his Silver Jubilee was an occasion of the greatest pomp and circumstance, and the greatest success. It was also one of the last great imperial occasions: in St Paul's Cathedral, the King sat surrounded by memorials to heroes of the Victorian empire such as Gordon and Kitchener.[41] 'King George V spanned the centuries', writes Kenneth Rose. 'At his christening in 1865 the minister in attendance on his grandmother, Queen Victoria, was Lord Palmerston. Shortly before his death in 1936 he handed the seals of office to a new Foreign Secretary, Anthony Eden.'[42]

Perhaps, though, it was the months following the death of George V that revealed just how attached the monarchy was to its Victorian moorings. Where the late King had successfully synthesised Victorian domestic probity with Edwardian public pomp, his son Edward VIII was far less keen on tradition. He was enamoured of the 'fast' life and, more specifically, of the married American heiress Mrs Wallis Simpson. By October 1936 Mrs Simpson had obtained her divorce; but the forces of tradition were already · rallying themselves. Those two arch-traditionalists Stanley Baldwin (who considered Mrs Simpson 'a respectable whore') and Archbishop Cosmo Lang led the campaign against the new King. They were not alone. It is clear that Edward VIII and his supporters overestimated the extent to which a 'modern' life of morganatic marriage would be viable in the 1930s. The King's subsequent abdication and succession of his brother George VI fittingly dramatised the backlash of Victorianism. George VI was a return to type. Sober, diffident and duty-bound, he was so conscious of his obligations that he set about taming a severe stutter in order to continue his father's broadcasts. He spoke of the monarchy as 'the family firm'.[43] Like his father (and as his daughter would be), George was steeped in Walter Bagehot's *The English Constitution*.[44] (Was it coincidence that the resolutely conservative historian G. M. Young gave Bagehot the appellation of the 'greatest Victorian' in 1938?)[45]

The date for the coronation of the new King – 12 May 1937 – fell strikingly close to the centenary of Queen Victoria's accession. Not surprisingly, these links were fully played up. A special film called *The King's People*, a eulogistic history of 'British character' and benevolent rule from Queen Victoria to George VI, was screened throughout the empire.[46] A comparable explicitness marked Hector Bolitho's biography of the new King. 'The cynicism of a new, lively century has made these laws of marriage unfashionable, but it has not made them untrue', he wrote. 'The rules of marriage and the example in domestic virtue which Prince Albert set, almost one hundred years ago, have become the abiding law of the members of the British Royal Family.'[47] In the coronation ceremony itself, all the fake-archaic paraphernalia of twentieth-century royal pageant – horse-drawn carriages, buckles and medals, ermine and jewels – was deployed. The music at Queen Victoria's coronation had been notoriously ill-executed, but on this occasion William Walton provided *Crown Imperial*, a glittering work in his best pastiche-Elgar mode. The message was clear: with George VI the monarchy was being re-established within a living tradition stretching back to Queen Victoria herself.[48] Such expansively regal pomp was also, of course, a conscious antidote to the mechanically drilled rallies then taking place in fascist Europe. Such elongated Victorianism may, as Piers Brendon has argued, have helped to mask the reality of Britain's 'perilous progress' on the world stage in the mid-1930s; but people felt a genuine imaginative connection with tradition which would stand them in good stead as the decade came to its grim close.[49]

Those who served the monarch were no less rooted in the attitudes of yesteryear. Sir Alec Hardinge, Private Secretary to successive Kings between 1920 and 1943, had royal connections stemming back to the pre-war age. The Ponsonby family had even lengthier attachments. Sir Henry Ponsonby had been appointed Private Secretary to Queen Victoria in 1870; his second son Frederick was an equerry to the Queen, and subsequently, under George V, became Treasurer of the Household and Keeper of the Privy Purse.[50] Outside court circles and specialised departments of Whitehall such as the foreign service, older assumptions about links between government office and the landed classes were, admittedly, waning under the strain of aristocratic decline. But seen in another light these might be taken as triumphs for Victorianism in themselves. Meritocracy in the civil service and armed forces had, after all, been consolidated in the last thirty years of the nineteenth century. And an older definition of Victorianism, that associated with social privilege, continued to flourish at the same time: for these new career civil servants, lawyers and army officers were hardly the diligent grammar school boys of a later generation.

Background still mattered. Most civil service postings went to those who had enjoyed the benefits of a good school (probably private) followed by Oxford or Cambridge. Here the Northcote-Trevelyan Report of 1854, establishing the idea of an efficient and impartial civil service run along meritocratic lines, held sway and would continue to do so for the rest of the twentieth century. But the flaw in this tradition was a culture in Whitehall that exchanged the dilettante air of the aristocratic club for the cloistered atmosphere of the Oxbridge common room. An ethos of gentlemanly values emanated from the corridors of power long into the twentieth century, and indeed it was not until the 1940s that standard 'etiquette' books for civil servants and ministers were drawn up at all. However meritocratic the selection process may have been, those who showed what Sir Charles Trevelyan in 1854 had termed 'superior docility' to the prevailing ethos of public duty stood the best chance of recruitment.[51] Those who had been schooled (often literally) to make conventionally 'Victorian' noises in this area enjoyed a distinct advantage. And there was no shortage of such people in the early twentieth century.

In the highest circles of church and politics, the key positions were also occupied by individuals of a distinctly Victorian hue. Randall Davidson, Archbishop of Canterbury between 1903 and 1928, did not come from patrician stock, but he was steeped in the values of tradition and would eventually resign over parliamentary refusal to accept revisions to the Prayer Book. The first modern archbishop to visit troops at the front line during the war, Davidson had also been an intimate of Queen Victoria. His successor was Cosmo Lang, incumbent until 1942, and we have already witnessed the extent of his traditionalism in the Abdication Crisis. It was also with Lang that the Gladstone sons, as we shall later see, sought to preserve the posthumous standing of their father by presentation of his diaries to Lambeth Palace.

The Prime Ministers of the inter-war years were comparably Victorian. Once again, the transition from landed patriarchs like Lord Rosebery or Lord Salisbury to plutocrats and professionals should not blind us to their regard for the past. Andrew Bonar Law, in his espousal of Unionism, has been called 'a Victorian survival'.[52] Historians continue to debate whether Neville Chamberlain was hopelessly old-fashioned in his attempts to reach a gentlemanly agreement with Hitler over appeasement.[53] But it was above all Stanley Baldwin and Ramsay MacDonald who enshrined the triumph of traditional values in inter-war Britain.[54] Although they inhabited opposite sides of the political spectrum, Baldwin and MacDonald both espoused moderate policies. Baldwin cultivated a conciliatory style, informed by deep religious belief, to promote national unity; MacDonald respected the monarchy highly, and believed the empire to be 'a great family'. Both, as products of non-patrician families, believed in the merits of honest hard work. And both venerated the countryside at a time when it was being promoted as a repository of spiritual values. Baldwin wrote introductions to the series of books on 'English Heritage' after 1929, and MacDonald wrote the commendations.[55] And it is worth adding that both were public-spirited rather than nostalgic in their love of tradition: this was no unfocused atavism.

Here a very distinctive feature of the years up to the Second World War emerges. Although the aristocratic mien of the establishment had begun to pass away, there remained a deep commitment to public duty amongst those in positions of power and influence. This was unmistakeably a Victorian phenomenon, a marriage between educated opinion and the anxiety that those with new-found privileges like the vote might not exercise them intelligently. We tend to think of debates about the influence of American culture and the tyranny of mass opinion in the light of the twentieth century: but these issues first appeared in works like J. S. Mill's *On Liberty* (1859) and Matthew Arnold's *Culture and Anarchy* (1869). Middle-class intellectuals in the late Victorian period, keen on encouraging social harmony and spreading the gospel of 'sweetness and light' to be found in 'the best that is known and thought' (both phrases from Arnold), set about their work with truly evangelical zeal.[56]

An important feature of these intellectuals was the interconnected nature of their lives, whether through birth, marriage, social circles or calling. Lord Annan once famously traced an 'intellectual aristocracy' in Victorian Britain which, with dizzying complexity, linked T. B. Macaulay, Charles Darwin, G. M. Trevelyan (a grandson of Sir Charles Trevelyan), John Maynard Keynes, Aldous Huxley and Ralph Vaughan Williams, to name but a few, into a large network of familial connection.[57] (It is striking that the Blooms-bury Group, most of whom in fact appear in Annan's network, echoed this arrangement, albeit with the commitment to public virtues often inverted to private pleasures: a suggestive irony which may underline further their latent Victorianism.)

With the dawning of the twentieth century, intellectuals became increas-ingly professional in outlook and vocation. But this did not mean that personal interconnections, or the old commitment to the propagation of civilised values, ceased to be important. Many networks continued. In the National Trust were involved not only Baldwin and MacDonald but Lord Grey, Lord Halifax, G. M. Trevelyan, R. C. Norman (Director-General of the BBC between 1935–39) and Oliver Brett (son of Lord Esher, who had been so heavily involved in the staging of royal ceremonials since the days of Queen Victoria).[58] Bertrand Russell, G. M. Trevelyan, J. M. Keynes, E. M. Forster and Leonard Woolf had all been members of the Apostles at Cambridge, and in later years drew upon shared membership of that private discussion group for influence in public affairs. Sir John Reith, first Director-General of the BBC, consciously echoed Victorian notions of public duty by striving to transmit 'into the greatest possible number of homes everything that is best in every department of human knowledge, endeavour and achievement' while omitting 'things which are, or may be, hurtful'.[59] At the BBC he built up a team of like-minded colleagues, and nurtured important connections with the political establishment, broadcasts of royal ceremonies becoming a particularly notable feature.[60]

Amongst critics who upheld Arnoldian notions of literary culture in the age of cinema, mass advertising and frivolous escapism was a network including T. S. Eliot, I. A. Richards and the husband and wife team F. R. and Q. D. Leavis.[61] (Significantly enough, *Culture and Anarchy* was influentially reissued in the early 1930s.)[62] A recent study has also identified Henrietta Barnett (social campaigner), G. A. Lefroy (Bishop of Calcutta), Raymond Unwin (architect and town-planner), Eleanor Rathbone (social campaigner), Leonard Woolf, J. M. Keynes, John Reith, J. B. Priestley and John Summer-son (architectural critic) as sharing a commitment to public duty. The Victorian liberal faith in social stability harnessed from individual freedom, material progress and bourgeois domesticity may have been challenged on each of these grounds by the early twentieth century, but that was why it was all the more important to search for new definitions of 'sweetness and light', and to present them to an illiberal world.[63]

What all of these networks and individuals had in common was a profound belief in the importance and virtues of civilisation. How they defined 'civilisation' was of course another matter, and some of those who drew upon the legacy of Victorian ideas about public duty were not necessarily enamoured of the past in all of its trappings. John Maynard Keynes is an outstanding example of such ambiguity. He was deeply attached to private pleasure, yet sought to integrate this with an equally passionate belief in improving the lot of mankind through economic theory. Could the probability of inducing refined pleasure, he wondered, act as a guide to economic policy? Could the private values of Bloomsbury be wedded to the hard realities of public finance? It is a measure of Keynes's genius and humanity that he considered such questions in the first place. But it is also a measure of his innate sense of the past. 'Our generation', he wrote to Virginia Woolf in 1934, two years before the publication of his masterpiece, *The General Theory of Employment, Interest and Money*, 'owed a great deal to our fathers' religion. And the young ... who are brought up without it, will never get so much out of life. They're trivial: like dogs in their lusts. We had the best of both worlds. We destroyed [Christianity] yet had its benefits.' [64] Post-Victorian in his atheism, Keynes could also be neo-Victorian in substituting pleasure in life as a religion, and evangelising it through his theories.

For some, the Victorian past became more directly and unambiguously relevant after the Russian Revolution and First World War. In this respect, it may have been that one of the great legacies of the war was not so much to tarnish perceptions of the Victorians as to enhance them. Where monarchies had been toppled by war and its aftermath in Russia, Germany, Austria and Italy, the British monarchy and parliamentary tradition glowed as an even brighter beacon in a dark world. Not that observers were unconcerned about the future. Bolshevism was considered a particularly dangerous threat in the 1920s. One anonymous writer, calling himself only a 'later Victorian', pondered in 1921:

Will the youth of to-day be able to look back with equal satisfaction, thirty years hence, upon the years 1918–21, or on those which seem likely to follow? Surely our grandchildren will prefer to turn for guidance to the traditions of Victorian days ... It may well be that the issue of the present upheaval in Russia will decide the fate of European civilisation; but it is hard to believe that the England of Victoria, the England of Peel and Palmerston, of Gladstone and Disraeli will relapse into medieval barbarism. May we not hope that a future generation, grown wiser through bitter experience, will look back with envy to those halcyon days of contentment and security to restore at least some portion of their glory? [65]

W. R. Inge, the reactionary Dean of St Paul's from 1911 to 1934, subsumed nostalgia for the Victorian age within his cosmically pessimistic outlook on life (he was dubbed 'the Gloomy Dean' by the *Daily Mail*).[66] In his 1922 Rede Lecture at Cambridge, he commented on the opprobrium heaped on Tennyson by some of the younger critics for his antipathy to the French Revolution. Sidestepping logic (and history) by linking the Jacobins with the Bolsheviks, Inge went on to argue that 'Years will bring a relative sanity to our young Bolsheviks; they will then, I hope (for I wish them well), begin to read Tennyson'.[67] Ten years later the Victorian period was still being invoked as a prophylactic against Bolshevism. Annabel Huth Jackson's memoir *A Victorian Childhood* (1932) was written in conscious reaction against 'the present Bolshevistic point of view raging in England and on the Continent' which, she believed, was threatening to destroy all vestiges of venerable tradition.[68]

For all the atavism of Baldwin and MacDonald, others felt that part of the danger lay in the desultory nature of domestic politics after the war. Some wanted a return to Victorian values. We have already seen Arthur Baumann's self-categorisation of himself as 'a Victorian Tory, naked and unashamed'. Baumann also advocated reviving 'some of the civic virtue of the last century': a time when 'the government of the country was conducted by men round whom the confidence of the country had gathered during many years of public service'.[69] Baumann was echoed here by G. M. Young, who closed his 1936 *Portrait of an Age* with quite unashamed comments on contemporary society and its 'daily clamour for leadership, for faith, for a new heart or a new cause'. 'But the great [early and mid-Victorian] age is not so far behind us that we must needs have lost all its savour and vigour', Young reflected, evidently urging emulation.[70] In his 1938 essay on 'The Greatest Victorian', Young wrote of 'the most precious element in Victorian civilization, its robust and masculine sanity'.[71]

Some felt that robustness had been squandered in the unnecessary compromises of inter-war politics. It is surely no coincidence that the reputation of Sir Robert Peel, hitherto castigated within the annals of Tory history as a 'traitor' over Catholic Emancipation and the Repeal of the Corn Laws, was reassessed in an age when it was not always entirely clear for what the Conservatives stood.[72] Historians in these years framed that famous question about whether Peel put party or nation first. The same thing was being asked of Stanley Baldwin, and it is striking that the famous denunciation of appeasement, *Guilty Men* (1940), would accuse Baldwin of putting party before nation over rearmament.[73] Some observers felt that the rot had begun lower down. 'Nowadays', lamented Howard Coote, erstwhile Lord Lieutenant of Huntingdonshire, 'the first question which appears to leap from the lips of an industrialist, a farmer or a working man is, "What is the Government going to do for me?" Whereas the Victorian was more apt to enquire, "What can I do for myself?" – a question much more likely to produce practical results.'[74] Anticipating Margaret Thatcher by nearly half a century, this appeal to Smilesian values yet had the distinctive timbre of one who had direct acquaintance with Victorian practice.

Revivalism abounded between the wars. There were, naturally, the grumblings of the older generation: that 'there is little left now [1919] to the imagination; and this is a mistake'; that 'ballroom dances of the mid-Victorian era were both more varied and animated [than] the monotony of the eternal tom-tom rhythm which has so afflicted the dancing of our post-War years'; that 'modern fiction, modern films, and other intellectual sewers that used to be closed ... are now open' – one imagines it all intoned by Nancy Mitford's Uncle Matthew, who has already gnashed his way through four sets of dentures.[75]

It is really the revivalism of members of the younger generation which gives pause for thought. 'Victoriana' (the term was first used, strikingly enough, in 1918)[76] enjoyed something of a revival during and after the First World War.[77] This manifested itself most famously amongst a circle of Oxford undergraduates in the early 1920s. One of these was Henry Yorke, who recalled:

> We collected Victorian objects, glass paperweights with coloured posies cast in them, little eternalized baskets of flowers in which nothing could break ... and large piles of waxed fruits under high glass domes ... A number of us bought spotted dogs in china from Staffordshire, one or two had figures of the Prince Consort in the same material.[78]

There were Cambridge aesthetes, too. Frances Partridge recalls tales from George ('Dadie') Rylands about an undergraduate who painted his rooms scarlet and black, resided behind permanently drawn curtains, and 'lunched off vodka and oysters while a gramophone played a Victorian polka'.[79] This makes Wilde's endeavours at Oxford to live up to his blue china seem positively plebeian.

What is most striking about this revival of Victoriana is not so much the camp affectedness, the very restricted nature of its following, or even the anticipation of a later market for Victorian collectables, but the emotional quality of this relationship with the past. Beneath the fripperies and frills of those like Harold Acton who dressed as early Victorian gentlemen, there was an acute anxiety about modern life. They turned to the past for escape, if not for serious guidance: and it was not to late Victorian decadence (a certain cult for Wilde apart) or to the more recent experiments of the

1. Victoria with her mother, the Duchess of Kent, in 1834. Writers have increasingly become interested in the young Victoria and how she became the monarch of legend. Engraving by George Hayter. (*Royal Archives*)

2. The opening of the Great Exhibition on 1 May 1851. The emblem of Victorian confidence and prosperity, the Exhibition cast a long shadow over the twentieth century.

3. The British Bee Hive. This view of society was fine if you happened to be somewhere near the top. Drawing by George Cruikshank, 1867, reflecting the controversy over the Second Reform Act.

4. The scarcity of welfare provision for the Victorian poor would be a savagely criticised aspect of twentieth-century views of the age. Detail from Sir Luke Fildes, *Applicants for Admision to a Casual Ward* (1874). (*Royal Holloway, University of London*)

5. Charles Dickens at his writing desk in 1858. (*National Portrait Gallery*)

6. William Ewart Gladstone in tree-felling mode. A rare moment of repose – or another photo opportunity?

7. Oscar Wilde, posing as himself. (*National Portrait Gallery*)

8. Four generations of monarchy. Queen Victoria and the future Edward VII, George V and Edward VIII in 1899. Staring the camera (and modernity) in the face, Edward VIII was to suffer the consequences of ignoring his great-grandmother's example in royal probity. (*National Portrait Gallery*)

Bloomsbury Group that they turned, but to the freshness and optimism of
the early Victorian period. As Acton explained, in the disorientating aftermath of war, 'We wanted Dawns, not Twilights'.[80] Bliss was it in that Dawn
to be alive: that may have been the cherished hope of members of this circle
like the young Evelyn Waugh, whose bright young things throw 'Victorian
parties', but his early novels are as vulnerable beneath the surface as they
are funny.[81] One thinks, too, of that other Oxford aesthete, John Betjeman,
forlornly clutching Archibald (later pirated by Waugh for Sebastian Flyte's
Aloysius).

The frivolities were, in any case, to end in the 1930s when a new austerity
was imposed on Oxford undergraduates by the Great Depression.[82] More
generally, as the 1930s wore on, the Victorian past increasingly took on a
burnished glow. It was not only that the trauma of war and the subsequent
efflorescence of anti-Victorianism had died down; it was also that the
nineteenth century now seemed rather far away, especially under the dark
storm clouds that scuttled across from Europe. John Galsworthy, who had
begun his *Forsyte* novels in 1906 with a harsh depiction of Soames Forsyte,
the rapacious 'man of property', closed it in 1928 with a much softer view
of him in the pointedly titled *Swan Song*. Galsworthy, of course, remained
a great favourite with working-class audiences in the inter-war years, partly
because they had never felt disaffected from history. Other contemporaries
also waxed lyrical about their Victorian origins in the late 1930s. Ralph
Vaughan Williams, anxious about the spectre of fascism in Europe, completed his *Dona Nobis Pacem* in 1936, at one point setting the words of John
Bright in 1855: 'The Angel of Death has been abroad throughout the land ...'
The work was frequently performed by choral societies in the tense interval
before the outbreak of war; Vaughan Williams 'had caught, with unerring
accuracy, the mood of the times', one observer has written.[83] And Arnold
Bax, soon to be appointed Master of the King's Music, included in his
majestic, ruminatively nostalgic Seventh Symphony of 1939 a passage that
he referred to as 'a real 1840 romantic wallow'.

Society remained underpinned by Victorian practices and attitudes, and
yet there were those who felt that the past should have even more influence
over the present. There are, of course, nostalgic people in every age. But
the nostalgia that flourished in the 1930s had a particular piquancy, and, it
might be argued, a hard-won justness. One writer who had certainly earned
his nostalgia was Siegfried Sassoon. Writing in 1928 about his happy rural
childhood, he used a felicitous phrase to describe what it was that could
make the Victorian past so attractively clear to people: 'the sunshine of ...
clarified retrospection'.[84] Ten years later, and only a fortnight before Neville
Chamberlain flew to Munich, Sassoon published *The Old Century*, to great

acclaim. Readers seemed not to mind its unashamedly lyrical escapism; here they read that 'time's wavering shadows are falling across the glade; but there will be no sunset for that pictured afternoon'.[85] The place of the Victorian age, in the general scheme of this nostalgia, was made even more explicit in George Orwell's novel *Coming Up for Air*, published the following year. Its subject is the final trip made to his childhood village by a fictional everyman, George Bowling. 'Before the war,' he reflects,

> and especially before the Boer War, it was summer all the year round. I'm quite aware that that's a delusion. I'm merely trying to tell you how things come back to me ... What was it that people had in those days? A feeling of security, even when they weren't secure. More exactly, it was a feeling of continuity. [86]

That sense of continuity was one thing that would change forever as the bombs began dropping on Britain.

# 4

# *War*

'As I write, highly civilized human beings are flying overhead, trying to kill me.' So wrote George Orwell in the summer of 1940, amidst the thundering bombs and wailing air-raid warnings of the Blitz. Orwell was exploring, in these troubled times, what it was to be English. The outcome was *The Lion and the Unicorn*, published the following year and destined to earn a reputation as one of one of the most probing analyses of national character ever penned. What Orwell concluded about society in 1940 was this:

> England is not the jewelled isle of Shakespeare's much-quoted passage, nor is it the inferno described by Dr Goebbels. More than either it resembles a family, a rather stuffy Victorian family, with not many black sheep in it but with all its cupboards bursting with skeletons. It has rich relations who have to be kow-towed to and poor relations who are horribly sat upon, and there is a deep conspiracy of silence about the source of the family income. It is a family in which the young are generally thwarted and most of the power is in the hands of irresponsible uncles and bedridden aunts. Still, it is a family.[1]

For all the fashionable jibes of Strachey and his kind, Orwell realised, society in 1940 remained profoundly Victorian in character. This would serve the nation well in many ways, for it had been plunged into a struggle in which its physical and emotional resources would be tested to the very limit. There was none of the bright-eyed enthusiasm of an earlier generation when the slow, mournful voice of Neville Chamberlain issued from wireless sets across Britain in September 1939. Now, as the war turned in 1940 towards the Blitz and the Battle of Britain, civilians found themselves caught up in a 'People's War'. It was a war, they were told by the politicians, to save civilisation. But this they had already sensed themselves.

They had sensed another thing, too. It also soon came to be seen as a war to *change* civilisation. Early in the war – perhaps as early as June 1940, between the Dunkirk débâcle and the Blitz – the political climate seems to have changed in Britain. A spirit of 'never again' worked its way into the consciousness of people.[2] And this was not simply a determination to avoid the horrors of the Doodlebug and the miseries of the ration queue. What

people had most in mind were the deprivations of the 1930s, that 'low
dishonest decade' over which the Conservatives had presided. Where a
cultivated observer like G. M. Young had called in 1936 for a return to
Victorian values in order to solve the problems of contemporary life, the
agenda had been completely rewritten within the space of four years. The
war became the greatest challenge yet to the lingering influence of Victorianism on British society, and so to the way in which the Victorians were
seen.

At first glance, the war and its aftermath seems, if anything, to have
strengthened the bonds of Orwell's Victorian family. The war was, after all,
effectively won by a Victorian. Winston Churchill, descendant of the Duke
of Marlborough, son of Lord Randolph Churchill and veteran of the Boer
War, was steeped in the proud martial spirit which had won and kept for
Queen Victoria an empire. He was no less suffused with the spirit of the
Victorian gentleman-amateur, turning his hand with great success to journalism and even more so to the writing of history. It was this sense of the
past that was the very essence of Churchill. His memory has become the
site of fierce controversy in the years since 1945, with many historians arguing
that his backwards-looking premiership was disastrous not only for the
Conservatives but for the nation as a whole. Yet, in 1940, it was precisely
this atavistic mindset – historical-minded and deeply conservative – that
was needed. The great speeches, with their rolling cadences and dramatic
pauses, the inimitable husky brays and control of dynamics, seemed to make
themselves part of history the moment they were delivered.

What listeners responded to was not simply a theatrical presentation of
their precarious situation, but the voice of history itself. Churchill's was
the art that hid artifice. His oratorical style had been honed over many
years from close perusal of Johnson, Gibbon and Macaulay; and his
speeches, for all their apparent spontaneity and ability to take sudden wing,
were drafted with the most fastidious care. On his side he had not only
natural eloquence but a deep feeling for the past. 'The key to Winston',
wrote his colleague Leo Amery in 1929, 'is to realise that he is a Mid-
Victorian.' A year later Churchill himself lamented that there were so few
successors to the great statesman of the 'Victorian Epoch' (himself, presumably, excluded).[3] Churchill possessed what Isaiah Berlin has called 'a
historical imagination so strong, so comprehensive, as to encase the whole
of the future in a framework of a rich and multicoloured past'.[4] This was
the voice of continuity, a voice whose elaborate rhetoric turned the clock
back on two decades of neo-Stracheyan sniping. And, of course, the nation
responded to this oratory during the war. Most people, as we have seen,

never subscribed to fashionable debunking of the past. They were, after all, the grandchildren of people who had heard Gladstone and Disraeli deliver similar speeches.

Churchill showed a less sure historical touch in 1945 when, in the election campaign, he warned that a vote for Labour might as well be a vote for a new Gestapo. The result was a famous landslide victory for Labour. In its wake there followed the welfare reforms which would underpin society for the remainder of the twentieth century. The National Health Service was a break with existing welfare legislation which was still recognisably Victorian in character: by the late 1920s up to 140,000 people were still dependent on the Poor Law.[5] The Beveridge Report on which these reforms were based, appropriately enough, deployed language straight out of A Christmas Carol: the 'giants' to be slain were want, sickness, squalor, ignorance and idleness. Government spending and nationalisation also brought elements of Keynesian economics charging in to slay the old dragon of Victorian finances.

Still, the election of the Labour government and the end of the war should not be characterised too sharply as a break with the past. Churchill's bewildered defeat at the polls has a rich suggestiveness about how this scion of the Marlborough family was felt to be out of touch with the contemporary mood. Yet the premier who replaced him was in some ways even more emphatically a Victorian figure. Clement Attlee was a member of that last generation of Victorians, born only three years after Lytton Strachey. He was, as he put it himself, the son of 'a typical family of the professional class brought up in the atmosphere of Victorian England'.[6] A sense of public duty, gained as much from reading William Morris as from the Victorian aura of Haileybury School, stamped itself on him from an early age.[7] He was moved as a student at Oxford to take up work at Toynbee Hall, the mission house in the East End. The product of a respectable middle-class education, he manfully served in the First World War, and despite his socialist connections was known for years afterwards as 'Major' Attlee. A politician's politician, he said in retirement that he thought Lord Salisbury the finest Prime Minister to have held office during his lifetime.[8] Attlee was far from unique in such archaisms. His Chancellor of the Exchequer between 1947 and 1950, Stafford Cripps, was fired by profound religious convictions. Ernest Bevin, the plain-speaking Foreign Secretary, had certain Palmerstonian credentials and favoured 'sharp and forceful action' on a number of matters.[9] And Aneurin Bevan, the mastermind of the NHS, was the son of a miner weaned as much on the Victorian autodidact culture as on the Welsh dissenting tradition.

Nor was there discontinuity after 1945 with some of the initiatives made during the war to bolster morale and spread a little Arnoldian 'sweetness and light'. The Council for the Encouragement of Music and the Arts was set up in 1940, providing factory workers around war-torn London with inspiring orchestral concerts and enabling the Old Vic theatre company (bombed out of its metropolitan home) to tour Lancashire and South Wales. In December 1941 the new President of the Board of Education, R. A. Butler, offered the chairmanship of CEMA to one of the great devotees of public duty, John Maynard Keynes. Under Keynes, CEMA continued to flourish, and in 1946 it was relaunched for the post-war world as the Arts Council of Great Britain. There were, admittedly, some tensions from the outset about how funds should be distributed. Should enterprises be supported in London or in the provinces? Should money be given to amateur groups or professional organisations? Although Keynes died early in 1946, he ensured that the answer in each of these cases tended to be metropolitan and professional: 'the best which has been thought and said in the world', felt this neo-Victorian, should surely be couched in the tones of the established experts.[10]

It was also in 1946 that the BBC renewed its commitment to cultural excellence through the foundation of the Third Programme. Plans to consolidate the artistic and intellectual items in broadcasting, previously mixed up with lighter fare, had been gathering pace for some time. It may have been that the wartime separation of the BBC into 'Forces' and 'Home Service' networks encouraged the subsequent division into the Home Service, Light Programme and Third Programme. Enthusiastic audiences for the activities offered by CEMA also suggested that a station for 'persons of taste, of intelligence, and of education' would be viable. But for all the patrician overtones of such thinking, it should be remembered that the original architects had in mind a fully Arnoldian perspective on broadcasting. William Haley, Director-General at the end of the war, was a compulsive autodidact who was said to devour three Victorian novels a week. He envisaged a pyramid of tastes to be embodied in the three stations, with the ultimate design of 'a BBC through the years – many years – which would slowly move listeners from one stratum of this pyramid to the next'.[11] The first controller of the Third Programme was George Barnes, a Cambridge aesthete and friend of E. M. Forster. His successor in 1948 was Harman Grisewood, who defended the station from charges of snobbery by commenting: 'The attacks on the Third reflect the kind of philistinism which Matthew Arnold and many others have accused the English of ... I believe in elites, because they are simply the best. And I think the best is the right thing to have.'[12]

The Victorians, appropriately enough, featured heavily in the early schedules of the Third Programme. Most notable here was the 1948 series 'Ideas and Beliefs of the Victorians'.[13] It ran for four months, with a number of supporting features in the *Radio Times*, and opened with a long discussion between Bertrand Russell, G. M. Trevelyan, Lord David Cecil and Christopher Dawson.[14] In the same year there was a selection of readings from Victorian sources on the theme of female emancipation.[15] And in 1951 the BBC supported the Festival of Britain with a special '1851 Week'. As Peter Laslett, the Cambridge historian who masterminded the project, commented: 'Everything which you will hear during this week in 1951 was heard in England during 1851.' This included music played in that year, theatrical successes from the 1851 season, and news items of the day. 'The purpose of this is ... to use the wireless to recapture the aesthetic atmosphere of the Great Exhibition year.' As Listener Research showed, the scheme was a triumph. 'This has been a most interesting week of programmes', commented a science lecturer. 'Could we have some "history without tears" this way occasionally?' A machine tools apprentice was even more impressed: 'The atmosphere was brilliantly achieved ... to such a degree that my father thought that the 1851 news item was *Today in Parliament*, till mention was made of the Rt Hon. W. E. Gladstone.'[16]

At the beginning of the 1950s, with the physical appearance of the nation pockmarked by war, with the continuation of rationing, and with the old men still in charge, little may appear to have changed. Quietness – even drabness – hung like a pall over the post-war world. 'Sunday', writes one observer, 'was still essentially Victorian in character – a day for a large family dinner, quiet relaxation and religious worship.'[17] Margaret Forster recalls how working-class families in Carlisle during the 1950s continued to believe in the importance of a respectable 'send off':

> Carlisle people seemed to treat funerals with a Victorian intensity – lots of big, gleaming black cars, all crawling along bumper-to-bumper; masses of flowers, lavish wreaths and crosses; every single mourner in black, and many of the women heavily veiled. I was fascinated by these spectacles and resented my mother closing our curtains out of respect, when I wanted to position myself in the window so that I could see everything.[18]

Further south, Lorna Sage recalls, the village of Hanmer in North Wales existed in 'a time warp, an enclave of the nineteenth century' for which the war had not counted at all:

> The war had changed [awareness of the outside world] to some extent, but not as much as it might have because farming was a reserved occupation and sons hadn't been called up unless there were a lot of them, or their families were smallholders with little land. Hanmer in the 1940s in many ways resembled

Hanmer in the 1920s, or even the late 1800s except that it was more depressed, less populous and more out of step – more and more islanded in time as the years had gone by.

Sage endured a miserable childhood in such a village. Her escape came through reading, but even there the book she read most was an anthology of nineteenth-century verse first published seventy years before.[19] Older writers of at this time, however, often had fonder recollections of their own genuinely Victorian childhoods. These years were a good time for fond recollections of the past, as enchanting memoirs by Katharine Chorley and Gwen Raverat show.[20]

In other respects, though, the tide had already turned. Wartime trends favourable to the rehabilitation of Victorian attitudes proved to be short-lived. One of the prime casualties here was the audience for Victorian culture which been stimulated during the war, partly because of the constraints on leisure imposed by black-outs, but also no doubt on account of the certainty it seemed to offer. By 1944 Dickens and Hardy were the second and third most regularly borrowed novelist from the Bristol public libraries, and the ordered mid-Victorian world of Trollope also attracted many readers.[21] Noticing this trend, F. R. Leavis talked in 1948 of 'the present vogue of the Victorian age'. In the same year Humphry House pondered: 'Are the Victorians Coming Back?'[22] The answer was no. There were certainly breakthroughs in biography and historical scholarship, but the popular renaissance was to flag. The Hardy and Dickens novels were returned to the library; WEA attendance dropped off; and people began to accuse the BBC of elitism.

The Third Programme struggled to retain an audience even as the old guard remained in charge. Its listening figures in December 1946 of 6 per cent of the population had rapidly dwindled, so that by the time of the '1851 Week' it sometimes failed to attract more than 100,000 listeners each night.[23] In the more egalitarian climate of post-war Britain it was widely accused of snobbery. The ghost to be exorcised here, of course, was that of Matthew Arnold. As one journal commented in 1951, when Harman Grisewood and E. M. Forster gave talks to celebrate the fifth birthday of the Third Programme, they sounded 'like aristocrats making dignified speeches from the scaffold before having their heads chopped off. The execution has been postponed but the baying of the Philistines still lingers in the air.'[24]

Symptomatic here were responses to the Festival of Britain, held on the South Bank of the Thames in 1951. What most people remembered from the Festival was its hopes for the future, not its celebration of the past. The BBC may have highlighted the centenary of the Great Exhibition, and attracted some favourable comments on its scheduling, but most who visited the South

Bank and gazed up in wonder at the Skylon were little troubled by the demise of Victorian values. As Jeffrey Auerbach has written, 'nineteenth-century liberalism no longer seemed relevant in the post-war, democratic-socialist society'.[25] The section commemorating the Great Exhibition (an afterthought in itself) was accordingly modest: a somewhat unimaginative scale-model of the Crystal Palace. For the organisers, too, the Festival was about celebrating the present and designing the future, not recalling the past; if anything, contemporary critics thought their plans not enough of a break with tradition.[26] The last Victorian generation may still have ruled the roost after 1945, but ordinary people had been changed irrevocably by the experience of war. How had this come about?

The tumultuous events of wartime damaged many of the traditional features of society. Bombs were no respecters of social niceties. Middle-aged people who had been brought up to observe fine Victorian class gradations now found themselves crammed against strangers from all walks of life in the air-raid shelter or Underground sleeping-place. The jury is still out on whether this experience really helped to break down class barriers.[27] Some in the East End felt so aggrieved at the disproportionate level of bombing they faced that they were heard to wish some of it on those who lived in better-heeled districts. The idea of a 'Blitz spirit' – of warm generosity towards strangers and humorous stoicism – may in part be a myth; but it had considerable basis in actual behaviour, and was no less useful for being romanticised.

Individual people could, in often appalling circumstances, make a difference. There was no shortage of people like 'Auntie Mabel', the Underground shelter marshal who chirruped to Mass-Observation in 1943: 'Never a cross word all the time I been down 'ere. Know everybody, I do.'[28] And Virginia Woolf, not otherwise known for her class sensitivities, was also struck by a new spirit of camaraderie. She and Leonard once took refuge in a pill-box on Wimbledon Common. A couple was already occupying it, making a cup of tea. 'We were invited to join them', recalled Woolf. 'In two minutes we were all chatting happily like old friends.'[29] (One wonders whether Woolf might, in hindsight, have thought of revising her statement about human nature changing in December 1910. Should it have been June 1940?) Sometimes cross-class encounters took place in the most striking of environments. Part of the Victoria and Albert Museum, the hallowed repository of historical memory, was converted into a canteen to feed labourers who had come down from the north to rebuild London.[30] These war-enforced encounters between privilege and poverty, past and present, seem to mark a watershed in social attitudes. In the brave new world of Attlee's government, everybody was supposed to be accorded greater personal significance.

Even the physical setting for post-war life was new, for the war changed the face of a Britain which, in 1939, had still literally been Victorian. This dramatised attitudes to the past, and created one of the first debates about the place of 'heritage' in modern society. Bombing had ravaged many towns and cities, reducing to rubble Victorian slum tenements in the East End as well as many parts of nineteenth-century industrial powerhouses like Birmingham, Coventry, Manchester and Sheffield. For the 'never again' generation, this meant an ideal combination of need and opportunity to move away from moribund living conditions.[31] The drive to moral and physical reconstruction shines through many of the reports initiated even during the course of the war. The *County of London Plan* (1943), for example, reflected that: 'London was ripe for reconstruction before the war; obsolescence, bad and unsuitable housing, inchoate communities ... all these and more clamoured for improvement before the enemy's efforts to smash us by air attack stiffened our resistance and intensified our zeal for reconstruction.' 'To rebuild the city on the old lines', the town-planner Thomas Sharp also subsequently concluded of Exeter, 'would be a dreadful mistake.'[32]

Some landowners, hit as much by crippling costs and a prescient sense of the drive to egalitarianism as they were by bombs, also saw that they would have to cut their losses after the war. R. G. Proby, a prominent landowners' representative, admitted in 1942 that that while efforts should be made to preserve great estates like Arundel and Wilton, 'there are many Victorian barracks [in them] which I think might well be demolished without great harm being done'. This was very much the pattern that was to follow, as schemes in the 1950s and 1960s to open stately homes to the public were made more viable by closing down Victorian and Edwardian wings in favour of the Georgian parts.[33]

Post-war rebuilding, then, encouraged not just a transformation of the physical environment but a simultaneous imaginative retreat from the past. Victorian mansions cleared away from Roehampton by the London County Council in 1957 were condemned as 'crumbling, decaying and totally uneconomic'.[34] Victorian brickwork continued to be held in low esteem, perhaps from a society which had more recently grown used to prefabricated housing. Glass, concrete, high-rise flats and open spaces were to be dominant motifs in urban existence in the 1950s and 1960s. This was the age of 'New Brutalism', a phrase tellingly adopted by younger architects in the 1950s – individuals scornful of the 'Dickensian' trappings of the past, considered by turns dirty, dangerous and twee. Contemporary efforts to soften this angular, massively functional aesthetic were derided in terms of avoiding a return to William Morris.[35] (His name was invoked partly, perhaps, because of the successful 'Victorian and Edwardian Decorative Arts' exhibition at the Victoria and Albert Museum in 1952.)[36]

Controversy raged, but young designers enamoured of 'Brutalism' made progress in high places. Particularly ironic, here, were the designs by James Stirling for the History Faculty of Cambridge University, resulting in a large greenhouse-like building. Several generations of students have since been dripped upon in December and lightly grilled in June. Stranger still was the fact that Stirling was trying to do for the post-war age what Victorian architects had done for the nineteenth century. 'One has only to compare the Crystal Palace to the Festival of Britain,' he wrote in 1958, 'or the Victorian railway stations to recent airports, to appreciate the desperate situation of our technical inventiveness today, compared to the supreme position which we held in the last century.'[37] Such veneration, however, did not extend to anything like emulation.

The appearance in 1963 of Asa Briggs's *Victorian Cities* – a study of London, Birmingham, Leeds and Manchester (amongst others) – was closely related to many of these concerns. Briggs had already written a history of Birmingham ten years before; but *Victorian Cities*, he wrote, was designed 'to illuminate some of the themes which are of interest to the many different kinds of specialists who approach "*the* city" from quite different angles'.[38] Everyone, it seemed, had ideas about what cities should be like, and few of these incorporated a sympathetic historical dimension. To a concerned and highly intelligent scholar like Briggs, this was a cause of unease. 'Year by year we are pulling down the older parts of our cities', he wrote, 'with a savage and undiscriminating abandon which will not earn us the gratitude of posterity. If the detailed study of Victorian cities is not pursued at this perilous moment of time, when we are still poised between the nineteenth and twentieth centuries, it may be difficult to pursue it at all.'[39] 'Images and Realities' was the pointed subtitle of a study on Victorian cities published a decade later.[40]

Some parts of Victorian cities, on the other hand, deserved to be consigned to oblivion and were not. In the Lower Broughton area of Manchester, houses condemned as unfit in 1965 were purchased three years later by the council and rented to those who could not afford anything else. Lavatories were not installed until 1971, and before that buckets had still been emptied into the street. 'If Engels could see it now', sighed Polly Toynbee of an area which that writer had in fact described back in the 1840s. It was the kind of thing to give Victorian cities a bad name: small wonder that elsewhere there was a rush to tear them down.[41]

For more salubrious Victorian houses which survived the combined onslaughts of the Luftwaffe and the London County Council, interior fashions in the 1950s and 1960s favoured a style far removed from that of their original inhabitants. As post-war restrictions and drabness gave way in the later 1950s to a consumer culture there was a new emphasis on light and space in the home. Out went Victorian darkness and clutter; in came stream-lined furniture and formica, patio doors and plastic – all show-cased in the brightly optimistic Festival of Britain back in 1951. 'A Victorian interior with everything from aspidistra to whatnot', declared the style journal *Everybodys* earlier that year, 'to us is the worst of taste.'[42] What the subsequent Festival emphasised in its section on 'Homes and Gardens' was, not surprisingly, 'the problem of space'. The showcase room for the parlour, that great mainstay of Victorian homes, showed how any lingering wish for a room in which to relax might be met 'in twentieth-century style and without any trace of frowstiness'.[43] Twenty years of consumer culture and Do-It-Yourself would see the Victorian cobwebs chased vigorously away in a great many homes. In certain respects, what Lytton Strachey had failed to achieve, formica did.

Here, of course, the generational perspective was absolutely crucial. The coronation of Elizabeth II in 1953 was a spectacularly successful event, and also a symbolic one: for it seemed, to many, to hold out the promise of a heady 'New Elizabethan' era. And it is surely no coincidence that the last generation of those who had been born Victorians was dying out in the 1950s and 1960s. Cosmo Lang, David Lloyd George, J. M. Keynes and Stanley Baldwin had already been carried away in 1945–47; there followed in 1950 George Bernard Shaw (in his nineties an even older Victorian); in 1958 Ralph Vaughan Williams; in 1962 G. M. Trevelyan; in 1965 Winston Churchill, accorded the first state funeral since Gladstone; in 1967 Clement Attlee and Siegfried Sassoon; and in 1970 two other long-lived Victorians, E. M. Forster and Bertrand Russell. These are, of course, only some of the big names. Many died even earlier. But by 1970 very few born in the 1880s or earlier had managed to cheat death. And everywhere, in all households, this would have been the pattern. With the rising tide of fashion, it is not difficult to see how Victorian domestic life as a lived reality passed away within a generation after the Second World War.

Many of the public realities of Victorianism were also beginning to fade away or be challenged in the decades after the war. Britain's resources had been stretched to the very limit (and beyond) by the war; yet victory in 1945 seems to have blinded politicians to the likelihood of its reduced status in the world.[44] The war had stimulated the mechanical, chemical and electronic industries, but they did not look set to be given the necessary support to replace the weakening Victorian sinews of coal and steel. (Ironically it was Germany and Japan, the countries worst affected and with least cause for inflated national pride, which rebuilt and innovated with the greatest effectiveness after 1945.) The generation of Churchill and Attlee, the last Victorians, had grown up with the empire; they saw little serious need for a rapprochement with Europe and its nascent economic community until it was really too late. To be sure, imperial trade links in 1950 were more lucrative than those with a still decimated Europe. But even so, in the coming few years, there was a wilful disinclination to probe both the nature of Britain's declining influence and its reliance upon the 'special relationship' with America.

It was therefore with a shock of sudden recognition that the Suez crisis of 1956 held a mirror up to the futility of Britain's lingering imperial pretensions. Anthony Eden may have felt that he was confronting another little Hitler in Colonel Nasser, but as much as anything else he was echoing Palmerston's style (and literal practice) of gunboat diplomacy. More pertinent still was the connection with an earlier Conservative Prime Minister. 'Memories of the route to India, that jewel in the Imperial Crown,' writes Robert Blake, 'and of Disraeli's purchase of the Canal Company shares blurred post-war realities.'[45] The public reaction was, famously, divided; and it was a defining moment for many who were coming to political and historical awareness just as old presumptions about the empire were dying away.[46] In John Osborne's *The Entertainer* (1957) – a requiem for the Victorian music hall in itself – a British soldier dies offstage. The passing seemed doubly symbolic. The critic John Raymond felt that the play was 'a grotesque cry of rage and pain at the bad hand history was dealing out to what was once the largest, most prosperous empire in the world'.[47]

By this stage the empire was already shrinking fast, a fact which was hardly disguised by use of the polite euphemism 'Commonwealth'. Most instructive here was the progression to independence of India and Pakistan in 1947. The jewel in the crown had long since ceased to pay for Britain. Moreover, Attlee, with his atavistic mindset, felt that the work of the Raj had been accomplished: India would be capable of civilised self-rule. But the British had not accounted fully for the differences between Nehru's Indian National Congress and Jinnah's Muslim League; deep divisions over land and religion were to tear negotiations apart. Viscount Mountbatten, the last Viceroy, sent to retrieve the situation and to ensure potential allies against Communism, hardly proved to be the ideal choice. This great-grandson of Queen Victoria approached the crisis with a combination of old-world suavity and Disraelian wile.[48] And what is striking is the extent to which this old-fashioned and scrappily personal approach failed, or at least gave rise to lingering doubts about the speed with which Britain retreated from imperial shores.

In such an emerging climate it is hardly surprising that there was an efflorescence of post-imperial guilt. Victorian entrepreneurs were penitently resurrected in the 1950s and 1960s as possible guides to economic development in Africa, the continent which Britain was just in the process of evacuating.[49] E. M. Forster's *A Passage to India* was adapted for the stage in 1960, and enjoyed a hugely successful run in London. The *Times* review of the play commented on Forster's message about the incompatibility of East and West.[50]

Another post-imperial play with equally complex themes was *Funnyhouse of a Negro* by the African-American writer Adrienne Kennedy. Kennedy, descended from a white grandfather, was fascinated by the dynamics of empire. Before travelling to the newly independent West Africa in 1960, she visited London, and was transfixed by the memorial to Queen Victoria outside Buckingham Palace – 'the single most dramatic, startling statue I'd seen'. The statue returned in *Funnyhouse*: the 'funnyhouse' being the hall of mirrors, distorted and grotesque, that was the Victorian view of black racial identity. In the play a black woman struggles with the desire to assimilate herself into white 'civilisation', and eventually hangs herself in front of the statue of Victoria. It is, in one way, a last bitter legacy of Victorian imperialism; but even here the victim is finally released from the literal gaze of Victoria, and in having sacrificed herself to the statue, transforms it into an icon of African tribal art.[51]

Meanwhile in 1966 Jean Rhys published *Wide Sargasso Sea*, her 'prequel' to *Jane Eyre*. The novel explores the fate of the first Mrs Rochester, the Creole heiress driven to madness by the oppressive colonial society in which she lives. Rhys's exasperated comment on reading Charlotte Brontë was to stand as a motto for study of Victorian imperialism in the next generation: 'That's only one side – the English side.'[52] The empire had struck back. In many former outposts during the 1960s, statues of Queen Victoria and other dignitaries could be found lying toppled amidst the heat and dust. In their newly recumbent positions, missing an arm or a nose, they now seemed bereft of power and life: totems which had lost their magic.

Closer to home, the talismans of traditional intellectual authority were also under attack. Another of the public values of Victorianism to be challenged after 1945 was the commitment to an Arnoldian mindset. It was in the late 1940s and 1950s that many of the Victorian assumptions about aesthetics, refinement and social progress began to be challenged. Debates in wartime within CEMA about how funds should be distributed, as we have seen, anticipated this. So too did emerging criticism of the elitism of the Third Programme. The key debate in all of these things was that over the meaning of 'culture'. Matthew Arnold had described it as the best that is known and thought in the world. He used it in an active sense, feeling that culture was not simply something to acquire passively – a check-list of artistic and factual references – but a dynamic force within a progressive society. That was very much what William Haley and the architects of the Third Programme had in mind with the post-war BBC. Listeners were supposed to work up the pyramid of stations until they reached the exalted heights of the Third Programme. The intellectuals, despite an occasional wariness about the new-fangled medium, had followed their sense of public duty and flocked to the microphone.

They were too late. In debating the relevance of culture to society after the war, critics increasingly realised that they would need to take account of the retreating tide of the past. To many of these critics 'culture' still ultimately meant the vision of progressive society: Attlee's Britain was, after all, supposed to be the 'New Jerusalem'. How that progress was to be measured and achieved was a very different matter. There were some, like F. R. Leavis and T. S. Eliot, who were almost unreconstructed Arnoldians. But there was a younger generation which was more radical, and which related itself to the Arnold-Leavis tradition in an ambivalent way. What this new generation stood for was a more inclusive definition of culture, one which was committed to spreading the gospel of literature without the patrician overtones and assumptions of the past. This was to be the pursuit of the 'full rich life' without the 'peg-on-nose' approach;[53] culture in a realistic setting, from critics who knew and respected the mental habits of 'real' people.

This was a generation whose most prominent members included the literary critics Richard Hoggart and Raymond Williams, and the historian E. P. Thompson. All had been involved in adult education teaching. Extramural teaching was in fact itself a Victorian phenomenon, the progeny of the Oxbridge social conscience and the earnest self-improving tradition of the working classes. It had fast assumed a rather radical character, as any movement to promote plebeian self-awareness was bound to do. But, by 1945, there was heated debate within the WEA (for whom Hoggart, Williams and Thompson all taught) about the direction it should take after the war: should adult education raise class-consciousness, or should it be about developing the individual's sense of self?

The question was complicated further by evidence that the working classes were ceasing to find adult education 'relevant'. In 1937–38 just over 48 per cent of WEA students had been workers; by 1958–59 this had dropped to 28 per cent. Partly, perhaps, this was because Butler's Education Act of 1944 had made it easier for bright working-class children to receive better education in school (and even at university). But there were other, worrying, signs of a loss of interest in self-improvement. Working-class audiences had once cheerfully joined in with Shakespearean actors as they spoke their lines; by the 1950s, few had even heard of Portia or Lysander, and fewer still attended the theatre: possibly because they had been taught in 'better' schools that Shakespeare was 'difficult'. In 1956, the editorial director of the Dent Everyman series conceded that 'Already during the fifty years of the Library's existence it has been perfectly clear that the standards of "immortality" have been changing'.[54] It was, nevertheless, literature rather than politics which won the debate about the future of the WEA.[55] This was a triumph for the Victorian notion of cultural progress, which valued self-cultivation and impartial knowledge above selfish political concerns. Still, it was a triumph highly circumscribed by the altered circumstances of Britain by the late 1940s.

Literature prevailed partly because of the fresh possibilities to be explored in a wider definition of 'culture': in a more egalitarian climate, other sources like newspapers, popular romances and crime novels could be studied as well as (and in relation to) Austen, Thackeray and Hardy.[56] Absolute standards continued to matter, but 'culture' was now a more anthropological concern: it was about why some books were better than others, and about how ordinary people might relate them to the reality of their lives. The key works here were Hoggart's *The Uses of Literacy* (1957), Williams' *Culture and Society* (1958) and Thompson's *The Making of the English Working Class* (1963). The last was a Marxist study of the way in which the Industrial Revolution created class-consciousness, and an attempt to rescue ordinary experience from its marginal place in the historical record. Eight years earlier Thompson had written a weighty biography of William Morris, the intention of which had been to revive his status as a socialist thinker and moral idealist.[57] Previously the great Victorian sage had only been re-evaluated in a *kitsch* context: Evelyn Waugh, John Betjeman and Osbert Lancaster had rediscovered Kelmscott Manor with what Fiona MacCarthy calls 'a shriek of joy', creating around it 'their own fantastical version of a Pre-Raphaelite soap opera'.[58] George Bernard Shaw had kept the flame of Morris's memory burning for socialists, but it was Thompson who most vigorously and seriously interpreted Morris for a modern age. His later book built upon these initiatives and was a corrective to both past and present: to the past, for having marginalised Morris's revolutionary status; to the present, for the British Communist Party's dalliance with Stalinist thuggery.[59] (Like many belonging to the 'New Left', Thompson was to break with Communism in 1956.)

The Arnoldian tradition had been qualified a great deal already by these new perspectives on culture. But they in turn came to find themselves under pressure from changing social patterns. One of the greatest challenges to Victorianism, and to enduring regard for Victorian individuals, was to emerge in the 1950s as consumerism. Needless to say, the 'culture' of consumerism shared very few of the features of 'culture' as it would have been recognised (for all their individual slants) by Matthew Arnold, William Morris, G. M. Trevelyan, F. R. Leavis and even members of the Bloomsbury Group. In the years of post-war boom, with Harold Macmillan's famous rallying-call to the shoppers ('You've never had it so good'), new levels of disposable income found ready outlets in mass-produced and technologically-advanced goods. Televisions, vacuum cleaners, refrigerators and automatic washing machines undoubtedly improved the quality of life of a great many people. But it was not necessarily all gain. For the dynamics of modern consumerism proved, in the eyes of those attached to older definitions of culture, to be responsive to worrying tendencies in human nature. The promise of economic freedom did not always mean intellectual and emotional fulfilment.

Quite the reverse, felt concerned commentators like Richard Hoggart, who lamented the way in which a traditional working-class tendency to sceptical wisdom was being dulled by commercial exploitation and trite sensationalism. 'There are plenty of people more able than ever before to provide for them at the level of the lowest common denominator of response', he reflected in 1957. 'In many parts of life mass-production has brought good; culturally, the mass-produced makes it harder for the good to be recognized.'[60] Appropriately enough, Hoggart invoked Matthew Arnold on the dangers of a lack of discrimination leading eventually to complete indifference. Relativism flourished after the 1950s as public moralists of the old school were swamped by changing social attitudes to culture and authority, the proliferation of mass education and intellectual specialisms, and the changing identity of the very nation and empire upon which they had based their prescriptions.[61] The Britain of the well-connected arbiter of good taste and order, of J. M. Keynes, G. M. Trevelyan and Sir John Reith, was fading fast.

The culture of consumerism, mass entertainment and moral relativism was here to stay. A. J. P. Taylor once commented that the coming of commercial television in the late 1950s, and therefore the ending of the BBC's monopoly, was 'the biggest knock respectability has taken in my time'.[62] Looking back on the cumulative effect of these retreats from the public world of the Victorians – hierarchy, empire, public duty, 'the best that is known and thought' – Raphael Samuel observed in the early 1990s: 'the grand permanences of national life are no longer those of altar and throne, nor, as in the "Whig" interpretation of history, constitutional government, but rather those of the nuclear family'.[63] This was history according to the generation of home-owners and home-improvers. And by inexorable but no less ironic logic, the future of the Victorians outside academia would lie in large part in their packaging as products.

# 5

# *Youth*

Completed in 1928, privately printed by a Florentine publisher, ruthlessly pirated, judged indecent, expurgated, smuggled into the country, its very title a by-word for the titillating and smutty.[1] Few books have had such an extraordinary lifetime as D. H. Lawrence's *Lady Chatterley's Lover*. The single most remarkable moment of this lifetime came, surely, on 20 October 1960, when the trial of *Regina* v. *Penguin Books Limited* began at the Old Bailey. The trial was to be a key moment in the changing reputation of the Victorians. For what it represented was the clash between past and present: between quiet respectability and the increasingly outspoken voice of youth and permissiveness. Lawrence's novel had been banned under Victorian obscenity laws, the great precedent being the Hicklin case of 1868. There it had been decided that publications could be banned if they were 'proven' (and genteel Victorian juries often did not take much convincing) to suggest thoughts of 'a most impure and lustful character', especially if it were available on street corners to 'all classes'. Language such as 'contamination', 'pollution' and 'impurity', as used in that case, reflected a characteristic late Victorian concern with national efficiency and the risks of degeneration.[2]

The political and intellectual establishment of the 1950s, as we have seen, remained steeped in a Victorian mindset. And it clung all the more desperately to these values in the face of what it felt to be a wave of post-war crime and immorality. The smoke and the Rachmaninov may have swirled around Trevor Howard and Celia Johnson as they retreated, with accents of clipped anguish, back into middle-class respectability at the close of *Brief Encounter* (1946), but theirs was an increasingly less common scenario. Having apparently defeated the forces of modernity in the Abdication Crisis, the establishment suffered an irreversible blow with the huge rise in divorce rates after 1945: a phenomenon which, ironically, it had itself facilitated with the granting of legal aid to enable the sensible unpicking of wartime misalliances.

Between 1926 and 1930, there had been an average annual divorce rate of about 4000; between 1951 and 1954, the figure soared to about 33,000.

'Until recent years', reflected one commentator in 1957, 'Christian teaching has dominated all discussion of marriage and divorce and has determined the standard of accepted behaviour.'[3] Church attendance continued to plummet. Some, no doubt, saw a connection between this and the rising tide of 'immoral' activity. (Detection of immorality, needless to say, was dependent upon the vigilance of authorities.) Between 1948 and 1961, indictable heterosexual offences rose from 588 to 1218, and homosexual offences from 1405 to 2513.[4] Much of this, concerned observers felt, was attributable to post-war developments. In 1952, a social survey by Seebohm Rowntree and G. R. Lavers expressed fears that medical advances in the NHS promising to eradicate venereal disease would only inaugurate a new era of immorality.[5]

To add insult to injury, some of the younger members of the establishment were themselves turning away from the hallowed traditions of the past. Sometimes the damage done to Victorian notions of public respectability occurred by default, as in the defection of the Cambridge spies or, more resonantly still, the Profumo scandal of 1963. The real advances, though, were made by a disparate group of politicians and intellectuals who campaigned for legal reform to take account of the way in which attitudes to morality, behaviour and authority were altering in a more egalitarian post-war world. This was a group including Sir Alan Herbert (chairman of the Society of Authors), the journalist C. H. Rolph, John Trevelyan (secretary of the British Board of Film Censors, and yet another descendant of the man who had co-written the Northcote-Trevelyan Report) and Roy Jenkins (Labour backbench MP, and subsequently Home Secretary). Just as notions of 'contamination', 'pollution' and 'impurity' were designed to strengthen the fibres of empire, so Britain without an empire (and the ideological baggage that went with it) had less need of such outdated ideas. The retreat of the empire in the 1950s and 1960s was mirrored by a deconstruction of the laws which had upheld it; decolonisation and decensorship were, in many respects, two sides of the same coin.

Sir Alan Herbert and Roy Jenkins had been troubled especially by the old-fashioned law regarding obscenity, and the way in which it condemned good literature along with pornography. At no time was this more evident than in the 1950s, when the moral panic had led to farcical prosecution of a number of novels from respectable publishers like Secker and Warburg, Hutchinson and Heinemann. The Herbert Committee, set up in 1954 to campaign for the rationalisation of the obscenity law, gained the ardent advocacy of Jenkins, and succeeded in pushing the Obscene Publications Act through Parliament in 1959. The Act changed legal procedures in two ways. First, it ruled that literature being prosecuted on the grounds of obscenity had to be considered in its entirety. This was a response to the

Hicklin precedent of merely 'proving' the obscenity of a piece of literature: prosecutors had hitherto been free to select individual passages out of context. And, secondly, juries were allowed to acquit any work (even one containing obscene passages) provided that its publication would be 'in the interests of science, literature, art, or learning, or of other objects of general concern'. Expert witnesses could now be called to establish such merits.

The scene was therefore set for the trial of Lady Chatterley – the first major prosecution brought under the new law. Penguin Books, proposing to bring out an unexpurgated version of Lawrence's novel, deliberately precipitated the case by providing the police with twelve copies to hand on to the Director of Public Prosecutions. This, they knew, counted in legal terms as an act of 'publication', and what they had in mind was a confront-ation before the book went on sale and copies could be seized for destruction. It was also, though, a deliberate challenge from a liberal-minded younger generation to the Victorian propriety of its elders. Oddly enough, then, it was the prosecutor, Mervyn Griffith Jones, who advised the jury in his opening address: 'Do not approach this matter in any priggish, high-minded, super-correct, mid-Victorian manner. Look at it as we all of us, I hope, look at things today.'[6]

Nine members of the jury were in favour of acquittal from the outset, and they needed little persuading. In any case, the prosecutor's words were little more than a sop to modern opinion, a rhetorical device before the full extent of his conservatism was revealed. Building upon one of the elements of Victorian law to have survived reform, the notion that obscene literature is that with a 'tendency' to corrupt vulnerable readers, Griffith-Jones showed his patrician colours in expressing consternation at the cheap price of the proposed edition (3s. 6d.) – would this not pervert the working-classes as well as the young? (The humble paperback helped to expose Victorian hypocrisy further: 'deluxe' hardback editions of classic bawdy works tended to be looked upon with a blind eye, and this became an issue after 1960.)[7] The case for the prosecution took a further turn for the worse (though provided the jury with titillation: individuals were seen to smirk) when Griffith-Jones asked, with an extraordinary lack of awareness, 'Is it a book that you would even wish your wife or your servants to read?'[8]

The defence found little difficulty in presenting their case after such self-inflicted wounds. The commitment of Sir Allen Lane, chairman of Penguin, to providing the masses with good literature at affordable prices was pointed up. The implicit anti-Victorianism of Lawrence's four-letter words was emphasised in a way that was bound to bring sympathy. 'It is plain, in my submission,' commented Gerald Gardiner, one of the leaders

of the defence, 'that what the author intended to do was to drag these words
out of the rather shameful connotation which since Victorian times they
have achieved.' 9 And to guarantee victory, a veritable barrage of thirty-five
expert witnesses was presented to establish the status of *Lady Chatterley's
Lover* as an important and even puritanical work of art. This latter suggestion
– an artful occupation of the moral high ground commanded by the
prosecution – was put forward by Richard Hoggart, and verified by the
elderly E. M. Forster. Hoggart remembers the 'small, rather stooped figure'
in the witness-box being presented with his claim, and looking round the
courtroom whimsically, before announcing: 'I think the description is a
correct one, though I understand that at first people would think it para-
doxical.' The jury, anyhow, had already sat up in anticipation, when Forster
took the box, or when the title *A Passage to India* had been read in
establishing his identity.10 It was difficult to see the jury failing to acquit
Penguin Books, and acquit them it did. Two million copies of the unexpurgated *Lady Chatterley's Lover* were sold within the year, many to readers
who professed themselves rather at a loss to understand what all the fuss
had been about.

After *Lady Chatterley*, the deluge. Attitudes to Victorian sexuality were
greatly affected by the appearance of Steven Marcus's *The Other Victorians*
(1966) and John Fowles's novel *The French Lieutenant's Woman* (1969). As
one historian pointed out in 1967, scholarship had long been hampered not
only by the Victorians' own relative reticence but by the surprisingly strong
reticence of later scholars.11 Since then, study of the Victorians and sex has
never looked back.12 Marcus used sophisticated Freudian analysis to probe
the emotional dynamics of prostitution and pornography in the Victorian
age, emphasising the social constraints which had paradoxically encouraged
them to flourish. For Marcus, pornographers like the pseudonymous 'Walter' were heralds of the modern age of permissiveness. 'The issues raised in
this writing,' Marcus writes, 'the fantasies played out in it, the conflicts
which it tries to evade and the problems with which it struggles, have, as I
have tried to show, come down to us. They are part of our civilized legacy.' 13
The sexually subversive, for Marcus, were both far-sighted and emotionally
stunted: even they, despite their saving 'otherness', could not help being
'Victorian' in their lack of maturity. And they had a message for the modern
world: pornography and prostitution were safety valves for mankind as it
progressed towards sexual enlightenment. The implication was that only
emotionally immature people (like many Victorians) needed them.

It is ironic but not surprising that the publication of Marcus's book
encouraged Arthur Dobson, a Bradford bookseller and publisher, to bring
out an edition of Walter's *My Secret Life* in 1967. Readers of *The Other*

*Victorians* would have known that this was an account by a Victorian gentleman of encounters with 1200 different women and girls, and one which did not stint on detail (running to over 4000 pages) or explicitness. Dobson was arrested and prosecuted in February 1969, with John Mortimer acting for the defence and the services of Steven Marcus himself procured as expert witness. He was joined in court by a distinguished line-up of historians: E. P. Thompson, J. H. Plumb, Geoffrey Best and others. But even this very strong team failed to ensure an acquittal for *My Secret Life*, largely it seems because the literary merit of the work was risible in comparison with that of *Lady Chatterley's Lover*.[14] It was obvious enough, too, that Dobson was not so much seeking to inform society about Victorian sexuality as to make money from it.

Like the study by Marcus, Fowles's *The French Lieutenant's Woman* had a curious ambivalence towards Victorian sexuality and its relationship to the present. As the blurb of a 1971 edition remarks, Fowles tells the story of a couple 'seeking escape from the cant and tyranny of their age', an 'allegory on the decline of the static Victorian ethos and ... the birth of the twentieth-century passion for freedom'. That is one perspective, the teleological march to permissiveness. Another view emphasises Fowles's ambivalence towards the Victorians. The style of the novel, with its largely omniscient narrator, is both an honest imitation of Victorian literature and a knowingly ironic commentary on the nature of pastiche.[15] The narrator's voice has the inescapable colouring of hindsight, a retrospective attitude towards the Victorians which in the 1960s found it difficult to evoke their attitudes to sex without emotional distance. *The French Lieutenant's Woman* is therefore both a sympathetic attempt to understand the strangeness of Victorian behaviour and a rumination on the barriers to such empathy. 'We have, in destroying so much of the mystery, the difficulty, the aura of the forbidden, destroyed also a great deal of the pleasure', comments the narrator at one point; but earlier the same voice shudders at 'that strangely Egyptian quality among the Victorians; that claustrophilia we see so clearly evidenced in their enveloping, mummifying clothes, their narrow-windowed and -corridored architecture, their fear of the open and naked'.[16]

Theatrical censorship also ended in an explicitly Victorian flurry. Since 1737 plays scheduled for performance on the public stage had been submitted to the office of the Lord Chamberlain for approval. Victorian propriety reached its height at the turn of the twentieth century, when the Lord Chamberlain's blue pencil was working overtime on the scripts of Ibsen, Wilde and Shaw.[17] By the 1960s, with few significant alterations, it was still scratching away at contentious references to politics, sex or the monarchy. In the days of Gillray's cartoons, and then of often savage criticism of Queen

Victoria, there had been a certain logic behind such precautions. But not only had attitudes to the monarchy softened since the late Victorian period; the days of exaggerated deference were themselves also over. With a mischievous wink to the Lord Chamberlain, Joe Orton – 'the Oscar Wilde of Welfare State gentility' – made the plot of *Loot* (1966) dependent on a character signing herself 'Queen Victoria'. He got away with it.[18] In the more open climate of the 1960s, attitudes to sex had also shifted irrevocably. Things would clearly soon have to change.

In July 1967 Roy Jenkins, then Home Secretary in Harold Wilson's government, informed the current Lord Chamberlain that his post would be terminated after the unanimous decision of a joint select committee. Wilson himself had misgivings at the prospect, fearing the unfavourable representation of his kind on stage (the perennial worry of Prime Ministers since Walpole had introduced censorship in the eighteenth century). The anxieties of Wilson were compounded in November 1967, as reform of the law was going ahead, by submission to the Lord Chamberlain of Edward Bond's new play *Early Morning*. Almost every conceivable Victorian taboo was broken in it; and they were broken in a specifically Victorian setting. There was Queen Victoria; there was Gladstone and Disraeli; there was sex: not just between the Queen and one of her Prime Ministers, but between the Queen and Florence Nightingale; and, if all this had not sent surviving Victorians into cardiac arrest, there was even cannibalism. Needless to say, *Early Morning* was refused a licence; but not for long, given the imminent changes, and when public performances began in 1969 there was (as with *Lady Chatterley's Lover*) relatively little fuss. That the law had been old-fashioned and hypocritical was only underlined by the realisation that audiences had seen it all before (even the cannibalism) in *Titus Andronicus* or *The Duchess of Malfi*.[19]

All of these developments should be considered against the backdrop of a series of reforms passed in the 1960s, largely under the impetus of Roy Jenkins and like-minded colleagues such as David Steel. They were convinced that the permissive society was also a civilised society. 'All of the "reforms" of the late fifties and sixties marked a retreat from social controls imposed in the Victorian era by evangelicalism and non-conformity', writes Arthur Marwick, pointedly calling one of the chapters in his social history of post-war Britain 'The End of Victorianism'.[20] These reforms included the legalisation of abortion, the provision of free contraceptives by local authorities, and the decriminalisation of homosexual acts between consenting adults in private (all in 1967); the suspension and then abolition of capital punishment (1969); and divorce reform which made a more efficient and equitable split possible for couples (also 1969). In legal terms, the direct influence of the Victorians had, to all intents and purposes, faded in Britain by the 1970s.

Running parallel to all these developments were pressures from below. Youth culture had developed in the late 1950s as a result of affluence, technological innovation and international awareness (especially of the music and fashions of the United States): *Paris-Match* reflected in 1960 that 'war, the aeroplane and cultural exchange with the continent [have] liberated the British from their ancient Victorian complex'.[21] The new youth culture was not, of course, monolithic, as could only be expected from a phenomenon sensitive to the very idea of fast-moving fashion. Spread over two decades, it had many complex interweavings, from the teddy boys of the 1950s to the feminists of the 1970s. For all the imaginative liberation of these years, there was also deep division and ill-feeling between different elements of fashionable young opinion: mods and rockers clashed, hippies abhorred the materialism of their image-conscious peers.

For those who passed their days in marijuana infumed rooms (even for those who did not inhale) there is little evidence of coherent stigmatisation of the Victorian past. Indeed, for LSD-buffs, the 'psychedelic' canvases of the Pre-Raphaelites floated into view as something wondrous to behold. Aldous Huxley had already enjoyed the Blakean doors of perception opened up on old art works by mescalin. Blake, forefather of the Pre-Raphaelites, was adopted as the presiding spirit of the ground-breaking International Festival of Poetry held – resonantly enough – at the Royal Albert Hall in June 1965.[22] Part of the youth culture also sought out Victoriana to be bought cheaply on the Portobello Road in the 1950s and 1960s. By the end of the 1960s there were about two thousand stalls or mini-shops in the area, many of them selling Victorian jewellery or bric-à-brac. One celebrated emporium for Victoriana, Alice's, made a speciality of Victorian brass bedsteads and stripped furniture (anticipating a later 'heritage' look). Clothes might also be found in the Portobello Road or Carnaby Street: the 1967 film of *Far from the Madding Crowd* encouraged a certain camp following for Terence Stamp's costume of scarlet tunic and tight pantaloons.[23]

There was nevertheless a serious theme to youth culture: the willingness to question authority, tacitly or otherwise, and often this meant the values of the last generation of Victorians which was dying out in the 1950s and 1960s. Even their children were not to be trusted. 'Never trust anyone over thirty' became a mantra of the 1960s.[24] A greater level of wealth and exposure to mass media meant that middle-class adolescents were simply less dependent than before on their parents, assuming adult status at an earlier age.[25] Intelligent young people became the natural audience for the satire boom of the 1960s, with *That Was The Week That Was* and *Private Eye* both beginning to churn out acidic comment in 1962. Joan Littlewood's *Oh! What a Lovely War* (1963) resurrected music-hall techniques to debunk the war-mongering of pre-1914 Britain. The publication of Michael Holroyd's biography of Lytton Strachey in 1967–68 also encouraged an appreciative audience for his subject's flouting of Victorian conventions. Such was Strachey's new-found celebrity that one of his risqué stories even appeared in *Playboy* in 1969: surely one of history's more improbable meetings.[26] 'With his pacifism, homosexuality and that split between the classical mind and romantic imagination,' writes Holroyd, 'Strachey might have become a folk hero of the 1960s.'[27]

A number of youth subcultures challenged authority and tradition quite explicitly. Guilt about the empire flowered in a generation which not only had few imperial assumptions but lived anxiously under the shadow of the Bomb. Bertrand Russell, the old establishment scourge who had enjoyed reading *Eminent Victorians* in prison during the First World War, gamely endured another spell there at the age of eighty-nine. The Campaign for Nuclear Disarmament, to which Russell was mentor in the 1950s, failed to attract much working-class support and soon split internally. For a time, however, past had joined hands with present: for the flower-power gener-ation, noted Frances Partridge in a diary entry in 1967, Russell had 'described the moment of almost mystical revelation when as a young man he realized the value of love and understanding and became a pacifist, which he has always remained'.[28] The culture of Bloomsbury anti-Victorianism was almost resurrected anew in the 1960s. Passionate members of CND and other protest groups were, no doubt, too preoccupied with the present fully to engage with the historical dimension of Bloomsbury; but the new-found popularity of Strachey and Russell can only have encouraged further the tendency to dismiss as 'Victorian' anything authoritarian or constrictive.

Not surprisingly, the reputation of Virginia Woolf also enjoyed a signifi-cant boom in the 1960s. People were no longer, to paraphrase the title of Edward Albee's 1962 play, afraid of Virginia Woolf. By 1966, over 50,000 copies of *To the Lighthouse* were being sold annually; the following year her collected essays were published in four volumes. In 1969, an informal talk on Woolf by J. J. Wilson at the San Francisco Public Library (and we should remember the international perspective to youth culture) brought readers flocking in their hundreds. 'All of them', wrote Wilson, 'were ... fascinating private people who claimed Woolf as their personal saviour and were almost dismayed to find her become so popular.'[29] The key element here, of course, was the feminist revival of the 1960s and 1970s.

The historical dimension was inevitably foregrounded in post-war feminism. In the 1950s, women had found opportunities as nurses in the NHS; but those openings had been circumscribed by the traditional view of women as 'carers', and romances almost inevitably ended with the heroine's marriage and return to the domestic sphere.[30] In 1950, strikingly enough, Cecil Woodham-Smith published a biography of Florence Nightingale, and the following year Herbert Wilcox made his film *The Lady with a Lamp*. It starred Wilcox's wife Anna Neagle (who had previously played Queen Victoria on screen) as Nightingale. Although it might in one sense be viewed as testimony to women's part in the brave new world of the welfare state, it also embodied a conservative view of femininity. As one commentator has pointed out, Neagle's career was devoted to 'creating an image of British womanhood that was well-bred, patient and resolute, finding fulfilment in a life of service and sacrifice'.[31] And in 1962 G. M. Carstairs, Professor of Psychological Medicine at Edinburgh, reflected on gender roles as part of his Reith Lectures. He suggested that tradition still determined gender roles, and that the consumer culture had in some ways trapped rather than liberated women. Even so, there were welcome signs of change:

> Society has not yet abandoned the Victorian ideal of the fully-domesticated mother and wife, destined to find satisfaction only through service for others. Because of this lingering conception, remorselessly perpetuated by all women's magazines, women are still made to feel guilty if they seek for themselves satisfactions which come from fulfilment of their own peculiar talents and potentialities.[32]

A conscious sense of the past carried momentum further. It was at a History Workshop meeting at Ruskin College, Oxford, in September 1969 that Sheila Rowbotham and Sally Alexander proposed a conference on women's history for the following year. This first national Women's Liberation conference, as it became, led to a campaign for equal pay and educational opportunities, free contraception and abortion on request, and child care facilities for working mothers.[33] But the uses of history within the Women's Liberation Movement of the 1970s were complicated, and cannot easily be characterised as either a rediscovery or a renunciation of Victorian feminist trends. There certainly was rediscovery. *Spare Rib*, the influential feminist magazine, carried articles on aspects of Victorian feminism such as the life of Josephine Butler and the campaign against the Contagious Diseases Acts.[34] A steady flow of publications about the experiences of Victorian women began to appear with titles like *Silent Sisterhood* and *One Hand Tied Behind Us*.[35] (In both titles one notes the emphasis on shared experience: past joining hands with present.) Intellectual inheritances were reclaimed in other ways, too, with an occasional helping hand from people like Dr Freud. In 1979 Sandra Gilbert and Susan Gubar published

*The Madwoman in the Attic: The Woman Writer and the Nineteenth-Century Literary Imagination*, a work which put forward the argument that Mrs Rochester is Jane Eyre's *alter ego*, a reflection of the heroine's unconscious rage and madness at living in a male-dominated world.[36]

Others, like Germaine Greer, Juliet Mitchell and Sheila Rowbotham, found the Victorian inheritance problematic. They saw that Victorian and Edwardian feminists, though often inspirational, were themselves hidebound by traditional outlooks on race and class: attitudes which did not sit comfortably alongside ideas from the civil rights movement. And, they tended to feel, would not rejection of the traditional male perspective on women only consolidate it by taking it too seriously? The result, in something like Greer's *The Female Eunuch* (1970), was a view inspired by the past but very careful in its handling of it. The book caused a stir with its argument that feminists should rebel against 'the civilizing process' handed down by tradition. Women, Greer argued, would only continue to underline old-fashioned gender divisions if they defined the struggle in terms of liberation from men; the emphasis instead ought to be on unlocking female desire and creativity. This radical-feminist perspective simply did not speak the language of Victorian separate spheres. The drive to equality had only just begun: but the first blow had been struck in a distinctively post-Victorian context. Within a decade Britain would have its first female Prime Minister – one who used 'Victorian values' to *her* own advantage.

In cultural terms, youth was also asserting its own voice. The reaction began with what the contemporary press called the 'Angry Young Men' of the late 1950s. This was a generation of writers including Kingsley Amis, John Braine, John Osborne and Alan Sillitoe – people who took violent exception to the seemingly mediocre and old-fashioned assumptions of post-war society. They were appalled by Eden's gunboat diplomacy at Suez and (unlike some of their peers a decade later) detested the fey pretensions of the Bloomsbury Group. The shining parapets of the 'New Jerusalem', they felt, had simply not been erected in post-war Britain – the pre-war elite, with all its dated values and complacencies, continued to hold sway. In Amis's *Lucky Jim* (1954), the repellent sons of Jim's departmental head are suspiciously Bloomsburyesque, one a bearded pacifist painter and the other an effeminate writer. Their father, Professor Welch, is 'tall and weedy, with limp whitening hair'. At work he habitually answers the telephone with the solemn words 'History speaking'.

> [Jim] pretended to himself that he'd pick up his professor round the waist, squeeze the furry grey-blue waistcoat against him to expel the breath, run heavily with

him up the steps, along the corridor to the Staff Cloakroom, and plunge the too-small feet in their capless shoes into a lavatory basin, pulling the plug once, twice, and again, stuffing the mouth with toilet-paper.[37]

So much for reverence towards the voice of history.

With their provincial settings, explicit language, sexual daring and exploration of educational opportunity, novels like Braine's *Room at the Top* (1957) and Sillitoe's *Saturday Night and Sunday Morning* (1958) directly challenged the prevailing conservatism of the age. For Raphael Samuel, the *Lady Chatterley* trial only underlined the implicitly anti-Victorian nature of these writers:

> Through the Lawrence revival and the *Lady Chatterley* trial Northernness was associated with the cause of sexual frankness, the practice of post-Victorian morality, and the desacralization of marriage. Socially, too, Northernness came to stand for a new and emancipatory openness.[38]

*Saturday Night and Sunday Morning* is set in the Nottingham of Lawrence and Sillitoe. It traces the weekend lifestyle of the factory worker Arthur Seaton, a man intent on escapist Saturday night pleasure after the deadening routine of the week; after hardworking respectability comes drink, promiscuous sex and plain speaking. All of this is couched in Sillitoe's colloquial, often hard-hitting prose – prose that moves far away from Lawrence's Victorian-mystical style, which Sillitoe tended to pillory. Times had moved on even before the *Lady Chatterley* trial, which may well explain why readers of that novel in 1960 found it disappointingly chaste. What was needed, felt Sillitoe, was a voice to articulate these changes: 'The country was dead from the neck up, and the body buried in sand, waiting for someone to illuminate those views and values which [people] were being told in a thousand ways were something to be ashamed of and ought never to be expressed.' [39]

Theatre in the first post-war decade remained dominated by the voices and production values of yesteryear. The established voices – William Somerset Maugham, T. S. Eliot, Noël Coward, Terence Rattigan – echoed across the boards in tones which would have been familiar to pre-1914 audiences, let alone to pre-1945 ones: as Simon Callow puts it, Maugham was 'yesterday's playwright, or the day before yesterday's'.[40] Then, in 1956, came John Osborne's *Look Back in Anger*. Osborne had a curious relationship with the past. In one respect hankering after the certainties of pre-1914 England (his two volumes of autobiography are called *A Better Class of Person* and *Almost a Gentleman*), he also violently attacked the complacencies of tradition. Measured, thoughtful, even slightly elegiac in his appearance on the BBC 'Face to Face' series in the early 1960s, Osborne's was the voice of a generation of intelligent and passionate young people which had been dispossessed of the certainties as well as the abuses of the nineteenth century. In *Look Back in Anger*, produced at the Royal Court Theatre in the year of the Suez Crisis, it is the disaffected hero Jimmy Porter who cries 'there aren't any good, brave causes left', and abuses his father-in-law (a retired colonel) and the 'Edwardian brigade' he represents. Just the following year, in *The Entertainer*, Osborne would be saluting the music hall. Like Peter Cook's affectionate but (by contemporary standards) slightly irreverent mocking of Harold Macmillan's Edwardianism in *Beyond the Fringe*, this was a profoundly ambivalent attitude towards history.[41]

At around this time, in the late 1950s and early 1960s, the Pop Art movement began to emerge. This showed the influence of mass media and the United States. For all the variations between, say, Richard Hamilton, Peter Blake and David Hockney, it was bright, egalitarian, irreverent and self-consciously gimmicky. It was everything that high Victorian art was not: where Victorian painters had produced expensive canvases for private clients on lofty subjects, the followers of Pop Art produced work which was cheap, mass-produced and deliberately ephemeral in subject. Here was a movement, recalled the critic John Russell in 1969:

> Against the old-style museum-man, the old-style critic, the old-style dealer and the old-style collector ... Pop was meant as a cultural break, signifying the firing squad, without mercy or reprieve, for the kind of people who believed in the Loeb classics, holidays in Tuscany, drawings by Augustus John.[42]

One of the most effective ways of dealing with the Victorian legacy was to recycle it (like the trinkets on the Portobello Road) as *kitsch*. This testifies partly, perhaps, to nostalgia in a listless post-war world; but it was a nostalgia very much on its own terms, defusing any of the lingering potency of tradition by using Victorian images in a self-consciously ironic manner. Peter Blake's work 'combined folk art styles such as fairground painting with imagery drawn both from Victoriana and from his idols among his contemporaries, such as pop singers, pin-ups, and film stars'.[43] His design for the cover of the Beatles album *Sergeant Pepper's Lonely Hearts Club Band* (1967) has Oscar Wilde brushing shoulders with Marlon Brando, Edgar Allan Poe looking over Marilyn Monroe's shoulder, and Sir Robert Peel casting a beady eye over Aldous Huxley. (The group Cream also had a psychedelic album cover in 1967 bearing the title *Disraeli Grins*.) Some of the images, meanwhile, could really shock. In 1963 the American Bruce Conner unveiled an assemblage called *Couch*, 'a decaying Victorian sofa on which there appears to be a rotting and dismembered corpse'.[44]

It was perhaps in textile and wallpaper design that the legacy of the

Victorians became most prominent in the 1960s, arguably extending some way beyond *kitsch*. By the mid-1960s many had grown weary of the austerity of modernism, and had begun to look to other cultures and to the past for inspiration. Textile and wallpaper design benefited especially from the excited rediscovery of the late Victorian style of 'Art Nouveau'. In 1964 John Line produced a book on wallpaper patterns called *Epoch*, featuring such categories as 'Victorian Style' and 'Art Nouveau'. Two years later a design journal commented that 'the modest Victorian flower designs which sparked off the print stampede blossomed into bold, vigorously designed prints reflecting the current preoccupation with Art Nouveau and Geometrics, in vivid Byzantine colours.'[45] Late Victorian patterns underwent an extraordinary transformation: the delicate pastel fronds of a Morris design emerged for the flower-power generation with exaggerated swirls and blasts of turquoise, purple and bright green. Morris and Company itself had been disbanded in 1940, but some of its fabric blocks found their way to Liberty, where the designs were transferred to silk screens and marketed at affordable prices from the 1960s. ('Morris and Company' itself survived as a trademark of Sanderson, and continues to flourish today.) Laura Ashley was also originally part of this movement. She began printing tea-towels with a Victorian motif in 1953, and so well did the first batch sell at John Lewis in Oxford Street that she soon set up business on her own. By the 1970s the 'Laura Ashley look' – a kind of back-to-nature chic – had become a recognisable phenomenon in its own right.

This mixture of apparent nostalgia and *kitsch* recycling emerges as one of the most distinctive uses of the past in the 1950s and 1960s. These were also the years which saw the growth of a serious market for Victorian antiques. But youth culture was not in the thrall of history. It went its own way, especially where human relations were concerned. This was the result of a heady combination of circumstances: war had underlined the emotional distance from the past; the last generation of Victorians was dying out; and consumerism enabled the past to be packaged in new ways. The outcome was often a repudiation of Victorianism, and a frenetic bid to catch up with years of lost pleasure. Sexual intercourse, as Philip Larkin put it, began in 1963: between the end of the *Chatterley* ban and the Beatles' first LP. Here, for some, was a lifestyle of personal fulfilment glimpsed in the smiling sepia tints of the Bloomsbury Group.

Youth culture was also a popular replaying of the lifestyle of the 'Bright Young Things' of the 1920s and 1930s. Those people had enjoyed dressing up for 'Victorian' parties and collecting glass paperweights. A later generation, more socially inclusive and consumer-orientated, also enjoyed donning Victorian tunics and collecting tea tins emblazoned with union jacks and reproductions of Lord Kitchener. And just as Evelyn Waugh and his friends felt a hollowness beneath the high jinks, so did members of the wider youth culture experience disorientation in the post-war world. Despite higher levels of consumer wealth, Britain had been bankrupted by the war, had lost its place in the world as a great imperial power, and now was overcast with the long and gloomy shadow of the Bomb. Unsurprisingly, then, it was not all angry renunciation of Victorian taboos in the 1950s and 1960s. There was, mixed in with it, an uneasy nostalgia for the days of relative certainty, if not of human repression. People were beginning to discover in the Victorian age the values that they wanted to find.

# 6

# *Heritage*

'The facts?', protested the lady with the handbag (and soul) of iron, 'I have been elected to change the facts!'[1] The reputation of the Victorians underwent a curious but oddly symptomatic phase during the 1980s. Margaret Thatcher famously brought home for a consumer-orientated, post-imperial society a neatly packaged version of 'Victorian values'. She was determined to challenge and rewrite the 'facts' which had dominated British society since 1945: Keynesian economics, the dominance of the Welfare State and half-hearted consensus politics. These, she felt, had created a nation which was by turns unnecessarily poor, lazily dependent and led by weak men.

By contrast Thatcher offered a return to the values of her youth, steeped in the lingering Victorianism of working-class life that we have traced in earlier chapters. Born in Grantham in 1925, she was the daughter of Alderman Roberts, a self-made man and zealous autodidact of the old school. His grocery shop, and the Methodist chapel nearby, was to be the school for the Victorian values that Thatcher preached half a century later:

> We were taught to work jolly hard. We were taught to prove yourself; we were taught self-reliance; we were taught to live within our income. You were taught that cleanliness is next to godliness. You were taught self-respect. You were taught always to give a hand to your neighbour. You were taught tremendous pride in your country. All of these things are Victorian values. They are also perennial values.[2]

Yet Thatcher, the science graduate, was no historian. From the very beginning, political rivals like Neil Kinnock had countered her Victorian values with those of cruelty, misery, drudgery, squalor and ignorance (a list which resonantly echoes the Dickensian 'giants' to be slain in the Beveridge Report). And David Lodge, in his 1988 novel *Nice Work*, took issue with any simplistic notion of Victorian values, producing a work that resurrected the Victorian condition of England novel (there are allusions to Disraeli, Dickens and Mrs Gaskell) to criticise the emerging 'two nations' of Thatcherite Britain (north and south, entrepreneurs and academics).[3] In recent years a small historical industry has emerged devoted to correcting Thatcher's 'abuses' of the past.[4]

The 1980s became a good decade for reassessment of the nature of Victorianism, just as the 1950s had been for an earlier generation.[5] This may not be a coincidence. For the 'facts' which Thatcher was dedicated to changing were those established after the social and imaginative watershed of the Second World War. Thatcher's overturning of post-war consensus politics, an act of political archaeology supposedly to unearth a forgotten Victorian tradition, naturally encouraged a review of the foundations on which society had been built since 1945. But what this excavation revealed was not a clear break with tradition in 1945 so much as signs of deep-rooted continuity. Attlee's vision of post-war Britain was more genuinely Victorian in character than that of Thatcher: as one historian has suggested, the Welfare State was 'the last and most glorious flowering of late Victorian liberal philanthropy'.[6] Of course it is easy to establish Thatcher's claims as a 'conviction' premier in the mould of Gladstone; yet Gladstone, devotee of European civilisation and ready payer of overseas compensation, would have been appalled by Thatcher's Little Englandism and handbagging of the EEC over agricultural rebates. Gladstone was an intellectual in his own right, driving for disinterested (albeit rudimentary) enlightenment of the masses; Thatcher (though clever) distrusted thinkers, and sought to put a market price on education. One of the historical studies that attained political popularity in the early 1980s was a book by Martin J. Wiener arguing that Britain's industrial decline owed itself to the Victorian obsession with gentrification. Too many entrepreneurs, he argued, had been lured by the temptations of the gentlemanly life, and retired to the countryside or sent their sons to public schools and Oxbridge, where they were allegedly inculcated with effete anti-industrialist views. Wiener's thesis has since been all but disproved, but at the time it was grist to Thatcher's mill.[7] She did not see the irony of its implicit anti-Victorianism.

It may actually be that Thatcherism had many of its roots, like that of the post-war consensus it set out to demolish, in the grim years of the 1930s – the years when little Margaret saw at first hand just how difficult life in a Britain shorn of Victorian certainties could be. After all, it was in the inter-war period that the distinctive Thatcherite creed of anti-socialism had first been anticipated within Conservative party practice.[8] Much of this original anti-socialism, as books from those who described themselves in those years as surviving 'Victorians' testify, was partisan in nature. If surviving Victorians like G. M. Young could be partisan about Victorianism, then it comes as no surprise that people like Margaret Thatcher could be more partisan still fifty years on. Did Thatcher genuinely believe her rhetoric about Victorian values? Or was it, as Raphael Samuel suggests, that Victorian values were little more than a smokescreen for Thatcher's profoundly radical political agenda? 'Mrs Thatcher's traditionalism allowed her to act as an innovator', he writes. 'By turns radical and reactionary, modernising and atavistic, she moved from one register to another with the dexterity of a quick-change artist.'[9]

What was symptomatic about Thatcher's 'Victorian values' was the way in which the past could be commodified and used by the 1980s. The last generation of Victorians had died out in the 1950s and 1960s; attitudes towards social expectations and morality had begun to change; the law had lost its existing Victorian character; rising levels of personal wealth had encouraged a youth culture to emerge. All of these factors were connected. Perhaps most important, though, was the consumerism which underpinned the youth culture especially. Youths of the 1960s are, of course, the middle-aged people of today. Inevitably their attitudes to many social and political issues are likely to have mellowed and become more conservative. Yet to them, and to their children, many of the basic assumptions with which they grew up have become established as social orthodoxy.

Nowadays the past is often considered as 'heritage', a commodity to be marketed and used according to need or pleasure, but always with nostalgic overtones. We are not entirely unique here. In the United States there has been a similar attempt to recapture 'Victorian virtues'.[10] Looking backwards, the Victorians themselves had also 'used' the past, as their obsession with ancient civilisations or the Gothic revival shows. The Pre-Raphaelites, whom we tend to consider quintessential Victorians, were seeking to return to a style literally pre-dating Raphael in the fifteenth century. William Morris, one of the great icons of the modern 'heritage industry', was himself obsessed with the medieval past. The Victorians were interested in the past partly on grounds of escapism in the face of a disorientating present. But, unlike us, they also used the past as a springboard for the future, giving expression to their atavism in the great institutions and buildings which they trusted would carry progress into the twentieth century. Throughout Queen Victoria's reign politicians debated issues in a Westminster rebuilt in the Gothic style; and the royal couple themselves were painted by Landseer as Edward III and his Queen for a costumed ball in 1842. Other Victorian manifestations of 'heritage' – the *Victoria County Histories*, the National Trust or the *Dictionary of National Biography* – were also geared towards an essentially progressive view of the nation's past in relation to its future.[11]

How did our conceptions of 'heritage' alter in the late twentieth century? The answer, perhaps, is twofold. The first important context was the simultaneous (and probably not unrelated) fragmentation of the historical profession as old views of Britain's dominant place in the world were lost.

Post-imperial Britain no longer ruled the waves, and views of the past changed to accommodate these sober realities. Emphasis was taken away from the drum-and-trumpet style of history which had given children an optimistic overarching vision of national (and imperial) progress. The second context, since the late 1950s, was the gradual but inexorable commercialisation of notions of 'heritage'.

One fascinating feature of this commodification of the past has been its impact on our sense of nostalgia. 'Nostalgia' in its original sense, coined in 1688 by Johannes Hofer, referred to the maladies developed by sailors and travellers abroad. (Often these were illnesses picked up through deprivation at sea or contact with foreign climes, but some psychosomatic responses also seem inevitable.) Nostalgia (from the Greek: νόστος, return to native land; ἄλγος, suffering or grief) literally meant homesickness.[12] It was in the nineteenth century that views of nostalgia began to become more abstract and interior, as people were removed from the 'homeland' of their birth by industrialisation and urbanisation.

But it was the twentieth century which witnessed the great apotheosis of nostalgia. The age of Freud encouraged people to think of their personal histories, full of traumas and longings, and, once views of the national past receded after the 1960s, it was such histories that remained. People learned that self-exploration and self-fulfilment are important things. At no time was this more meaningful than in the late twentieth century, when individuals felt menaced by mounting uncertainty in the workplace and widening chasms of moral relativism. 'Heritage', as David Lowenthal has pointed out, 'is not an inquiry into the past but a celebration of it, not an effort to know what actually happened but a profession of faith in a past tailored to present-day purposes.'[13] It is the Whig interpretation of history for the consumer age: the utopia of shopping has replaced the utopia of democratic progress. Nostalgia in such a climate has increasingly come to feed upon material artefacts and the recreative experience.

The Past Times chain of high street shops has become especially prominent where objects are concerned. Founded by John Beale in Oxford in 1986, the chain aims to offer elegant imitation artefacts with 'carefully researched descriptions'. The emphasis is primarily on lifestyle: the Victorian section of shops typically includes games, shawls, writing implements and lamps. Perhaps not surprisingly, given this domestic emphasis, four out of every five customers in the early 1990s were women.[14] Photographs, too, have come to adorn pubs furnished in 'period' style, or to decorate the family home. The Victorians are ideal subjects for hanging on walls, and not only because theirs was the first age to be documented in photography. The appeal of Victorian photographs may lay in the aesthetics of the camera itself: photographs capture an irretrievable moment that is history as soon as it is taken. Victorian photographers knew this, and it appealed to their sense of nostalgia; that nostalgia, like some 150 year-old brandy, has only matured and become richer as the years have passed. Photographs are also, of course, a commodity in which the viewer's privileged eye has power over the subject: it is a way, quite literally, of domesticating the past.[15]

This process of domestication tends to favour the visual, trendy or immediate above the written and cerebral. William Morris wallpaper and tea-towels sold at a tremendous rate in the 1990s while copies of *News from Nowhere* languished in second-hand bookshops. Neither E. P. Thompson's radical reading nor Fiona MacCarthy's fine biography seems to have dented Morris's iconic status within the 'heritage industry'. The centenary exhibition at the Victoria and Albert Museum in 1996 played up Morris's socialism and poetic leanings, but it is probable (and understandable) that most visitors went away with memories of the exquisite fabrics that had been draped from the heights in several large rooms. Reproductions were, of course, on sale in the exhibition shop. 'Morris and Company' continues to be used as a trademark of Sanderson, marketing furniture, fabrics, wallpaper and paint 'designed to bring classic style to any home'. 'The company's designs have never been more widely appreciated than they are now', their brochure comments. Although only 'inspired by the Morris & Co. design archives', Sanderson, having bought the original wallpaper blocks in 1940, claims to guarantee 'authentic versions of those enduring designs'.[16] 'Inspired by' and 'authentic' do not sit altogether happily together, but it is the very stuff of the 'heritage industry'. ('Authentic' here seems to mean a genuine emotional frisson: though whether that excitement comes from connection with the past or consumer exclusiveness it is less clear.)

John Ruskin, one of Morris's idols, has suffered a similar fate. Indisputably one of the great Victorians, an influence on Gandhi, and deemed worthy of a centenary lecture by George Bernard Shaw in 1919, he enjoyed only marginal status within the 'heritage industry' at the end of the twentieth century.[17] Again, Tim Hilton's acclaimed biography appears not to have changed popular perceptions (or the lack of them).[18] At best there is a certain esteem for what we might call Ruskin's 'green' attitude to the environment, and it may be oddly appropriate that the Guild of Saint George, a communitarian farming enterprise masterminded by Ruskin in the 1870s, continues to exist as a charitable foundation for educational purposes in the age of the eco-warriors.[19]

It is not all bad news. For if in one sense the 'heritage industry' may be a de-historicised (and often de-intellectualised) reflection of post-imperial gloom or the triumph of commercialisation, in another it is a reflection of an emotional attitude towards the past. That attitude can be refined to add depth and meaning to life. The 1960s and 1970s, the point at which modern commercial trends in 'heritage' were beginning to assert themselves, are especially instructive here. These were years of satire and *kitsch* borrowings from the past. But they were also years of profound nostalgia and some extraordinarily resonant connections with the world lost in 1914. On television there was the remarkable success of *The Forsyte Saga* and *Upstairs, Downstairs*. Joseph Losey gave us the haunting film of *The Go-Between* in 1970. Jacqueline du Pré recorded her bestselling account of the Elgar Cello Concerto, and Sir John Barbirolli his incandescent Elgar Second Symphony. André Previn added youthful insight and transatlantic glitter to the Vaughan Williams symphonies, while Sir Adrian Boult recorded all of this repertoire with his blend of gentlemanly poise and supreme wisdom. Most of these efforts, still available as 'heritage' products on video or compact disc, are by any standard commanding intellectual and emotional achievements.

Nostalgia is inclusive and evocative, and may in its warmth draw people into a more nuanced study of the past. We need to remember, too, that nostalgia is not simply 'bad history': 'heritage' is an *attitude* to the past, and does not claim to be history.[20] Consumers smitten with 'heritage' products can go on to deepen their acquaintance either with a period or with a novel that was the basis of a television or film adaptation. Publishers now issue paperbacks of classic novels that have been adapted, and these must presumably sell well. (Certainly the BBC/Penguin tie-in of *Pride and Prejudice* did. Within a couple of months of the television adaptation in 1995 it had sold over 150,000 copies.)[21] Viewers of Iain Softley's subtle 1997 film of *The Wings of the Dove*, with Linus Roache and Helena Bonham Carter, may thereby come to gain acquaintance with the even greater subtleties of James's original. Consumers may in any case be more sceptical of the 'heritage industry' than we have allowed. The tendency of the 1980s to adopt a puritanical and negative attitude towards it, perhaps in part a reaction against Thatcherite trends, has since been tempered.[22] A few years on, we appreciate that people can enjoy nostalgia without subscribing to any 'post-imperial' agenda or being duped by its de-historicised feel.

Even where scepticism is not clearly in evidence, the very nature of the post-1960s 'heritage industry' has helped to limit its own abuses. The cost of 'heritage', we all know, is a highly selective view of history. But this is a selectiveness which applies increasingly to all periods of the past. One distinctive feature of the post-1970s 'heritage industry' has been the foreshortening of the threshold of nostalgia. Whereas people up to the 1960s and 1970s might have located a golden age in the years before 1914, the nature of consumer-orientated nostalgia subsequently encourages people to wax lyrical about events only a decade or two before the present. (The royal wedding of 1981 has been widely analysed as a historical, rather than simply historic, event; songs from the same period have already become the pop equivalent of 'classical' music.) Fashion is ever-reliable in its fickleness. Those at the end of the twentieth century who were nostalgic about the 1960s and 1970s became, to the younger generation, hopelessly *passé* – time-worn figures whose tiresome mantra about 'growing old disgracefully' seemed as dated as anything that issued from the lips of Queen Victoria. The generational perspectives which dominated earlier attitudes to the Victorians have collapsed. 'Heritage' was by the 1990s, often literally, an open shop for all ages and generations. For those inclined to think more carefully about the nature of the 'heritage' they were being offered, and to explore history further, the Victorians could be viewed through possibly the most objective eyes yet.

The evolution of these objective eyes took a long time. The Oxford aesthetes in the 1920s were the first people to begin collecting Victoriana, but theirs was a minority occupation that reflected primarily upon their attitude to their parents. In anticipating the later fascination for Victorian photographs, it may have been that resurrecting Julia Margaret Cameron's famous images of Herschel, Darwin and Carlyle in the 1920s was a way of ridiculing history. Introducing a 1926 collection, Roger Fry wrote of the 'naive confidence of these people' and 'of the abyss of ridicule which they skirt'.[23] It was only in the 1950s, that good decade for clearer reassessment of the Victorian age, that the craze for Victoriana began properly. Although the term 'Victoriana' had been coined back in 1918, Asa Briggs suggests it came into wider use in the 1950s.[24] One commentator in 1954 remarked how eccentric Arnold Bennett had been considered thirty years earlier for collecting papier-mâché furniture with scenes of Balmoral in inlaid mother-of-pearl. 'Today tables and chairs of this kind command high prices in the saleroom and are the prized pieces in cultivated living-rooms', he went on. 'It is, in a word, once more "done" to admire Victoriana.'[25]

Victoriana, 'the Cinderella of Antiques' according to C. W. Drepperd's 1950 guide, became transformed with a magical wave of the auctioneer's gavel to things of rare beauty. And rare beauty meant high prices. Already, by 1959, Briggs felt that the craze concealed hidden dangers:

> During the last twenty years the 'Victorian revival' has done much to rehabilitate many Victorian objects – from monuments and buildings to bric-à-brac. Indiscriminate praise has taken the place of indiscriminate blame, pilgrimages to Victorian sites are undertaken, and collectors have forced up the prices of many objects which earlier in the century were relegated to the dust heap or the lumber room.[26]

In the 1960s and 1970s the market for Victorian antiques expanded exponentially, and many books appeared acting as guides to the amateur collector. Judith Miller became an important figure here, and she has written recently of the historical and market forces driving the business of Victoriana:

> When I started out [antiques] were something of a minority interest, for the most part appealing to only specialist collectors, academics, and the more affluent sections of society. All that has changed. Indeed, since the late 1970s they have enjoyed what can only be described as an explosion of popularity. Various developments have combined to fuel this phenomenon. One has certainly been the tremendous expansion in the type of object either labelled antique, or considered collectable. For example, when I started out, only something that had been made before 1840 was considered an antique. This rigid definition was gradually softened to accommodate pieces over 100 years old.[27]

In other words, Victorian items came within the generally agreed definition of 'antique' just as a popular growth in consumer spending occurred. Victorian trinkets which had sold cheaply as *kitsch* on the Portobello Road in the 1950s came to command serious prices amongst antique-hunters. In the late 1990s, a modest glass butterfly brooch from the late Victorian period would cost up to £200, a small 1880 bust of Gladstone by Robinson and Leadbeater up to £400, and a glass-paste paperweight of Victoria and Albert from the mid-Victorian period up to £600. A reclining 'Morris' chair from 1870, with the original upholstery featuring birds and a floral design in pastel greens, would set back the late twentieth-century purchaser up to £4000.[28]

The expansion of the market for Victoriana was complemented in these years by a growth in the preservationist instinct. As we have seen, it was not always the floundering stately homes that benefited most from renewed interest in the nineteenth century: often the Victorian wings were the first to be closed down in favour of older parts. The National Trust had been driving to rescue country houses since the 1930s, and Hugh Dalton (the new Chancellor of the Exchequer in 1945) did much to acquire for that body the estates of impoverished landowners through tax concessions.[29] But few of the new acquisitions – Knole, Petworth, Sissinghurst – were Victorian houses, or houses with significant Victorian additions. It was really the post-war assault on Victorian architecture and engineering that did most to generate the impetus for protection and rehabilitation. In the 1950s Nikolaus Pevsner set out on his mammoth traversal for *The Buildings of England*: an endeavour of truly Victorian magnitude in itself, a kind of architectural *Dictionary of National Biography*. His aim was to draw the attention of ordinary people to the splendours, intimate as well as grand, of the buildings around them. Eloquent and often opinionated, the imposing émigré with the slight German accent illuminated readers about where original Morris stencils might still be found, or laid down the law where additions to old buildings did not work aesthetically. The Victorian Society also developed an intricate network of architectural walks in towns and cities across the nation, an initiative designed to make people more aware of the history literally beneath their feet and before their eyes.

John Betjeman was doing a similar thing in his bouncy, less systematic way. Like Evelyn Waugh, the early parody-Victorianism became almost a parody of itself as Betjeman became ever rosier about the architecture of the nineteenth century. He had once, of course, greatly preferred Georgian architecture to anything since the mid-Victorian period, and in *Antiquarian Prejudice* (1939) had launched one of the earliest attacks on what we would call the 'heritage industry'. Fear of and distaste with the post-war world subsequently sent his work scuttling back into Arcadian nostalgia. In the post-war *Shell Guides*, in poems, on radio and television, Betjeman enthused volubly about all manner of Victoriana, from villas to railways. When *Ghastly Good Taste* was reissued in 1970, one of the new illustrations (by Peter Hesketh) was of the demolition eight years before of the arch at the entrance to Euston Station. Betjeman and the Victorian Society had both campaigned in vain for its preservation.[30]

Like Betjeman, Pevsner had a mixed record when it came to appreciating the Victorians. Betjeman's early reservations were the product of a reaction against his upbringing, while in later years (like Waugh) he seemed unable to dissociate country houses from the lives led in them. Pevsner had none of this emotional baggage, nor any romantic notions about the squirearchical existence. He praised in English history the interplay between practicality, dynamism, fantasy and fluidity. The Victorians had not been short on dynamism, nor on fantasy; but it was often difficult to combine the two effectively. This was why he held William Morris in such high (if not total) esteem. The wariness about artistic genius Pevsner did not much like; the sensitive craftsmanship he did. 'We owe it to [Morris]', he wrote, 'that an ordinary man's dwelling-house has once more become a worthy object of the architect's thought, and a chair, a wallpaper, or a vase a worthy object of the artist's imagination.'[31] That left much in the nineteenth century that was whimsically impractical or barbarically utilitarian. And there were dangers, too, in the modern world, where design was often self-consciously democratic and committee-bound rather than the product of dynamic innovators. 'We can live in hope', Pevsner commented in 1956, with urban planning and Henry Moore in mind. 'But there is also the danger of timidity and inertia and of the unquestioning faith in the majority vote.'[32]

Perhaps it was with such anxieties about the future that Pevsner agreed to become the first chairman of the Victorian Society, a body founded in 1958 to campaign for the preservation of Victorian and Edwardian architecture. In the early years the society reflected Pevsner's general lack of interest in small Victorian houses, and concentrated instead on the preservation of public and commercial buildings. Where domestic interiors had been the setting for a particular kind of anguished anti-Victorianism, these public edifices had attracted most of the flippant architectural criticism before 1939: Rupert Brooke traced a bout of conjunctivitis to gazing on the neo-Gothic buildings of Rugby School, while Sir Thomas Beecham (in one of his unique double-barrelled insults) described Elgar's First Symphony as being the musical equivalent of St Pancras Station. St Pancras itself was upgraded from a Grade III to a Grade I listed building in 1968 after agitation from the Victorian Society. There had been less success in saving Euston Arch, even with support from figures like Betjeman, earlier in the decade.

Other buildings remained under threat, despite the initiatives of the preservationists: in the case of the Albert Dock in Liverpool, a Grade I status achieved in 1968 did not put developers off the scent until the mid 1970s, when a property crash made building unviable. Here the Victorian Society and other preservationists had to pick their way carefully through the cultural politics of the emerging 'heritage industry'. In the 1970s and 1980s a trend amongst affluent professionals towards the 'period look' encouraged the refurbishment of dockyards, warehouses and erstwhile slum terraces. Often, though, this meant preservation at a price: aesthetic or historical. Too fastidious or protective an approach could condemn buildings to a kind of antiquarian vacuum, neither used nor appreciated. And already prejudices lingered about certain types of Victorian buildings, especially those built from brick. Brick-cleaning methods had become widely used in Britain in the 1960s, but it was not until the early 1970s that work on the Royal Albert Hall signalled similar benefits for Victorian buildings. The cost and slowness of many such endeavours reflected an even greater challenge to the preservationists. Reliant upon the vagaries of government and private assistance, it is perhaps inevitable that bodies like the Victorian Society concentrated itself more upon raising historical appreciation than setting itself impossible financial goals. That tended to be left to the property-developers. As Raphael Samuel reflected, the triumph of the preservationist instinct in the late twentieth century was essentially a consumer-led phenomenon.[33]

The closest contact that many people have had with the Victorians since the end of the twentieth century has been through television and cinema adaptations of classic novels. Here complex cultural politics are at play, suffusing the vision of the past being presented on screen. Before screen adaptations there was a long tradition of Sunday teatime broadcasts on the wireless. These broadcasts – of *David Copperfield* in 1925, or of *Barchester Towers* in 1938 – had not been a conscious part of any recognisable 'heritage industry'. What they represented was a more or less direct link with the Victorian age, for they were part of Sir John Reith's campaign to enlighten as well as to entertain. Moreover, there is evidence from questionnaire returns that listeners actively called for such adaptations – a responsiveness which, given the thriving autodidactic culture in Britain up to the 1930s, should hardly surprise us.[34]

Nor should it surprise us that early attempts to translate classic tales onto the screen were wreathed in Victorian assumptions. When the British Board of Film Censors was set up in 1912 it included as grounds for censorship scenes of 'indecorous dancing' or the depiction of 'native customs in foreign lands abhorrent to British ideas'.[35] Thomas Hardy, having given up writing novels in the 1890s amidst a torrent of abuse about the immorality of his characters, managed to recoup some of his losses by negotiating with film companies interested in adapting his works. And of course they were thoroughly respectable adaptations, even after harmless liberties were taken, such as setting part of *Tess of the D'Urbervilles* in a nightclub. (Asked by a visitor whether he had seen it, the octogenarian writer gave 'one of his rare shy smiles and shook his head'. No doubt he found wry amusement in such a spurious attempt to give his novel 'relevance'.)[36] The first television adaptations of classic novels in the 1940s and 1950s were equally suffused with old-fashioned practices and attitudes. By necessity programmes were transmitted live, and performers were often those who had served their apprenticeship on stage. Bransby Williams, who had learnt his craft amidst the grease-paint and gas-lamps of the music hall, and had been performing Dickens monologues since 1896, was still going strong fifty years later: on Christmas Day 1946 he treated television audiences to his rendition of Scrooge. Fidelity to the text and family values remained a key part of the rationale behind broadcasting.

Things began to change in the late 1950s, when the BBC monopoly was broken by commercial television. Thereafter pressure began to mount for more ambitious or more 'adult' adaptations of classic novels. The BBC version of *Oliver Twist* in 1962 depicted the murder of Nancy so violently that a debate was sparked in Parliament (the Postmaster General described the scene as 'brutal and quite inexcusable') and a final shot of Sikes's body hanging from the rope was excised.[37] More palatable – indeed triumphant – was the BBC's adaptation of John Galsworthy's *The Forsyte Saga* five years later. Part of the tremendous success of this version was the ambitious tailoring of its scope to a contemporary fascination with domestic Victoriana. Its twenty-six episodes, each of fifty minutes, attracted regular audiences of over 18,000,000, and clergymen would change the time of evening services to avoid painful clashes of conscience. Again, there was public debate: this time, however, politicians found themselves so caught up in the Victorian 'soap opera' that they argued not about television ethics, but about whether Soames Forsyte (played by Eric Porter) had been justified in forcing his attentions on his estranged wife (Nyree Dawn Porter).[38]

Colour, so important a feature of later 'heritage' adaptations, was first deployed in a 1967 serialisation of *Vanity Fair*. Spectacle, sweep and human interest were pushed to the fore in the 1970s, albeit sometimes in a way that sowed seeds of doubt about the nature of people's attitude to classic novels. The BBC's 1974 version of *The Pallisers*, Trollope's great arch of novels about political life in Victorian England, is a case in point. In its scope (again, twenty-six episodes of fifty minutes each) it was evidently an attempt to formulate another *Forsyte* success. There was lavish supporting material in the *Radio Times*, including plot synopses and family trees, and there was one of the now ubiquitous tie-in publications of Trollope's original novels from Panther. Yet it was not the triumph it had been orchestrated to be. Partly, no doubt, this was because Trollope is not wont to be sensational, and there are few passionately heated Forsyte-moments in his somewhat gentler pages. Raymond Williams also suggested that whereas the Forsytes had been recognisably middle-class, the Pallisers were alien in their aristocratic ways. The cast and crew, he argued, had difficulty getting inside the idiom.[39]

Some of this unease was shared by John Drummond, then head of arts programmes for BBC2. For whereas the BBC was only too keen to adapt Victorian novels for television, it seemed strangely indifferent to historical or biographical context. Part of the problem was that young producers, people not always in thrall to Victorian culture, were in charge. 'When the BBC spent a large sum on the serialization of Trollope's *Palliser* novels,' Drummond recalls, 'it seemed to me important to provide a fuller picture of Trollope as a novelist who also had an interesting life. But there were no takers: nobody was in the least bit interested in him.'[40] It was a similar situation with Dickens, who over the years had provided so many palpable hits for the BBC. An unsatisfactory dramatisation of his life, with Anthony Hopkins as the writer and Arthur Lowe as his Micawberish father, had been made for the centenary year 1970. And over at the Victoria and Albert Museum, Roy Strong found his kingdom-to-be in languid form. Here basic lack of interest had been replaced by a plodding dutifulness. 'The Dickens exhibition opened', he recorded in his diary, 'a disappointing affair with far too many items and no visual excitement. Someone said that it was like having the footnotes without the book.'[41]

Viewers increasingly expected adaptations of classic novels to be relevant to the age in which they lived. *The Forsyte Saga*, with its exploration of female experience, comfortable material life and inter-generational tensions, had been ideal for the late 1960s. So too was the exploration of instinct against social order in John Schlesinger's challenging 1967 film of *Far from the Madding Crowd*. Julie Christie, its heroine, had already achieved iconic status as a fashionable free-thinking actress; Terence Stamp, as we have seen, also turned eyes (male and female) with his dashing soldier's outfit. Further adaptations followed in the next decade, perhaps most notably Dennis Potter's 1978 screenplay for *The Mayor of Casterbridge*. Potter's reading emphasised the commodification of women by men, and deliberately portrayed Michael Henchard (played by Alan Bates) as a manic-depressive. Hardy had already become one of the key authors for 'heritage' on screen, ever-reliable for idyllic pastoral settings and tales of powerful psychological or sexual obsession. In 1967 the Hardy Society had been founded, and visitors began flocking to Dorset on the Wessex pilgrimage. In many ways this was the inevitable outcome of a trend initiated in the 1921, when the Progress Film Company had shot a silent version of *The Mayor of Casterbridge* on location in Dorset. Hardy himself had helped with the spelling of the Wessex dialect for the title cards, thereby creating one of the first entertaining clashes between whimsical 'heritage' and sober reality. 'Hardy read the script,' writes Matthew Sweet, 'made notes and corrections, and told no one, presumably, of his habit of inventing dialect terms.'[42] But if people did not notice (or mind) in the 1920s, they certainly did not fifty years later.

The era of Thatcher and 'Victorian values' witnessed further engagement with classic novels on screen. Ironically, though, one of the first victims of 'Victorian values' was the presentation on screen of the Victorians themselves. Thatcher wanted financial accountability from the BBC; the BBC responded, perhaps inevitably, by becoming more acutely ratings-conscious than ever before. In the 1980s and early 1990s it tended to play safe with adaptations of classic novels, although its splendid 1982 *Barchester Chronicles* may have been something of a covert comment on the age – Thatcherite boardroom politics amongst the rooks and bells of Trollope's cathedral cloisters. (Nigel Hawthorne, the scheming Archdeacon Grantly, reprised his deliciously knowing performance in modern dress for *Yes, Minister*.) More generally, the BBC came to rely upon a stable of regular authors, notably Dickens and Hardy. It clung all the more fiercely to such reliable writers when independent rivals like Granada, unfettered by funding difficulties, were producing lavish blockbusters like *Brideshead Revisited* and *The Jewel in the Crown.*

This may be an appropriate moment to ponder the relationship between history, the screen and the 'heritage industry'. Often it is claimed that the 1980s and 1990s were the nadir of historical sensitivity on screen. From much that has been written, it might be concluded by someone who has never seen a 'heritage' film that adapters of classic novels worked only to regulations about the requisite number of dances in country houses, or of sepia shots of fields being harvested. Certainly the quantity of productions was notable, keeping adapters like Andrew Davies working overtime. Some of these productions (not, incidentally, those by the gifted Davies) were disappointing, drawing attention to their cynically market-driven nostalgia. It has become commonplace to dismiss all 'heritage' productions as a reflection of the late twentieth-century obsession with the lost glories and certainties of yesteryear. The arch-offenders here have often been cited as Merchant Ivory: to be 'Merchant Ivory' is to be prettified and to value surface above content.

Such thinking is curiously unreflective. For one thing it does not do justice to the accomplishments of many adaptations. Merchant Ivory films may make a high priority of surface finish, but they generally manage to complement this with intelligent scripts and skilled acting. In consistency of thoughtfulness, they seem in fact to be decidedly superior to many other films of the 1980s and 1990s. Often, too, Merchant Ivory took commercial risks. To their excellent versions of *A Room with a View* (1986) and *Howards End* (1992) they added *Maurice* (1987), which had its Cambridge architecture and its Allegri *Miserere*, but also what James Ivory called a 'dark, cold, masculine look' and some distinctly un-'heritage' male nudity.[43]

Individual viewers are bound to disagree about particular points of interpretation in such adaptations. They are likely, too, to experience a certain unease about even the most enjoyable of translations onto screen. There has long been a feeling that films are rarely as subtle as novels. If they are subtle, then they are subtle on their own terms, and this almost always involves moving away from the letter of the original novel.[44] At the end of the twentieth century, fear of violating some unwritten contract with textual fidelity – or its reverse: a tendentious bid to make old books 'relevant' to the modern age – could leave adaptations struggling to engage originally with the source material. The pressure for marketability accentuated these trends, and here the demands of the overseas viewers (voracious consumers of costume drama) became increasingly important. One result of this, even where adaptations were successful, was a market-dominated process of canonisation in which the same authors – Austen,

Dickens, the Brontës, Hardy – would appear time and again, with an experiment (*Nostromo* in 1997, *Wives and Daughters* in 1999, *The Way We Live Now* in 2001) only every few years. Put this way, the drawbacks of the 'heritage industry' owed themselves not so much to post-imperial nostalgia as to the difficulty of approaching the Victorians with imagination and originality in an age where the ruffling of feathers was discouraged. Thatcher's era of 'Victorian values' ought to have liberated the past from the deadening grip of imaginative and financial caution; many producers must have felt, however, that they were the nail in the coffin.

Yet in the later 1990s, once the less happy outlines of the post-Thatcherite landscape had become clear, adapters of Victorian novels often managed to achieve 'relevance' as well as an intelligent engagement with the source material. For one thing they became more self-conscious about the potential pitfalls and evasions of the 'heritage industry'. And so, whereas the clichéd rendition of a classic novel had beautiful costumes, forelock-tugging yokels and happy endings, many of the versions of the 1990s were darker, consciously challenging stereotypes about presentation of the Victorians on screen. They also reflected life in Britain at the end of the twentieth century, with renewed awareness of the nature of materialism, career insecurity and family dysfunctionalism. Appropriately enough, several actors who had starred in Merchant Ivory films reinvented themselves in darker roles in the 1990s: Helena Bonham Carter, who had been an angelic Lucy Honeychurch and otherwordly Helen Schlegel, found a superb role as the coldly scheming Kate Croy; Rupert Graves, who had been a puppyish Freddy Honeychurch and alluring Alec Scudder, showed a more unsettling side as Arthur Huntingdon.

That last role, in the BBC's 1996 adaptation of *The Tenant of Wildfell Hall*, involved unapologetic scenes of wife-beating and marital rape. (The *Daily Telegraph* praised the way it 'spoke to the modern viewer on feminist issues within the spirit of the original'.) [45] The role of Helen Graham was taken by Tara Fitzgerald, an excellent actress who had carved out a name for herself in a number of gritty northern dramas. Another highly skilled actor with a similar background was Christopher Eccleston, who in 1996 starred in Michael Winterbottom's dark and uncompromising film of *Jude the Obscure*. From its opening scene – a barren furrowed field with crows wheeling overhead – the version powerfully translated Hardy's bleak worldview into visual terms. For the Victorians, and for sanitised 'heritage' adaptations of Hardy, babies may have appeared under gooseberry bushes; cinema-goers of the 1990s were reminded of the reality of the forces of nature in a disturbing childbirth scene with Kate Winslet.

Lighter in tone, though also appropriately tart, was the BBC's adaptation of *Vanity Fair* in 1998.[46] This had powerful resonances for contemporary audiences in its portrayal of Becky Sharp (Natasha Little) as a splendidly shameless opportunist in a male-dominated world: a phenomenon known at the time, in certain circles, as 'girl power'. Instructive, too, was its knowing mockery of 'heritage' conventions. The music made no attempt to be elevating, or to pastiche early nineteenth-century styles, but with jazzy syncopations and flatulent rasps announced its modernity and satirical cut with relish. Those who watched the end credits roll saw them imposed not on some vista of beautiful landscape, but on a large pig snuffling in mud. Edginess prevailed. At the end of 2001 the BBC dramatised Trollope's *The Way We Live Now*, with David Suchet as the shady foreign financier Augustus Melmotte. The sly transfer of Thatcherite boardroom politics to the cloister had given way to an explicitly millennial gloom, the legend on the front of the *Radio Times* saying it all: 'Sex, Lies and Victoriana'. Many critics pointed out that Melmotte, who tries to buy his way into the status of an English gentleman, has very clear parallels with the life of Robert Maxwell; and indeed, in preparing for the role, Suchet read every available biography of Maxwell.[47] Less sharply observed, in the standard assumption that 'heritage' productions habitually strive for relevance, was the fact that Trollope has put his finger on a set of ethical issues that have never been resolved. The Victorians, Andrew Davies's subtle screenplay suggested, not only anticipated but invented us.[48]

Mention ought finally to be made of museum practice within the so-called 'heritage industry'. Here, again, the origins of trends in the late twentieth century can often be traced back to a time before the consumer revolution of the late 1950s and 1960s. Lucasta Miller has followed the emergence of a Brontë cult dating from the nineteenth century itself, when Elizabeth Gaskell's biography of Charlotte inadvertently created the idea of the sisters as tragic, repressed individuals living on the windswept Yorkshire moors. Their home, Haworth Parsonage, soon became a site of pilgrimage; as early as the 1920s one commentator claimed that 'for every single individual who reads [Charlotte Brontë's] books to-day, it is probably true to say that there are a hundred who find an absorbing interest in the story of her life'.[49] The parsonage was opened to the public as a museum in 1928. Souvenirs sold at a spiralling rate, and visitors itched to touch tables, clothes and scraps of paper that had once been in contact with Brontë skin. Inevitably, television and mass-marketing accelerated these trends further. In 1974, in the wake of Christopher Fry's dramatisation *The Brontës of Haworth*, the parsonage museum attracted 221,497 visitors. Brontë bookmarks, ashtrays, tea towels and biscuits have long been available for purchase. (The bookshop at

Haworth, by sad irony, closed down as a result of declining sales.) [50] It was a similar case for nineteenth-century writers elsewhere, especially those associated with particular geographical areas like Hardy and Wessex or Wordsworth and the Lake District.

The two key elements of such pilgrimages were marketing and the privileging of personal experience. These were linked, and were the legacy of both consumerism and of changing attitudes to the past. Social and economic history, as we shall see, came to replace traditional political narratives; and in schools empathy with historical figures became one of the most valued goals of study. These found their outlet in pilgrimages and the increasingly interactive nature of many museums, which had educational programmes specifically geared towards school study. In some places visitors no longer peered at artefacts behind glass cases or from a roped-back distance. Instead they handled reproductions and experienced re-enactments: at Jorvik one could be a Viking; at Canterbury one could travel with Chaucer's pilgrims; at the Imperial War Museum one could be Blitzed. At Whitechapel there was (and is) a popular 'Jack the Ripper' walk: a guided tour of the murderer's haunts by enthusiasts who evince a sometimes disturbingly detailed knowledge of the topic. For those underwhelmed by modern-day Whitechapel, escape to the narrow-alleyed, fog-bound, muffled-hoof place of a century before could be found in computer games like *Sherlock Holmes and the Case of the Serrated Scalpel*: a game which not only brought Holmes and Watson in on the Ripper case, but allowed the player to move around locations (the morgue, Holmes's laboratory, a victim's room) at will.[51]

Some took their enthusiasm for living in the past even further, dressing in up in period clothes. Television and film productions often employed such people (usually without payment) as extras to be chopped down by cannon fire or to stroll nonchalantly by as some crucial scene was enacted in the foreground. Television at the end of the twentieth century also provided a curious spectacle in *The 1900 House*. This series followed the struggles of a family to adapt to life for three months in a painstakingly reproduced Victorian home. In some respects it was the apotheosis of history-as-personal-experience, for although it forced the family to engage with the material reality of life in a middle-class Victorian home, it was the very anachronism of their attitudes that made it such compelling viewing. Of public life there was nothing. They never discussed Prime Minister Salisbury. The Boer War did not impinge on this household, even though the husband served in the armed forces.

For museums which kept to more traditional ways of presenting the past, the Victorian age remained no less interesting, even if again it was often the social and economic side that was emphasised. In 2001, for example, the

Victoria and Albert Museum held a centenary exhibition called *The Victorian Vision: Inventing New Britain*. It was designed both to show 'how an era shaped our world' and to present 'the Victorians as they saw themselves'. By doing so the curators evidently intended to bypass many myths and stereotypes: hypocrisy, snobbery, prudery and social exploitation were scrupulously avoided. Whether they were right to do this remains a point of debate. In flagging these themes, they may simply have revived unexamined prejudices; or they may have tackled them directly, and used them to add nuance to the exhibits before visitors' eyes. There is no clear solution to such difficulties. Throughout, the emphasis remained that of progress and variety, and the exhibition unfolded into six sections: 'royalty', 'society', 'nature', 'the world', 'the army' and 'technology'. It was a positive, wittily designed and often very atmospheric exhibition.

It was, however, problematic. Since visitors had been invited to consider the Victorians 'as they saw themselves', it was a point of interest rather than pedantry to consider *whose* vision of society was being offered. (Not to mention at which point in the reign: as Asa Briggs noted in the accompanying book, the Victorians had different conceptions of public and private time, even without our retrospective parcelling of the age into 'early', 'mid' and 'late'.) [52] This was a middle-class view of the Victorian age for middle-class visitors. There was very little on working-class life. The section on 'the world' downplayed controversies about imperial exploitation, presenting instead an evasive multi-cultural perspective. Science and the rise of evolutionary theory featured prominently, but religion was almost entirely omitted. Striking, too, was the eco-friendly profile of the section on 'nature'. 'They admired the majesty of wild animals, yet had no hesitation in hunting and stuffing specimens', one caption testily remarked. The point was driven home by juxtaposition of Landseer's *Monarch of the Glen* against a ghoulish chair fashioned from antlers. Hindsight was more obvious still in the attention given to changing views of women and children, and especially to the royal family. The opening section on 'royalty' seemed, on reflection, to have been overtly political: a defence, almost, of the very idea of monarchy in post-Diana days. Typical was the avoidance of any mention of the controversy caused by Victoria's seclusion after the death of Prince Albert. There was a statuette of John Brown, though again the caption was resolutely discreet, and one felt that the presence of a bust of Albert in the same cabinet implied a likely absence of discord in heaven.

Combining nostalgic appeal with presentation that will encourage more nuanced historical or intellectual engagement is clearly not an easy thing to achieve. The Victorians were certainly not the only people to suffer from the tensions between 'heritage' and history at the end of the twentieth century. The 'heritage industry' is implicitly materialistic and consumer-orientated, and has a tendency to collapse different periods (even very recent ones) into one commodified version of the past. Potentially this breaks down old imaginative barriers and links us to the past in ways that had not been common before the Second World War. The dangers, meanwhile, speak for themselves: a vision of the past which lacks subtlety and nuance, and in doing so fails to respect the complex humanity of people who lived in a different age. History is about difference as well as similarity; and it is the challenge (amidst distracting demands for marketability and crude 'relevance') of strengthening and deepening this balance which emerges as perhaps the most crucial for the future of the Victorians.

7

*History*

At the end of 1913 Lytton Strachey wrote to an old friend who had been one of his contemporaries at Trinity College, Cambridge, and a fellow member of the Apostles. Strachey took him up on the nature of historical writing:

> I agree with what you say about history, thus far at least I think it would be more difficult now to write a large scale history of all aspects of a neat period, especially of course a modern period. But by limitation of scope great things could still be done if there were men like Gibbon, Macaulay or Carlyle. Meanwhile, even if the age and the future be unfavourable to decent history, it is all the more reason to do the best we can before we fall into [the] utter barbarism of unenlightened learning. I expect you agree with this.[1]

The recipient of this letter was G. M. Trevelyan, already set on the path to a most eminent career in the historical profession which would culminate in 1927 with his election to the Regius chair. Almost certainly Trevelyan agreed with the sentiments being expressed by Strachey. Earlier in the year he had published *Clio: A Muse*, a version of the essay initially written in retaliation against J. B. Bury's advocacy of scientific history in his inaugural lecture as Regius Professor in 1903.[2] For all their differences, and the differences that would later arise over their uses (and sometimes abuses) of the Victorian past, Strachey and Trevelyan were agreed on one thing. History ought to be about real people; it ought to be the product of imagination and feeling; and it ought to be written with artistry and verve. The rise of scientific history, by contrast, threatened to supplant the wisdom of sympathetic historical appreciation with a dull recitation of facts for their own sake. This was to be an argument played out at greater length throughout the twentieth century, and one which would profoundly affect ways in which the Victorians were seen.

Strachey and Trevelyan, both members of that 'intellectual aristocracy' which was so important in Britain up to the Second World War, gained their view of the past through the historical writing of the Victorians and their own predecessors. (Indeed, Trevelyan was bodily linked to the tradition, for his great-uncle was Lord Macaulay.) Most nineteenth-century scholars had been amateurs of independent means unattached to any academic establishment. Prose had flowed with remarkable confidence and ease from tables in comfortable libraries, the quills pausing only while the appropriate classical reference or witty turn of phrase was pondered. Unencumbered by obscure methodologies or fetishes about archival sources, scholars like Gibbon and Macaulay had explored history as a constant dialogue between past and present, finding therein plentiful opportunities for humour, drama and instructive insights into human nature. And yet there were shortcomings to their work: sometimes it elided the differences between past and present too smoothly; often it recalled the lives of princes but not of paupers; and certainly there were sources lying in dusty archives which might profitably have been used.

It was partly for such reasons that the historical profession began to ex-perience systematic organisation towards the end of the nineteenth century.[3] In Germany, scholars like Leopold von Ranke placed emphasis on the study of the past *wie es eigentlich gewesen* – as it really was, rather than how we might like it to have been, and his example in the impartial probing of sources came to be widely emulated.[4] There were impulses, too, from the greater involvement of the state in the provision of education after 1870. Much of this, to be sure, was rudimentary. But there was also a felt need for a distinctive national identity in the heyday of imperialism, a reflection perhaps of Kipling's comment about what they should know of England who only England know. In 1868 the Royal Historical Society was founded, achieving a recognisably 'modern' status (reflected in its *Transactions*) in the late 1880s with the marginalisation of its early dilet-tante style by an influx of academic historians.[5] In 1872 and 1875 the history tripos was set up at Oxford and Cambridge respectively. The appoint-ments to Regius chairs of Sir John Seeley (Cambridge, 1869) and William Stubbs (Oxford, 1871) is generally taken to signify the beginning of the quasi-scientific study of history in those universities. In 1886 the *English Historical Review* was inaugurated, while in 1896 Lord Acton began presiding over what was intended to be the summation of Victorian historical knowledge, written by the finest professionals in their field, *The Cambridge Modern History*.[6] The Historical Association was founded by A. F. Pollard in 1907 to stimulate an integrated sense of national and imperial identity amongst teachers of history at all levels, its journal *History* being published from 1916.[7] A plethora of new universities – including Manchester, Leeds, Liverpool and Sheffield – was set up in this decade, while in 1917 and 1920 doctorates of philosophy were finally introduced at Oxford and Cam-bridge. Also in 1920 the Institute of Historical Research, attached to the

University of London, was founded; its *Bulletin* was published from the following year. The Cambridge Historical Association and its *Journal* came into existence in 1922.

Intellectual changes were afoot, too. Lewis Namier's *The Structure of Politics at the Accession of George III* (1929) and *England in the Age of the American Revolution* (1930) showed new 'professional' standards at work by focusing on history not as the onwards march of progress, to be measured by great happenings, but as the product of individual actions and everyday practice. The reaction against the old view and practice of history was, of course, implicitly anti-Victorian, and owed much to the profound imaginative shock of the First World War. Scholars like Macaulay had seen history as a gradual revelation of the greatness of Britain since the Glorious Revolution – a red-carpeted progress towards the investiture of democratic, liberal ideals at some stage in the near future. The blood and the carnage of the Western Front revealed the hollowness of such myths, even if at the time scholars like Gilbert Murray pretended to themselves that they stood for wisdom and culture while their German counterparts were pedlars of the obscure and pedantic.[8] Herbert Butterfield's *The Whig Interpretation of History* (1931) went even further. His book launched a coruscating attack on the tendency of historians to study the past exclusively in the light of contemporary concerns, in the process omitting inconvenient details and adopting a moral stance towards the past.

But history as it would have been understood by Strachey and Trevelyan did not completely pass away during their own lifetimes, and that has implications for how the Victorians were interpreted in the early twentieth century. One of the dangers in tracing the origins of modern historical practice lies in the temptation to define 'professionalism' by our own standards. 'Professional' practice in the early twentieth century would not seem all that professional by modern standards; it may make more sense to think in terms of a co-existence of old and new ways.[9] The irony of such unprofessional behaviour would, surely, not have been lost on Strachey; and, indeed, it was he who reflected on the dilemma facing historians around 1918 in the preface to *Eminent Victorians*. That preface is best known as a manifesto for modern biography, but it was also a thoughtful statement about the options and difficulties facing scholars when they came to write about the Victorians:

> The history of the Victorian Age will never be written: we know too much about it. For ignorance is the first requisite of the historian – ignorance, which simplifies and clarifies, which selects and omits, with a placid perfection unattainable by the highest art. Concerning the Age which has just passed, our fathers and our grandfathers have poured forth and accumulated so vast a quantity of information

that the industry of a Ranke would be submerged by it, and the perspicacity of a Gibbon would quail before it.[10]

There is a serious generational point here, as well as an informed comment on the crossroads at which historians found themselves in 1918, unsure whether to take the scientific route of Ranke or the humanist route of Gibbon, and knowing that neither individually would yield success.

Strachey's less well-known thoughts on Hume, Gibbon, Macaulay, Carlyle, Froude and Creighton also repay consideration.[11] In the 1929 piece on Creighton, for example, he regards the rise of 'professional' historians with typical ambivalence, neither unaware of its worthy insights nor of its deadly dullness:

> Born when the world was becoming extremely scientific, he belonged to the post-Carlyle-and-Macaulay generation – the school of Oxford and Cambridge inquirers, who sought to reconstruct the past solidly and patiently, with nothing but facts to assist them – pure facts, untwisted by political or metaphysical bias and uncoloured by romance.[12]

In hindsight, the publication two years later of Butterfield's *Whig Interpretation* might seem to have won the case for this post-Carlyle-and-Macaulay generation. But this was not entirely true. For one thing, Butterfield's tract was not universally acclaimed. Often it was not reviewed at all. And for those notices it did receive, there were reservations about its repetitiveness and intellectual inconsistencies. For example, Butterfield castigated Whig historians for omitting detail, yet he was forced to admit that 'the art of the historian is precisely the art of abridgment'.[13] The issue of *what* detail to omit was, of course, the crucial one; but it was not clear that it was the 'professional' historian's prerogative to decide such matters, or that he was free from subjectivity himself. 'He hardly seems to be the master of his thesis', one reviewer noted laconically.[14]

There were other reasons why 'professional' standards did not completely supplant older perspectives on the past. The habits of tradition proved difficult to shake off. While the First World War may have disillusioned those of an optimistic persuasion, victory only served to reassure many that Britain had been bound to win on account of its august tradition of liberty and constitutionalism.[15] The philosopher R. G. Collingwood, in one way an implacable critic of Whiggish positivism, in another was a profound believer in the moral superiority of the British Empire over German expansionism. He felt that it was the responsibility of pedagogues to educate the future rulers of nation and empire.[16] And he was not alone. School textbooks in the early twentieth century were designed to inculcate children with a number of nationalist, racialist and imperial assumptions about Britain's place in the world.[17] To be sure, progressive educationalists after the trauma of the First World War did advocate a move away from the militaristic strains of drum-and-trumpet history. However, as Patrick Brindle has shown, classroom practice in the inter-war years did not follow suit; teachers enjoyed no special training and allowed pre-war assumptions to filter back into their lessons.[18] Others were unrepentantly Victorian, encouraging noisy talk of kings and battles to echo around the classroom. One textbook of the 1930s even had separate indices for battles, wars and peace treaties.[19]

This was very much the world of *1066 and All That* – and indeed the humour of that work fed directly upon contemporary readers' experience of history lessons. (The fact that few children today appreciate its jokes tells us much about how attitudes and practices have changed.) Even pupils who attended modest academic schools seem to have had a good working knowledge of the Victorian past, from which we can infer no great disaffection on the part either of teachers or their charges. In 1918, a recognition exercise in Sheffield revealed widespread awareness amongst working-class people of the Industrial Revolution, the 1832 Reform Act, and the names Gladstone and Darwin.[20] Those educated at more socially selective schools inevitably found themselves even more subject to a version of history based upon dates, names and a series of triumphalist assumptions. G. H. Blore, an assistant master at Winchester, produced a book called *Victorian Worthies* in 1920: a study of figures such as Shaftesbury, Bright and Rhodes designed to show 'the spirit of public service' in action.[21] Another textbook crooned as late as 1939: 'Queen Victoria was the best, the noblest, the purest, the kindest-hearted sovereign that ever sat upon the throne of the country.'[22] Such overkill almost rendered Stracheyan deflation unnecessary.

The *raison d'être* of studying history at university was perhaps even clearer. 'Self-reliant and self-propelled,' writes one commentator, 'the graduate who translated his education into specific public service would continue to give the university its principle of justification until the 1930s.'[23] This was particularly true of history at Oxford and Cambridge.[24] The cultivation of sound judgement was considered more important than acquiring research techniques or knowledge for its own sake. Many undergraduates were content simply to take the pass degree, or even no formal qualification at all, and as late as 1913 only 62 per cent of Cambridge undergraduates were honours candidates.[25] More ambitious or accomplished Oxbridge students stood a good chance of coming to influence public opinion after graduation. Of the 543 (out of 7852) Oxford graduates who took first-class honours degrees in modern history between 1873 and 1929, fifty-six went on to attain entries in the *Dictionary of National Biography*, and it has been estimated that at least a further twenty-seven became 'major figures, especially in the teaching and writing of history'.[26]

At Cambridge, the history tripos of the inter-war years focused predominantly upon the constitutional, economic and imperial development of Britain. This reflected not only the time when the study of history had been shackled to jurisprudence, but a strong continuity of attitude about Britain's place in the world. Undergraduates were directed in reading lists to works such as Walter Bagehot's *The English Constitution* (required reading for most twentieth-century monarchs, as we have seen); Queen Victoria's letters; and political biographies of Gladstone and Disraeli by John Morley and G. E. Buckle. Only in 1940 were E. L. Woodward's *The Age of Reform, 1815–1870* (1938) and R. C. K. Ensor's *England, 1870–1914* (1936) – both recognisably 'modern' works of scholarship – added to the list.[27] Inevitably students would have turned to the relevant chapters of *The Cambridge Modern History*, that great summation of Victorian historical knowledge; and there they would have been reassured that 'Great Britain has built up a model system for the administration of an oversea empire' which conferred upon its subjects 'the benefits of Western knowledge and Western ideals of government'.[28] Small wonder that one undergraduate of the 1920s, W. H. B. Court, lamented that 'the chief want of the Cambridge Historical School in our day' was 'general ideas on man and society adequate to explain historical change'.[29] Exam questions were riddled with Whiggish assumptions. 'Comment on the results of the outbreak of the French Revolution on English constitutional development and the dangers which it threatened to that development', tripos candidates were instructed in 1936. The ghosts of Burke and Macaulay haunted Cambridge common rooms long into the twentieth century.

As in so many other areas, the Second World War fundamentally changed how the Victorian past was studied and taught. In time, the more egalitarian spirit of post-war society would make itself felt. So too would the opportunities offered by Butler's Education Act to bright children from humble backgrounds, many of whom in the 1960s and beyond became radical teachers in their own right. But in the short term the war served simply as an imaginative watershed. It provided people with an opportunity to look back on the Victorians and their legacy without the fierce partisanship either of the early critics or the survivors of the age. By the 1950s the Bloomsbury Group was defunct, and those who had called for a direct return to the values of yesteryear had passed away. The last generation of Victorians – Churchill and his peers – were, of course, still around; but their days were numbered, and they were forced to exist in a climate where deference and public duty were fast being supplanted by consumerism and private fulfilment.

The Bloomsbury Group, before the beginning of its rehabilitation in the 1960s, lay in the doldrums during the late 1940s and 1950s. This was, in fact, symptomatic of a reaction in favour of the Victorians during these years. For although the influence of Victorianism itself was passing away from society, the scholarly and biographical reputation of the Victorians enjoyed a golden period in the decade or two after the war. These apparently contradictory trends may, of course, have had an entirely predictable logic. Anti-Victorianism and nostalgia before 1945 had been heated affairs precisely because society remained steeped in the values of the past. The gradual distancing of time and the imaginative impact of the Second World War changed all that. A society less in the thrall of particular values has better opportunity to consider them impartially and to reset balances. Anti-Victorianism did not gain that much of a hold on minds in the early twentieth century, but as a dominant intellectual fashion historians were inevitably sensitive to its jibes and insinuations. And so, where historical scholarship was concerned, there was much work to be done.

Where Victorian scholarship before the war had been (by our standards) patchy, having itself been suffused with old-fashioned priorities, historical writing in the 1950s often had the best of both worlds. It could combine, in the works of J. H. Buckley, Asa Briggs, Walter Houghton and W. L. Burn, the literary grace and wide erudition that marked much older scholarship with a newer clarity of focus and academic rigour.[30] Much of it also took more seriously the study of social attitudes. Economic and social history, as we have seen, had been gaining momentum in the early years of the twentieth century. Its tone, however, was often too readily critical of Victorian industrialism, and correctives to pessimistic writing about dark satanic mills had not been greatly helped by the predominance of drum-and-trumpet history. But in the post-war world, with the optimism of the Welfare State and slowly rising levels of consumer wealth, the time was ripe for more expansive and engaged overviews of lives measured beyond politics and battles. Asa Briggs, the doyen of Victorian studies, first established his name in the 1950s; he has been described as 'the Lord Macaulay of the Welfare State'.[31]

Two of the great achievements of this scholarship are worth singling out. The first of these was a sophisticated probing of the very definition of Victorianism itself. Earlier writers, with the notable exception of G. M. Young, had usually invoked a definition of 'Victorian' to suit themselves and their often partisan purposes. Critics like Strachey had been the worst offenders here, perhaps partly because they knew of their own tendentiousness. Young, on the other hand, is alleged to have breathed 'we're in for a bad time' when he read *Eminent Victorians*. 'I was constantly being told that the Victorians did this, or the Victorians thought that,' he wrote in the second edition of his *Portrait of an Age*, significantly reissued in 1953, 'while my own difficulty was to find anything on which they agreed: any assumption which was not at some time or other fiercely challenged.'[32] Young's message, and his profound belief in the need to 'listen' sensitively to the multi-layered voices of different generations within Victorian England, was taken up by scholars in the 1950s.

'Victorian taste is intelligible only in a context of thought and feeling which defies easy explanation', wrote J. H. Buckley in 1952, taking as his starting-point Ruskin's comment about taste being the ultimate arbiter of character. Like many of his contemporaries, Buckley went on to point out that the Victorians were often their own best critics – a volubility which would have unfortunate consequences in the twentieth century:

> Now, however a post-Victorian world may have chosen to regard other Ruskinian dogmas, many a 'moral' indictment brought by the twentieth century against the Victorian character has rested squarely upon some generalized impression of Victorian taste ... 'Victorianism' was undoubtedly, at least in part, a monster created by rebellious spirits and bequeathed to a posterity which all too frequently is content to regard the spirits as the monster's children.[33]

With similar sensitivity to the tricks of memory and the abuses of hindsight, Walter Houghton's study five years later opened with Strachey's comment about the impossibility of writing the history of the Victorian age because too much was known about it. 'The truth', Houghton notes, 'was rather that in the full tide of reaction it was impossible to achieve a detailed and broad perspective.'[34] His own book, *The Victorian Frame of Mind*, went someway towards this by exploring manifold contradictory tendencies within the Victorian frame of mind: optimism and anxiety, the critical spirit and philistinism, love and hypocrisy, and so on.

The second achievement was a new appreciation of the internal chronology of the Victorian age. The terms 'early' 'mid-' and 'late' Victorian had been used increasingly towards the end of the nineteenth century itself, and then by subsequent critics or admirers of the age. But their use was essentially qualitative, so that the connotations of 'mid-Victorian' in the 1920s, as we have seen, were either those of golden bygone days or of an age half-mired in barbarism. Renewed awareness of the Victorians as critics of themselves drew attention to their struggle to adjust to the legacy of pre-1837 society, and to the ferocity of dissent at the end of the nineteenth century. This naturally encouraged concentration on the mid-Victorian years: the crucial time-frame occupied by Houghton's *The Victorian Frame of Mind*, singled out by Buckley, and later the subject of Burn's important *The Age of Equipoise*. Perhaps, too, the mid twentieth-century perspective drew scholars to the corresponding period of the nineteenth century, especially when (the Crimean War apart) that age was coming to be widely interpreted as one of peaceful harmony and relative prosperity.

In any case, though Young had clearly been well-disposed to the mid-Victorian period, it had simply not been adequately studied before 1945. 'The period of English history which begins with the Great Exhibition of 1851 and ends with the Second Reform Bill of 1867', wrote Asa Briggs in 1954, 'is one of the least studied and least understood chapters in English history.'[35] Briggs's *Victorian People*, an exploration of these years through a series of case studies, did much to make up lost ground and suggest new avenues for others to follow. A later book, *The Age of Improvement*, not only put the early and mid-Victorian periods into a larger timespan, but celebrated them as the deeply interesting and (largely) positive culmination of earlier trends like evangelicalism and the entrepreneurial spirit. The Hammonds, it is worth remembering, had called their study of Britain on the eve of the mid-Victorian period *The Bleak Age*. Lord Briggs remains aware of the period feel of his book, writing about the preparation of a revised edition in 2000 that he was disinclined to change too much in the text. 'I believed rather that the first edition ... should stand as a record of how a young historian – on the eve of a transformation in the study of history – thought and felt about what was just beginning to be regarded as a critical but hitherto somewhat neglected period in British history.'[36]

Amidst these initiatives to re-engage with the Victorians, and to expand study of the age into new areas like social and intellectual history, one name continually emerged to be firmly cut down to size. 'It is over forty years since Lytton Strachey decided with a flourish that we knew too much about the Victorian era ...'; 'Strachey ... conveniently dismissed [Victorian biographies] as part of the cortège of the undertaker'; 'Lytton Strachey's elegant libels ...'[37] Ironically, it was perhaps such complaints that ensured Strachey's notoriety in the second half of the twentieth century, and the scholarly exaggeration of the extent to which Strachey's ideas tarnished the attitudes of his contemporaries in the first half. At any rate, as early as 1958, the historian John Clive noticed a worrying tendency in scholarly and biographical writing towards reinflation of the subjects previously targeted by Strachey's barbed arrows. 'Is the pendulum perhaps beginning to swing too far the other way?', Clive pondered.[38] Forty years after the publication of *Eminent Victorians*, it seemed that the reputation of the Victorians might not only be safe but comfortable, too.

'Once the cadaverous ghost of Strachey had been exorcised, probably in the 1950s,' one scholar has reflected, 'specialists began to weave a seamless web of historical knowledge that embraced everything the Victorians did and stood for.'[39] Walter Houghton in 1966 assembled a team of scholars to begin identifying the authors of some 89,000 articles (most of them anonymously signed), feeling that the Victorians could best be studied in their own words. The resulting five-volume *Wellesley Index to Victorian Periodicals*, completed in 1989, outlines for researchers the contents of forty-three reviews and journals: a veritable cornucopia of Victorian voices and attitudes. Interdisciplinary history would indeed begin to flourish in these years, as the pages of *Victorian Studies* demonstrate. From its inception in the late 1950s, that journal has typically crossed boundaries to explore the links between literature and politics, gender and class. More recently it has been joined by the *Journal of Victorian Culture*. Courses in 'Victorian Studies' can now also be taken at universities, with modules typically including options on Victorian cities, women writers in the nineteenth century, media adaptations of Dickens novels, and the cultural context of the Pre-Raphaelites.[40] All of these developments have depended upon the expansion and diversification of a body of now fully 'professional' historians. Clearly it is impossible to describe the full extent of Victorian scholarship since the 1960s, but it may be instructive here to consider a few areas.

Social and economic history flourished in the 1960s, with E. P. Thompson's *The Making of the English Working Class* (1963) the great intellectual landmark of the decade. Acute interest was taken in ideas about class identity, radicalism and the ways in which society diffused the threat of revolution after the grim deprivations of the Industrial Revolution. The importance of culture, language, religion and region were all played up in order to rescue ordinary people from what Thompson called 'the enormous condescension of posterity'. Studies of local villages and individuals proliferated, but bolder overviews were offered, too. Harold Perkin traced the gradual emergence of a professional spirit in Victorian Britain, viewing history not from the perspective of great men and events, but from that of class.[41] Such works offered an overarching view of the nineteenth century, developing ideas about the mid-Victorian decades as a plateau of relative class harmony flanked on either side by turbulent years of unrest. But these were not the golden decades identified by memoir writers in the 1920s who had spoken of their own 'mid-Victorian' characters; for many of these interpretations were inflected with Marxism, and explored the period as a time of class betrayal and assimilation. Eric Hobsbawm, for example, put forward the idea that skilled workers – potential leaders of a revolution – had been placated and assimilated through such trappings of bourgeois gentility as parks, libraries and notions about respectability.[42] The underside of politics and party formation was also probed in works which explored not the stately progress of democracy but the world of calculating individuals, wily manoeuvring and the razor-sharp pursuit of political advantage.[43] In avoiding the conservative assumptions of their Victorian predecessors, historians managed to shed light on some areas of that age hitherto shrouded in darkness.

At much the same time, and coinciding with a wider growth of post-imperial guilt, scholars began to burrow deeper beneath the once confident façade of Victorian imperialism. As late as the 1940s, Attlee had liked fondly to believe that part of the rationale behind decolonisation lay in the satisfactory completion of the Victorian mission to civilise the world. Questions had long been raised about the ethics of imperialism by social democrats and Marxists, who tended to see it as a vehicle for capitalist exploitation. To these had been added in the 1950s the suggestion that the Victorian empire had satisfied the cravings of members of the landed order who could find no gainful employment at home.[44] Now, in the post-Suez years, the argument was put forward that the empire should be considered without moral judgement or hazy romanticism; for Ronald Robinson and John Gallagher, the Victorian presence in Africa had been purely strategic, with the safeguarding of the route to India uppermost in mind.[45] After 1956, it seemed clear that the Egyptian nationalists who had given Gladstone such trouble were the forerunners of Colonel Nasser. On both occasions (though to very different effect) a flexing of the imperial muscles had been deemed vital; what had begun with attempts to uphold order a century before, proposed some scholars by the 1970s, resulted in a protracted imperial adventure the banal endgame of which had only just been played.

By the same token, the study of Victorian femininity benefited enormously from contemporary developments in the Women's Liberation Movement. As we have seen, the first national Women's Liberation conference grew out of a History Workshop meeting. And indeed, not only was a sense of the past important to feminists, but the *way* in which it was studied had a formulative influence, too. The History Workshop series began as an attempt by socialist historians to take account of previously unseen or marginalised human experience. Women readily qualified for such treatment, especially since socialist writers like E. P. Thompson had foregrounded class rather than gender. Sometimes this encouraged new readings of Victorian feminism, and sometimes it moved away from those traditions. (Scholars like Sheila Rowbotham and Germaine Greer felt the suffragette tradition to be inspirational but now dated and politically suspect.) But scholarship was permanently altered, and historians now neglected to take into account female experience at their peril. (Some, however, seemed to manage it.)

The next generation of scholars built in turn on these insights into class, politics, empire and gender. Old arguments about the nature of Victorian class and politics were qualified or undermined. Marxist history, already moribund, did not survive the collapse of Communism at the end of the 1980s. In any case, it had long been felt that class-struggle was a rather reductive way of examining the Victorians. This was especially the case when it became fashionable amongst scholars in the 1980s to downplay the impact of the Industrial Revolution. Removing the central prop of the Marxist argument – that the traumatic rapidity of industrialisation had created a working-class identity – undermined many old notions about Victorian history. Class still mattered deeply, of course, and never more so than for the highly class-sensitive Victorians; but its reappearance in scholarship of the 1990s took place in the context of explorations of how the Victorians used class, not of how class used them.[46] New readings of the workings of the Victorian political system continued to abound, some of which profoundly altered our views of how statesmen saw the world around them.[47]

But nowhere did historians break more with their predecessors than where theory was concerned. Here it was the theory of language, which had been on the rise since the 1960s, that came into its own. Where it had once been fashionable to view political agitation as a reaction to the squalor endured by the oppressed of the Victorian age, historians increasingly looked to the role played by language. Gareth Stedman Jones, for example, suggested that a movement like Chartism flourished when the right *language* for protest was found, rather than when living or working conditions were especially bad.[48] Such ideas encouraged a dramatic overhaul of studies on the Victorian age, with a new emphasis upon how language was used and identities were constructed. In a climate like this, great demagogues (from the fiery Chartist Feargus O'Connor to the indomitable William Gladstone) came to be studied as much for the melodrama of their stage presences as for the political content of their speeches.

Scholarship on the empire was reinvigorated not only by new explorations of its development, but by works unravelling how imperial identities and attitudes were shaped. A sense of imperial identity, we learned, was as much a matter of mental manipulation as it was of genuine understanding or pride.[49] Study of women's history gave way to an emphasis on gender, so that ideas about Victorian class and masculinity were brought into the feminist fold. Particularly important here was the work of Leonore Davidoff and Catherine Hall, which opened new avenues into the study of what the Victorian middle classes felt about home and the place of the two sexes within it.[50] Valuable, often cliché-destroying, research was carried out into Victorian masculinity.[51] It was argued, for instance, that the legendary hypocrisy of Victorian men was time-honoured and only stigmatised as hypocrisy in a home-loving culture. Judith Walkowitz, meanwhile, literally mapped accounts of sexual deviance and temptation onto the thoroughfares and alleyways of late Victorian London.[52]

The Victorians and sex had been an almost frenetic area of scholarly activity since the 1960s; it showed few signs of abstinence a generation later. At the end of Queen Victoria's centenary year, 2001, the most prominent exhibition in London devoted to her age was *Exposed: The Victorian Nude* at Tate Britain. The exhibition encouraged visitors to think about the emotional dynamics of viewing the Victorians voyeuristically, in one darkened room literally stepping into private pools of light shared with the exhibits, or standing alongside other visitors peering through slots in a square box in which was being projected an early pornographic film. Here was a consciously modern take on Victorian physicality, 'highlighting concerns about sexuality, desire and censorship that are still relevant today'.[53] In its way, *Exposed* reflected what modern historians of gender had been exploring for some years: the way in which sexuality was constructed, commercialised and policed in the nineteenth century.

Identities and their construction were everywhere. Fresh interest was found in issues of patriotism and the rhetoric of 'Englishness'.[54] The Victorians, we were made to understand, could be both patriotic and fierce critics of the government. It was shown that 'patriotism' was annexed by Disraeli in the age of mass democracy as an effective vote-winner for the Conservatives; previously, as Dr Johnson was wont to complain ('Patriotism is the last refuge of a scoundrel'), to be a patriot was to be a troublesome thorn in the side of 'Old Corruption' (government, in other words).[55] Such work was undertaken at a time when Margaret Thatcher was trying to put a Conservative spin on 'Victorian values'. Equally, renewed fascination with the issue of national identity should be seen against the backdrop of devolution and an increasingly wary attitude towards Europe. In asking what the Victorians felt about patriotism, or about their 'Englishness' or 'Britishness', historians were of course asking fundamental questions about themselves and us and how we have come to be who we are. This was – and is – a most fruitful and rewarding interaction with the Victorian age, a genuine dialogue between past and present.

This brief glance at some scholarly trends since the 1960s does, nevertheless, suggest a fundamental drawback. Since the 1960s we have come to know more than ever before about the nineteenth century. But just as the emotional rehabilitation of the Victorians in the 1950s was dependent upon the imaginative distance placed between past and present, so 'professionalisation' was dependent upon a final move away from the 'amateur' attitudes of the past. The triumph of this professional spirit bequeathed certain problems. It became difficult for scholars to stake out new ground in an increasingly over-populated field: in 1997 alone, some 1143 pieces of work on Britain between 1815 and 1914 appeared – a rate of production unmatched by historians of either the eighteenth or twentieth centuries.[56] Not only was it difficult to keep up with this veritable flood of material from the presses, but the rapidly-changing tide of intellectual fashion made scholars nervous to venture beyond projects of a very limited scope. Like so many sorcerers' apprentices, it was easy amongst the dizzying whirl of articles and books for historians to forget their public.

In the rush to keep up with the latest trends, in the anxious search to find new areas of the Victorian age hitherto unmapped by scholarly explorers, in the post-Thatcherite culture of academic 'accountability' (which effectively meant funding by word-count: quality was quite a different matter), the public often suffered. Scholars like Asa Briggs, Raphael Samuel, David Cannadine and Simon Schama were able to command large and appreciative readerships. They did this by wearing their erudition lightly, weaving nimbly between different disciplines, yet bringing their findings together with clarity and an unfailing feel for the significant and the humanly engaging. Much scholarship, however, was devoted to obscure topics, the resonance of which to ordinary readers was never made plain. Packed with dense jargon, it succeeded only in making readers feel dense.

What, indeed, was happening to awareness of the Victorian past amongst ordinary people after the 1960s? Steeped in Victorian assumptions themselves, teachers at school and university up to the Second World War had imparted a vision of history which emphasised great men (and usually only men), great events and general progress. The move away from such assumptions after the 1950s, and the enthusiastic embracing of a more interdisciplinary approach, inevitably played down these drum-and-trumpet resonances. The influence of social and economic history made itself powerfully felt in school lessons and BBC programmes of the 1960s and 1970s. Empathy and a feel for the everyday life of ordinary people in the nineteenth century came to be dominant fashions within these circles. Where the Industrial Revolution had once been recounted as a confident progression of Smilesian innovators, children were now encouraged to imagine themselves amongst the deafening roar and dangerous machinery of a Coketown factory. In many respects a liberation for ordinary experience, it may well have given a spur to the huge craze which set in during the 1980s for family and local history.

There was, however, a price to pay. As the great men and great events receded from classrooms, popular knowledge of significant people and important events became ever patchier. G. M. Young's *Portrait of an Age* was reissued in a scholarly annotated edition in the 1970s, but one scholar was pessimistic about its likely audience. 'The Uncle Toby obsession with old battles and battlefields may well inhibit the development of an appreciative audience for Young. As Victorian England goes, so goes Young', wrote Sheldon Rothblatt. 'It would be easy, if boorish and wrong, to fasten upon him the charge of guilt by association.' [57] Others were also sensitive to the dangers of losing sight of the basic facts about history, albeit for different reasons. Margaret Thatcher, so keen to resurrect 'Victorian values' in the 1980s, encouraged her education secretary Kenneth Baker to reassert something like drum-and-trumpet history as part of the core curriculum for schools. Thoughtful observers like Raphael Samuel not only protested at the conservatism of this plan but cast doubt on its viability after the proliferation of so many new approaches since the 1960s.[58]

The scheme did not, however, take off. In the National Curriculum of the 1990s, children by the age of eleven were expected to know about 'The lives of men, women and children at different levels of society in Britain and the ways in which they were affected by changes in industry and transport'. By the age of fourteen, those studying Britain between 1750 and 1900 would be acquainted with the growth of trade, the empire and its impact on Britain and the colonies, industrialisation and its impact on different social classes, and have a rough sense of political chronology. Personalities were very much given a supporting role, even if it were possible to study Gladstone and Disraeli at slightly greater length. Where children of a similar age eighty years before had learned about great men, battles and the general greatness of Britain, pupils now learned the importance of critical analysis and independent conclusions.[59]

Modern textbooks exemplify these profound changes of emphasis. Chapters in works for children at primary school typically include even-handed accounts of how life differed for each social class, evocations of life in factories and towns (often providing an opportunity to discuss social reform), and an emphasis upon advances in science and technology. The empire is usually glossed as an interesting encounter with the wider world, and sources focus on the emigrant's feelings. There are, though, occasional nods towards post-colonial scholarship. 'In all parts of the empire', one textbook notes reprovingly, 'the British took very little notice of the ways of the people who were already living there. British rules and ways of life were brought in.'[60] Religion, one of the great mainstays of Victorian culture, tends to be noticeable by its absence – perhaps not surprisingly, given the multi-cultural and secular nature of the young readership. Wars are explored, if at all, in the light of what it had been like to serve in

Victorian armies, or as a way of introducing Florence Nightingale and medical reform. Gladstone and the Whigs may be mentioned, but rarely Palmerston or the aims of the Chartists.

Needless to say, we should not expect too much detail or sophistication from these works. They seem on the whole to fulfil admirably the tasks of encouraging empathy and a feel for the differences within human experience, L. P. Hartley's 'foreign country' of the past. Even one children's book with a very unpromising title, *The Vile Victorians* (1994), proves in fact to be no worse than a series of odd anecdotes accentuating how strange the period would seem to present-day visitors, and ends with a sober quote from Dickens.[61] (It becomes clear, too, that the title is selected on alliterative rather than qualitative grounds: there are, after all, also *The Terrible Tudors* and *The Slimy Stuarts* to scrutinise.) Still, such works are light years away from the style which had predominated until the Second World War. The great cost has been not so much in terms of the Whiggish reverence which was once devoted to the story of Britain's greatness. Nor has it been in the emphasis on acquiring analytical skills over knowledge of the lives of Victorian worthies. But when, as was the case only a couple of years ago, some teenagers were unable to place the decade in which the Second World War began, or suggested that it might have lasted for as long as six months, alarm bells ought to have sounded.

Popular awareness of the Victorian past has benefited from the low-key diffusion of social and economic history into classrooms. The lives of ordinary people are no longer ignored; false assumptions about Britain's place in the world are no longer propagated; sources are no longer taken at face value. Historical empathy, the educationalists rightly appreciate, brings the past alive. But advocating empathy in a culture devoted to materialism and private fulfilment can sometimes only endorse extreme subjectivity, and then mere indifference, to anything beyond the scope of the individual's imagination. This is more dangerous still when children up to the age of fourteen (many of whom do not study history further in school) are not given the necessary factual framework through which empathy should be channelled. It is not, of course, a matter of celebrating Britain's greatness again, or even of hiding from our decline in the world through jolly classroom re-enactments of life in a Victorian village school. What a due sense of political chronology and the agency of individuals provides are the markers – temporal and human – against which students can gauge continuity and change, or the role played in history by particular people. The paradox of Victorian scholarship in the past fifty years may be that we have come to know too much: there are so many potential perspectives, and so many grounds why we might prefer one to another, that it has become extremely difficult to find a *modus vivendi* between each approach. Strachey's complaint in 1913 about the tensions between 'decent history' and 'unenlightened learning' seem, by comparison, enviably straightforward. We have settled, at least in schools, for the sensible if still contentious criterion of 'relevance'.

The definition of 'relevance' at A-level, ironically, appears to embrace the very opposite of the largely non-political agenda set by study earlier in school. Here it is tempting to see the presence of an older generation: of teachers (and syllabus makers) who themselves were taught by people who formed a 'take' on study when social and economic history was still in its infancy. At A-level today students will almost invariably study, where Britain is concerned, either the Tudors or a chunk of political history carved out of the late nineteenth and early twentieth centuries. The standard course on British history between 1867 and 1918, its very dates circumscribed by famous political events, is resolutely old-fashioned. As one headmaster has recently reflected, wide-ranging and lively textbooks like Peter Clarke's *Hope and Glory: Britain, 1900–1990* (1996) simply appear 'irrelevant' to the average A-level student intent on mugging up the chronology of the suffragette movement or the rise of the Labour Party. 'This sorry syllabus', writes Martin Roberts, 'bears no relation to the kind of history now being written by university historians.'[62] The great challenge – and it may well prove to have a generational solution – will be to combine the fresher sense of interdisciplinary study when pupils are young with the rigour of factual mastery at A-level. For it seems certain enough that the blackboard, exercise book and school trip have far from exhausted the Victorians.

PART TWO

*Lives*

# 8

# *Biography*

Biography remains the bestselling literary genre in Britain, appealing to readers' fascination with the intricacies, triumphs and indiscretions of an individual's life. Not only does it provide a compelling glimpse of how others have struggled to make sense of their lives, but in the biographer's art it can also offer a wonderful literary performance. New biographies by Peter Ackroyd, Victoria Glendinning, Michael Holroyd and Richard Holmes – regardless of the subject – are literary events in themselves. Biography flourishes so well today partly because we live in an age dedicated to self-expression and voyeurism. It is also benefiting from cross-fertilisation with the genres of autobiography and family history, so that writers like Margaret Forster and Lorna Sage have given us memorable accounts of life in post-war Britain, while Martin Amis in *Experience* (2000) has written a latter-day *Father and Son*.[1]

Such influences apart, there has been a strong tradition of biographical writing in Britain.[2] This is a tradition that does not shrink from criticising its subjects, probing into delicate personal areas, or reflecting intelligently on the often bizarre business of reconstructing a 'real' life. Holmes, an especially articulate and wry commentator on this business, has talked at some length about his method of trying to become 'haunted' by his subjects, whether traipsing the same dirt tracks as Robert Louis Stevenson or looking out over the same Italian lakes as Percy Bysshe Shelley.[3] (In the case of Shelley it seemed to work: while working on the biography Holmes absent-mindedly dated a cheque '1772'.)[4] Or there is Geoff Dyer, manically pursuing the ghost of D. H. Lawrence from Nottingham to Sicily and Mexico. But he, too, is a literary performer, and for all his entertaining honesty he offers a diffuse portrait of Lawrence between the lines of a surface failure to do so.[5] Biography, it has been resolutely established, is an art. A. S. Byatt's novels *Possession* (1990) and *The Biographer's Tale* (2000) have done for biography and the Victorians what John Fowles's *The French Lieutenant's Woman* (1969) did for views of the Victorians and sex, blending art and history with an intelligent and subtle appreciation of the ways in which we fabricate written lives.

A great deal of this appreciation indirectly owes itself, in fact, to the theme we have been pursuing. For it was Lytton Strachey who effectively reinvented the biographical tradition for the twentieth century in *Eminent Victorians* (1918), simultaneously criticising his subjects and the mode of biography which their age had handed down. Although the style of *Eminent Victorians* has received wide treatment, the nature of its innovations, and its implication for the changing reputation of the Victorians, have attracted disappointingly ungenerous comment. It is usually depicted as a savage repudiation of the Victorians, in the words of Peter Clarke a work that subjected the past 'to an exquisite literary assassination by a thousand digs'.[6] Any lingering signs of esteem for history were delivered the brutal *coup de grâce* by Strachey's numerous and generally less nimble imitators.[7] Even the format of these neo-Stracheyan biographies may have been an insult in themselves, the truncating and lumping together of lives in collective biographies testifying to what A. S. Byatt has called the desire 'to see human beings as parts of large social structures whose mechanisms and inter-relations we can uncover and describe': the Victorians put behind glass cases.[8]

This is an unfair and inaccurate estimation of the place of *Eminent Victorians* in history. Certainly the book had its crude imitators who did not do the Victorians a service; and certainly, with all these lesser versions in tow, it encouraged a salutary counter-reaction amongst historians: strongest, as we have seen, immediately after the Second World War. But it is possible to argue that Strachey's contribution to the art of biography was ultimately to prove beneficial to the reputation of the Victorians, and not just in the counter-reaction of G. M. Young and subsequent writers. Like most critics of the Victorians in the early twentieth century, Strachey had too many emotional links with the age to repudiate its figures completely. He was also too interested in them as human beings to indulge in the flippant caricatures with which he has often been charged. Indeed, part of his irritation with the past lay in the way that the Victorians themselves had failed to discuss the human vitality of contemporaries in their own biographies; the iconoclasm of *Eminent Victorians* was generic as much as anything else. Once the genre had been reinvented, the Victorians – for better or worse – would come to stand in clearer light for reassessment. We therefore need to consider carefully the context in which Strachey launched the great twentieth-century experiment in biography.

The preface to *Eminent Victorians* has been described as 'a manifesto for modern biography'.[9] In it Strachey advocated psychological probing, an absence of 'tedious panegyric', 'a becoming brevity' based upon artistic selection, and 'a freedom of spirit' on the part of the biographer.[10] This was

a response to the standard two-volume biographies of the nineteenth century
– works which Strachey acknowledged to have provided him 'not only with
much indispensable information, but with something even more precious
– an example'. (In the draft version, filed away at the British Library with
all the notebooks and scraps of paper showing just how much Strachey had
gleaned from these biographies, he originally wrote 'dreadful example'.) [11]
Such biographies made little attempt at authorial intervention in the sources
used. Still less was there any strong inclination to probe beneath the surface
of the subject or to court controversy. These biographies were consciously
written as a record of worthy endeavour which readers might emulate.[12]

Strachey waged war on all this. It is important, though, to put the
originality of *Eminent Victorians* into proper perspective. From the long
perspective, it was less an act of biographical iconoclasm than one of
restoration. Strachey idolised the eighteenth century, and in *Eminent Victorians* attempted to return to Johnsonian principles. As he had commented
as early as 1906, 'It is sufficient for us to recognize that [Johnson] is a
mountain, and to pay all the reverence that is due.' [13] Indeed, the extent to
which Strachey's directives had been anticipated by Dr Johnson nearly two
centuries earlier is striking. It was he who had first insisted that biography
is an art. Like Strachey, Johnson believed that it was 'the business of the
biographer' to avoid 'uniform panegyrick', to 'lead the thoughts into domestick privacies', and to avoid narratives assembled only from 'publick papers'
so that the work degenerated into 'a chronological series of actions or
preferments'.[14]

Since Johnson's day things had changed in two respects. First, the Victorian period had interposed itself and presented biographers with a long
stretch of time unprecedented in complexity and documentation. As Strachey put it in the arresting first sentence of his preface: 'The history of the
Victorian Age will never be written: we know too much about it.' [15] The
second change offered writers like Strachey the solution. In the late nineteenth and early twentieth centuries, perceptions of 'domestick privacies'
had been revolutionised by psychological realism and Sigmund Freud.
Strachey's own response was to write biography which cut a swathe through
the mass of material to get at the 'essence' of his subjects by alighting on
particular aspects of their personalities. His own celebrated metaphor –
lowering a bucket into 'that great ocean of material' and bringing up 'to
the light of day some characteristic specimen' – suggests a Freudian agenda.[16]

Lytton Strachey was familiar with Freudian theory, not least via his brother
James, who was to be Freud's principal translator into English. But Strachey
himself was ambivalent about psychoanalysis. Although he would make
*Elizabeth and Essex* (1928) a Freudian drama, suggesting that Elizabeth

suffered sexual neurosis on account of her father's unorthodox marriage arrangements, he was sceptical of psychoanalytical 'insights'. In early 1924 he spent an 'appalling' weekend at Garsington Manor, the home of Philip and Ottoline Morrell, where he found that conversation was dominated by a German psychoanalyst offering 'cures' for homosexuality. (No doubt he figured that Garsington, a regular congregation point for Bloomsbury, would be a good place to ply his trade.) Strachey escaped to his room at one point, writing to Dora Carrington (then Mrs Ralph Partridge): '"Psycho-analysis" is a ludicrous fraud.' [17] It was Dostoevsky's psychological realism which, as with so many early twentieth-century intellectuals, was to prove the more formative influence. Reviewing Constance Garnett's celebrated translations in 1914, Strachey paid tribute to the way in which the novelist's lacerating humour was 'the key to his sympathetic treatment of character'.[18]

This state of human understanding reached through biting character analysis and caustic humour was what Strachey strove to achieve in *Eminent Victorians*. By reviving Johnsonian values and adapting them for the twentieth century, he managed to get closer to the Victorians than had often been the case before. Strachey deserves – and was given by contemporaries – credit for this. But his 'reinvention' of biography also needs to be seen from the perspective of the longer tradition of attacks on the Victorians traced earlier on. This is not to downplay Strachey's innovativeness. Rather it is to put it into context with earlier works which had begun that process of emotional negotiation with the past which we call anti-Victorianism. Looking back from 1939, Virginia Woolf traced a line of descent through J. A. Froude's *Carlyle* (1882–84) via Edmund Gosse's *Father and Son* (1907) to Lytton Strachey.[19] Harold Nicolson in 1927 had similarly suggested that the 'Victorian fog' of earnestness which descended on biography with A. P. Stanley's 'egregious' *Life of Arnold* (1844) had begun to lift by the 1880s.[20]

Many works after the 1880s eschewed hagiography and embraced ambivalence, using selectiveness and sometimes irony to shape narratives that were essentially *portraits* of the subject. By producing portraits, biographers were liberated from the expectation of providing works that were both eulogistic and exhaustive in surface detail. As portrait painters they involved themselves in the artistic process, thereby making it possible to explore their own feelings about their subjects to an even greater degree. Increasingly it was becoming clear that a history – or histories – of the Victorian age could be written, if the task was approached through biography. Of course, the truth-telling in this new biographical format would be selective, and in less accomplished hands it could degenerate into mere caricature. It is significant, however, that the great exemplar of this new style, *Eminent Victorians*, stopped short of such crudity. Its quintessential anti-Victorianism embraced the ambivalence which lay at the heart of much contemporary criticism of the past, and enriched it with Strachey's abiding interest in human nature.

'Human beings are too important to be treated as mere symptoms of the past', Strachey wrote in the preface to *Eminent Victorians*. 'They have a value which is independent of any temporal processes – which is eternal, and must be felt for its own sake.' [21] Strachey's deep preoccupation with human nature may be traced in large part to G. E. Moore's *Principia Ethica*, the appearance of which in 1903 heralded what Strachey called 'the beginning of the Age of Reason'.[22] Moore, the Cambridge philosopher and doyen of the Apostles, argued in this work that good exists in the world but does not give itself easily to analysis. Ethical conduct, therefore, ought to be dictated by a watchful common sense. The final two chapters argued that the only sure sources of intrinsic value, since they demonstrably did no harm to others, were 'certain states of consciousness, which may be roughly described as the pleasures of human intercourse and the enjoyment of beautiful objects ... it is only for the sake of these things – in order that as much of them as possible may at some time exist – that any one can be justified in performing any public or private duty'.[23]

Such beliefs were of course central to the Bloomsbury identity. But they struck a particularly resonant chord with Strachey's remarkable blend of rationality and human warmth. His belief in rationality – in part a reflection of his enthusiasm for the Age of Reason – is well-known, and was demonstrably affected by the First World War. In August 1918 Strachey declined an invitation to write for the *New Statesman* on account of its 'blackguardly' policy of 'unconscious jingoism'. He also objected to its rough treatment of Lord Lansdowne, who in the previous year had attacked government propaganda: Strachey felt that he was 'an honest man, and a man who is at any rate trying to use his reason'.[24] Strachey's discreetly affectionate nature is less often recognised, especially amongst historians intent on characterising him as a cynical denigrator. Others such as Charles R. Sanders have commented more kindly on this aspect of his personality:

What he liked was a way of life characterised by unaffected simplicity, by individual freedom, by that highest exercise of intelligence which he often calls 'sanity', by a sensitiveness to beauty in both nature and art, by an interest in people and a proper respect for the high potentialities of humanity, and by the glorification of the qualities of experience made possible by friendship and love.[25]

These qualities of rationality and warmth combined to make Strachey what one writer has dubbed 'the great *intimiste* among historians'.[26] Not only did he follow the example of Hume and Gibbon in admitting readers into a state of implied equality; he also judged historical subjects by his own exacting standards and by those of Bloomsbury and Moore. He anticipated by a decade what E. M. Forster would say about patriotism ('If I had to choose between betraying my country and betraying my friend, I hope I should have the guts to betray my country'), writing in *Elizabeth and Essex* of the different attitudes of Francis Bacon and Sir Charles Davers to the disgraced Earl of Essex:

> It was an occasion for the broad grasp of common humanity, not for the razor-blade of subtle intelligence. Bacon could not see this; he could not see that the long friendship, the incessant kindness, the high generosity, and the touching admiration of the Earl had made a participation in his ruin a deplorable and disgraceful thing. Sir Charles Davers was not a clever man; but his absolute devotion to his benefactor still smells sweet amid the withered corruptions of history.[27]

Or there is the unashamedly personal charge against Thomas Arnold, head-master of Rugby, in *Eminent Victorians*:

> Was he to improve the character of his pupils by gradually spreading round them an atmosphere of cultivation and intelligence? By bringing them into close and friendly contact with civilised men, and even, perhaps, with civilised women? By introducing into the life of his school all that he could of the humane, enlightened, and progressive elements in the life of the community? On the whole, he thought not. Such considerations left him cold, and he preferred to be guided by the general laws of Providence. It only remained to discover what those general laws were.[28]

Strachey confirmed the emotional proximity of figures from the past. He treated them as contemporaries, and saw little reason why eternal human dilemmas should not be judged by modern standards. In this sense he was literally a 'debunker': one who sets out to remove the accretions of time and myth but leaves the human essence intact. 'Between Lytton Strachey and most Victorian biographers there is a marked difference', A. C. Ward observed in 1930. 'Victorian biographers dehumanized their great men. We attempt to lay bare the humanity and leave the greatness to take care of itself, as it always will if the humanity is preserved.'[29]

Like so many early critics of the Victorians, Strachey's feelings about the past were profoundly complicated. We have already seen how ambivalent he felt about the gloomy Kensington home of his youth, and his own confession about the impossibility of coming to an impartial verdict on the Victorian age. Strachey had in fact originally planned a work around 1912 called *Victorian Silhouettes*, which was to have been a study of the lives of a dozen Victorian luminaries, some of whom – like J. S. Mill and Charles Darwin – he actively admired.[30] (The term 'silhouettes' also reflected Strachey's awareness of his own artistic perspective in biography.) We may reasonably assume that the course of the First World War sharpened Strachey's critical instincts and led him to write a more integrated denunciation of Victorianism.

The actual nature of the anti-Victorianism retained its close concern with human experience. The key, perhaps, came in Strachey's basic view of mankind: 'Human beings, no doubt, would cease to be human beings unless they were inconsistent.'[31] He perceived that people have an inexhaustible capacity for self-deception, and it is the harmful consequences of such evasions that brings to life the human comedy of *Eminent Victorians*. It is an elegy for those human values which Strachey felt had been sacrificed by the age: intelligence, humour, intimacy. He implies that the Victorians diverted their emotional energies too exclusively into public concerns, and that here the drive came from a strange concoction of worldly ambition and evangelical zeal. These are the two central themes that run through *Eminent Victorians*, complemented by a counterpoint of respectability, humanitarianism, public school education and imperialism.

It is striking, though, that in addition to being the perpetrators of Victorianism, Strachey also depicts his subjects as its victims. Public duty is presented as a means of escape from the private horrors of their upbringing for Cardinal Manning, Thomas Arnold, Florence Nightingale and General Gordon; but given the lack of sanity and humour within the public face of Victorianism, it serves only to accentuate their underlying psychological problems. Manning's need to worship someone or something overflows into barely concealed worldly ambition. Nightingale throws herself manically into humanitarian work to escape from the fate of becoming an 'Angel in the House'. Arnold never really recovers from his father's excessively high expectations (who would, being given Smollett's twenty-four volume *History of England* to read at the age of three?). And Gordon struggles to appease the demons that lead him to his own immolation at Khartoum.

By interweaving these common themes Strachey came to paint an integrated and ultimately tragic portrait of the age – an angry, deliberately exaggerated counterpart to Young's chaste, scrupulously nuanced vision. It was bad history, and in as far as written lives are deemed to require factual accuracy, questionable biography too. But as an intelligent engagement with an era that still cast a long shadow over the twentieth century it was a masterpiece. And in its daring attitude towards the established method and tone of biography it was little short of revolutionary. Significantly enough, most reviewers responded positively to *Eminent Victorians* when it was published in May 1918. Gosse, as we have seen, was perplexed by its tone, and there were a number of pedantic complaints about the exact length of Arnold's legs or the nature of Gordon's fondness for brandy. Most reviewers, however, were highly complimentary. The *Nation* quoted no fewer than thirty lines from the groundbreaking preface, while the *Times Literary Supplement* even praised Strachey's 'detachment'.[32] The former Prime Minister H. H. Asquith spoke of his admiration for 'Strachey's subtle and suggestive art' in a lecture at Oxford that summer.[33] And G. M. Trevelyan wrote to the author: 'I don't think the book "cynical"; Gordon and the Bird [Nightingale] both emerge heroes, far more living than other treatment would make them. Manning was what you represent him – and so, by God, was the Oxford Movement!'[34] *Eminent Victorians* became a bestseller. By the time of Strachey's death in 1932 it had sold 35,000 hardback copies in England and 55,000 in the United States. It had also been translated into six other languages, including Polish, Romanian and Japanese.[35]

It is perhaps the fate of innovators to suffer a backlash after death. In the case of Lytton Strachey, though, the natural reaction of the 1930s coincided with a growth in esteem for the Victorian era. Young's *Portrait of an Age* appeared in 1936, partly as a reaction against Strachey. Young was characteristically discreet on the matter, but had commented in a little-known 1932 essay (a sketch, really, for his fuller *Portrait*) that Strachey had 'much to answer for'.[36] In the year that Young did publish his *Portrait*, an observer condemned Strachey as 'one of the most pernicious influences in modern biography'.[37] Such supporters as Strachey had – Guy Boas, Virginia Woolf, Max Beerbohm – were obliged to take the defensive.[38]

During the Second World War, the stock of the pacifistic Bloomsbury Group was predictably low: this was an age that called for grandiloquent rhetoric not rarefied gossip. The starchy F. R. Leavis even informed Cambridge undergraduates that Strachey had caused the Second World War, explaining this singularly improbable theory by alluding to his supposed influence over J. M. Keynes, and therefore over the government's guilty attitude towards the Versailles settlement.[39] (It seems that Leavis was even less of a historian than Strachey.) How odd it is that Strachey and the rest of the Bloomsbury Group came to enjoy unprecedented popularity at the end of the twentieth century, while a figure as great as Winston Churchill attracted often shamefully carping biographical treatment.

Such, however, are the vagaries of a biographical tradition liberated from Victorian traditions of worthiness and distance. Even in the 1950s, when the reaction against neo-Stracheyanism was at its height, biographers did not attempt to retreat back into multi–volume veneration of the past. As John

Clive complained in 1958, some were too defensive of Strachey's erstwhile subjects, and showed a temporary swing back towards hagiography. But the new agenda had already been set, wrote Clive: 'We have discovered new dimensions in the great Victorians. Figures once irritatingly ebullient, confident, and self-satisfied we now find more and more frequently staring at us in anguish out of some strange and awful chiaroscuro. And our hearts go out to them.'[40] This was happening with sensitivity, intelligence and learning in works like Noël Annan's *Leslie Stephen* (1951), Philip Magnus's *Gladstone* (1954) and Roy Jenkins's *Sir Charles Dilke* (1958). Such works probed beneath image and myth to explore the psychological complexities of their subjects, selecting with almost artistic care quotes gleaned from new sources, notably letters and diaries.

Indeed biography and history, once bonded to one another in a rather unsatisfactory marriage of life-and-letters, pursued different but complementary tracks. As the years passed, the sum total of letters and private papers in the public domain increased to an ever greater number. Many of the immediate family members of eminent Victorians, and those mentioned in a sensitive context within correspondence, had died by the 1950s. Accordingly, a number of great projects were initiated to publish the letters and diaries of many Victorian luminaries. Most notable here was the phenomenon of the *Gladstone Diaries*, a huge fourteen-volume edition covering more than 25,000 entries, initiated by M. R. D. Foot in 1968 and completed in 1994 by H. C. G. Matthew. A figure of Victorian industry himself, Matthew also presided over the early stages of the *New Dictionary of National Biography*: testimony not only of the enduring influence of at least one Victorian 'institution', but of the co-existence of detailed factual knowledge alongside post-Stracheyan biographical artistry. (The *DNB*, first edited by Virginia Woolf's father Sir Leslie Stephen, survived her mischievous comment that 'The true length of a person's life, whatever the *Dictionary of National Biography* may say, is always a matter of dispute.' *Orlando* was, of course, her light-hearted reprimand to any biographer who thinks that facts alone can convey the essence of a life.)[41] Projects of a similarly large scope included the ongoing Edinburgh-Duke edition of the letters of Thomas and Jane Carlyle, and an edition of the Brownings' correspondence from an obscure publisher in Kansas which has optimistically projected volume forty-four to appear in 2009.[42]

Other projects included the Pilgrim edition of the letters of Charles Dickens, begun by Humphry House in 1951 and seeing publication of its first volume in 1965. Eleven volumes had been published by 1999, and yet the project was still not complete: painstaking in detail, some of the volumes covered only two or three years' of the author's life. 'The plan', writes Angus

Easson, 'was to publish all of Dickens's letters, however seemingly trivial a mere refusal or an appointment time might be deemed, to offer the fullest detail of the pattern and significance of Dickens's life and a sense of his engagement with his age.' [43] (And as if all this were not sufficient, there was a parallel drive from the 1990s to publish all of Dickens's journalism in a Dent edition overseen by Michael Slater.) A similar push to exhaustiveness can be traced in the published correspondence of Oscar Wilde. The titles tell their own story: in 1962 Rupert Hart-Davis published *The Letters of Oscar Wilde*; then in 1985 came his supplementary volume, *More Letters of Oscar Wilde*; and in 2000 came *The Complete Letters of Oscar Wilde*, edited by Hart-Davis and Merlin Holland. The last included everything that had been published before, together with 300 letters either discovered since 1985 or rejected by Hart-Davis at the time as insignificant. At the end of the twentieth century, it was clear, nothing relating in any way to the lives of eminent Victorians could be deemed insignificant.

This gathering flood of published letters and diaries has been used to enrich biographies of the Victorians. The urge to publish (and increasingly to publish exhaustively) may at first glance seem a matter of pedantry, almost a return to the life-and-letters pedestrianism that Strachey had put off its stride in *Eminent Victorians*. But of course times had changed, and the letters and diaries were used to probe areas of a subject's psychology in new ways. Modern views of Thackeray owe much to the endeavours of Gordon N. Ray, a young American scholar who collected together four volumes of Thackeray's letters in the 1940s, and worked his findings into an important two-volume biography (1955–58).[44] Wilkie Collins's private life – the drugs and multiple mistresses – was also gradually pieced together from a series of manuscripts, leading to literary rehabilitation and an interest in themes like 'identity' in the novels. The issue of 'identity' loomed large, too, in readings of Robert Louis Stevenson's *Dr Jekyll and Mr Hyde* (1886), Oscar Wilde's *The Picture of Dorian Gray* (1891) and Bram Stoker's *Dracula* (1897) – all now widely seen as a reflection of profound duality in those late Victorian authors. 'The contrast between Harker and the vampire', writes one commentator on *Dracula*, 'might also be sought in Stoker's own divided personality: the feeble child and the vigorous youth; the dutiful lawyer and the reckless globe-trotter; the respectable married man and the passionate idolater of men like Whitman and Irving.' [45]

Biography both fed, and fed upon, this growing fascination with who the Victorians were. Here the drive to exhaustiveness was important. The publication of as much private material as possible occurred not just because it had been liberated from a largely illustrative role in works of the life-and-letters genre, but because it was increasingly prized in itself. The personal connection with historical figures, as we have seen, became an important part of the 'heritage industry'. Readers wanted to come into contact with words written by the Victorians without the excessive mediation or selection of an editor. Ideally, of course, they would have liked to handle the original documents themselves. One innovative solution to this demand was the production of luxurious facsimile editions of various works. In 2000 the British Library was selling, at £125 each, eighty-page facsimiles of the manuscript of Wilde's *De Profundis*: a poignant and highly collectable item, even if the cheap lined notepaper of the original had evidently been replaced by a superior brand. (One suspects that Wilde would have approved.) More generally, many new biographies of Victorians – especially those who were writers – include reproductions of their handwriting from letters or manuscripts.

The extensive publication of letters and diaries was welcomed, too, by biographers and historians. Partly this was because many were biographers *and* historians, feeling the need to acquaint readers with historical context as that awareness receded from living memory, or correcting misapprehensions. One of the unseen presences in many biographies of famous Victorians is the popular afterlife of their subjects. William Gladstone remains famous for talking to prostitutes; John Ruskin's unconsummated marriage is probably the best-known biographical 'fact' about him; Oscar Wilde's afterlife as a gay icon often all but blots out the human reality. Afterlives say much about the society in which they exist: in these cases, the Victorians have remained in the limelight through our commodification of sex. If only in dealing with such ideas, as any responsive and responsible writer should, biographers find their narratives informed by the agenda set down by modern rumour and myth.

This is where drawing on as much first-hand material as possible can be so valuable – whether to confirm, to refute outright, or to comment that the archives will not sustain a particular theory. Where the Brontë sisters are concerned, Lucasta Miller has produced a fascinating book about the multi-faceted nature of their collective afterlife: as victims of themselves, victims of others, mystics, domestic saints and proto-feminists. (As early as 1905, Henry James complained that romantic notions about the tragedy of the Brontës' lives amidst the windswept moors, a view that distorted appreciation of the robust literary merits of the novels, was 'the most complete intellectual muddle ... ever achieved, on a literary question, by our wonderful public'.) [46] Miller discovered that even the archive had been distorted by myth. 'In her quest to establish an accurate text of Charlotte's letters,' she writes, '[Margaret] Smith also had to cope, among other obstacles, with weeding out forgeries, which began to enter the market in response to the demand for Brontë memorabilia.'[47] The 1990s were clearly, though, a golden period for Brontë scholarship: a number of biographies appeared, including Juliet Barker's *The Brontës* (1994), the product of eleven years' immersion in archives and a systematic trawl of unusual sources including local newspapers and parish records. Three years later she produced an important 'life in letters' collection.[48]

Of course we now also feel that lives, let alone archives, are problematic. Even if it were possible to locate, verify and make accessible every item ever written by a particular individual, contemporary attitudes to biography would still find the writing of lives problematic. Lytton Strachey used original sources very sparingly in his biographies, preferring to paraphrase letters and invent conversations in order to bring his subjects to life from a particular artistic angle. Here he was trying not only to avoid the cumbersomeness of the Victorian biographies that must have loomed in multi–volume menace over *Eminent Victorians* when it appeared in bookshops in 1918, but also to humanise his subjects. That process of humanisation, as we shall see, reached its delightful apogee in *Queen Victoria* (1921). The twentieth century later kept Strachey's emphasis on humanisation, but filled out biographical narratives with more detail: partly, of course, to counteract some of the worst neo-Stracheyan tendencies. Strachey's own biography – a quite magnificent and intensely human work by Michael Holroyd – originally appeared in multi–volume format in 1967–68, amounting to 1229 pages. The revised 1994 edition, by these Boswellian proportions, runs to a positively gaunt 780 pages. More ironic still was Strachey's enshrinement as part of the 'heritage industry' in a sunny and highly enjoyable 1995 biopic. It was adapted from the Holroyd biography by Christopher Hampton, and starred Jonathan Pryce as Strachey. His recreation of the part – exquisitely fey but consistently concerned – was so good that the nonagenarian Frances Partridge, who had known Strachey very well, was said to have gasped in amazement at the opening scene.[49]

Lengthy or not, however determined to uncover the human reality of their subjects, the archives do not yield their secrets easily. Sometimes that is because they are invariably incomplete in themselves: even the 1270 pages of 'complete' Wilde letters shed no new light on a question that has increasingly come to concern biographers. As with Tchaikovsky, the cause of whose death (cholera or suicide?) has divided musical scholars, the nature of Wilde's final illness has become a matter of fierce contention. Richard Ellmann, in his virtually definitive 1987 biography, was of the opinion that Wilde died of a syphilis-related disease. (He suggested that Wilde may have contracted it from a prostitute while at Oxford, and that his discomfort at showing his teeth resulted from the black staining that was associated with a mercury cure.) The Wilde estate was so unhappy with Ellmann's theory, itself favouring a meningitis-related cause, that he inserted a footnote admitting the inconclusiveness of the medical evidence. More definitely a mistake, though one for which the dying Ellmann can hardly be blamed, was inclusion by the publisher of a photograph supposedly of Wilde in cross-dress as Salomé. In 1994 it was established that the photograph was one of the Hungarian opera singer Alice Guszalewicz.[50] 'When you look again it is not very much like him', reflects Alan Sinfield. 'It is part of the modern stereotype of the gay man that he should want to dress as a woman, especially a fatally gorgeous one.'[51] Archival misreadings hold up a mirror to our biographical preoccupations.

These are venial mistakes and difficulties associated with biography. Far more vexing is the issue of whether, after a century's distance and the publication of so much source material, the archives can furnish viable lives of the Victorians. For what Dr Johnson knew, and what Lytton Strachey reminded people in the decades after Victoria's death, was that biography is essentially an art. It is not (or should not be) about invention, but it is about creation. As Peter Ackroyd has reminded us, 'every biography is a prisoner of its time'; but one constant across the twentieth century has been a move away from the faith in quasi-scientific methods held by the Victorians.[52] And indeed, just as the variety of biographical perspectives on any individual (especially if they are creative or deemed important) have proliferated since the 1950s and 1960s, so has the cumulative sense that all these different views make the reality of a life almost impossible to grasp. Postmodern theory, which thrives on the open-ended readings made possible from the huge collections of published source material and simultaneously denies any single definitive reading, has encouraged us to be even more cautious. For some it is not simply that the reality of a life cannot be contained within the covers of any one book: it is whether that reality exists at all.

Mercifully most historians and biographers stop short of such nihilism, an initially admirable sensitivity to nuance and ambiguity within historical interpretation raised (or lowered) to the point of catalepsy. Biographies of the Victorians, whether in inventive new readings from particular angles (Trollope and gentlemanliness; Queen Victoria and feminism; Peel and posthumous fame; Darwin and literature),[53] or in bold overviews for the general reader (often more inventive still than the angled monographs), continue to be written. They are often written, though, with a deep sense of the artistry involved in biography, and of the intellectual responsibilities it carries. Heirs to Dr Johnson and Lytton Strachey, they tend to live up to these responsibilities through verbal play, engaging directness of utterance and fantastic digression. So celebrated had Richard Holmes's

method of following in the footsteps of his biographical subjects become
(he subtitled his 1974 biography of Shelley 'The Pursuit') that D. J. Taylor
opens his 1999 biography of Thackeray with a marvellously evocative account of searching out his subject's grave, attended 133 years earlier by a
grief-stricken Dickens: 'Kensal Green, 10 December 1996: a freezing morning, the sky quite opaque. A threat of snow. Walking north through
Ladbroke Gove, past parked cars with "for sale" notices taped to the rear
windscreens and down-at-heel West Indian takeaways, one picks one's way
through what seems like the litter of centuries.'[54] Later, he splices the
narrative with two 'interludes', 'Thackeray: The Pursuit' (a slight Holmes-
parody: 'I have always been suspicious of the idea of writerly "presences"
that supposedly hang about in the ether long after their originals have
disappeared'),[55] and 'Why Thackeray Matters'.

What recent biographers of the Victorians have tended to do is to immerse
themselves in the habitat and contemporary culture of the subject. The
indefatigable Peter Ackroyd read all the available novels, journalism and
letters three times over in preparation for *Dickens* (1990). In this way, rather
than despairing at the impossibility of recreating a life, biographers appreciate to an even greater degree the protean nature of their subjects. 'The same
man is not always the same man', writes Victoria Glendinning of one of
her subjects. 'It depends on how you look at him and on what you want
to see, and on how he sees himself, and on what day of the week it is, and
any number of other variables.'[56] They develop, too, something of a personal
relationship with the subject – not that the intention here is to attempt to
see things through that other person's eyes: Holmes calls this 'the first crime
in biography', and Holroyd has reflected on how the biographer 'must
continually lead two separate but overlapping lives – his own and that of
the person about whom he is currently writing'.[57] The result, in the subtlest
of hands, is a compelling blend of a life and a sense of the inventiveness
that this life demands from the biographer. The biographer, as artist, both
controls his material and is controlled by it. The Victorians had little sense
of this artistry; Strachey glided over it disingenuously ('Je n'impose rien; je
ne propose rien: j'expose': 'I impose nothing; I suggest nothing: I reveal');
but many modern biographies of the Victorians revel in such imaginative
requirements.

Peter Ackroyd's *Dickens*, for example, resurrects the subject to interrogate
his biographer about the aims and methods of the work as it unfolds. What
may at first glance appear a gimmick is of course an inventive way of
furthering the biography, and an illuminating insight into what Ackroyd-
as-Dickens feels about Ackroyd-as-biographer. Here is a sample of one of
their 'conversations':

Dickens:  'How could you understand me when I do not even understand myself?'

Ackroyd:  'The biographer – '

Dickens:  '– Oh, biographers. Biographers are simply novelists without imagination!' He looked across at me with that full, direct glance which I had come to know so well; and then he smiled. 'Forgive me. As I said, I am tired. And some of my best friends are biographers.'

Ackroyd:  'When you say that you do not understand yourself, do you mean that you don't care to?'

Dickens:  He snatched at the word. 'And there's another thing. I never really know what I *mean*. That is the question I can never bring myself to ask anyone when they talk about my writing. But what does it mean? What does it mean?'[58]

A similar, if necessarily less sophisticated, approach has also become common in school teaching. Again, this relates very much to history as a branch of personal experience. A guide to educational websites on Dickens recently indicated two striking locations. One was 'The Biography Maker': 'Students are guided through the process of writing a biography, in a fun and interactive way.' Another was 'It's Good to Talk': 'Allows students to "talk" to famous figures, including Dickens.'[59]

By the end of the twentieth century it had become clear that biography of the Victorians was flourishing. As in Lytton Strachey's day, biography was one of the main ways in which people connected with the Victorian age. Strachey had been impatient with the Victorians, and with how they represented themselves to one another (and to posterity) in worthy life-and-letters volumes – biographies 'as familiar as the *cortège* of the undertaker, and wear[ing] the same air of slow, funereal barbarism'.[60] Posterity was having none of it. Yet, even here, Strachey and his more intelligent followers were fundamentally concerned with the human legacy of the Victorians; and, though some of the tricks may have been cheap, the underlying seriousness of engagement was never in doubt. It was precisely this seriousness, and this accompanying originality of method, that ensured for the Victorians a lively afterlife on the biographical shelf as soon as *Eminent Victorians* appeared. No doubt, without Strachey, writers would have returned to a form of Johnsonian biography on their own: we cannot entirely credit him with modern trends. But neo- or post-Stracheyan biography, whether in its mounting insistence on human honesty or in its restorative reactions against flippancy, has undoubtedly made attitudes to the lives of eminent Victorians one of the most exciting areas of historical interest at the beginning of the twenty-first century.

# 9

# *Victoria*

The life of Queen Victoria lies at the heart of attitudes to the age bearing her name. As icon and myth she not only continues to inform ideas about the Victorians, but enjoys a retrospective afterlife of her own. It is a measure of her symbolic resonance that this is an afterlife burnt onto the retina: until the 1960s and 1970s there were many who recorded having seen Victoria at one of her official functions. G. M. Young glimpsed her twice; Virginia Woolf, aged fifteen, was enthralled by the pomp and ceremony of the Diamond Jubilee, recording in her diary: 'Troop after troop   one brilliant colour after another … The Queen … smiled and nodded her poor tired head.'[1] We can now see for ourselves early film of that day – images so evocative that the absence of sound and colour seems scarcely to register at all. There is something curiously apposite, too, about the uneven speed of the film, emphasising the otherworldly quality of the little old woman sitting dwarfed in what appears to be a huge carriage.

What all of these sightings have in common is the elderly imperial matriarch that Queen Victoria became. This image of Victoria – grand-motherly, dutiful and unamused – became the standard view of her in the twentieth century. That was partly because those who were old enough to have seen Queen Victoria in person were themselves born only near the close of the nineteenth century. In the end, so to speak, was the beginning: the longevity of Victoria preceded her, colouring twentieth-century attitudes to a life that for a long while eluded anything like real understanding. Knowing that Queen Victoria set an influential example, the sight of her vaguely petulant mouth, pouting cheeks and regally forbidding eyes served for many years subtly to underpin assumptions about the dourness of the age. But a sense of dourness has increasingly given way to human interest, and to an appreciation that the life of Victoria has instructive lessons for the present and future as well as for our attitudes to the past.

It is this Janus-faced profile – looking to both past and future – that is most striking about the highly enjoyable 1997 film *Mrs Brown*. Starring Judi Dench as Queen Victoria and Billy Connolly as her Highland gillie John Brown, the film deals with the decade or so after Prince Albert's death in 1861. Queen Victoria effectively went into seclusion in the 1860s, refusing to attend almost all royal ceremonies and social occasions on account of her tattered nerves. There was an element of Miss Havisham in this (Dickens's novel, in fact, having just appeared), exceeding by far the elaborate Victorian etiquette concerning what widows should wear in the two or three years after their husbands' passing. This John Brown saw and endeavoured to change. Victoria took well to his undeferential manner, coming to count him as a close personal friend. Others, including the public, were not so sure; even at the time there was speculation about the precise nature of Victoria's relationship with Brown, and fiercer criticism still of the constitutional implications of a monarch's neglect of her duties.

Out of this turbulent decade can be traced the emergence of Queen Victoria in her final 'role' as the dutiful mother of nation (and soon to be empire). So, too, can be traced the modern monarchy and a set of constitutional debates associated with it. Queen Victoria is initially shown in *Mrs Brown* at her least able. But then she comes to her senses, casting off Brown and her nervous exhaustion to assume the mantle for which the twentieth-century would remember her. Her fault in the 1860s had been to neglect the fundamental duty of the monarchy in fulfilling what Walter Bagehot called its 'dignified' role in society. Bagehot was a constitutional expert whose study *The English Constitution* appeared in 1867, the year of the Second Reform Act. The Act came at a time when the monarchy was already under fierce attack on account of Victoria's withdrawal from public appearances; in 1864 a wag had pinned a notice to the railings outside Buckingham Palace reading: 'These commanding premises to be let or sold, in consequence of the late occupant's declining business.'[2] Not for the first time Victorian politicians became obsessed with the prospects of revolution. Bagehot, however, analysed the situation clearly and soberly. Politics, he argued, now gave 'efficient' power to Parliament and 'dignified' power to the monarchy. The royal family should therefore play its role in constitutional government by becoming a symbolic figurehead: something which the people could admire and respect. Any abandonment of that role – whether through invisibility or mismanagement of ceremony – risked the very future of the monarchy.

Certainly the makers of *Mrs Brown* must have had some of these thoughts in mind when they released the film in 1997. By sad coincidence, that year witnessed the sudden death of Diana, Princess of Wales, and a reaction against the monarchy that must have had anxious advisers at Buckingham Palace reaching for their Bagehot. The backlash had, of course, been some years in the making. Since the 1980s members of the royal family had been trying to 'modernise' and demystify a monarchy whose very essence resides in archaism and mystique. Queen Victoria, though no advocate of demystification, found this out to her cost in the 1860s. And indeed the parallels between Victoria and Elizabeth II are striking. Both have been scrupulous in their personal integrity. Both have reigned over periods of dramatic change in Britain without seeking to appear spuriously 'relevant'. Both have been faced with relatives whose more relaxed moral standards and search for 'relevance' have shone an unflattering light on the royal family. Elizabeth II was shown, on the fortieth anniversary of her accession, leafing through one of Victoria's diaries, and she is clearly well-attuned to (or well-advised on) the importance of precedent. Small wonder, perhaps, that she headed the gathering at Sandringham on the centenary of Queen Victoria's death. 'May we uphold in our lives those principles which made her a great human being and monarch', the rector of Sandringham urged his unusual congregation, also evidently aware of history.[3]

The centenary in January 2001 brought similar comments from the constitutional expert Vernon Bogdanor. He wrote of Queen Victoria as a sovereign of a new sort, one who had weathered anti-royal feeling as well as dramatic change to bequeath to the twentieth century an example in monarchical dignity. 'In modern times,' he observed, with a cartoon of Victoria casting a watchful eye over Westminster, 'constitutional democracy has come to sustain democracy, not to threaten it'.[4] For that reason alone Queen Victoria has thrown a long shadow over the twentieth century. She was not, admittedly, a perfect example of Bagehotian impartiality, being too stubborn and spirited even in later years to take a less than transparently personal attitude to her prime ministers. She disliked William Gladstone intensely, because she felt that he treated her too much like a public institution (which, as a sensible Bagehotian, he did): at his last interview with her, after his sixty years of devoted political service, she uttered 'not one syllable on the past'.[5] Benjamin Disraeli, by contrast, succeeded in winning Victoria's admiration and affection: when it came to the monarchy, he drawled, you should lay the flattery on with a trowel.

It is clear, nonetheless, that Queen Victoria came to set a commanding example in personal probity and the execution of the 'dignified' parts of the Bagehotian constitutional equation. All twentieth-century monarchs have been conscious of it. Here, though, it has not always been a simple matter of emulation. For although the media has been used increasingly to consolidate the symbolic aspects of royalty (the first great landmark being television coverage of Elizabeth II's coronation), it can also extract a heavy price. As early as 1960 the *New Statesman* reflected on the dangers as well as the merits of media interest. 'The monarchy in Britain is established and safe', it suggested on the marriage of Princess Margaret. 'Indeed, the age of mass-communication has brought it a degree of popularity which would have seemed inconceivable even to the Victoria of the Jubilee. But for this reason, it cannot afford to make mistakes.'[6] Mistakes, or at least misfortunes, it did however suffer in the next four decades: and all in the glaring light of television coverage. Since the early 1990s certain members of the court circle have been speaking about the threat of 'QVS': Queen Victoria Syndrome – a long-reigning monarch out of touch with her people.[7] Media intrusion, ironically, has created this semblance of distance; for, if one thing is sure, Elizabeth II has been as conscientious in her execution of public dignity as anyone steeped in Bagehot could have hoped. What Bagehot did not have an answer for was the modern obsession with informality and youth. Here it appears that past and present look set to part ways before much longer.

We have conspired to make a simple retreat into Bagehotian 'dignity' impossible for the descendants of Queen Victoria, for we have become used to a much more human Victoria than her subjects knew. If, on the balance of evidence, we have come to appreciate her personal application to the difficult role of being monarch in an era of tumultuous change, then we have also helped to demystify the very trappings of power that Bagehot was so keen to shroud in spectacle and atmosphere. The twentieth century, striving to understand the Victorians, sought to do away with such obstructions. And so for posterity the greatest challenge to an understanding of the human Victoria was felt to have emerged even while she was alive. Eminent Victorians were generally accorded laudatory biographies; with Queen Victoria, the most eminent Victorian of all, the hagiography was made to work overtime.

Early views of Victoria depicted her as a latter-day Gloriana presiding over the unblemished success story of nineteenth-century Britain. Inevitably this was a habit accentuated by the Jubilees of 1887 and 1897, events which furnished observers with an opportunity to indulge in readings of the Queen's life decked out in full Whiggish fig. One writer in 1887, making little attempt to disguise his own Unionist and imperialist affinities, concluded his biography with an elaborate roll-call of the areas in which progress had been made throughout the century.[8] The journalist W. T. Stead proved to be no less myopic in his patriotism when it came to the Diamond Jubilee. He dubbed Victoria the female 'high-water mark of realised success in the Evolution of Humanity'.[9]

As far as reverence would allow, biographers also tended to adopt a mawkishly sentimental attitude towards their subject. Titles such as *Victoria the Good* (1901) by Clare Jerrold or *Victoria the Well-Beloved* (also 1901) by W. F. Aitken speak for themselves. Much of this sentimentality was directed

towards Victoria's earliest years, because it was in childhood anecdotes that
biographers thought that they could detect the origins of Victoria's subsequent benevolence as Queen and Empress. They thereby projected a
contemporary adoration back onto the earlier life of Victoria, and in so
doing revealed to posterity more about themselves than they did about their
subject. Psychologically penetrating they were not. The fault was not necessarily that the Victorians were pre-Freudian, but that they were too fond of
whimsy and of the idea of great men (and, as here, the occasional woman).
They are to be found at their least perceptive in such writings about Victoria's
childhood.

David Campbell, for example, told readers in 1901 that 'delightful little
stories' would 'give promise of that generous humanity which was a notable
feature of Victoria's maturer years'.[10] John Campbell, ninth Duke of Argyll,
and coincidentally son-in-law of his subject (he married Princess Louise in
1871), went further, saying that these childhood stories 'cannot be passed over
and omitted as mere nursery tittle-tattle ... They indicate character; they
often show the germs of that excellence which became afterwards apparent
to all the world'.[11] Another purveyor of 'pretty stor[ies]' belonging to this
period' went on to shape the story of Victoria's adolescence as a Walter
Scott romance. He presented Prince Albert as a latter-day knight-errant:

> The moment had arrived to send the Prince to the rescue of the maiden Princess
> whom he had loved from boyhood ... Enchantments of all kinds, evil tongues,
> and the plots of self-interested courtiers, would all vanish at the touch of that
> Ithuriel's spear – true love. And what maiden could help loving this perfect knight,
> spotless as Launcelot? – bringing with him, too, the memory of first affection and
> girlish hopes.[12]

With writing like this one wonders whether Lytton Strachey need have said
anything at all. Such sentimentality was not extended quite so widely to the
rest of Victoria's life, though many could not resist the temptation to
produce purple prose about the Queen's last years, when she seemed to be
the benevolent mother of her people – a 'fairy of the awe-inspiring sort', as
Campbell imagined, echoing Disraeli.[13]

There was, admittedly, good practical reason for such obsequiousness.
Biographers and scholars (even those steeped in Bagehot) knew relatively
little about the inner workings of monarchy, or about Victoria's private life,
especially after her widowed seclusion. Her correspondence did not begin
to appear until after 1907, and such sources as biographers could draw upon
– most notably the autobiographical *Leaves from the Journal of Our Life in
the Highlands* (1868) and *More Leaves* (1884) – were, for all their artless
candour, largely unrevealing. It is notable that these writers downplayed the

effects of Victoria's withdrawal from public affairs after 1861, not just from lack of knowledge about what went on behind closed palace doors, but also because it fitted in with their predominantly laudatory accounts of the reign. At its worst, opposition to Victoria's seclusion had run to republicanism, with critics attacking the exorbitant cost of a monarchy which was not fulfilling its public functions. Some eighty-four republican clubs were set up between 1871 and 1874, and in the light of such developments Argyll's comment only a generation later that 'people ... were inclined to grumble at the representation of the royalty not being adequately brought before the public' seems distinctly disingenuous.[14]

Greater appreciation of the public and private sides of Queen Victoria could only come about, however, through humanisation of the figure subjected to such obsequious sentimentality in her own time. Victoria's death unleashed mixed feelings of sorrow and relief: sorrow because she had become a popular monarch by the 1890s, and had created a semblance of continuity; relief because, for all the affection, many felt that she had reigned too long. This was the original 'QVS'. G. M. Young, that most sympathetic of commentators on the age, noted in 1936 that, although an 'idol' to her people, Victoria 'had come to press with something of the weight of an idol, and in the innermost circle of public life the prevailing sentiment [at her death] was relief'.[15] Arnold Bennett, a shrewd observer of ordinary feeling, also noted in his diary on 2 February 1901: 'This morning I saw what I could, over the heads of a vast crowd, of the funeral procession of the Queen. The people were not, on the whole, deeply moved, whatever journalists may say, but rather serene and cheerful.'[16]

There followed in the Edwardian age a time of sharper reaction against many aspects of Victorianism. This appears to have been reflected in biographical interest in the Queen herself. After Sir Sidney Lee's fine 1902 biography it is striking that there did not follow a major study of Victoria's life for some years. This is not to say that Victoria was ever forgotten. Sir Theodore Martin, the biographer chosen by her to write the laudatory life of Prince Albert, produced an equally laudatory memoir of the late monarch in 1908. Access to Victoria's private diaries enabled Viscount Esher to write *The Girlhood of Queen Victoria* (1912), and Clare Jerrold her trilogy *The Early Court of Queen Victoria* (1912), *The Married Life of Queen Victoria* (1913) and *The Widowhood of Queen Victoria* (1916). Yet these works maintained the distance which had always separated readers from the Queen, and which had been confirmed by her death. While avoiding the sentimental excesses of earlier biography, they were too respectful to engage analytically with their subject, and were still sketchy on the later years.

It was in such a climate that Edward VII attempted to encourage greater awareness of his mother's personal achievements. A. C. Benson and Viscount Esher were authorised to produce an edition of Queen Victoria's letters in 1907.[17] The aim of this collection, the editors wrote, was 'to bring out the development of the Queen's character and disposition', but there was a curious failure to achieve this in an edition which covered only the years up to 1861. Readers were already well-acquainted (albeit in sentimental depictions) with Victoria's early years, and it was the controversial period after Albert's death that remained obscured from view. No doubt part of the reason why further work was not immediately undertaken on this period was because it was so near to the present. It is highly unlikely that Edward VII relished having his turbulent private life discussed in print, and of course many of those discussed in Victoria's often candid letters would still have been alive.

Whether revelations about Victoria's later years would have encouraged more biographical work to be undertaken in the Edwardian period it is difficult to say. One is tempted to think not. The dynamics of emotional distance were such that, although Victoria was never forgotten, her life was as yet too close to be considered appropriate for analysis, and certainly too close for nostalgia. Both of these things were to change within a generation. By the 1920s and 1930s, as we shall see, people became far more interested in her life, and this interest went hand-in-hand with new biographical revelations and perspectives. But before that it was necessary for society to have a breathing space in which to contemplate its relationship with Victorianism and its eponymous ruler. As the essayist, aspiring politician and biographer Philip Guedalla commented on Victoria and Gladstone in 1933: 'There was an interval of indifference, almost of disrespect, in which their names were greeted with a thin derision. But increasing distance restores a just perspective; and as the age recedes, its two leading figures resume their true proportions.'[18]

Biographical writings on Queen Victoria show how a greater level of knowledge about the private lives of the Victorians became a crucial factor in their eventual rehabilitation. Close as many people were to the Victorian age in the inter-war years, they often knew less about its eminent figures than we do today. This is one of the paradoxes of historical knowledge: discretion, posthumous loyalty and government secrecy frequently conspire after an event or death to keep people in the dark about happenings within their own lifetime. There was the added obstacle, where Victoria was concerned, of biographical tradition and royal reserve. A case in point was her widowhood. When Lytton Strachey came to write his 1921 biography *Queen Victoria*, he was disarmingly honest about the difficulty of depicting his subject after 1861:

> The first forty-two years of the Queen's life are illuminated by a great and varied quantity of authentic information. With Albert's death a veil descends. Only occasionally, at fitful and disconnected intervals, does it lift for a moment or two; a few main outlines, a few remarkable details may be discerned; the rest is all conjecture and ambiguity ... We must be content in our ignorance with a brief and summary relation.[19]

This problem was addressed in the late 1920s and early 1930s, and these are consequently the key years when it comes to locating a recognisably 'modern' view of Victoria's life. Above all it was the publication of the second and third series of Letters of Queen Victoria, edited by G. E. Buckle between 1926 and 1932, which transformed contemporary scholarly views of Victoria.[20] It is scarcely an exaggeration to use the term 'transformed', because these letters dealt with the hitherto shadowy period in Victoria's life after the Prince Consort's death. A number of writers drew upon them to produce works that analysed Victoria from a Bagehotian perspective: Frederick Ponsonby and Frank Hardie, for instance, showed how the Queen had managed to influence politics even though 'efficient' power resided in the late nineteenth century with Parliament.[21] As Hardie commented, Queen Victoria had been even more dutiful, industrious and artful than popular impressions allowed.

Emotional distance and the growth in knowledge about Queen Victoria could, of course, have brought double-edged consequences where the subject of her personal character was concerned. Laurence Housman wrote in 1934, introducing his series of royal plays Victoria Regina:

> As successive volumes of her letters and diaries are made public, with a frankness hitherto unexampled in the official editing of Royal remains, it becomes more and more evident that she was the mourning widow, not only of a beloved and worthy Consort, but of a whole set of cherished notions, which in the 'sixties and 'seventies were already moribund ... the mind of Victoria was sedentary, and did not move.[22]

Potentially this offered rich opportunity for sarcasm, and certainly the Victoria who emerged from these thirty miniature theatrical pieces is temperamental, inflexible and all too easily flattered. But she is also shrewd, hard-working and often touchingly vulnerable, such that the last image presented is of a 'great, wonderful, little old Lady' being slowly wheeled away after the celebrations of 1897.[23] Even those conscious of 'QVS' could not help admiring the elderly Victoria, whatever the constitutional implications may have been.

It is noteworthy that images such as the Diamond Jubilee proved to be very popular when Victoria Regina was granted a stage licence in 1937.[24]

9. Giles Lytton Strachey, pondering the grave responsibilities of the biographer. (*Estate of Lytton Strachey*)

10. Virginia Woolf in 1902. She found the 'experiment in living' dominated by the Victorian age. (*National Portrait Gallery*)

11. E. M. Forster in his rooms at King's College, Cambridge, during the 1950s. Some of the furniture dates back to his childhood home of the 1880s. (*King's College, Cambridge*)

12. Philip and Edmund Gosse in 1857. Fifty years later Edmund Gosse would recount how he asserted 'a human being's privilege to fashion his inner life for himself'. (*National Portrait Gallery*)

13. Winston Churchill in 1881. Eighty years later, he would still be wearing the look of Victorian confidence. (*Imperial War Museum*)

14. The modern face of Dickens: the Freudian love triangle of the BBC's *Great Expectations* (1999). Ioan Gruffudd as Pip, Charlotte Rampling as Miss Havisham and Justine Waddell as Estella. (*BBC*)

15. Stephen Fry as Oscar Wilde in Brian Gilbert's 1997 biopic. Constance (Jennifer Ehle) is at his side, but 'Bosie' (Jude Law) hovers ominously in the background. (*Samuelson Productions*)

16. The Albert Memorial. Splendidly restored in the 1990s, it exemplifies our tendency to view the Victorians as 'heritage'. (*A. F. Kersting*)

There had, admittedly, been a certain amount of trepidation about the impact the play would have upon perceptions of the past. 'A magnified and distorted picture of the Queen will be conveyed to the British people, and indeed to the whole world', the historian C. K. Webster prophesied. 'It may influence profoundly their attitude not only towards the Crown as an institution, but towards the whole Victorian age.'[25] Such had been the anxiety of the political establishment for many years already; and, as we have already seen, the Lord Chamberlain would still be censoring plays about Queen Victoria thirty years later. But in the event the play proved to be a critical and popular success. *The Times* referred to it as 'a sketch at once candid and affectionate ... a brilliant pageant, quick in emotion, but as restrained as it is just'.[26] Housman is reputed to have made £15,000 from the centenary performances which opened on 21 June 1937 at the Lyric Theatre.[27]

The work of Housman is characteristic of the tone of much inter-war biographical treatment of Victoria, where the distinctive breakthrough was one of sympathy. 'QVS' was increasingly downplayed in favour of a human emphasis. And for the first time, Queen Victoria came to be seen as a fully human being. This was a status that necessarily entailed a sense of her fallibility, but proved for that very reason to be more enduringly positive than the eulogies offered by earlier biographers. As George Bernard Shaw had quipped in 1886: 'A few faults are indispensable to a really popular monarch.'[28] The debunkers were getting to work on the 'dignified' façade erected by their predecessors.

Lytton Strachey was the key figure in the attack on the Victorian biographical genre. It will come as little surprise, then, that it was his 1921 biography of Victoria that proved to be the most important work in setting the tone for later studies of the Queen, even if only through biographers' decisions to eschew Strachey's approach. It sold well from the outset, and in Britain the book went through five impressions within a year.[29] The American edition, published by Harcourt and Brace, proved to be so popular that Strachey regretted having sold them the copyright for a fixed sum of $10,000. 'The sale has been much larger than expected,' Strachey wrote in September 1921, 'and promises to continue.'[30] So iconic did the work become that the Oxford aesthetes – those avid collectors of Victorian artefacts – planned a ballet of Victoria's life, with Martin Harvey as the Queen and Harold Acton as Strachey. Part of the choreography was to include 'Strachey' secreted beneath a couch in the act of observing and taking notes on Victoria's private life – a striking acknowledgement of the degree to which people were coming to appreciate the art of the biographer.[31]

Strachey's Victoria, although hampered by bourgeois philistinism, is a fundamentally sympathetic figure. And that is how he consciously set out to portray her, having once written to his cousin Edith Plowden that he considered Victoria a 'great queen'.[32] As Michael Holroyd suggests, this discreet affection may partly have been because Strachey associated Victoria with his own mother: when the biography was published Lady Strachey was eighty-one, the exact age to which Victoria had lived.[33] For such a project, Strachey adopted a different technique from that of *Eminent Victorians*. He made this biography more akin to a romantic novel, using Victoria's psyche as a centripetal ordering presence so that other characters (though sharply etched) complement and show different angles of the main subject. Victoria's delight in the attentions of Melbourne and Disraeli is fulsomely conveyed, and even in old age the mind is shown to be lively and responsive; the Queen in her dotage is allowed 'a long evening ... mild, serene and lighted with a golden glory'.[34]

As a homosexual, Strachey clearly took vicarious pleasure in Victoria's feminine traits, and wrote with particular lyricism about Victoria's adoration of handsome Prince Albert. Stranger still, where Albert was concerned, is Strachey's mixture of wish-fulfilment and empathy. With some fey asides about Albert enjoying 'close yet dignified' contact with 'distinguished men', Strachey hints at a repressed homoeroticism.[35] Although a self-evident interpretative liability, there can be no question of hostility here. For surely, in the Prince's loneliness, that of a 'conscious and unrecognised superiority', we see much of Strachey's own outlook on the world.[36] (Even on his deathbed Strachey was heard to utter: 'If this is dying, then I don't think much of it.') Few writers had dared to broach the difficult topic of the Prince Consort's unpopularity in England; nobody had empathised with him, as Strachey did. With this biography Victoria (and Albert) became human beings more fully than ever before. The *Times Literary Supplement* enthused: 'Far better is a Queen no longer muffled by the veils and trappings of her state – far better, certainly, to read about.'[37]

Such humanisation of Queen Victoria was galloping ahead by the 1930s. Reflecting on the prospect of the opening night of Housman's *Victoria Regina* in 1937, *The Times* noted that the question 'who was Queen Victoria?' had only become more resonant still as the decades had passed:

A hundred years have allowed for the memory of Queen Victoria to survive that period of depreciation which follows excessive adulation for all the great; and her true eminence may be taken as firmly established. Her correspondence has been published, illuminating her faults as well as her virtues, her narrowness and prejudices as well as her commanding breadth of mind. Tonight for the first time authority permits her person to be represented on the public stage. She no longer needs protection from the risk of calumny. She abides our question, and we may welcome the aid of any help that science or art can give for the illumination of her character.[38]

This balance of sympathetic deflation, fresh archival insights and new angles of interpretation was consolidated in the generations that followed. The archives continued to be plundered, enabling the publication of editions of the Queen's correspondence with public figures like Palmerston and with private relations including Princess Victoria (the mother of Kaiser Wilhelm II). The latter became the theme of one of the largest projects after 1945: the five-volume edition of correspondence between Queen Victoria and Princess Victoria edited by Sir Roger Fulford between 1964 and 1981.[39] This fascination with the lives of Victoria's daughters (of whom there were five) was indeed emerging in the 1930s and 1940s as one of the most prominent by-products of the engine pouring out new material on the Queen. Developing from an interest in surviving members of Victoria's family (the last died in 1944), and perhaps from rueful consideration of the dynastic links that had failed to prevent carnage throughout Europe, the tale of her daughters' lives remained compelling reading in the post-war years.

It was compelling precisely because so many of the constraints under which they had lived were now beginning to fade away. Admiring as the tone of biographies such as David Duff's *The Shy Princess* (1958) may have been, there is little doubt that its subject was seen as a martyr: virtually unmentioned in her mother's journal, yet constantly required to dance attendance, Princess Beatrice emerges as yet another victim of Victoria's temperament.[40] Six years later, Lady Longford would concur about Victoria's possessiveness towards Beatrice, a girl so strictly chaperoned and censored that she 'dared not discuss any subject beyond the weather without an imploring look at her mother'. Victoria was anxious about losing her youngest daughter through marriage, writes Longford; but that does not prevent her from a quietly severe judgement. 'The Queen's behaviour was a gloomy example of the selfishness to which, under stress, she could descend.'[41] Needless to say, such behaviour sat oddly against traditional views of Victoria as the ideal 'mother' figure, and stored up for her reputation some contradictions with which feminists of the next generation would struggle to accommodate themselves.

Nevertheless, it was still the human Victoria who dominated the biographical landscape in the 1950s and 1960s. The most important biography of these years, and perhaps since that of Strachey, was Elizabeth Longford's *Victoria R.I.* (1964). In her preface Lady Longford signalled her knowledge of Strachey's *Queen Victoria* – 'a portrait which in its own way is inimitable' – in rather ambiguous terms. The rationale for producing her own biography,

however, was simple. Much new archival material had been made available
in recent years, and even more importantly she had been granted 'unhindered
access' to the Royal Archives at Windsor. This was a major watershed. The
notes for the biography, accordingly, are peppered with references to source
materials, many of which had never before been deployed. With more space,
far greater access to archives and less of an inclination to Stracheyan artistry,
Longford was able to probe many of the old myths and rumours about
Queen Victoria, comparing different sources on particular points.

   Longford convincingly suggests, for example, that Victoria's relationship
with Disraeli was less a case of flattery laid on with a trowel than one of
mutual whimsy. 'The Queen had the measure of her Prime Minister's foot
also,' she observes, 'and together they savoured the delicious fictions of their
relationship with as much gusto as they brought to the facts.' [42] Prince Albert,
shorn of homoerotic innuendo, receives equally discriminating and sympathetic treatment. Not fighting shy of the deficiencies in Albert's character,
or of the tensions between the royal couple, Longford manages to convey
a sense of some of the magic that kept the Widow of Windsor in mourning
for the last forty years of her life. One of the sources used by Longford is
Victoria's rapturous description of her wedding night. After a nerve-racking
and exhausting ceremony, Victoria returned to Windsor with Albert, and
they explored 'the new suite of rooms together, running like children from
one to the other'. Then Victoria sinks with a headache; but it is not to have
a typically Victorian outcome:

> But ill or not, I NEVER NEVER spent such an evening!!! My DEAREST DEAREST
> DEAR Albert sat on a footstall by my side, & his excessive love & affection gave
> me feelings of heavenly love & happiness, I never could have *hoped* to have felt
> before! – really how can I *ever* be thankful enough to have such a *Husband*! [43]

With such quotes the young, vulnerable, headily impressionistic Victoria
springs immediately and touchingly to life: material like this would surely
have been grist to Strachey's mill. And indeed both books share a kind of
feminine intuition, grace of execution and profound interest in the contradictions of human nature. Longford's biography is certainly the more
impartial and scholarly, but again, the tradition of sympathetic humanisation
of the Queen lays essentially unbroken over the span of forty years. Longford,
too, felt that Victoria was (as Strachey put it) 'a great queen', and her
biography strives to establish that, for all Victoria's foibles, she rose to the
challenge of being monarch with spirit, shrewdness and above all an enormous sense of duty. 'Enough is known of her today to see her as she was',
the author concludes. 'The extended view will modify but not obliterate the
impression of greatness she left with the country and the world.' [44]

A generation later, the humanisation of Queen Victoria was a project still compelling to writers and readers alike: testimony, no doubt, to fascination with an individual whose life continued to haunt the popular imagination and evade easy categorisation. Increasingly, though, the nature of humanisation was becoming literally more intimate. Lady Longford's gracious biography tactfully considered the question of Victoria's health. But medical matters came back with renewed vigour and breezy transatlantic openness in a 1987 biography by the American scholar Stanley Weintraub. 'Medical knowledge affords us new insights,' Weintraub observed, 'and former reticences about matters once deemed private or even unspeakable can be discarded.' [45] His reading, accordingly, probed into matters such as the consequences of Victoria's frequent ill health for those around her in politics and (especially) at court. The domestic life and dynastic connections of Victoria's children had often been traced, but never in such detail the day-to-day business of conception, pregnancy and child-rearing in the early years of the Queen's reign. And it was indeed often a day-to-day business – 'throughout the 1840s Victoria was pregnant almost as much as she was regnant', remarks David Cannadine.[46]

This abiding interest in painting human portraits of Queen Victoria, then, has developed a momentum of its own. The tradition initiated by Strachey, largely confirmed by Longford and continued in the present day by writers like Weintraub, looks set to continue for some time. But there are signs that the urge to reveal the human side of Queen Victoria has begun to reach saturation point, and not only because most of the archives have been exhausted. When it comes to biographies musing over the accuracy of a contemporary medical diagnosis for a minor indisposition, it seems reasonable to conclude that the subject has been comprehensively documented at the personal level. Historians have also, though, lamented that such biographies, though sympathetic and useful, run the risk of underplaying exactly how Victoria's personality interacted with the age to which she gave her name. An almost exclusive preoccupation with humanisation ignores, most importantly, the reality of the Queen's role in Victorian politics. The publication of many of Victoria's letters by the 1930s and subsequent access to the Royal Archives generated the possibility of biographies which might have integrated the human and the political sides of the Queen; increasingly, though, biographers have specialised in the former, and historians in the latter.

The sheer strength of the neo-Stracheyan tradition may help to explain this bifurcation, especially when there is an understandably wide readership for continuing exploration of Victoria's personal character. But it is not just literary skill and human interest that has kept this tradition strong. The tantalising prospect also dangles itself before writers and readers that the puzzle that is Victorianism might possibly be solved if the secrets of Victoria's heart and mind are unlocked; not for nothing do Longford and Weintraub make vague metaphysical statements about the Queen's determination to 'be good' as an embodiment of her age, or of Victoria 'becoming' England.[47] The almost exclusive preoccupation with personal matters may therefore seem a worthwhile investment, the specific shedding light on the universal.

Still, it remains fair to say that few individuals are gifted enough to be good biographers as well as good historians. And the tradition of writing that has humanised Queen Victoria has been dominated by biographers who have not been professional historians. At a time when specialised knowledge of the Victorian age has reached unprecedented levels, biographers often struggle to integrate their insights with the latest research. This is not for one moment to detract from the artistry and humanity of the tradition, which looks sure to continue and to produce studies that are compelling and full of insight. But how well largely personal biographies of the Queen will fare once the corner of significant Victorian anniversaries has been turned remains to be seen. After the centenary year 2001, the next obvious anniversary will be 2019, the two hundredth birthday of Queen Victoria; and almost exactly a century on from Strachey's groundbreaking biography it will be fascinating to see where we stand on the subject of Victoria as a human being.

Biographical perspectives on Queen Victoria have, in fact, since the 1970s and 1980s already begun to move in dramatically new directions. In the last thirty or so years the agenda has increasingly been dominated by the contemporary themes of sex and gender. Historians have yet properly to probe the topic, but it would be interesting to know how far this modern agenda has been set by the reign of the first female monarch since Queen Victoria, and from the 1980s by the experience of the first female Prime Minister – an even more formidable figure, and one (at least on paper) committed to 'Victorian values'.

More certain is the way in which these perspectives have depended upon the humanisation of Queen Victoria that had been taking place for the previous fifty years or more. But human nature, and the very business of history and biography, was becoming more complicated as the biographical priorities the Victorians themselves had held began to unwind in the post-war decades. It was no longer enough to write about how Victoria set about fulfilling her duties, or even to make Victoria a straightforward biographical project. The rise of theory put paid to this: in history, scholars wrote about the ways in which people like Queen Victoria entered into 'dialogues' with previously unseen forces like gender expectations; while for biographers, the idea that identities could be 'created' and manipulated, or might only exist in the mind of the viewer, cast doubt upon the ability to recreate a life at all. For the most part, however, biography has been enriched by these new approaches: many of the most distinguished biographers working today have accommodated the challenges of post-modern theory with positive and witty results. Feminist scholarship, too, has risen to the challenge. We have yet, though, to be offered a study that matches Strachey's *Queen Victoria* for wit: gaiety of spirits seems not to rank terribly high amongst those writing about Victoria from the feminist perspective.

Such sobriety is hardly surprising given that Victoria presents a particular challenge to those who would interpret her as a key figure within the struggle for women's rights. For while it is certainly true that Victoria was a woman presiding over an age overwhelmingly dominated by men, and frequently played upon her femininity as mother and wife, she herself echoed many of the prejudices of the time. Her place as monarch, it seems clear, was a triumph for the principle of royalty safeguarded by parliamentary democracy, not for the principle of women's rights. As feminist historians have been keen to point out, many observers in 1837 were very taken with the idea of having a queen. In living memory was the sordid affair of Queen Caroline, forcibly debarred from her husband's coronation in 1820, and the subsequent outpouring of fury at the apparent slur on Britannia's person.[48] And when Victoria acceded to the throne, popular associations were made with those earlier icons of strong female leadership, Queen Boadicea and Elizabeth I.

Yet it is clear that much of this enthusiasm came at the prospect of youth rather than femininity, and innocence rather than debauchery: the optimism at Victoria's succession needs to be seen in terms of the contrast she offered to her elderly and self-indulgent uncles. Although the young Queen's femininity was crucial to this image of freshness and purity, it is difficult to make a convincing case for any revolution in gender roles in 1837. If anything, the Victorian age witnessed the zenith of female oppression with the sanctification of the 'Angel in the House'. Queen Victoria, a woman dedicated to domestic piety, distanced herself from anything that threatened this middle-class idyll: she opposed the extension of the vote to women, dismissing the very notion as 'mad, wicked folly', and thought that Lady Amberley, a supporter of the cause, 'ought to get a good whipping'.[49] Victoria was not alone amongst women with such sentiments: but she had the luxury of being exempt from most of the laws that bound wives to tyrannical husbands, and never experienced the difficulties that other women did in establishing their voices in the public sphere.

It is precisely this smooth fusion of 'private' (wife, mother) and 'public' (Queen, Empress) personas, with an emphasis on the dependency of the public on the private, that feminists have claimed as a blow struck for women by Victoria.[50] But this was at best a pyrrhic victory, and such readings fail to convince on grounds of the wilful suppression of Victoria's profound conservatism. In response to this criticism, many scholars since the 1990s have begun to modify their perspectives. This may also partly be a reflection of unease on the part of Anglo-American feminists about their own position within academia, which oddly resembles that of Queen Victoria within her age. Now firmly established and influential, with their insights taken seriously, feminist historians sometimes feel that they have allowed themselves to be assimilated within a patriarchal establishment, just as Victoria did a century before.[51] Post-modern theory, too, has confirmed that thinking in terms of gender (male versus female) is a form of intellectual entrapment.

Whatever the reason may be, studies of Queen Victoria and gender have lately become more nuanced. And so, instead of leading the campaign for female liberation, it is Victoria's artful use of her own sex to wield power that has been emphasised, thereby creating an alternative tradition: one not so much of victory, but of feminine influence. In these readings all sorts of unusual sources have become subject to (re)interpretation, including the visual. Take, for example, Mary Loeffelholz's interpretation of an 1887 drawing entitled *Victoria Refusing to Sign Recognition of Southern Confederacy*:

> The minister in the foreground gestures aggressively with his right hand, its index finger pointed directly at Victoria and positioned over the official document on the table behind them, its seal dangling toward the floor, while his left hand is opened more supplicatingly toward the Queen. Half turned away from the confrontation, Victoria raises one hand in rejection of the document and the minister's pointing finger, while the other protectively or retreatingly gathers her veil up to her waist, a gesture that also, along with her sash, calls attention to her ample maternal bosom.

For Loeffelholz, this is a deliberate visual embodiment of 'Victoria as the imperial but feminine savior of American union'.[52]

This is an 'invented' Queen, and it is surely no coincidence that several female scholars in recent years have written about how the young Victoria 'became' both her real self and a feminine icon. Lynne Vallone, for example, has traced how the sentimentalised Princess Victoria so popular with loyal audiences at the end of the nineteenth century – the girl absorbed in her sketching and reading, or playing with her spaniel Dash – was created through cartoons, portraits and writings. Re-examination of Victoria's childhood exercise books, journals and sketches, meanwhile, shows the less cherubic but more endearing reality of an inquisitive, outspoken and pleasure-seeking little girl. The Princess who was supposed to be a model of good manners and dutifulness was also the plump child who, at seven, wrote a story about a girl who is 'naughty, greedy and disobedeent [sic]', but has the charm and guile to evade chastisement and even to secure a plate full of sweetmeats: royal prerogative literally as having one's cake and eating it. Queen Victoria 'became' herself in a personal as well as a mythical sense, which only serves to deepen interest in her as the figurehead of an age.[53]

Queen Victoria is now seen not just as a symptom of Victorianism, but as a shaper of it too. Margaret Homans and Adrienne Munich have been particularly influential in putting 'Victoria back into [the] Victorian', and in doing so they have found new areas of interest without making exaggerated claims about her as a feminist icon. Her gender and personality, they argue, acted instead as a kind of mirror:

> Victoria reflected back to her subjects their own values to reassure them about the comprehensibility of their lived reality; they in turn created her in their image to serve their social and economic needs. Queen Victoria, her subjects around the globe, and even those outside the empire collaboratively made her into a myth and an icon.[54]

What they demonstrate is that Queen Victoria meant many things to many people, and was consciously 'marketed' as such. After all, almost everyone would have had at least one image of the Queen in their home by the end of the nineteenth century, whether it was a regal image on a Jubilee mug or a sentimental print of the youthful Victoria. Images implied a particular view of Victoria, such as the strong but benevolent Mother of Empire, or the eager and dutiful young Queen. In an age of great change and upheaval, onlookers responded to this range of overlapping views, inferring from particular favourites or at particular moments the qualities that appealed and reassured.

Popular views of Queen Victoria, too, have remained preoccupied by the general theme of how it was that she ruled in an age dominated by men. Here there has been less awareness of feminist and post-modern perspectives, and rather more awareness of the subjects of sex and royal display. Once again, the long drive to humanise Victoria has inevitably thrown up a good deal of material, especially where sex is concerned. Strachey, in his genteel way, revelled in the Queen's sexuality; Longford was honest but tactful; Weintraub was direct and analytical. At every stage openness has grown upon the subject, and by the 1970s and 1980s it was clear that Victoria was in the process of being re-eroticised. Books like Theo Aronson's *Heart of a Queen: Queen Victoria's Romantic Attachments* (1991) were published, detailing her feelings towards Melbourne, Albert, Napoleon III, John Brown, Disraeli and the Munshi. 'Never, not even in old age', Aronson reminds us, 'was Queen Victoria the dour, censorious puritan of popular imagination: through her complex character ran a bright thread of romanticism.'[55] More down to earth, perhaps, was the emphasis on Victoria and Albert as 'enthusiastic patrons of the nude' in *Exposed: The Victorian Nude* at Tate Britain at the end of 2001.[56]

General awareness of Queen Victoria's amorous feelings has grown exponentially and (surely significantly) in tandem with revelations about the marital irregularities of certain members of the present royal family. But of course there is an essential difference here. For the notion that the adoring Victoria could ever have been unfaithful to Albert is positively risible; and indeed, even as a widow (and many widows remarried), it is likely that in body she was not even unfaithful to his memory. As Dorothy Thompson has remarked, scandalmongers are likely to gain little return from investigation of Victoria's relationship with John Brown. Not only is the evidence thin, but an idiomatic reading of it would suggest at most a connubial affection.[57] For this reason, and with an awareness of popular interest in the lives of the royal family, recent presentations of Queen Victoria on film and television have focused upon the nature of her amatory feelings and its implications for the constitution. That is the context in which *Mrs Brown* needs to be viewed.

There is a striking comparison here with a film made sixty years earlier: Herbert Wilcox's *Victoria the Great*. In this depiction Queen Victoria, played by Anna Neagle, was given unashamedly romantic and admiring treatment. Not for Wilcox the humanised Victoria that had emerged from the pages of Strachey, although in the final scenes she is portrayed as the 'grandmother of the great family of mankind'. But the conservatism of approach to the Queen's person, contrasting so markedly with that of *Mrs Brown*, did not owe itself to any simple psychological naivety in the 1930s. For, like its successor, *Victoria the Great* should be seen against the backdrop of contemporary politics: only the year before its appearance, the royal family had been rocked by the Abdication Crisis. Many observers contrasted Edward VIII unfavourably with his great-grandmother and the respectable domestic values for which she was seen to stand. George VI, by contrast, was positively Victorian in his sense of family duty. And significantly enough, he took an active part in the preparation of the 1938 sequel, *Sixty Glorious Years*. He gave access to various royal estates for filming, encouraged his daughters to follow the shooting process, and even prompted Lady Antrim to coach Neagle in the body language of his great-grandmother. It is noteworthy that Queen Victoria, as an emblem of Victorian values in the 1930s, was fully appreciated. The *Star* reported in November 1937 that *Victoria the Great* was being seen by schoolchildren in block-bookings of 350 at a time; and a year later, *Today's Cinema* thought *Sixty Glorious Years* contained 'a message for today that cannot be ignored'.[58]

The place of Victoria's sexuality in views of her constitutional status has, unsurprisingly, become far more heavily emphasised in a climate that is attuned to such matters. Yet there has also been considerable continuity across the years, since however much speculation may have become orient- ated towards the details and psychology of Victoria's private life, it remains true that she possessed an acute sense of constitutional decorum. It was not, of course, flawless: in refusing to change her ladies of the bedchamber to suit standards of political impartiality, in her callous dismissal from the royal household of Flora Hastings (wrongly accused of illegitimate pregnancy), in her shabby treatment of Gladstone and her occasional interference in politics, her record was not unblemished. But, with the exception of her withdrawal from public life in the 1860s and early 1870s, Victoria's deter- mination to raise the profile and standing of the monarchy was indisputable. It is one of the many ways in which Victorianism – if we put Victoria back into the 'ism' – dominated public life in the twentieth century, and continues to do so today.

A case in point is the BBC dramatisation *Victoria and Albert* shown on television in 2001. Like *Victoria the Great* and *Mrs Brown*, it contained a number of pointed political themes that resonated immediately in a modern setting. In this version Victoria (Victoria Hamilton) may have been charm- ingly re-eroticised, not turning a hair when Albert ( Jonathan Firth) is outraged by the accidental discovery of a courtier *in flagrante delicto*; but it is she who is sensitive to public opinion, she who lectures on the importance of correct constitutional procedure (even if her own blunders are downplayed), and she who has much to say to the wayward Prince Bertie. '*Victoria and Albert* is a love story,' wrote one reviewer, 'not just between man and woman but between queen and country, a reminder that duty is not necessarily the enemy of domestic happiness. Modern royals could do worse than watch it.'[59] By such processes has Walter Bagehot – G. M. Young's 'greatest Victorian' – been all but restored to public discourse. Very few people on the street would be able to name the foremost con- stitutional expert of the Victorian age, but almost all are familiar with the debates he did so much to frame in the nineteenth century: the distribution of real power between Parliament and the monarchy, the role of ceremony

and public relations, the 'purpose' of the monarchy in general. The questions remain, and for all the difficulties of understanding Queen Victoria's
complex personality, it is evident that she continues to prove a hard act
to follow.

# 10

# *Dickens*

Appropriately, for a novelist so keen on the home, the language of Charles Dickens forms part of the mental furniture of every person in the English-speaking world. From Fagin to Pickwick, Scrooge to Pecksniff, the gallery of characters created by Dickens looms large in the imagination and in our retrospective sense of the Victorian age. To a still greater degree has Dickens invested the twentieth century with a number of haunting images of the society of his day. Etched into the collective memory is Oliver and his bowl of workhouse gruel, or the prison hulks moored off the misty marshes, or the mud and fog swirling outside Lincoln's Inn. Dickens, clearly, is crucial to our sense of the Victorians. Indeed it may even be felt that Dickens in some way is the key to the Victorian age; 'Dickensian' often illuminates 'Victorian', rather than vice-versa. 'For many people,' Gordon Marsden has written, 'Charles Dickens *is* the Victorian era.'[1]

What, if anything, did Dickens *mean* in his work? We ponder this in unprecedented depth and detail today, and use any guides we can on the matter. Even photographs of Dickens have become subject to close analysis and the kind of treatment that suggests the rich complexity that we now find about this most extraordinary of Victorians. In the entrance to the Charles Dickens Centre at Rochester, for example, we confront an enlarged photographic image of the writer. It is a famous face: the hair in exuberant clusters about the forehead, the long beard and moustache, the deeply-lined face, the melancholy and slightly wary eyes. 'Who is Dickens?', we are asked, and as we move along the image is reproduced some half a dozen times, on each occasion looking at an area of the face in ever greater detail. What we are left with is a hugely magnified eye: still tired and vulnerable, but now also probing and utterly inscrutable.[2] Who, indeed, is this Dickens of ours?

The supplement to the *Oxford English Dictionary* cites the first use of 'Dickensian' as from 1881, a decade after the novelist's death. But as early as 1856, while *Little Dorrit* was appearing, observers were using terms like 'Dickenesque' to describe his style of writing; clearly some sort of relationship had been forged between Dickens and his audience. This audience was notable in itself, for at a time when multi–volume novels were prohibitively expensive, Dickens managed to reach a far greater number of readers through serialisation. All of his novels originally appeared in serial form, published at monthly intervals (usually over twenty months) at a shilling an issue. From the earliest it was a triumph: with *The Pickwick Papers* in 1837, the twenty-five-year-old Dickens was reaching a monthly audience of 40,000 people.[3] What, twenty years later, did these people understand by 'Dickenesque'? It is difficult to be sure, especially given the range of readers that must have been accommodated by such large figures. But we know that Dickens exploited the medium in which he worked, structuring his novels to deliver the maximum frisson at particular moments. In large part it was this frisson to which readers responded, whether in terms of drama or emotion. The obvious modern parallel, of course, is the television soap opera; and there is something oddly familiar about the excited gathering of people, a mass of whispers and anxious speculation, waiting at the docks in Boston and New York for the arrival of the issue of *The Old Curiosity Shop* that would tell them whether Little Nell had lived or died.[4]

Still, although Dickens has flourished in television and cinema adaptations for many years, it is unlikely that we appreciate his novels in quite the same way as his contemporaries did. Even in 1930 Aldous Huxley had dismissed the sentimental parts of *The Old Curiosity Shop* for 'their lack of understanding [which reveal themselves] with a vehemence of florid utterance that is not only shocking, but ludicrous'.[5] Before we dismiss this in turn as an excessive piece of early twentieth-century anti-Victorianism, it is worth bearing in mind that the novel has not in recent memory been adapted for television or film. Even Hollywood, one suspects, would fight shy of the lachrymose quasi-mysticism of Nell's deathbed scene. Dickens believed that the free play of the imagination encouraged sympathetic and humane feeling; and there were certainly some, like Dean Stanley in his obituary sermon at Westminster Abbey, who spoke of how they were 'roused by him to a consciousness of the misery of others'.[6] But it would be another century before Dickens's 'technique' of engaging with social concerns through sentimentality was fully probed by scholars. For many of Dickens's contemporaries, he was simply the spinner of magical yarns. That, at any rate, was what Thomas Carlyle, the dedicatee of *Hard Times*, thought of the 'little man'. Although they were on affectionate terms, Dickens's veneration for Carlyle's fiery social criticism was not reciprocated.[7]

Our sense of the range and depth of Dickens's vision has coalesced in the years since his death. So, too, has our understanding of the complexities of the Victorian age. Hindsight tells us that neither is as straightforward as we once might have believed, and that the relationship between them is equally complex. And so it is really in the twentieth century that the term 'Dickensian' seems to have taken off, both as a descriptive term and as an emotional attitude towards the age about which Dickens wrote. The foundation in 1905 of the *Dickensian*, the journal of the Dickens Fellowship set up three years before, may have done much to consolidate the word as the standard Dickens adjective, and to make it a palimpsest upon which manifold readings of what Dickens 'meant' have been inscribed. It is for this reason that the rather neutral *OED* definition of 'Dickensian' does not greatly matter: it states that it is something or someone 'marked by conditions or features resembling those described by Dickens'. This is not as flat a definition as it at first sounds. For there is built into it, with the word 'resembling', a careful concession to the way in which the term has been borrowed from a purely literary context. This is a matter of relating to history through the 'Dickensian': it has a descriptive power, based upon our knowledge of the novels (and visual memory of film or television adaptations), as well as an evocative resonance which is slightly harder to pin down, yet often even more important.

Raphael Samuel, for example, peppers the first volume of his *Theatres of Memory* (1994) with references to the 'Dickensian' nature of the Victorian age (usually in that form, with inverted commas to signal its use in a wider context than just the novels). Often Samuel uses the adjective 'Dickensian' to invoke physical surroundings both visually and affectively, thereby implying an emotional attitude towards them. Hence we have '"Dickensian" tenements and the basement dwelling ... thought of as a breeding-ground for TB'; or discussing the cinematography of David Lynch's *The Elephant Man*: 'The townscape is thoroughly "Dickensian", with narrow, dripping alleys, and cobbled, gas-lit streets.'[8] Samuel's feel for Dickens is palpable, and this is by no means the only way in which he uses the term. Nevertheless, it is clear that for Samuel, in John Keegan's words 'full of concern for the underdog, the unhappy, the lonely, the overlooked', 'Dickensian' often related to the dark and downtrodden, and to his (as well as Dickens's) attitude to such things.[9]

Such readings have many precedents, the notion of Dickens-as-social critic having enjoyed particular currency at times in the twentieth century when there was less faith in economic and social progress. During the First World War it was the novels of Dickens, alongside the posters of Kitchener and the music hall songs, that jostled in the minds of soldiers as they marched off to the trenches. The wartime president of the Dickens Fellowship, W. W. Crotch, even went as far as to claim that 'Any study of Dickens means a spiritual arming of the people for Democracy'.[10] One Labour MP subsequently claimed, in the uncertain years after the Versailles Conference, that his party was committed to 'making our great nation into one family', adding that behind this aspiration 'stands the form of Charles Dickens'.[11] Such a dream, however, had still not come true a decade later. And so in the Depression-ridden 1930s, when the gulf between rich and poor widened sharply, it was again to Dickens that many people turned. As the *Daily Worker* exclaimed in 1932: 'Scrooge still lives! ... The modern Scrooge is a monster, whose malice far surpasses that of his miserly namesake.'[12] George Bernard Shaw stated in 1937 that *Little Dorrit* was a more seditious book than *Das Kapital*, while in the same year Thomas Jackson published a notorious Marxist reading of Dickens that claimed – fairly improbably, it has to be said – that its subject might easily have become a socialist or communist.

Most commentators, however, valued Dickens in these years not for his stigmatisation of poverty and exploitation, but for his emphasis on kindliness and warmth. Links with Dickens's own age became valuable commodities as people born in the late Victorian period recalled Christmases of their youth for children in the 1930s.[13] Charlie Chaplin, who grew up in recognisably 'Dickensian' poverty in London in the 1890s, made a fortune in the depressed inter-war years playing the underdog; he was obsessed with *Oliver Twist*, and his take on it became *The Kid* (its young star, Jackie Coogan, later took the logical step and actually played Oliver Twist).[14] Many cinematic adaptations in these years, such as the 1935 *David Copperfield* starring W. C. Fields as Mr Micawber, consciously played up the lighter side of Dickens so as to offer temporary escape from the grim economic circumstances in which people found themselves – Jeffrey Richards has referred to them as 'fantasies of goodwill'.[15]

Dickens also remained widely read in these years. One investigation of the Newcastle public libraries in 1920 revealed that on a randomly selected day some fifty-three (out of a possible seventy-five) Dickens novels were on loan.[16] Most readers before the Second World War seem to have preferred the sunnier novels, but there were some who revelled in a perceived Dickensian radicalism. Discontented working-class readers actively preferred Dickens to Marx, the name appearing time and again in autobiographies which showed what an important role his novels had played in expanding intellectual and political horizons precisely for being so 'recognisable'. (Marx, by contrast, was too abstract and of course far too foreign.) 'All the tyrants and fools could be transmogrified into Dickens characters,' wrote M. K. Ashby, the son of a Warwickshire farm labourer, 'and once you had smiled at your enemy you could think the better how to deal with him.'[17]

It was that tradition of finding Dickens 'so real' (as the son of a Cumberland tailor put it) that came into its own in 1933, when Fleet Street editors locked horns in a remarkable tussle over readers. Various schemes were mooted to increase circulation and score an advantage over rival newspapers. The *Daily Herald* hit upon the idea of offering registered readers a sixteen-volume set of Dickens, and this inevitably threw down the gauntlet to the *Daily Mail* and *Daily Express*. Over 300,000 readers took up the offer of Dickens sets for ten shillings each, constituting a huge but apparently justifiable short-term loss to the newspapers concerned.[18] So topical did the struggle become, and so ubiquitous were rows of pristine Dickens novels in many households, that even the politicians took note. Neville Chamberlain, then Chancellor of the Exchequer, quipped in 1934 that the nation had just finished the tale of Bleak House and could now sit down in prospect of Great Expectations. It is difficult to imagine any present day politician making such literary allusions.

No doubt that is partly because our keen sense of 'Dickensian' squalor was deflated by the Second World War and its consequences. The Luftwaffe played an important role, reducing to rubble areas of London that had remained almost unchanged since Dickens had written about them. Post-war rebuilding, of course, did not restore the Victorian habitat; and it testifies to the extraordinary power of Dickens's vision that his dirty slums and narrow alleyways have continued to exist in an imaginative afterlife, even for those who have not read many of the novels. In the immediate decades after the war, however, such 'heritage' notions held little sway, and there was a concerted effort to move away from 'Dickensian' living conditions. Nowhere was this more dramatically signalled than in the Beveridge Report, which mobilised Dickensian language against the troubled legacy of Victorian living conditions. In *A Christmas Carol*, written almost exactly a century before, Dickens had invoked the spectres of two 'yellow, meagre, ragged, scowling, wolfish' children: Ignorance and Want.[19] Beveridge, taking advantage of the wartime popularity of classic novels, included these amongst the 'giants' that were to be slain: want, sickness, squalor, ignorance and idleness. And, to a large extent, slain they were in the 1950s and 1960s.

Then came the 1970s and 1980s, and the realisation that progress had its discontents. The radical Dickens again came to the fore, working his way particularly into television adaptations of the 1970s and later, which, by that stage, had become a more powerful medium for social comment than the written word. There were television versions of *Our Mutual Friend* in 1976, and, with what must have been painful contemporary resonances, of *Hard Times* in 1977. Some have argued that Dickens was used in the 1980s as a weapon with which to attack the culture of individual gain encouraged by

Margaret Thatcher. There was a superb BBC adaptation of *Bleak House* in 1985, as powerful a condemnation of greed, social indifference and legal cumbersomeness as any imaginable. In its way, the version of *Nicholas Nickleby* staged by the Royal Shakespeare Company in 1980 also seemed to run counter to many of the emerging Thatcherite trends. In its warmth and inclusiveness, its steadfast refusal to be rushed and to collapse Dickens's rich language and characterisation into convenient generalisations, it had a generosity of spirit not easily forgotten by those who experienced it. 'It is a great crackling fire, radiating joyous energy, warm-hearted affection, generous indignation, devouring interest in the variety of the human species, and a sense of hope', wrote Irving Wardle in *The Times* in 1981, 'everything that is claimed for Dickens, and everything that modern Britain is not'.[20]

This *Nicholas Nickleby* clearly fell into another category, too. For many others in the twentieth century, Dickens has connoted not so much social criticism as escapism or the simple enjoyment of life. These were the qualities emphasised by probably the best critical commentator on Dickens in the early twentieth century, G. K. Chesterton. And indeed his 1906 study of Dickens was a deliberate corrective to that of George Gissing a few years before, a work saturated with that writer's habitual gloominess. But for Chesterton the essence of Dickens was ebullience, unforgettable characterisation, passionate indignation and above all sheer cosiness. His novels, argued Chesterton, were patriotic in the old-fashioned sense of criticising 'Old Corruption', but they were patriotic too in their exploration of a quality that is uniquely English:

> [Dickens strikes] the note of comfort rather than the note of brightness; and on the spiritual side, Christian charity rather than Christian ecstasy ... This ideal of comfort belongs peculiarly to England; it belongs peculiarly to Christmas; above all, it belongs pre-eminently to Dickens ... The word 'comfort' is not indeed the right word, it conveys too much of the slander of mere sense; the true word is 'cosiness', a word not translatable. One, at least of the essentials of it is smallness, smallness in preference to largeness, smallness for smallness' sake. The merry-maker wants a pleasant parlour, he would not give twopence for a pleasant continent.[21]

And so through a dim, frost-encrusted pane we glimpse the glow of the crackling Christmas fire: in its way one of the richest legacies to the twentieth century.

Chesterton's comments also remind us vividly of the perceived Englishness of Dickens. That has been one of the agendas which, at different times and for different reasons, has served to focus our attention on Dickens's humour and high-spirited fascination with eccentrics. During the First World War, the critic André Maurois observed that 'Frenchmen were often surprised, observing English officers and soldiers, by this innocent, almost childish, cheerfulness, that joy of action, that urge to organize a game in any circumstances – all Dickensian traits'.[22] Making the best of a bad business, it is touching (and entirely credible) that soldiers shivering in the trenches preferred to mimic the Dickens characters they had seen re-enacted in music hall routines rather than read the poetry of Siegfried Sassoon or Wilfred Owen. And in the Second World War, as we have seen, readers on the home front also flocked to Dickens novels for diversion and morale-boosting. Since then, Dickens's Englishness has re-emerged in yet another context: that of the issue of European integration. When *Our Mutual Friend* was adapted for television by the BBC in 1998, it was noteworthy that the chauvinistic Mr Podsnap was excised altogether; certainly one can imagine that his way of speaking to Frenchmen 'as if he were administering something in the nature of a powder or potion to the deaf child' might have been deemed less than likely to further amity towards our European neighbours.[23] That was a telling Dickensian omission; but an equally suggestive commission was the placing of Dickens on the £10 note, the backdrop being the inimitably English scene of the cricket match at Dingley Dell.

The cheerier, or at least more evocative, side of Dickens has also featured heavily in the 'heritage industry' of the 1960s and beyond. A generation after 'Dickensian' was a dirty word, used to attack the insanitary and old-fashioned, it was back in vogue as what Raphael Samuel calls 'retrochic'. Covent Garden was redesigned in the 1970s to carry a deliberately archaic atmosphere, along with 'Dickensian' window-panes for the shops, Victorian street lamps and cobbled forecourts.[24] A similar project was undertaken in the Victorian Quarter in Leeds city centre, a place that now exudes Pickwickian warmth and plenty (despite – or perhaps because of – the beggars on the streets outside). But it was above all in Dickens's home town of Rochester that the commodification of his name took hold. A wander through that attractive but strange little city, with many of its buildings still those upon which Dickens had gazed, reveals that every second shop or café bears a name culled from the novels. It is a city that plays up its historical associations, but in some ways one feels that it is in Miss Havisham-like thrall to 'heritage'. Perhaps significantly, the original Satis House is close to the high street; smaller than Dickens's rambling version, it is no less lugubrious with its barred gateway and dark windows.

Still, there can be no doubt that many have gained from an emphasis on Dickens as an emblem of 'heritage'. Numerous adaptations, from Lionel Bart's *Oliver!* (1960) to Christine Edzard's film of *Little Dorrit* (1987) and Stefano Giannetti's 1999 ballet of *Great Expectations* (to music by Elgar, another icon of both 'heritage' and Englishness) have been identified in this respect. Edzard's film, though serious and strongly cast, worried some viewers with its fastidious approach to period detail.[25] It was not, perhaps, so much the meticulous costumes, hand-prepared and exhibited and photo-graphed for the accompanying Penguin paperback, so much as the meticulous attitude to dirt. There is indeed something rather odd about paying lavish attention to grime, for although it is necessary for the context of Dickens's novels, one feels a vague unease about returning to the condi-tions (even if only in reproduction) that the novels did so much to criticise and surmount. It is one of the paradoxes of the 'heritage industry' that consumers are so keen on experiencing Victorian dirt: but of course, if they could not do this from a safe distance, the 'heritage industry' would not exist at all. In 'heritage' views of Dickens, dirt has been transmuted to gold.

Just as often, though, the sunnier side of Dickens casts few shadows over our modern attitude to him. Dickens has always brought to mind warmth and exuberance, and rightly so. Dickens – in Frank Muir's words the 'epitome' of English humour when it was 'in the middle of a century and a half of being polite and warmly sentimental' – occupies more space than any other writer except P. G. Wodehouse in the span of the five centuries covered by *The Oxford Book of Humorous Prose*.[26] Muir recalled getting into a scrape in the 1960s talking to an audience of students in the Soviet Union about Dickens. Inevitably they were used to Marxist readings of Dickens, 'clearly a Party hero' at the time of Muir's visit. The talk, however, proved to be something of a comic parody of one of Dickens's own readings, not least since Muir spoke no Russian. 'As I had no idea what he was saying', he writes of being introduced to his audience, 'I tried to adopt a look of nonchalant amusement to give the students hope.' After forty minutes of 'waving my arms and leaping about to keep them awake', Muir gratefully moved onto questions, and found himself assailed about why he had not made more of Dickens's social criticism. He suggested that while Dickens detested nasty employers, he never suggested any viable solution to social exploitation beyond a generalised generosity of feeling.[27] Spoken in the heartland of left-wing belief, with 'Dickensian' grime all but eradicated at home, Muir had a point about the perennial freshness of the novels residing above all in their high spirits and glorious characterisation.

At first glance, these different perspectives on Dickens echo the contest that took place in the early 1980s over 'Victorian values'. Margaret Thatcher had eulogised them, but Neil Kinnock (perhaps with a nod to Dickens) qualified her positive reading by drawing attention to Victorian misery, drudgery and squalor. But the important difference between 'Victorian values' and those associated with Dickens is that the latter have been better integrated (without ever fully being pinned down) as the twentieth century has progressed. Dickens is now not only popular, but the subject of a huge scholarly industry. One of the achievements of this scholarship has been to draw together different themes within Dickens's life and work to paint a portrait of unprecedented detail and complexity. Prodigiously stocked as the Dickensian universe may be, the mind of its single creator has at least given itself to *some* tenable generalisations. For that reason it would be misleading to point up the polarities within Dickens, even though the emphasis may fall in different places according to the temperament and intention of the individual commentator. Scholars have grown used to thinking of these polarities as being all of a piece, so that it is not so much Samuel versus Muir as Samuel *and* Muir, as both writers would probably have been the first to attest.

This marriage of opposites and ambiguities has been dramatically enacted at the Charles Dickens Centre at Eastgate House in Rochester.[28] At one point, early on, the visitor enters into a warm, brightly lit room. It depicts convivial Christmas scenes from several of the novels and short stories. 'The word "Dickensian" has two contrasting meanings', the visitor's guide notes. 'Here we see its first meaning – hearty good cheer, warm friends, substantial meals, and the fellowship of family and friends.' But as soon as the visitor walks into the next room there is an effect, brilliantly achieved, of being plunged into cold and darkness. As the eyes adjust to the gloom, one perceives that the plush furnishings have given way to (imitation) rough brick and cobblestones: we have entered an alleyway in the slums. '"Dickensian" also means dark dirty grim grotesque sordid [*sic*]', the guide goes on. 'The mid-nineteenth century was Dickensian in this sense – insanitary dwellings, fever-ridden streets, narrow dark lanes. Dickens strenuously campaigned to improve living conditions for the poorer people of the big cities.' Further on there is another effective juxtaposition of rooms and themes. One room focuses upon prisons and Dickens's attitude to them; we see a model of Fagin cowering in the condemned cell, from the famous illustration by George Cruikshank. The next has talking models of Scrooge and Miss Havisham, and is about 'self-imprisonment'. 'Dickens also used the prison as a symbol. He realised that one way or another we are all imprisoned – by our past, by our fears, by the society we have created', the guide comments.

Today scholars think of Dickens much more in terms of such things as symbolism or psychological 'strategies' than used to be the case. Historicist readings, playing up the writer's engagement with issues of his day, now proliferate and show us how humour and sentiment is used in the novels to address serious matters.[29] Carlyle, as we have seen, did not think much of Dickens as a social critic because he dabbled in the 'frivolous' business of writing fiction; but it is ironic that, at a time when Carlyle is virtually unread, Dickens emerges as one of the supreme voices of Victorian satire. Dickens-as-social critic and Dickens-as-humourist are one and the same.

For Peter Ackroyd the essence of Dickens is his psychological strategy of humour, but it is a humour that complicates rather than simplifies our appreciation of the novels:

> There is only one certain and determining feature of Dickens's work, and that is its humour – this is the merest cliché, of course, but it does have an important bearing on the subject to hand. For it is not just ordinary comedy. It is a humour that dissolves ordinary categories, that explodes or defuses the most serious attempts at meaning; so it is that, when we talk of Dickens's themes and purposes, we must always be aware that they are likely to be diverted or ignored or overturned at any time.[30]

This echoes the conclusion reached by John Carey some years earlier in *The Violent Effigy*. The 'Dickensian', for Carey, is not really about social criticism or good cheer; it is about an imagination haunted by the inanimate and the grotesque, controlled and humanised only by humour. 'His humour serves as weapon and refuge', writes Carey. 'It allows him both to cut through the fake of the "real world" ... and to keep the terrors of his imagination at bay.'[31] Humour is also one of the 'siege weapons' tactically deployed against the reader's sensibilities in Malcolm Andrews's take on the Dickensian social conscience.[32] Dickens's language, often grotesque in its comic exaggeration, lacks any overt political 'message'; but in a sense the message *is* the language. The elusive, fertile imagination of Dickens therefore conspires to be many things at the same time: the cheerful, gloomy, sinister and satirical all coexist, though never in any pattern that can be easily predicted.

Readings like this are, of course, the province of specialised literary criticism, and few today would be likely to define Dickens in such a way. For most, the obvious resonances of 'Dickensian' – grim alleyways, humorous characters, Christmas cheer – will remain the most widely cited. But now, whether consciously or not, we have also grown used to a more complex Dickens. Because it complements contemporary attitudes about ourselves and our relationship with the past, this view of Dickens has been widely popularised, especially on television. A darker sense of the 'Dickensian' panders to our feeling for the prurient and the psychological. Needless to say, ratings are important in influencing the Dickens we are offered here. But in this medium Dickens does not always need much help: it has often been pointed out that his serialised novels were the Victorian equivalent of today's soap-operas. Indeed, it seems that producers and directors genuinely welcome Dickens for the extent to which he had 'anticipated' many modern concerns. At any rate, most television adaptations have managed, even where they do accentuate emotional trauma or psychological complexity, to remain broadly faithful to the text. This does not suggest a cynical attempt to make Dickens 'relevant' to modern audiences – a project destined for failure, as is any endeavour to make art (or history) 'relevant'.

Recent television versions of Dickens have shown a darker sensibility in action. *Great Expectations* was dramatised for the BBC in 1999 by Tony Marchant, a writer who had previously worked on gritty contemporary subjects. Indeed this version set out to break with the David Lean-inspired tradition, offering a 'darker and much less sentimental [view], reflecting the huge changes which have taken place since 1946'.[33] The production deliberately cast a younger and more attractive Miss Havisham in the shape of Charlotte Rampling, thereby making her relationship with Pip (Ioan Gruffudd) more obviously oedipal.[34] Much was also made of Pip's frustrated feelings for Estella (Justine Waddell), and of the emerging status of Magwitch (Bernard Hill) as a surrogate father. The legend on the cover of the video-cassette version reads: 'Desire, guilt and a young man's struggle for self-respect'.[35] (Dickens himself, it is worth remembering, was extremely coy about sex.) In Alan Bleasdale's television adaptation of *Oliver Twist* later that year, a long 'prequel' episode was added to show how Oliver came to be born in a workhouse, and to help viewers understand the inner motivations of his dastardly relatives. The 1998 BBC adaptation of *Our Mutual Friend*, while amplifying the social criticism of its 1976 predecessor about greed and social pretension, also made considerable play of the sexual jealousy of Bradley Headstone (David Morrissey) and his subsequent mental disintegration.

This more modern sense of Dickens from which literary criticism and popular presentations have been able to develop is a relatively recent phenomenon. For many years, long after the dip in esteem that commonly follows a writer's death, Dickens had languished in highbrow circles. This was partly because his novels did not accord with most of the Modernist principles that were at their height in the early twentieth century, though pause for thought might have been given by Dickens's influence on Dostoevsky, Kafka and Proust. But it was also, and perhaps more pressingly, because of the generational perspective that was such a crucial element in attitudes to the Victorians. One especially noteworthy reaction was that of Evelyn Waugh, a writer who has already emerged as one of the most telling examples in ambiguity towards the Victorian past. Waugh grew up to the sound of Dickens being read aloud by his father, an authority on Dickens and occasional chairman of meetings of the newly-formed Fellowship.[36] Father and son did not get on well, but in later years Waugh exacted his revenge on his father and Dickens.

In *A Handful of Dust* (1934) the hero, Tony Last, becomes lost in the Brazilian jungle and is rescued by a tribe presided over by the mysterious Mr Todd. He is persuaded, in a strange inversion of the filial relationship, to read aloud to Mr Todd every day from a set of Dickens novels (a topical allusion, perhaps, to the sets being offered by Fleet Street?). But Tony soon finds himself imprisoned by this routine, and it is Waugh's grim joke – underlined by the proximity of 'Todd' to the German *Tod* (death) – that it can literally be purgatory to read Dickens. And it is some measure of Waugh's obsession with the theme that he returned to it twenty years later, even as he himself was turning into a Victorian patriarch. In his penultimate novel, *The Ordeal of Gilbert Pinfold* (1957), Waugh describes a semi-autobiographical incident in which he was plagued by 'voices' during a cruise – the voices, apparently, having been induced by a cocktail of stress, sleeping tablets and alcohol. The first auditory hallucination features someone reminiscent of Mr Chadband, Dickens's obsequious clergyman; the ship's captain has the same name as David Copperfield's unfaithful friend, Steerforth; and Pinfold, turning the tables, tries to bore the voices into submission by reading aloud passages of mid-Victorian literature. Waugh had been reading Edgar Johnson's biography of Dickens in the months before his 'madness' in 1954.[37]

Waugh's profound ambivalence towards Dickens took place against the backdrop of a number of intellectual developments which were transforming his posthumous reputation. The recognisably 'modern' Dickens took shape around the 1940s, the years in which a distinctive breakthrough was made in appreciation of the artistry that underpinned his creative vision. This enabled people to probe beneath the surface of Dickens as never before, and to use the novels as a way of exploring new perspectives on the past. There are four interconnected factors or developments to be considered in this context.

First, there was the longstanding interest amongst intellectuals in psychological theory, particularly of the Freudian type. Freud's writings had begun to make an impact amongst a few readers before the First World War, but it was really in the inter-war years that his ideas made their influence felt. Freudian theory gave observers in the 1920s and 1930s another way of relating to history, and this was particularly important since attitudes to Victorianism were still being fiercely negotiated. The work of Dickens, it became increasingly clear, was not only one way of approaching this process of negotiation but was ripe for Freudian analysis in itself. Dickens was always powerfully concerned with the way that childhood experience can shadow, influence and sometimes erupt through the otherwise calm exterior of adult life: there are many people in the novels hampered by unhappy childhoods, or by 'repressing' an earlier life. *David Copperfield*, perhaps Dickens's most auto-biographical novel, and an innovative attempt to recreate and order the perceptions of a small boy, was one of Freud's favourite novels.

In Dickens's work there are no fewer than 318 children who lack at least one parent, and of course plenty of children with both parents but living in dysfunctional circumstances; and the connection between this and the writer's own life was not difficult to make.[38] There had been early trauma: at twelve Dickens had lost a sense of childhood innocence, and acquired a fear of poverty, when he was sent to work in a blacking factory while his father was imprisoned for debt. We can immediately see all manner of resonances: the impecunious Mr Micawber, the Marshalsea debtors' prison, Pip's determination (and guilt) about making a gentleman of himself, Dickens's own manic compulsion to work and earn money. In the age of popular psychoanalysis these themes came to the surface fully for the first time. Dickens had been so haunted by the blacking factory episode that he kept it even from his children during his lifetime. But he confided it to John Forster, his close friend, and the biography published a couple of years after Dickens's death in 1870 had disclosed it to the world. Seventy years later, the literary scholar Edmund Wilson drew upon this and subsequent reve-lations to interpret Dickens in an explicitly Freudian light.[39] Were not the novels, he argued, marked by an unconscious rage against parental figures? Did not Dickens's cheerful public face hide a much darker character within? And were not characters like John Jasper in *The Mystery of Edwin Drood*, the respectable public figure who may have murdered his nephew, actually reflections of the author's own divided soul? Those were the questions that readers were learning to ask by 1940.

The second factor relates to the growing professionalisation of literary criticism up to the Second World War. Until then, Dickensian scholarship had tended to be dominated by writing of three types. One was outright disparagement of Dickens's supposed vulgarity and lack of subtlety. Anthony Trollope, perhaps not without a trace of professional jealousy, referred to Dickens as 'Mr Popular Sentiment', and in 1872 G. H. Lewes commented that some Dickensian characters were like 'frogs whose brains have been taken out for physiological purposes'.[40] Another strand of criticism appreci-ated Dickens's radicalism. Marx thought that Dickens had 'issued to the world more political and social truths than have been uttered by all the professional politicians, publicists and moralists put together'.[41] After the Russian Revolution and the upheaval of the First World War such political readings inevitably continued, although there is little evidence that they were widely influential. The third type of criticism was the most widespread, and that was the kind that revelled in 'Dickensian' good cheer, comic eccentricity and sheer high spirits.

Dickens was rarely accorded the status of a serious novelist, partly because he attracted the attentions of readers obsessed with finding the original locations for scenes in the novels, or solving the mystery of Edwin Drood. Issues of the *Dickensian* dating from the inter-war years are full of such trivia. The professional critics left well alone. Percy Lubbock, the Jamesian disciple, placed great emphasis on the filigree construction of novels without some imposingly Victorian authorial voice. E. M. Forster in his splendidly chatty *Aspects of the Novel* (1927) took a less rarefied view, although was again not keen on the loudness of the Dickensian moral voice. 'Sometimes', he writes, comparing Dickens with Wells, 'the lively surface of their prose scratches like a cheap gramophone record, a certain poorness of quality appears, and the face of the author draws rather too near to that of the reader.' [42]

It was a perception of Dickens's very lack of moral seriousness, or rather his inability to find a sufficiently serious artistic framework for his morality, that meanwhile lay behind the criticism of F. R. and Q. D. Leavis. Queenie Leavis had already castigated Dickens for being a purveyor of 'crude emotional exercises' that were lapped up by the new middle-class audience for cheap serials. [43] F. R. Leavis even more famously kept Dickens shivering in the vestibule of his 1948 house-party of novelists in the 'great tradition' (Austen, Eliot, James, Conrad and Lawrence). There Dickens's *Hard Times* – his only 'completely serious work of art' – was relegated to an appendix. But subsequently the Leavises relented on the issue of the author's artistry, writing a more appreciative centenary study with the pointed title *Dickens the Novelist*. It is tempting to record that this lifelong ambivalence echoes that of Waugh: for little Frank Leavis had also been subjected by his father, a great enthusiast, to readings of Dickens. [44] It seems possible that Leavis, in an oddly Dickensian way, may have been influenced by the shadow of his childhood. There is a telling footnote added to a later edition of *The Great Tradition* that stands in relation to his earlier denigration of Dickens as merely an entertainer of genius. 'Childhood memory and the potent family-reading experience must be invoked to excuse what is absurd in this paragraph', he reflects. 'I now think that, if any one writer can be said to have created the modern novel, it is Dickens.' [45]

This breakthrough was anticipated by a new wave of critical readings around 1940–41: a series of interpretations that was coincidental in its timing, but benefited from many of the trends and disclosures of the previous couple of decades. Wilson's Freudian view of Dickens has already been mentioned, but also in 1940 there appeared George Orwell's superb essay which re-examined the writer from the radical-patriotic stance that would soon emerge in Orwell's own *The Lion and the Unicorn*. Orwell was a member of the so-called 'Auden Generation', and it may have been that, like many in the war-torn climate of 1940, he turned to the past for inspiration and for a guide to moral leadership. This he found in Dickens, but not in any straightforward or naive sense. For although he wrote about the ferocity of Dickens's attack on English institutions, Orwell also acknowledged his deeply Victorian conservatism. Of the depiction of mob violence in *Barnaby Rudge* Orwell observed: 'You might almost think you were reading a description of "Red" Spain by a partisan of General Franco.' 'The moralist and the revolutionary are constantly undermining one another', he concluded, celebrating instead Dickens's Little Englander quietism and emphasis on kindliness.[46] The path was being laid towards viewing Dickens as a social critic who used means other than simple moralising. Orwell's view was endorsed and developed by Humphry House in *The Dickens World* (1941), a work that deepened the sense of the symbolism and ambiguity within the novels. House went even further than Orwell in arguing that Dickens's moral sense was supported by a formidable artistic armoury: and so we learnt, for example, that the fog at the beginning of *Bleak House* may be a symbol for legal obfuscation, and that the dust-heaps that are a source of wealth in *Our Mutual Friend* may be a comment on the nature of that wealth (especially, as House noted, since Victorian dust-heaps generally contained human excrement).

Such new conceptions of Dickens owed a great deal to fresh biographical insights during the 1930s, the third factor to be considered here. This was part of the neo-Stracheyan impulse to look behind the confident façade of eminent Victorians, and to emphasise the underlying complexity of figures once thought not entirely human. Dickens provided ripe material for such investigations, especially in the light of the Freudian climate to which readers were becoming accustomed. It was speculation about the women in Dickens's life that proved to be so controversial. And the facts were well known: Dickens had split with his wife Catherine in 1858 after forming a liaison with the actress Ellen Ternan. Stranger still, Catherine's sister, Georgina, stayed on as the mistress of the house after Catherine had left Dickens. This caused many rumours at the time, and after Dickens's death it stimulated renewed interest in what he had felt about a third sister, Mary Hogarth, who had died in 1837 at the age of seventeen. Dickens was deeply traumatised by her death. Further evidence that Dickens had married the 'wrong' Hogarth sister emerged with interest in the sudden end of a love affair with Maria Beadnell, an event that was supposed to have sent the writer into the arms of Catherine shortly afterwards. All of these happenings have long been connected with Dickens's writing: after all, there are a number of adolescent girls (most famously Little Nell) who die prematurely in the novels. More generally there is a preoccupation with sexual innocence and purity: Freudian readings now trace the repressed aspect of Dickens's libido through dark characters such as Daniel Quilp, Bradley Headstone and John Jasper.[47]

John Forster had been discreet about Dickens's later years in his biography of 1872–74, and left out altogether mention of Ellen Ternan, but later writers felt less restricted by posthumous devotion and Victorian reticence.[48] In 1928 a biography written in the form of a novel by 'Ephesian' (C. E. Bechhoffer Roberts), *This Side Idolatry*, played upon the traumas in Dickens's life caused by his amorous impulses. Pressure was subsequently put upon Sir Henry Fielding Dickens, the last surviving son, to set the record straight about Maria Beadnell. He yielded, and a collection of correspondence between his father and Maria Beadnell appeared in 1936. The editor of that volume, Walter Dexter, also produced an important three-volume set of Dickens's letters for the Nonesuch edition of 1938. This correspondence appeared against the backdrop of ever greater fascination with Dickens's private life, and it is not difficult to perceive about them a corrective value. In 1934 Thomas Wright, an elderly biographer, published even more extensive revelations about Dickens's relationship in the *Daily Express*. (The newspaper may have seen this as an opportunity to claw back some of the money it had lost over the expensive sets of novels offered the previous year.) Wright claimed that Dickens had fathered a child by Ternan, and these allegations were confirmed in 1939 by a memoir of Kate Perugini, the last surviving daughter, adding for good measure that Dickens had been a bad father. Hugh Kingsmill thought at the time that the revelation of Dickens's relationship with Ternan was 'the most important contribution to the biography of Dickens in this century'.[49]

No longer, after all these revelations and recriminations, would Dickens be quite the same. Not could he be dismissed merely as the embodiment of Victorian sentimentality and high spirits. This darker Dickens was a driven soul: traumatised by his impoverished youth and unhappy marriage, often at odds with society, and a channel for all manner of dark symbolism and psychological resonance. The melancholy, inscrutable eye that stares at us in Eastgate House had started to come into focus. And strikingly enough, it was the visual that was the fourth factor in creating the sense of a modern Dickens. Innovations within cinematic theory and practice in the 1940s not only set the seal upon this new view of Dickens, but helped to popularise it. Cinematic adaptations of Dickens until then had been predominantly light in tone, full of pastoral associations and images of plenty. This reflected both a cheerier, old-fashioned attitude to Dickens, and, in the 1930s, a conscious drive to escape from the gloomy Depression-ridden circumstances of the day.

This changed quite dramatically in the 1940s. In 1944, Sergei Eisenstein published his influential essay on 'Dickens, Griffith and the Film Today'. D. W. Griffith, a popular as well as a critically-respected director, made only one Dickens adaptation (*The Cricket on the Hearth*, in 1909), but more generally acknowledged the writer's influence on the cinema, particularly with respect to montage. Within a couple of years David Lean had gone on to produce his superbly atmospheric, often lugubrious, versions of *Great Expectations* (1946) and *Oliver Twist* (1948). Lean was given the Nonesuch edition of Dickens as a birthday present in 1940, and had been devouring the novels ever since. As an admirer of Griffith, and being determined to bring the techniques of German silent cinema to British screens, Lean made sure that his adaptations were full of modernistic touches that would have been almost unimaginable a few years earlier.

Probably Lean was not familiar with the writings of House and Wilson, but it is interesting that he thought the key to Dickens his almost surreal characters, and that he began an extensive course of psychoanalysis during the shooting of *Oliver Twist*. Many critics found the films perplexingly cold and intellectual, not at all the Dickens to which they were used. Still, they scored commercial successes, even if some cinema-goers were confused by the talking cows at the beginning of *Great Expectations*. Lean defended himself by pointing out that 'We were not aiming at reality. What we wanted to create all the time was the world as it seemed to Pip when his imagination was distorted with fear. That, after all, was what Dickens himself did.' [50]

Just as Dickens engaged with the society of his time, so did Lean's adaptations show the imprint of their age. *Oliver Twist* is less striking here, although there was some consternation over the Jewishness of Fagin (played by Alec Guinness) in the wake of the Holocaust. Lean's bid for authenticity of feeling was also notable: it extended to employing a convicted burglar as a research assistant, and using the splendid Robert Newton as Bill Sikes. The problem with Newton was that he was consistently inebriated through-out shooting, affording, to those unaccustomed to the nimbleness of the habitually tipsy, a degree of anxiety over the rooftop scenes. But it is really the closing minutes of *Great Expectations* that suggests something about the nature of Lean's vision of history. Here film and novel diverge slightly in outline and greatly in tone. In the film Pip (John Mills) returns to a darkened Satis House, finding Estella (Valerie Hobson) rejected by Bentley Drummle and about to take up residence amidst the dust and shadows as another

Miss Havisham. But Pip, with much excitement about this being a 'dead house' and 'letting in the sunlight', dramatically tears down the tattered curtains, and saves Estella from repeating the past. The last shot shows them running out of the house into the sunshine.

For Raphael Samuel, this remarkable scene may have been 'to align it to the social-democratic vision of 1945, a dream of light and space'.[51] There might be much in this determination to clear away the dirt and darkness of the past, forbidding history to repeat itself; that was certainly one of the negative readings of 'Victorian' during the Second World War, and one against which the vision of a Dickensian social conscience had been invoked. Yet it may also have been simply Lean's instinct for a neat and psychologically resonant ending. Dickens himself, as it happens, had experienced trouble finishing the novel back in 1861. His first thoughts, echoing a sadly deflating encounter six years earlier with the now married and far less engaging Maria Beadnell, had been to have a brief meeting between Pip and a married Estella that ended with a parting under mistaken circumstances: Estella believes that Pip has married Biddy. Dickens was persuaded to make the revised ending marginally more optimistic, with Pip and Estella meeting up again at Satis House to pledge friendship to one another.

The more complex Dickens that we know today can therefore be traced to the years around the Second World War, as so often a significant dividing-line in attitudes to the Victorians. Relatively few readers will have had contact with the mass of scholarly publications that flow unabated from the presses, and few will have considered issues like cinematic technique. But we are all psychologists now. We have no trouble with the late, darker novels as our predecessors did sixty or seventy years ago. And to a surprising extent we have grown used to looking for high contrasts, contradictions and psychological depth within Dickens, from Lean's cinematic masterpieces to the juxtaposed rooms of Eastgate House.

Our relationship with Dickens is, of course, a two-way affair. For if we have invented a modern sense (or senses) of 'Dickensian', investing it with contemporary preoccupations about 'heritage', social and political life, and a deep interest in matters of psychology, sex and identity, then Dickens has also furnished us with a sort of *éducation sentimentale*. Many of his concerns are still with us: attitudes to Europe can have more than a whiff of Podsnappery (Little Englander as Dickens was); politicians are apt to strike the Pecksniffian pose; but, above all, issues of social aspiration, snobbery and exploitation of one kind or another continue to haunt our consumer-based culture.

Dickens himself can fall prey to this very consumerism, becoming an object of blind nostalgia or of adaptations which lack elements vital to his writing: bite and energy. In like fashion, 'Dickensian' can also be taken as a rather flat reflection of the Victorian age, or of an attitude to it which we feel compelled to adopt. As we have already noted, 'Dickensian' seems almost at times to come before 'Victorian'. Asked about the workhouse in the nineteenth century, our thoughts are bound to fly before long to *Oliver Twist*; asked about Victorian London generally, Dickens becomes virtually inescapable. This is where the great value of the modern, more complex sense of Dickens lies. Critics have often been keen to point out that he did not merely reflect his age, but engaged with it and helped to change it. That is why the life of Dickens remains important as well as interesting: for it is in his 'use' of the Victorian age, and in our subsequent 'use' of Dickens, that we can trace his contribution to modernity and the nature of our response to it.

# 11

# *Gladstone*

One of the many casualties of the First World War was the Liberal Party. The great Victorian party of progress, reform and moral conscience was never quite the same after Gallipoli, the Somme and Passchendaele. By the late 1920s, after a string of decimating electoral results, it was a pale shadow of its flourishing Edwardian self – the resounding voice of David Lloyd George, introducing old age pensions or rallying the attack on the House of Lords, now a mere echo. Historians, always apt to don the guise of the coroner, are still puzzled about this bizarre reversal of fortunes. The earliest coroner's report came in from George Dangerfield in *The Strange Death of Liberal England* (1935), a brilliant but flawed book that subsumed the author's own anti-Victorianism within a reading of history that sought to condemn Liberalism to the rubbish heap of the past.[1] For Dangerfield, Liberalism was quite simply a defunct creed by the turn of the twentieth century: feverishly rejected by hysterical suffragettes and suicidal politicians alike, the voice of Victorian moderation had no place in the modern world.

Victorian Liberalism, for Dangerfield, was as dead as a door-nail. But others, when his book was published in England in 1936, disagreed. A reviewer in the *Times Literary Supplement* noted that 'The most noble traits of the England he buried can be studied in last week's Hansard'.[2] The distinguished historian R. C. K. Ensor concurred, arguing that 'Not all of us believe progress to be an illusion or Liberalism to be dead in England'.[3] Such arguments have been replicated and developed ever since.[4] But the point about Dangerfield's attack on Liberalism, and the concerned defence of historians in the 1930s on both the left (like Ensor) and the right (like G. M. Young), is that they testify to an anxiety about the place of the past in the present. In the 1930s, as we have seen, there was a veritable flowering of nostalgia for the Victorian age amongst those who felt that Britain might be heading for the abyss. Liberalism featured in no small way, whether it was in the gradual move away from government economy at home or in comparison with the hectoring tone of fascism abroad. And it was, of course, above all William Ewart Gladstone who dominated these retrospective views of a golden age of Liberalism in Britain. Here is a suggestive paradox:

Liberalism as an organised political creed may never really have recovered its footing after the First World War; but Gladstone, its great colossus, towered over twentieth-century views of Victorianism. Constantly reinterpreted and reconfigured to suit new readings and needs, Gladstone has scarcely ever been out of sight. It is tempting to think that, had Gladstone not lived, we would have had to invent him.

For much of the twentieth century, at least while the values of public duty held sway within the corridors of power, Gladstone remained the Grand Old Man. Philip Magnus, in the first important biography of Gladstone after the Second World War, felt no unease about writing of his subject in unashamedly laudatory terms. 'He towered in moral grandeur over his contemporaries', Magnus reflected in 1954, 'and stood before the world as the inspired prophet of the nineteenth-century liberal experiment.'[5] To civilised writers of Magnus's ilk – he was a civil servant and magistrate, born in 1906 and schooled in gentlemanly values – this was indeed the example that Gladstone had lain down for posterity. And in many senses Gladstone's life, so rich in energy and contradiction, had something to offer everyone interested in the values of tradition. For Gladstone was a strange amalgam of Conservative and Liberal values, bridging the two in what was (initially at least) a non-partisan fashion to shape a core of 'liberal' values about which many who lived into the twentieth century were nostalgic. Certainly in later years he became adept at the game of party politics, scoring tactical points against his arch-rival Disraeli and the jingoistic policies the latter's followers had espoused. But essentially Gladstone remained a conviction politician, his convictions based upon a profound High Anglican faith and a perception of the world into which he had been born.

This was a very different world from that of the twentieth century, and there were elements of Gladstone's intellectual and emotional make-up that many found alien after his death in 1898: chiefly, of course, the astonishing and unquestioning moral fervour. That in part was a product of Gladstone's evangelical inheritance, having been born in 1809 the son of a one-time Calvinist who had moved to Liverpool and become a highly successful, if no less devout, businessman and Anglican. Gladstone was not alone in taking the step from evangelical Anglicanism to a High Church position in the years around the time of Queen Victoria's accession: these were, after all, the years of the Oxford Movement. The general evangelical legacy, however, remained: in Gladstone's profound conviction that he was directly accountable to God and perpetually teetering on the edge of sin, he was characteristic of a number of socially-conscious people at the time. One corollary, the commitment to public duty, was clear enough; indeed, without the vigorous activities of evangelicals like Henry Thornton and William Wilberforce, it seems doubtful that slavery would have been abolished in the British Empire as early as it was (in 1833). Strikingly enough, Gladstone's father was a beneficiary of slavery, owning sugar plantations in the West Indies which included black workers. Having entered Parliament in 1832 as a Tory MP for Newark, Gladstone's maiden speech on 3 June 1833 was both a defence of his father and a call for the gradual abolition of slavery.[6]

Such caution owed itself not only to filial reverence. For Gladstone had earlier opposed the so-called Great Reform Act, fearing, like many conservative-minded people, that it might lead straight to revolution. Gladstone was steeped in the writings of Edmund Burke, the politician and writer who had so castigated the French Revolution. For Burke, and subsequently for Gladstone, politics was about the responsible stewardship of a living organic state. This was always essentially to be Gladstone's outlook on politics, even after he began to advocate the granting of votes to working-class men in 1866, and even after many Liberals thought he had parted with his senses by advocating Home Rule for Ireland in 1886. In the first case Gladstone now perceived many working-class men to be responsible, and in the second he had internalised Burke's argument that the British Empire would be strengthened by encouraging not coercion but a more relaxed sense of shared identity. Whether as Tory or as Liberal, Gladstone was moulded by the circumstances of his youth and early reading. Like many men educated in nineteenth-century Britain, Gladstone's natural frame of reference was classical: from Aristotle he had imbibed a sense of the naturalness of the governing order; from Homer and Dante (the latter for the religious aspect) he had picked up the sense of a noble and elevated European-wide Christian order; and from Plato he had derived ideas about the perfectibility of politics as a human endeavour.[7] Few of his peers and successors were as scholarly as Gladstone himself, but at least until the Second World War the ethos of 'character' as schooled by the classics was a shared viewpoint amongst members of the political establishment. (G. M. Young, who dropped Greek quotations as if they were commonplaces, was even a little sniffy about Gladstone's merits as a classical scholar as late as 1936.)[8]

Even after 'the rising hope of those stern and unbending Tories' (as Macaulay dubbed him in 1839) wandered into the political wilderness in 1846, subsequently joining the newly-reorganised Liberal Party in 1859 and rising to become its most famous leader, there were strong elements of continuity across Gladstone's long and varied career. He was always 'conservative' (small 'c') every bit as much as he became more and more 'Liberal' (capital 'L'). The watchful martialling of economic resources, the belief in free competition, the commitment to moral causes: all, in a sense, reflected the loosely-defined 'liberal' belief in order and progress to which commentators of every non-extremist political hue after 1918 could lay claim. Particularly in an era in which there was no prominent political party to push for a cogently-defined set of practical Liberal policies, it is easy to see how Gladstone increasingly became a figure whose life could be selectively plundered for nostalgic contrasts between venerable tradition and squalid present-day practice.

So, too, must it have struck some more historically-minded observers that much of Gladstone's outlook was forged in the aftermath of an all-consuming European war: one of his first memories was that of the sound of cannons being fired from Edinburgh Castle in 1814 to signal the abdication of Napoleon Bonaparte.[9] Much of what followed in the Victorian age – the concern with economic efficiency after a hugely expensive war, the anxious eye for European stability and international order – was a consequence of the Napoleonic Wars. Gladstone's part in shaping the 'liberal' profile of politics from the 1830s down to his retirement in 1894 resonated powerfully with later generations whose own century would be scarred by the legacy of two world wars. At Versailles in 1919, when the map was being redrawn after five grim years of war and mass destruction, the allied plenipotentiaries found themselves sitting together during a lull in the proceedings. They talked about political reputations. Georges Clemenceau, the wily walrus-moustached French premier, leaned across to Lloyd George and asked: 'What about your Gladstone?'. 'He was a very great man', the Welsh wizard immediately replied, having himself just run a war (and split the Liberal Party) with an uncompromising missionary zeal that harkened back to his eminent predecessor.[10]

The absence of the Grand Old Man was even more ruefully noted as the inter-war period progressed, shedding its unhappy load of diplomatic recrimination and financial hardship. The League of Nations, founded in 1919, was set up along lines that recognisably echoed the ideal of the Concert of Europe cherished by George Canning, and in later years by his protégé Gladstone. It was this passion for European harmony and civilisation that contrasted so painfully with the juncture to which, in retrospect, diplomatic relations had come by 1914. What had gone wrong with British foreign policy? The answer for some, in a nutshell, was Disraeli. Gladstone and Disraeli had famously come head to head in 1876 over the issue of Bulgarian atrocities: Bulgaria had been witness to a massacre of Christian inhabitants by their oppressive Turkish overlords. Disraeli, ever shrewd and imperial-minded, saw (as many did) that the Ottoman Empire was a dwindling power: it had long been known as the 'Sick Man of Europe'. Its collapse would, in tactical terms, by no means be favourable to the welfare of the

British Empire; if the Turks lost their footing in the Balkans, the Russians might well expand into the vacuum and endanger crucial trading and military connections with the jewel in the imperial crown, India. And so, when the Russians declared war on the Turks, claiming pan-Slavonic empathy with the butchered Bulgarians, it was anti-Russian feeling that Disraeli orchestrated in Britain.

It was sufficient to bring Gladstone, eyes ablaze and hair in wild disarray, out of the retirement he had claimed for himself the previous year, vehemently denouncing the heathen Turks and barbaric Tories. In the event, although Gladstone revived a political career that would unexpectedly go on for another eighteen years, it was Disraeli's approach that prevailed. The Russian threat was contained, but with a brand of calculatingly modern diplomacy that was alien to the lofty post-Napoleonic atmosphere which Gladstone breathed. The Balkans were effectively fragmented so as to make it all the more difficult for them to be annexed by a larger external power. But fragmentation eventually led to the rise of nationalism; and the rise of Balkan nationalism set the fuse that would light the bomb of the First World War. In hindsight, some inter-war observers came to regret bitterly that Bismarckian *Realpolitik* had held sway in European diplomacy at the turn of the twentieth century. And, although times had inevitably moved on from those when Napoleon had been the great scourge of Europe, the ideal of a concerted effort to resolve diplomatic disputes seemed one that had been dreadfully squandered in the light of so many needless sacrifices and so many unresolved tensions. As the diplomatic historian R. W. Seton-Watson reflected, the year before Mussolini marched into Abyssinia and two years before Hitler remilitarised the Rhineland: 'the whole subsequent history of the Near East bears witness to the prophetic vision of Gladstone ... to the clear-sighted in 1878 [Balkan nationalism] was bound to end as we in 1934 see that it has ended'.[11]

It had ended in the bloodiest war yet known to man, and shockwaves that toppled monarchies like ninepins across Europe. There was, almost inevitably, a subsequent softening of hard-headed diplomacy within government circles: Piers Brendon writes that in the 1930s 'even the most flagrant practitioners of *Realpolitik* [clung] to the fig-leaf of morality'.[12] The link between Gladstonian morality and the League of Nations was clear. 'His principles are now accepted as commonplace at Geneva, the Hague, and Washington', Herbert Gladstone wrote of his father in 1928. 'Had the truth of them been realised earlier the world would have been spared the catastrophe of the Great War.'[13] But, where wars and rumours of wars are concerned, we must be careful not to presume that Gladstone would have been an advocate of appeasement. Some, admittedly, did think along these lines in the late 1930s. In H. R. Williamson's 1937 play *Mr Gladstone* the following scene occurs:

Gladstone: 'If Germany announced her intention to dominate Europe by arms in the cause of peace, should we allow it?'

Morley:   'I suppose not.'

Gladstone: 'You *suppose* not? You know not. Why, then, should we expect them to allow us? If we arm, everyone arms; and the end of that is war.' [14]

Britain was ill-prepared for war in 1937, but that was almost certainly more an issue of desperate financial hardship than one of Gladstonian morality. What may have been viable in the 1850s and 1860s was not necessarily viable seventy years on. 'How far and feeble are the voices raised in Europe to-day for this essential Liberalism, how many and strident those who decide it as a decadent survival from a past age', lamented one commentator in 1937.[15]

Neville Chamberlain, long collared as the guiltiest of the 'Guilty Men', was in fact sceptical of the ostensibly 'Gladstonian' attitude of the League of Nations, arguing that he saw little reason to go to war 'because of a quarrel in a far-away country between people of whom we know nothing'.[16] Chamberlain – 'the English fox' as Goebbels called him – was in no rush to adopt the high moral line that Gladstone had done when he called for the Turks to be booted out of Europe 'bag and baggage' in 1876. The ghost of Gladstone may have hovered over the League of Nations, but it was to the tune of Disraeli that foreign policy marched after 1914. At least, that is, until 1940 and the coming of Churchill. For Churchill – himself also a man who had belonged to both the Conservative and Liberal Parties – was an admirer of Gladstone; and, like Lloyd George a generation before, his leadership of the nation during a time of war was suffused with the language and rhetoric of Christian endeavour. Might Gladstone, too, have viewed the war against Hitler as a moral crusade? Later, when advocating something like European integration, Churchill would quote Gladstone on forgiveness – as Geoffrey Best comments, the key to Churchill in these years might have been his own comment: 'In Victory, Magnanimity. In Peace, Goodwill'.[17]

Another lost opportunity regretted in these years was Gladstone's policy of Home Rule for Ireland. His Bills, subject of the most heated and vehement debate in Parliament, had been defeated in 1886 and 1893. Gladstone split the Liberal Party on the issue, but it later reunited on the policy, introducing a further Bill in 1912 that would have become law (after characteristic delaying tactics from the Conservatives) in 1914. But the war intervened, rerouting the nationalist cause into the bloody path of the Easter Uprising and the breakaway of the Irish Free State in 1921. There followed a state of virtual civil war, with the assassination of Michael Collins and the attempted takeover by the IRA. In Ulster, too, the landscape of bitter Protestant-Catholic enmity was soon being mapped out. 'What fools we were not to have accepted Gladstone's Home Rule Bill', George V remarked to Ramsay Mac-Donald in 1930. 'The Empire now would not have had the Irish Free State giving us so much trouble and pulling us to pieces.'[18] Six years earlier, Churchill *fils* had uncharacteristically contradicted Churchill *père* ('Ulster will fight and Ulster will be right') by arguing that Ireland should have been granted Home Rule when Gladstone first attempted it.[19]

For all Gladstone's failure to accept the intransigence of Ulster and the mishandling of his own party over Home Rule, his reputation as a visionary remained undimmed amongst those still faithful to liberal causes. Francis Birrell, the son of the Chief Secretary for Ireland between 1908 and 1916, temporarily hung up his Bloomsbury credentials to admire the craggy profile of Gladstone as lone hero. He marvelled in 1933 at the idea of 'this old gentleman of seventy-six' grappling fearlessly 'with a shattering position'.[20] But this characteristically heroic vision of Gladstone was embraced most enthusiastically by J. L. Hammond in his landmark study of 1938. Hammond, alert to the slightest hint of exploitation in the nineteenth century, preferred the ideal of responsible patriarchal authority that he found in classical civilisation; and this in turn connected felicitously with Gladstone's own veneration of the classics. Gladstone became, in Hammond's view, a kind of Homeric protagonist in the Irish Question, fated to incomplete under-standing of his situation but battling with a 'large imaginative understanding' for civilised values. 'Gladstone saw the whole Irish problem with very different eyes from his contemporaries', Hammond explained. 'He saw on the horizon the shadows of the evils that fill the mind of all liberal Europe today; the dangers of an age in which the organized worship of the power of the State threatens to destroy all sense of spiritual values.'[21]

Such were the kind of views of Gladstone prevalent amongst politicians and historians up to the Second World War. Although, as we shall see, by no means without his critics in these years, he remained in essence 'Mr Gladstone': the grand embodiment of a lofty approach to the business of politics. It is a measure, however, of the extent to which the Second World War and the subsequent post-war settlement changed the very nature of politics that the Gladstonian tradition was markedly reconfigured after 1945. Public duty and the great mystique of 'character' were still, at least until the 1960s, highly valued qualities within government. But the political and economic terrain which had already altered since the death of Gladstone changed all the more radically in the era of the Welfare State and Cold War.

On these things the shadow of Gladstone could not be prompted to utter a great deal: neither his belief in government economy nor in international brotherhood sat easily alongside the climate of the 1950s and 1960s. Nor, even after the resurgence of the troubles in Northern Ireland in the 1970s, would any politician think it worthwhile to regret in public or at any length the passing of the Gladstonian moment in 1886: too many years had elapsed since then. In these years it was increasingly biography that dominated and revolutionised attitudes to Gladstone, and in a way made him more prominent than ever.

Then, as the post-war consensus began to break down amidst social and economic difficulties in the late 1970s, things began to change again. The arrival of Margaret Thatcher as Prime Minister in 1979 was a watershed, not least because she declared war on thirty years of neo-Keynesian practice by espousing 'Victorian values' of a recognisably Gladstonian hue. And of course she prosecuted her war on excessive government spending and the culture of dependency by resurrecting the language and style of 'conviction' politics that Gladstone had made his own in the 1870s and 1880s. There are indeed recognisable affinities between Thatcher and Gladstone in the shared belief that finance is intrinsically linked with morality. Gladstone, in his great budgets of the 1850s, had sought to make the payment of income tax commensurate with the holding of the vote, his hope being that this would encourage voters to put moral pressure on the government for financial accountability.[22] (His hopes were in fact almost immediately dashed: the nation rejoiced at news of an expensive outing to thrash the Russians in the Crimea.) Thatcher, too, wanted to put the moral incentive on citizens for political and economic responsibility by redrawing the line between state and individual.

With post-Thatcherite perspective, however, historians have become careful about glib comparisons with Gladstone.[23] Believing in an organic approach to politics, Gladstone sought to develop a flexible but naturally evolving approach to state authority; taking a divisive 'them' and 'us' attitude to politics, Thatcher radically hacked away at tradition. Thatcher the Conservative would probably have been too revolutionary for Gladstone the Liberal. Such a counterfactual speculation is, in any case, not terribly helpful: for Britain of the 1880s was a very different world from Britain of the 1980s. Political and economic strategies grow out of historical contexts, and Gladstone and Thatcher spoke different 'languages', even if the latter thought she could ventriloquise the former.[24]

What resonated more powerfully, especially with the lavish resources of the fourteen-volume *Gladstone Diaries* published between 1968 and 1994 and a flurry of excellent biographies, was the legacy of the Gladstone *style* within politics.[25] The old view of Gladstone as a great exponent of public duty and moral force within politics had, in a way, taken him out of the 'Gladstonian'. Here the problem was that Gladstone tended to be isolated within the historical imagination, seen as a force of nature rather than as an executive politician responding to the ebb and flow of the political tide. And, as the details of Gladstone's inner life and political timetable became clearer in light of the publication of the diaries, historians began to speculate on his manipulation of the party machine.[26] Traditionally Disraeli had always been seen as the Machiavellian mirror-image of Gladstone and the latter's saintly sense of purpose in politics. Increasingly, though, it was Gladstone who emerged in the 1980s and 1990s as the most fascinatingly 'modern' character where the practice of shrewd party politics was concerned. He was, after all, the first Prime Minister to make extensive use of technology and the media. The Midlothian campaign, which catapulted Gladstone back into power in 1880, was typical: a series of whistlestop speeches by train, with each brilliant oration supported by extensive newspaper coverage the following day.[27] 'Even if the speech itself was not delivered,' comments Peter Clarke dryly, 'the press handout was.'[28]

Gladstone became extremely adept at gauging the public mood and responding to it accordingly. There is no need for undue cynicism, given that he came to believe that God – always a mover in mysterious ways – spoke to him through the people. The evangelical inheritance was clear: just as Gladstone kept a rigorous diary account of his every waking moment for God's scrutiny, so God inscribed indications of divine will on the public mood of the day.[29] As early as 1832 Gladstone had already asserted: 'Restrict the sphere of politics to earth, and it becomes a secondary science.'[30] By the 1870s and 1880s, this perspective had blossomed into a full-blown love affair between 'the People' and 'the People's William'. But, as Jonathan Parry has noted, the love affair existed largely in Gladstone's own imagination: for his most ardent followers – trade unionists, dissenters and Celtic nationalists – were not terribly characteristic of 'the People', while 'the People's William' was a hall of mirrors that reflected different things back to different interest groups.[31] The siren-call of 'the People' was ultimately to lead Gladstone – Homeric hero that he felt himself to be – onto the rocks of political disaster, taking the Liberal Party with him.

In some senses, then, Gladstone's political acumen was dulled by the very efficiency of the party political machine that grew up around him during the 1870s. For all his intelligence and learning, Gladstone could be a bizarrely unselfconscious man. How else could he have embraced as enthusiastically as he did the near-idolatry of the mass meetings held in his honour during the 1880s, meetings which came perilously close to adopting the tone of a religious service? (Perhaps he reassured himself that these were indications of his followers' appreciation of the moral ecstasy of politics.) At the Free Trade Hall in Manchester during one meeting in 1886, the *Daily News* reported that 'The organ was played and the vast audience whiled away the time in singing right vigorously a series of songs, mostly in praise of the premier'. One of the Gladstone songs, from 1885, was sung to the tune of *Auld Lang Syne*:

> In Gladstone still, 'the People's Will'.
> Strong hand, brave heart, combine
> To send Lib'ral breasts a thrill, as in days of auld lang syne.[32]

It is perhaps difficult to imagine the success of an adaptation of, say, *Jerusalem* in praise of Tony Blair; but since his triumph in the election of 1997 it has again been Gladstone who springs to mind as the readiest point of historical comparison.

Blair is an admirer of Lord Jenkins, one of the two or three finest biographers of Gladstone in recent years. In a recent Gladstone memorial lecture, Jenkins observed that the Prime Minister harbours a 'regret that he read Law and not History at Oxford', and that he is a devotee of political biographies. New Labour has emerged, with certain caveats, shorn of its socialist heritage and embracing what appears in many ways to be a moderate Asquithian approach to politics.[33] Asquith, the great follower of Gladstone, attempted in vain to implement Home Rule for Ireland: Blair, equally, has been a dedicated protagonist in the search for peace in the Emerald Isle. And there is something Gladstonian, too, in Blair's greater openness towards Europe than has been the case since the premiership of Edward Heath.

Like Gladstone, Blair is an Oxford-educated High Churchman for whom, ironically, the pulpit style of evangelical politics has worn less effectively in our sceptical media-conscious age. But the moral imperative, whatever we might feel about the 'spin', is genuine. It is no longer possible for Britain to boot any government 'bag and baggage' out of power. In Blair's concerted efforts to garner international support for a moral 'war' against the alleged perpetrators of the terrorist attacks on New York in September 2001, however, the Gladstone mantle was seen to rest on his shoulders with remarkable and instructive ease. Here, as elsewhere, the rhetoric of 'the People', and the idea of People's Premiers, saw past and present link hands, as if the line of patrician Prime Ministers which had dominated the middle of the twentieth century had never existed.

Gladstone the private man has been no less prominent in twentieth-century eyes: indeed, it has been the growing correspondence between private emotion and public action that has revolutionised Gladstone studies since the *Diaries* began to appear in the 1960s. But the timing of their appearance needs to be seen partly against the backdrop of earlier writings and events that mediated public attitudes towards the Grand Old Man. As we have seen, it has commonly (and mistakenly) been argued that the values and attitudes of the Victorian age were repudiated in the wake of the First World War. Where Gladstone is concerned, it might be tempting for some to believe that an inter-war reputational eclipse could have been symptomatic of the decline of Liberalism – one of the 'lights that failed', to borrow a title from Kipling. And, not surprisingly, Gladstone does make a striking appearance in Lytton Strachey's *Eminent Victorians* (1918). In a brilliant five-page vignette, tucked away in the chapter on General Gordon, Strachey depicts Gladstone as a divided man, penetratingly intelligent yet strangely incapable of reflection on his inner motivations. It is not at all clear, Strachey ponders, whether he was 'the perfect model of the upright man' or 'a crafty manipulator of men and things for the purposes of his own ambition'.[34] Perhaps, Strachey seemed to imply, he was both, 'a chimera of the spirit'. Here Strachey was at one with a long line of Conservative resentment: Lord Salisbury, that dryly devastating analyst of the late Victorian political world, brusquely dismissed Gladstone's 'pulpit style of eloquence'; and Andrew Bonar Law, at the Versailles conversation in 1919, refuted Lloyd George by saying that Gladstone was not a 'very great man' but a 'very great humbug'.[35]

For most people in the early twentieth century, however, Gladstone would have been 'Mr Gladstone', the venerable patriarch of unshakeable moral conviction. This was an image that Gladstone himself had assiduously cultivated amongst the media and public from the 1870s; it served his purpose to be seen as the champion of the people.[36] The self-fashioning can be traced with equal potency through Gladstone's autobiographical writings, including *A Chapter of Autobiography* (1868), *Gleanings of Past Years* (1879), the *Later Gleanings* (1897) and the abandoned autobiography (1892–97). These writings, ingenuously or otherwise, did several things. They emphasised in Gladstone's life not flux and discontinuity, but evolution of thought and practice; and they allowed Gladstone to envisage himself as an instrument finely attuned to deep historical trends set down by God's hand. Both of these in turn complemented Gladstone's very real political priorities – above all Ireland – during the last two decades of his career. And these views fed into the host of biographies, many of them designated 'popular' and affordably priced, which began to appear from the late 1870s.[37]

The popular cult of 'character' which grew around Gladstone towards the end of his life was most powerfully embodied in the official biography published by John, Viscount Morley, in 1903.[38] This was to be for some fifty years the standard biography of Gladstone, attracting almost 100,000 sales before it went out of print in 1942, and nearly 50,000 sales of shortened editions. Morley was no disinterested biographer, and his close involvement in Liberal politics at the turn of the century led him to amplify rather than to deflate the nascent image of Gladstone as a national institution. Having been asked by the Gladstone family not to deal with the sensitive subject of religion on grounds of his agnosticism, Morley was only too ready to eschew dwelling upon what he called 'domesticities'. There were to be no private faces in public places here; and indeed this might well have pleased the subject who is reputed to have left Queen Victoria feeling as if she were a public meeting rather than a private individual. Instead Morley was preoccupied with a secular belief in progress and political evolution. This, together with his personal familiarity with Gladstone in august old age, led him to suggest that his subject's life had taken a largely predetermined course, its occasional setbacks and false starts having been corrected by iron fortitude of character. Such qualities, Morley felt, were sorely needed by the post-Gladstone Liberal Party, frustrated and marginalised at Westminster through years of Conservative electoral success.

Such, then, was the received biographical depiction of Gladstone around the time that Strachey published *Eminent Victorians* – a depiction which, as we shall later see, was reinforced by popular memories of the Grand Old Man. But this version of Gladstone as an essentially extrovert political animal also encouraged many educated observers after 1918 to ponder what lay behind the imposing surface image. With the growing popularity in intellectual circles of Freudian theory, people became sensitised to any trace of sensation or psychological inconsistency. Highbrow gossip about Gladstone monopolised this fascination with the inconsistencies of character in order to 'debunk' and to score cheap political points. Popular gossip inevitably showed the imprint of intellectual fashion less markedly, tending to consist of a few recollected rumours about Gladstone's relations with prostitutes: for it was, after all, in the 1920s that people began to speculate again on the Grand Old Man's preoccupation with 'rescuing' fallen women. This was to be a prominent theme throughout biographies after 1945, especially when the *Diaries* revealed the full extent of Gladstone's obsession with issues of sin and innocence amongst women. And even in the 1920s it was not difficult to imagine how such recollections might have supported more sophisticated dissections of Gladstone's character; at any rate, it is likely that Strachey would have amplified his insinuations about a divided mind had he been writing (or revising) *Eminent Victorians* in 1928 rather than 1918.

It was this complex, fraught context which faced the brothers who charged themselves with protecting their father's memory in the inter-war years, Henry Neville, Baron Gladstone of Hawarden (1852–1935), and Herbert John, Viscount Gladstone (1854–1930).[39] An effective team, with Henry's temperate thoughtfulness offsetting Herbert's fiery energy, they responded to the challenge of growing interest in the private life of their father in a variety of ways. One of these was to police archival material with an extraordinarily protective zeal. All material relating to Gladstone – family papers, correspondence, the diaries and so on – was at the beginning of the 1920s still kept under lock and key at Gladstone's old country home of Hawarden. This attitude seemed to be vindicated upon the publication of Peter Wright's *Portraits and Criticisms*, a rather weak neo-Stracheyan pastiche, in June 1925. The Wright case, as it came to be known, hinged upon what was in fact a brief digression from the topic of Lord Salisbury's political style. Wright claimed that 'Gladstone ... founded the great tradition since observed by many of his followers and successors with such pious fidelity, in public to speak the language of the highest and strictest principle, and in private to pursue and possess every sort of woman'.[40] This was a reference to a 'scraglio' which, Wright would later suggest when forced to set out his sources, had surrounded Gladstone towards the end of his career, thereby causing his political (and by implication personal) integrity to be compromised. That original digression was sufficient to incense Henry and Herbert Gladstone, who were eager to challenge him in court, no doubt sensing within Wright's claim about their father pursuing 'every sort of woman' – an echo perhaps of popular gossip – definite undertones of sexual innuendo.

What followed in legal terms can be summarised fairly quickly.[41] The brothers wrote a deliberately provocative letter to Wright on 22 July 1925, denouncing him as a liar, a coward and a fool. Wright sent this letter, together with a response setting out his sources in greater detail, to the *Daily Mail*, where they appeared on 27 July. The Gladstone brothers challenged Wright directly to sue them for libel. But Wright would not rise to the bait; and in any case this would not have been legally possible, given that Wright himself had sent their letter for publication to the *Daily Mail*. (Interestingly enough it was Lord Alfred Douglas, that veteran of libel cases involving Victorian sexual immorality, who advised Herbert Gladstone on this at an early stage. 'I know more about libel than many lawyers do', he commented wanly.)[42] The Gladstones were forced to pursue their quarry by other means. Complaining to the Bath Club that several of the letters relating to the controversy had been written by Wright on club notepaper, the brothers were able to tarnish his reputation sufficiently to cause his expulsion. Wright successfully brought a claim for damages against the club and, in the process, was obliged to sue Henry and Herbert Gladstone for libel. The five-day hearing, between 27 January and 3 February 1927, inevitably came to rest upon the original cause of the contretemps. Wright was unable to substantiate his claims about Gladstone's pursuit of women, and lost the case.

There was wide support for the Gladstone brothers throughout the trial, and this should give us pause for thought about the extent to which anti-Victorianism (and more specifically anti-Gladstone feeling) had gained hold in Britain by the 1920s. To be sure, a few individuals with long memories for sexual scandal did offer to provide Wright with evidence of Gladstone's immorality. W. H. Fox, for example, offered some popular gossip to Wright before the libel writ had even been issued. 'When news came through of the Phoenix Park murders,' Fox wrote, '[Gladstone] had to be sent for, and was unearthed from a brothel in Cecil Street, Strand.' [43] (It may indeed have been such 'evidence' which strengthened Wright's resolve to take the Gladstone brothers to court shortly afterwards.) But such a response was uncharacteristic. In many places ordinary people felt a direct connection with the Gladstonian tradition, and nowhere more so than in Scotland, the country from which Gladstone had relaunched his political career in the late 1870s. Thomas Cuthbert wrote about how he was 'born in Mid-Lothian … amid the Gladstone "tradition" which lingers there still among artisan thinkers'.[44] The Glaswegian butcher James Brechin, meanwhile, poured venom upon 'the unprincipled attack of a *pestiferous cur* on the memory of your illustrious father'. He then went on to offer his own particular style of support: 'the only kind of argument which can be used with that type of brute is physical chastisement and I shall gladly endeavour to inflict this if I ever meet the swine'.[45] Such indignation was not restricted to the Celtic fringe. 'Everyone worthwhile in England is glad of your action', wrote one correspondent to the Gladstone brothers, signing the letter simply 'One of The Multitude'.[46] When the verdict was given in court on 3 February 1927, *The Times* reported that there was applause in the gallery which was quelled only by Justice Avory threatening to commit any further offenders for contempt.[47] As the Gladstone brothers emerged afterwards into the Strand they were greeted with cheers from several hundred well-wishers.[48]

These legal proceedings in themselves are less important than the psychological and practical consequences of the Wright case. The Gladstone brothers, even with such evidence of support, were deeply disturbed by the controversy, preparing their side of the case with a level of thoroughness truly worthy of the adjective 'Gladstonian'.[49] Of course, they had much to lose if the libel case went against them, but it is surely significant that extensive research was underway long before the writ was drawn up in April 1926. The reason for this anxiety is not difficult to see. Gladstone's family was only too aware of the accusations which had been made against him towards the end of his life, and had themselves urged upon him greater caution in his 'rescue work'. Such had been the notoriety of the rumours that Gladstone had felt moved in 1896 to issue a solemn declaration of marital fidelity.[50] Henry and Herbert Gladstone initially suspected that the passage in *Portraits and Criticisms* alluded to their father's dealings with 'fallen women', though Wright denied knowledge of such rumours, claiming to have based his remarks about a 'seraglio' upon political gossip from Lord Milner.

Such comments were nevertheless sufficient to rattle the brothers, and to make them fearful of any other accusations that might resurface. This placed them in an acute dilemma. Until very shortly before the opening of the libel case they were decided upon producing the declaration in court as evidence. But there was a problem with it. Gladstone had written in 1896 that he 'limited' himself to denying 'infidelity to the marriage bed', and this peculiar phrasing might be taken to mean that he was unprepared to deny something approaching psychological infidelity. Herbert Gladstone was typically sanguine about this danger six days before the case was to be heard. 'Cross examination on this would have no terrors for me', he wrote to Henry. 'My view is that ... we could bring to the Court a true understanding of the declaration, and by anticipating hostile criticism put the other side at a disadvantage.'[51] But in the interim the brothers were persuaded by their solicitor Charles Russell not to produce the declaration for fear that such a tactic might backfire, and, as Henry remarked to Herbert, since Wright's allegations after all had not been based upon gossip relating to Gladstone's 'rescue work'.[52]

Nor were the diaries produced during the Wright case. On account of their extensiveness, and their oblique but revealingly intimate nature, these were an even greater source of anxiety to the Gladstone brothers during the 1920s. Herbert was intimately acquainted with their contents, having had an abridged copy of the diaries made in 1919.[53] 'What *is* our root difficulty?', he pondered seven years later to Henry. 'It is not in the letters and papers. It *is* in the Diary introspections, its spiritual misgivings and half accusations and in the fact that confessions of human weakness are definitely connected with the other sex.'[54] Small wonder that access to the diaries was denied to most historical researchers in the 1920s, even though G. M. Trevelyan, R. W. Seton-Watson and Arnold Toynbee joined one young historian in believing that 'if there might be any time for the publication of Mr G's diaries, it was now'.[55] But this was not to be for a further forty years. Even when J. L. Hammond consulted the abridged version of the diaries while researching *Gladstone and the Irish Nation*, it was under the strict proviso that he promised not to mention that he had even seen them.[56]

The diaries had in any case already been moved from Hawarden to the library at Lambeth Palace. The idea of placing them under the protection of the Archbishop of Canterbury had initially arisen while Cosmo Lang (then Archbishop of York) was stranded at Hawarden during the General Strike of 1926.[57] The minds of the Gladstone brothers were already much preoccupied at this time with the Wright case. In the intervening months, and even after the libel action against them failed, the nature of the introspections within the diaries remained a source of unease. One way of coming to terms with them was to urge upon the diaries the status of a work of religious introspection. And the natural repository for such a work would, of course, be in the safekeeping of the highest figure within the Anglican church. This was very much the line taken with Cosmo Lang. 'I cannot tell you how greatly honoured I feel', Lang wrote to Henry Gladstone in May 1927, 'at your having taken me into your confidence about the private papers of a "great Christian" for whom I had very real reverence.'[58] This was also the final line taken by the brothers before the handing over of the diaries and other sensitive material to Lambeth Palace in July 1928. Several months earlier they had written to Randall Davidson: 'The Diary shows that the life of Mr Gladstone is the life ... of a great Christian and a great Churchman.'[59] Even so, there was to be no access to the diaries without special permission, and although the Gladstone brothers eventually envisaged their publication, they stipulated that this was not to happen before the lapse of at least a further twenty-five years.

Need they have worried about what posterity would make of Gladstone's mind as revealed in the diaries and other personal material? For the most part not, for their publication in the 1960s benefited both from a less judgemental attitude towards issues of morality, and from fresh scholarly attitudes towards the Victorians. The diaries, as we have seen, could just as well support renewed assessments of Gladstone's sheer industry and sophisticated use of the party political machine. This has helped to make him a thoroughly 'modern' figure. There has been no major biography of Disraeli since Robert Blake's magisterial volume in 1966, and even though Thatcher emulated Disraelian jingoism rather than Gladstonian reserve during the Falklands campaign of 1982, the incentive to study of Gladstone's great rival has not been fully taken up.[60] Part of the reason, perhaps, is the very element of performance within Disraeli's life and career: sometimes we are not entirely sure that he had any coherent ideology or long-term political strategy at all. (Lytton Strachey told Hesketh Pearson, strikingly enough, that he had left Disraeli alone because he found him too inscrutable.) What Disraeli brought to the premiership in 1874 was charisma and vision, but not a great deal of practical energy. This was the man for whom power came, at the age of seventy, too late.

For Gladstone power could never come too late, as some would-be Liberal leaders who drummed their fingers impatiently knew only too well. And although the diaries fleshed out a sense of Gladstone's *use* of performance within politics, they even more abundantly testified to his astonishing sincerity and ingenuousness. Psychologically, few biographers or historians have felt daunted by the nuances and emotional intricacies of the diaries: rather, they have tended to look upon them as a clear pane through which to observe their subject. The more serious challenge is widely believed to lie in absorbing their sheer bulk: Gladstone scholars sometimes talk of one another as if they are mountain-climbers. When the Sir Edmund Hillary of Gladstone traversers, H. C. G. Matthew, died in 1999, one obituarist wrote of his editing of most of the diaries as 'a triumph of long-term planning and sustained organisation ... testimony to his personal application and self-discipline'.[61]

In the work of H. C. G. Matthew, Roy Jenkins and others, sympathetic and enlightening use has been made of the diaries. Again, for Matthew, it is the mountain analogy that comes uppermost. As the man who was probably most steeped in the diaries after Gladstone himself, his comments command attention:

> Its range, political, literary, religious, social, and personal, is extraordinary. No one will find it light work, and those seeking an easy read will be disappointed. The eclectic complexity and interrelated nature of Victorian culture pervades every entry. The reader approaching the diary will find it looming like some vast rock face seen from far off, some of it sunny and appealing, much of it bleak and uninviting. But closer inspection reveals a different aspect; it is, after all, a climbable face. The ascent is arduous, but reveals on the way a vast mosaic of events, views, descriptions, analyses, reports, changing social and intellectual relationships. As the end is gained, the pattern as a whole becomes clear.[62]

And for Matthew the essence of Gladstone was a fundamentally *public* achievement, the achievement measured in his relevance to the modern day.[63] He certainly did not neglect the private life or avoid issues like his subject's 'curious lack of self-awareness' – no reading of Gladstone so bedded on the rocks of the diaries could do otherwise – but there is something profoundly Gladstonian about this very emphasis upon a lasting body of achievement once the mortal body had passed away. The pattern of the life, for all its inconsistencies and blind spots, amounted to considerably more than the sum of its parts.

That view was shared by Roy Jenkins when he came to write his warmly engaging biography of Gladstone in the early 1990s. The typically supple, high-spirited and generous mind of the writer combined with Gladstone's own tendency to dogmatic seriousness and the *Diaries* to produce some delightful insights. Jenkins discusses, for example, one of Gladstone's recurrent 'religio-sexual emotional crises' in 1845, when he sought solace from sexual temptation at Baden-Baden by ensconcing himself in church for four hours. 'One feels that he must have been like a cinema-goer who saw the film several times round,' writes Jenkins, 'for it is difficult to believe that even in that age of relative fervour there were many subjects of Her Majesty who in a fashionable foreign spa town required that length of devotion.'[64] That splendid surreptitious humour only serves, however, to bring us closer to the serious business of assessing Gladstone the hero. And here Jenkins is unequivocal. Recounting a story that Clement Attlee (whose own favourite Victorian premier, as we have seen, was Salisbury) was repelled by Gladstone's high-toned marriage proposal to Catherine Glynne when he read the Magnus biography in 1954, Jenkins reflects:

> Gladstone was not a dreadful person. He was in many ways the greatest figure of the nineteenth century, and taken in the round the greatest British politician of that or any other parliamentary century. But he could be portentous and a little ridiculous, particularly when dealing with young women, and his twenties, which were nearly but not quite over when he wrote this letter, were not his best decade. It was understandable that Attlee should take against this letter, but it was both a little narrow and carrying his laconic dismissiveness too far to build a general censure upon it.[65]

So much for Attlee, normally a shrewd connoisseur of the past. Still, there have been those who have used the *Diaries* for the purposes of harder-edged scrutiny. Certainly there was to Gladstone a central psychological ambiguity, and that was fully evident in the diary entries he made day after day (indeed, it was evident in the very act of keeping such a painstaking record): this was the tension between worldly ambition and religious devotion. Gladstone imbibed both his father's driving business sense and his mother's profound evangelical religiosity. In a way, the two halves complemented one another, since evangelicalism urged the individual to action; but Gladstone, unsure in youth whether to enter the church or politics, never quite managed to reconcile them: it was a 'conflict', wrote Magnus, that 'lasted until the end of his life'.[66] He was evidently a man of prodigious energies, struggling to control these for most of his days, whether it was in keeping his temper in Parliament or resisting sexual urges. Contemporaries saw and knew this: Gladstone was frequently depicted in political cartoons with eyes ablaze and clothes askew, often in the process of some sort of movement or gesticulation.

All of these qualities have found their way into biographies after 1945, reversing Morley's simplistic notion in the official life that 'nobody had fewer secrets, nobody ever lived and wrought in fuller sunlight'.[67] In 1997 Travis L. Crosby published a psychoanalytical study of Gladstone that developed the theory of 'stress and coping' in his life. Gladstone, writes Crosby, 'fearing a loss of control and knowing its potential for harm in his political life, sought to gain a strict mastery over the circumstances of his life'.[68] And so Gladstone found outlets – in religious devotion, in 'rescue work', in rearranging his books, in chopping down trees, and so on. (Although it is an indication of the healthiness of Gladstone studies that the axe-wielding episodes could equally be read as another form of political theatre: they certainly became photo-opportunities, and viewers would have been reminded of cartoons from earlier in the century when reformers were depicted taking axes to the roots of the rotten constitution.)[69] Important, too, has become the issue of Gladstone's general attitude towards women. Here again Freudian views have tended to prevail. His beloved sister Anne died in 1829, throwing the young Gladstone into a bewildered state of shock. Like Dickens and Wilde, both of whom were deeply affected by the premature deaths of close relatives (a common occurrence in the nineteenth century), biographers have made a great deal of this. 'Throughout his life', observes Matthew, Gladstone 'saw women essentially as potentially noble creatures to be helped and lifted to a moral state as pure as that of his mother and his elder sister.'[70]

Not all biographers have formed such tactful conclusions. The two volumes of Richard Shannon's life of Gladstone, published in 1982 and 1999, presented its subject under a sometimes harshly analytical light. Gladstone, for Shannon, was indeed something of a 'control freak', sublimating the tensions of his life within an obsessive compulsion to action and self-realisation. He was a man who sacrificed nearly everything to his relationship with God, and his sense of God's purpose for him on earth. This made him a profoundly self-centred, if not actually selfish, individual: one who took account of others only if what they had to say bore relation to his current preoccupations. (Unsurprisingly, in the vignette of Gladstone around the age of thirty, Shannon quotes what Catherine Gladstone would famously and refreshingly say to her husband at a later point: 'if you weren't such a great man you would be a terrible bore'.)[71] Such a lack of self-knowledge sits oddly, in Shannon's mind, alongside Gladstone's intense drive towards emotional accountability and establishing the record for posterity.

What, in turn, are we to make of it? The forensic quality of Shannon's study has not gone down well with all readers, although he is far from unsympathetic, and is equally rigorous in quoting from authorities like M. R. D. Foot who attempted to soften the contours of his interpretation.

Shannon's dryness of wit where Gladstone's more idiosyncratic habits and attitudes are concerned marks him out as a modern writer. But more generally, the move in Shannon's biography is to emphasise the *strangeness* of Gladstone, the way in which we cannot read him in any straightforward sense as a contemporary figure. Shannon has criticised the biographies by Jenkins and Matthew as being respectively too Asquithian and too secular-progressive.[72] This is arguably to be somewhat overcritical of two very fine biographical achievements, but the point remains: since the 1980s we have been constructing Gladstone again very much in our own image. That has been true, as we have seen, of Queen Victoria and Dickens; and we shall see that in certain ways it is true of Wilde, too. But with all of these figures, the impulse to turn their lives into 'heritage' that can be plundered for 'relevance' ought to resisted. Whether Gladstone himself would have agreed with this it is difficult to say: for the very stuff of politics is enduring potency. There was, apparently, in the late nineteenth century such a thing as to be 'gladstonised': to be put under the spell of the Grand Old Man.[73] We may no longer be uncritical of Gladstone the private individual, but in some respects the spell holds its enchantment still.

# 12

# *Wilde*

History sometimes hinges on the most extraordinarily casual of scenes. A visitor to the Cadogan Hotel in London early on the evening of 5 April 1895 might have glimpsed through an open door the sight of a man drinking hock and seltzer. The man, slumped in gloomy silence, was tall and broad-shouldered, with a face that suggested that it had seen its share of earthly comforts. Glassy-eyed he sat as various people came anxiously to and fro: there was talk about whether it was too late to catch a train, terse recriminations about people who had been bad influences, discussion of what would come next. A suitcase, half-packed, lay on the bed. Still he sat, murmuring something about facing his sentence whatever it might be. And then, at about ten past six, a waiter brought two men to the door. They entered, there was an exchange of words, and they left soon after with the tall man. He looked ashen-faced, the worse for his wait, but composed and coherent.[1]

This was the moment, pregnant with anxiety but easily overlooked by the casual observer, in which an important piece of history was made. For the tall man was Oscar Wilde, and earlier that day his libel case against the Marquess of Queensberry had failed at the Old Bailey. The evidence that came to light during the trial proved sufficient for the prosecution of Wilde, and it was to arrest him that the two detectives had arrived at the Cadogan Hotel. Wilde was detained on the charge of committing indecent acts, and through the course of a spectacularly public criminal trial and prison sentence he was to change the history of moral attitudes in Britain. 'I was a man who stood in symbolic relations to the art and culture of my age', Wilde wrote during that grim prison sentence.[2] That is true; and it is also true that Wilde stood for much of the twentieth century in symbolic relation to the morality of his age. Wilde fell foul in the 1890s of a new and virulent strand of Victorian moral zeal, and his fateful encounter with it would shape not only attitudes to Wilde and the Victorians, but attitudes to sexuality and to the moral code handed down to us by tradition.

Wilde's downfall, after being taken away by the two detectives to Bow Street, was swift. Bail was refused, and he was remanded at Holloway Prison until trial at the Old Bailey. In the meantime there was a violent public reaction. Wilde's name was obscured on placards for his two plays that were running in London at the time, *An Ideal Husband* and *The Importance of Being Earnest*. Both, faced by dwindling audiences and 'discordant remarks' from the gallery, had closed by early May. His books disappeared from booksellers' windows and shelves, and would prove difficult to track down for the next decade and more. And where silence was imposed on the man's words themselves, a maliciously shrill noise was orchestrated in sections of the press. The *Echo*, rather than heeding its own injunction, noisily called for Wilde ('damned and done for') to 'go into silence, and be heard of no more'. The *Daily Telegraph* made similarly hypocritical play of how tedious the scandal had become, remarking that Wilde had 'been the means of inflicting upon public patience during the recent episode as much moral damage of the most offensive and repulsive kind as any individual could well cause'.[3] Even here we recognise Wilde as an icon of modernity, suffering at the hands of the 'New Journalism' of the 1890s that fed upon gossip and sensation. 'In the old days men had the rack', Wilde had written prophetically in 1891. 'Now they have the press.'[4]

Against the frightening public din there was the private tragedy. Tragic it certainly was: Wilde, the brilliant Greek scholar, must have been keenly aware of the dimensions of the downfall awaiting him. As he reflected to Ada and Ernest Leverson four days after his arrest: 'I write to you from prison, where your very kind words have reached me and given me comfort, though they have made me cry, in my loneliness ... With what a crash this fell!'[5] Fate was at work at home, too. Already a victim of her husband having become the most vilified man in London, Constance Wilde faced the further burden of legal costs for the failed action against Queensberry. Wilde had always lived (and would die) beyond his means, and with ticket receipts and book sales declining sharply, the financial situation became critical. On 24 April the Wilde residence at Tite Street was invaded by speculators and souvenir-hunters in a forced public sale of its contents. Bedrooms were ransacked. The children had their toys sold and were too young to understand why. Wilde's precious library, full of first editions with personal inscriptions, was dispersed for a pittance. Other items were simply stolen. The day before Wilde had written: 'I don't know what to do. My life seems to have gone from me.'[6]

Events were to take an even unhappier turn within the next week. Those events, enacted at the Old Bailey, were to flesh out for posterity what this whole tragic business had been about. Wilde was committed for trial on the charge of committing acts of gross indecency with various young men. These men were 'renters', working-class lads who offered their favours in return for trinkets and money. Wilde had been introduced to them through Alfred Taylor, the son of a cocoa manufacturer who kept what was effectively a male brothel at his exotically furnished rooms in Westminster. And Taylor in turn had been introduced to Wilde through the man on whom the entire misfortune seemed to balance: Lord Alfred Douglas, the beloved 'Bosie'. They had met in 1891, when Wilde, a decade of fame and notoriety already behind him, was just beginning his ascent as a hugely successful playwright, and Douglas, an Oxford undergraduate of strikingly delicate features, was carving out a literary career as a distinguished poet. Douglas's father was the Marquess of Queensberry, a man whose principal (and only) contribution to gentlemanly endeavour appears to have been the invention of the 'Queensberry Rules'.

Queensberry was a tyrant, and evidently volatile to the point of instability (a quality inherited, unfortunately, by his son Alfred). Queensberry and Douglas had an explosive relationship, and the father detested the son's very public association with Wilde. The rumours circulated, and Douglas was far from eager to suppress them on his father's behalf. On 18 February 1895 Queensberry left a card for Wilde at the Albemarle Club. Ten days later, when Wilde was handed the card by the porter, he found scrawled upon it the words: 'To Oscar Wilde posing Somdomite [sic]'. Illiterate or not, this was a public libel, and Douglas was jubilant: here was an opportunity to strike back at his father in court. On both sides the stakes of the vendetta, after all, had recently been raised: in October of the previous year, Douglas's brother Viscount Drumlanrig had shot himself after being implicated in an amorous liaison with the Prime Minister, Lord Rosebery.[7] It is not difficult to see how Queensberry and Douglas both sought revenge in different ways: Queensberry against perverters of public morals, Douglas against a bullying and judgemental father.

Wilde, despite the advice of many close friends, chose to proceed with legal action against Queensberry. Douglas's hand now seems clear in all of this: but at the time, although he strained in vain to be called as a witness, very few people saw how a private family feud would bring Wilde to ruin. Nor did Wilde help himself by presuming that he could win the case with clever words: with literary London at his feet, such hubris was understandable but unfortunate. And it was naive, too, to take such a disingenuous line with his solicitors over the accusation: for although Wilde had never been a sodomite, and although the intimacies with Douglas had long ended, his lifestyle had become far from 'respectable', and it was sufficient only for Queensberry to establish merely that he had 'posed' as a corruptor of youth.

The ruin announced itself during that first libel action against Queensberry, which opened on 3 April 1895. The defence for Queensberry was led

by Edward Carson, a shrewd and serious lawyer who would go on to achieve
celebrity as one of the most vociferous opponents of Irish Home Rule. He
and Wilde had been undergraduates together at Trinity College, Dublin,
and Carson had not thought much of his peer's flippancy even then. (Wilde,
appraised of Carson's involvement, reflected: 'No doubt he will perform his
task with all the added bitterness of an old friend.')[8] Carson caught Wilde
out on several small but fatally incriminating points, such as lying about
his precise age: a gentleman who was dishonest about his age might not,
after all, be entirely trustworthy. And surely the teasing preface to *The Picture
of Dorian Gray*, the one that proclaimed that there was no such thing as a
'moral' or 'immoral' book, threw into doubt Wilde's personal integrity?

Wilde succeeded in evading Carson temporarily and winning laughs from
a packed courtroom when cross-examined about his works, playing literally
to the gallery. But it was the sudden presentation of the renters that sent
shock waves around the court room, and made Wilde lose his footing. The
consummate performer, he must have sensed at this point that he was
beginning to lose his audience. Douglas had felt sure that his father would
not even know what a renter was: but the private detectives who had been
following him and Wilde certainly did. Asked whether he had ever kissed
Walter Grainger, a sixteen-year-old waiter from Oxford, Wilde replied that
he had not because Grainger was 'extremely ugly'. Carson wanted to know
why Grainger's ugliness or otherwise should be an issue. Wilde stumbled,
and the flow of clever words temporarily ceased. 'You sting me and insult
me and try to unnerve me', he blurted. 'And at times one says things
flippantly when one ought to speak more seriously. I admit it.'[9]

Thereafter it was downhill almost all the way for Wilde. Queensberry was
acquitted on 5 April, Wilde was arrested, and then on 26 April he was himself
put in the dock. The first trial ended inconclusively on 1 May, partly perhaps
because Wilde had given the jury pause for thought about the nature of the
crimes of which he had been accused. Against a rally of renters brought
forward to testify about Wilde's bedroom habits and financial arrangements,
the embattled defendant launched into an eloquent defence of 'the love that
dare not speak its name' (a phrase from one of Douglas's poems). After a
checklist of famous names – David and Jonathan, Plato, Michelangelo,
Shakespeare – Wilde invoked an image of Platonic love that any educated
Victorian would have recognised, at least in theory:

> It is in this century misunderstood, so much misunderstood that it may be
> described as the 'Love that dare not speak its name', and on account of it I am
> placed where I am now. It is beautiful, it is fine, it is the noblest form of affection.
> There is nothing unnatural about it. It is intellectual, and it repeatedly exists
> between an elder and a younger man, when the elder has intellect, and the younger

man has all the joy, hope, and glamour of life before him. That it should be so, the world does not understand. The world mocks at it and sometimes puts one in the pillory for it.

This speech was greeted with 'a spontaneous outburst of applause from the public gallery, mingled with some hisses'.[10] That mixed reaction was replicated in the jury, which was divided when it came to passing judgement.

Wilde was released on bail, and recommitted for trial on 20 May. Five days later he was found guilty of committing acts of gross indecency under section eleven of the Criminal Law Amendment Act of 1885. The presiding judge, Sir Alfred Wills, intoned darkly about this being 'the worst case I have ever tried' and about the maximum sentence he could pass being 'totally inadequate':

> Oscar Wilde and Alfred Taylor, the crime of which you have been convicted is so bad that one has to put stern restraint upon oneself to prevent oneself from describing, in language which I would rather not use, the sentiments which must rise to the breast of every man of honour who has heard the details of these two terrible trials. That the jury have arrived at a correct verdict in this case, I cannot persuade myself to entertain the shadow of a doubt.[11]

The charge was two years' imprisonment with hard labour. Wilde was seen to sway slightly, 'his face suffused with horror'. 'And I?', he mumbled faintly. 'May I say nothing, my lord?'[12] The verdict spread like wildfire and was greeted with savage exhilaration. As if for a moment transformed into Furies, prostitutes were seen to dance in the streets. Wilde, for his part, was taken away to Pentonville. Later he was transferred to Wandsworth, and then Reading Gaol. The last grimly telling moment in Wilde's fall came when he was moved from Wandsworth to Reading on 21 November 1895. 'Handcuffed and in prison clothing,' writes Richard Ellmann, 'he had to wait on the platform at Clapham Junction from 2.00 to 2.30 on a rainy afternoon. A crowd formed, first laughing and then jeering at him. One man recognized that this was Oscar Wilde, and spat at him. "For a year after that was done to me," Wilde wrote in De Profundis, "I wept every day at the same hour and for the same space of time."'[13]

How are we to make sense of this desperately unhappy sequence of events? What Wilde made of it was De Profundis, the long, moving letter written to Alfred Douglas under strict prison conditions between January and March 1897. Occupying a hundred pages in the Collected Letters of Oscar Wilde, it ranges widely over the writer's life, work, relationships and renewed interest in religious faith. Wilde portrays himself in De Profundis as both the repentant sinner and the Christ-like martyr: the act of immersing himself in spirituality blurs the line fascinatingly between self-abasement and self-absolution. Was Wilde not thinking of himself when he reflected, almost aphoristically: 'Christ, like all fascinating personalities, had the power of not merely saying beautiful things himself, but of making other people say beautiful things to him'? Were not the Philistines – they who upheld 'the heavy, cumbrous, blind, mechanical forces of Society' – all those who had ever criticised Wilde, and orchestrated his downfall at the Old Bailey? [14] And in *The Ballad of Reading Gaol* (1897) is there not an explicit reference to Christ's sacrifice in the lines about each man killing the thing he loves, the coward doing it with a kiss?

In fairness to Wilde, there is a great deal of conventional Victorianism here. Like many of his socially-sensitive peers, Wilde had always been interested in the figure of Christ: from the short stories to 'The Soul of Man under Socialism' images of Christian sacrifice can be traced with marked regularity. Wilde's sense of public duty was not restricted to keeping people entertained. He had always been an advocate of humane reform, and after his experience of prison redoubled his efforts in that area. 'The prison system is absolutely and entirely wrong', Wilde wrote in *De Profundis*. 'I would give anything to be able to alter it when I go out. I intend to try.' [15] Here, interestingly enough, he was at one with Dickens: he called for a set of the novels to be acquired for the library at Reading ('I feel sure that a complete set ... would be a great boon to many amongst the other prisoners as it certainly would be to myself'), and only days after his release on 19 May 1897 he wrote to the *Daily Chronicle* about the inhumanity of child imprisonment.[16] There is, nonetheless, an element of literary performance in *De Profundis*: less, perhaps, a matter of conscious conceit than one of helpless artistry. 'The first duty in life is to be as artificial as possible', Wilde had informed his public, that public ultimately being himself.[17]

What Wilde made of his demise – a mixture of classical tragedy, artistic martyrdom and Christian resurrection – is not what is made of it today. The terms of reference are completely different. Retrospectively we see that defence of Platonic love from the dock as a decoy against a society hostile to same-sex passion. The 'truth' is that Wilde was the patron saint of male homosexuality, a modern man adrift in a benighted age. Why else, after all, had he worn a green carnation, the emblem of homosexuals in decadent Paris? Why else had he written a homoerotic interpretation of Shakespeare's sonnets? Why, in his most celebrated play, had he sent out coded messages about 'bunburying' and used the name 'earnest', a well-known euphemism for homosexuals in late Victorian London? Why, to put it bluntly, had he bedded so much rough trade? But the answers to all of these questions tell us more about ourselves than they do about Wilde.

The problem, of course, is sex. Priapus certainly called for Wilde – 'what animals we are, Robert!' – he commented gleefully to his friend Robert Sherard after spending the night with a (female) prostitute in Paris.[18] And he spent rather a lot of time dwelling on the superior aesthetic merit of Greek nudes. (So much, we tend to think, for Plato.) But in point of fact Wilde's supposedly exaggerated and perverse libido seems to have been neither unduly pronounced nor odd: none of the encounters with renters extended beyond the activities practised by many 'experimental' heterosexual men throughout the twentieth century.[19] And even if his preferences had been more extreme in this respect, the point is that such matters ought to pale in comparison with a legacy of such generous, entertaining and often thought-provoking writing.

For there is, in addition to the 'gay' Wilde, the 'Irish' Wilde and the 'socialist' Wilde, another persona, the most exciting one of all: the 'category-defying' Wilde (in his age no less than ours). Academics since the 1980s have become accustomed to this last Wilde, but it is not a Wilde that has yet fully caught on with the public. There are, however, encouraging comments like this:

> That luxuriantly poisonous style … is, I suppose, not much more than literary drag, and, like so many drag acts, it can become tiresome. At any rate, it has nothing whatever to do with Oscar Wilde or his works. Indeed, such images are only part of what the current jargon labels the 'self-oppression' to which we are all prey. Wilde's courage lay not in his 'alternative sexuality' but in the freedom of his mind. To picture him primarily as a gay martyr *avant la lettre* is, I think, to play into the very hands of those who brought him down a hundred years ago.[20]

This comes from the ever-reliable Stephen Fry, whose splendid portrayal on film of Wilde is discussed below. Another actor who has done a great deal to foster intelligent views of Wilde is Simon Callow, who performed in a biographical play by his mentor Micheál MacLiammóir called *The Importance of Being Oscar*. One of the highlights was Callow's reading from *De Profundis* and, a century on from Wilde's death, he was to be seen on mainstream television extolling the virtues of this most civilised and humanly engaging of historical figures.

Wilde is far more interesting and challenging than any partisan reading based upon sexual orientation would suggest. History, according to a large number of commentators on sexuality, means the woeful tale of oppression in the days when the Victorians persecuted people like Wilde. Yet there is a curious naivety about such thinking, a presumption that history is a tale of onwards progress and mounting enlightenment about the human condition. We flatter ourselves that we know about the Victorians and sexual intolerance. But Wilde, too, was a Victorian, and an exuberant one at that. He built pathways under the instruction of Ruskin, sat at the feet of Pater, and wrote at a table originally owned by Carlyle. He was an occasional and admiring correspondent of Gladstone. He once considered, à la Matthew Arnold, becoming a schools inspector. His son remembered him as a loving Victorian paterfamilias. After his release from prison he held a party for French schoolchildren to celebrate Queen Victoria's Diamond Jubilee. All of these credentials sit uncomfortably alongside his status as an anti-Victorian icon. It simply will not do to rewrite the problematic aspects of Wilde's life – the happy family life, the blissfully heterosexual resolution to *The Importance of Being Earnest*, and so on – as an evasive concession to homophobic society from a gay man ahead of his time. In trying to liberate Wilde as a gay martyr, we only restrict him.

The modern reduction of Wilde to the status of gay martyr is not, in fact, greatly dissimilar to the attitude taken to him in 1895. The difference lies only in the slant put upon Wilde's sexual misdemeanours: where once he was vilified and pitied for his bedroom habits, now he is celebrated and 'understood'. But the central place of sex in popular views of Wilde has remained intact since the day he was arrested at the Cadogan Hotel. Rather too much has been made of the details of Wilde's private life, but, as an individual who brought down upon himself and posterity the full weight of the Victorian establishment, it is important that we dwell further on this issue of sexual morality. For, at least until the 1960s, it was one of the most potent legacies of the nineteenth century. Since then, its very reversal has taken place in terms dictated by the ghost of the past: any hint of reticence or rectitude is quickly interpreted as a retreat into 'Victorian' stuffiness. Quips at the expense of prominent figures in the late 1990s became common precisely because the BBC attempted to stifle them: Matthew Sweet writes with some incredulity about Nigel Hawthorne being silenced during a live interview in 1998 for comparing the situation of a certain cabinet minister to that of Wilde.[21] For better or worse, our views of private morality and public conduct are shot through with assumptions that were crystallised by Wilde's demise.

Promising signs have appeared on the horizon that we may be about to move away from anachronistic ideas about Wilde as a gay martyr. Since the 1980s a number of readings, marked by a more critical distance about the 'construction' of identities, have emphasised his downfall as a key moment within the very formation of modern ideas about homosexuality. One of the most striking things that we should bear in mind is that in Britain in 1895 the word 'homosexual' was scarcely used at all: throughout the trial transcripts edited by Montgomery Hyde there is no mention of the term.

It had, in fact, been coined in 1868 by the German-Hungarian writer Hans Benkert, and did not appear in English print until the 1892 translation of Richard von Krafft-Ebing's *Psychopathia Sexualis*.

In Tom Stoppard's *The Invention of Love* (1997), one of the ways in which love is 'invented' is in the formation of the word 'homosexuality', a hybrid of Greek and Latin. This greatly annoys the hero of the play, the austere A. E. Housman, famed for dismissing books of poetry that carried so much as a misprinted comma; conjoining two different languages he considers to be an unutterable act of linguistic vandalism. But what the play also does is to dramatise a particular moment in what retrospectively would be called gay history: this is a moment in late Victorian society when modern views of same-sex relationships had yet to coalesce. Medical terminology like 'homosexuality' was beginning to be deployed, but the stereotypical homosexual did not exist. The options were broad: Housman and Wilde – both now identified within the gay 'canon' – were very different figures, yet they were alive and flourishing at the same time. They did not meet in life, but Stoppard brings them together in an extraordinary scene near the end of the play. The dry, oblique scholar converses with the airy, verbose socialite amongst the debris of the Diamond Jubilee party Wilde held for children at Berneval shortly after being released from prison. Housman comments that Wilde's life has been 'a chronological error'.[22] For a moment we are tempted to infer that Housman is referring to Wilde as the 'true' homosexual that we tend to think him. But Housman is talking about a subject close to Wilde's heart – ancient Greek civilisation – and we realise that possibly he, too, might have grumbled at the clumsy new-fangled word 'homosexuality'. Wilde's own 'invented love', Stoppard makes radiantly clear, was the deliberate transformation of banal reality into beautiful meaning.

This scene helps to illustrate how imaginatively restrictive the new term 'homosexual' was. Part of the reason for employing the word may have been precisely to simplify and group together those elements that were considered harmful to social stability. And the late Victorians were certainly becoming more conscious of the tensions within their world. Evolutionary theory and medical advances began to generate the idea that same-sex relationships, long stigmatised as immoral, might also be indications of biological impurity. But the great anxiety of the 1880s and 1890s, the period coinciding with Wilde's rise and fall, was not directly associated with same-sex relationships at all. Worry gathered itself over the empire and the idea of national efficiency. Britain saw the possibility of being overtaken in the imperial and economic stakes by countries like Germany and the United States. What if Britain, small by comparison with many other nations, failed to produce human stock to run its affairs and defend its shores with the requisite vigour

and character? Muscle and morality was what the Victorians increasingly
liked to see demonstrated in their menfolk. They were concerned, though,
about alarming indications that society was not all that it might be. Was
not the birth-rate falling? Were not women getting above themselves? Had
not social surveys revealed the plight of the destitute and sickly? And where
was all the virile masculinity and noble endeavour?

Onto the stage, straight from the pages of Gilbert and Sullivan's *Patience*
(1881), skips Wilde in full aesthetic dress, walking down Piccadilly with a
poppy or a lily in his medieval hand. The triumph for Wilde, where views
of his dandified period in the 1870s and 1880s were concerned, was in making
people believe that he might have walked down Piccadilly with a lily in his
hand whether he had done so or not. All publicity was good publicity. Wilde,
then, had made himself a legitimate target for the forces of conservatism.
It is not difficult to see why the Marquess of Queensberry chose as his form
of slander '*posing* as a sodomite'. Posing does not seem, in a modern context,
especially controversial; but to the Victorian middle classes, obsessed with
respectability, any hint that an individual consciously flouted standards of
public deportment was a grave matter indeed. Although Wilde's libel action
was driven partly by consideration of Douglas, there is every reason to
believe that he was genuinely affronted at the slur on his good name. Wilde
clearly expected to win the case: might it have been that he thought this,
too, would be good publicity? If so, it was one of the most tragic miscal-
culations of the Victorian age.

What Wilde, overestimating his own verbal fireworks, so badly underes-
timated was the extent to which the establishment had become preoccupied
with issues of masculine virility. Wilde had already been the subject of a
chapter in Max Nordau's *Degeneration* (1893), a work that put forward the
argument that 'degenerate' lifestyles – lifestyles given over to self-indulgent
pleasure – threatened the very fabric of society and the future of mankind.
It was translated into English with uncanny prescience just before Wilde's
trials took place, and enjoyed an understandable vogue in the summer of
1895. Before that there was the Cleveland Street affair – the 'Victorian
Watergate' as it has been called – which involved a male brothel, an English
lord, several telegraph operators and an embarrassing cover-up operation
by Salisbury's government.[23] *The Picture of Dorian Gray* had begun to be
serialised shortly afterwards. Not for nothing did one reviewer criticise Wilde
as being fit to write for 'none but outlawed noblemen and perverted
telegraph boys'.[24]

Still, with all these ominous rumblings, Wilde's inability to see the dangers
ahead is understandable. For the fact is that, although late Victorian society
deemed same-sex relationships to be immoral and unnatural, it was not a

homophobic society. And it was not homophobic because homosexuality did not really exist; or rather, even after the Cleveland Street affair, it had not been given a public face. The public face it was to assume was, of course, that of Wilde. But before those remarkable events at the Old Bailey in 1895 there was a surprising degree of haziness about same-sex relationships. In 1871, for example, there was a criminal prosecution involving two transvestites, Fanny (Fred Park) and Stella (Ernest Boulton). The authorities simply did not know how to go about establishing that their relationship was illegal. After much scratching of heads and inconclusive medical examinations, one anonymous writer suggested that they consult the work of a foreign sex-expert called Tardieu. The doctor assigned to the case followed up the suggestion, but without enlightenment. This did not go down at all well with the authorities, though it did confirm their suspicions that Paris was the very hub of moral depravity. The prosecution was subsequently attacked for having recourse to 'the newfound treasures of French literature upon the subject – which thank God is still foreign to the libraries of British surgeons'.25 Gathering up their skirts, Fanny and Stella walked free.

Fourteen years later things were to change in a small but decisive way. In 1885 the Criminal Law Amendment Act was passed, primarily with the intention of reducing female prostitution and protecting girls from the advances of men. This was part of the general drive towards sexual morality. In an amazing publicity stunt that almost certainly aided the progress of the 1885 legislation, the newspaper editor W. T. Stead had drugged and kidnapped a girl simply to show that it could easily be done. (Apart, conceivably, from a certain distress, the girl came to no harm; but Stead was put behind bars, and for years afterwards would wear prison clothes on the anniversary of his committal.) 26 An individual of comparable moral drive was the radical MP Henry Labouchère. It was he who managed to have appended to the Criminal Law Amendment Act a section eleven which criminalised 'acts of gross indecency between men'. This was to be the law of which Wilde fell foul, and it would remain in place until 1967.

Much has been made of the Labouchère amendment. For a number of modern observers it represents a watershed in attitudes to homosexuality. Certainly it is true that some aspects of same-sex relationships, as with so much in the age that prided itself on scientific progress, were slowly being brought under the eye of medical scrutiny. In 1861 the old religious law against sodomy, punishable as a capital offence since 1533, had been brought under secular criminal jurisdiction. Perceptions of mental and emotional degeneracy increasingly came to exist alongside ideas about same-sex relationships as a moral evil. And what the Labouchère amendment may have done, in criminalising *any* sexual activity between men in public or private, was to attack not simply a type of activity but the 'type' who committed that activity. The medical as well as moral profile of the 'invert' or 'pervert' was being mapped out. So runs the argument of several commentators.[27] But this may be to privilege a rather modern perspective on the stigmatisation of same-sex practices in Britain. There is striking evidence that what Labouchère had in mind in his amendment was only the abuse of children (boys as well as girls), and not the activities of consenting adults.[28] More striking still, though Labouchère's journal *Truth* would be virulently anti-Wilde in 1895, the man himself had helped to organise Wilde's American tour of 1882, arguing that a dose of hyper-aestheticism was exactly what the United States needed to counter its own hyper-materialism.[29] The camp Wilde 'pose', evidently, was not automatically associated with suspect sexual behaviour.[30] People like Labouchère and Stead may have thought badly of Wilde's flippancy, but there seems little question of any sustained or coherent attack on him and his 'type'. Indeed in 1905 Stead wrote of how, after Wilde's release from prison, he had 'the sad pleasure of meeting him by chance' in Paris, greeting him 'as an old friend' and stopping to talk for a few minutes.[31]

Perhaps what brought Wilde down in 1895, then, was not any recognisable homophobia (a modern concept) so much as unease about the moral example he was setting to the next generation of young men.[32] There was something improper about his relations with renters, but it was not just that same-sex activities resonated as vaguely immoral or unnatural: it was that Wilde was a respectable public figure who had been shown to take advantage of his social inferiors. Class mattered a great deal in the Wilde trials, as it would matter in 'Victorian' legal cases down to the point in 1960 when jury-members were asked whether they would be happy to allow their servants to read *Lady Chatterley's Lover*. (How many, one wonders, thought at that point of Wilde?) Carson sneered at Wilde's insistence that he found the company of working-class lads stimulating, but was his claim that he had 'a passion to civilise the community' entirely disingenuous?[33] Gender mattered as well, at least as far as the habitual misogyny of the Victorian establishment was concerned. Effeminacy had traditionally meant spending too much time with women, the implication being that something of their putative irrationality and fragility would rub off on male associates.

This was where Wilde's public manner (as much as his private preferences) landed him in such hot water: even to pose as someone who took a less than manly attitude to life, who refused to shoulder the burdens of conventional duty and morality, who spent his time doing less than respectable things with less than respectable boys, was a threat to public order and the establishment. Wilde was, in many respects, one of them. Of course they knew about indiscretions involving gentlemen and members of their own sex, but those gentlemen at least were tactful enough to leave the country before any scandal broke. That was clearly what had been expected of Wilde, too, on the day his libel action against Queensberry had failed. When the police applied to Sir John Bridge, the Bow Street magistrate, for an arrest-warrant on the afternoon of 5 April, he had carefully inquired after the time of the boat-train's departure, fixing the time of application for fifteen minutes afterwards. The place that Wilde might have occupied was taken by any one of six hundred gentlemen who apparently decided on the spur of the moment to take a holiday in France.[34]

Why Wilde chose to stay, knocking back hock and seltzer at the Cadogan Hotel before the detectives arrived, remains perhaps *the* question of his life. Writers in the twentieth century speculated at enormous length on what must have been going through his mind as the half-packed suitcase lay on the bed. Just some of the interpretations have included a Hamlet complex, a Jesus complex, a Greek-tragedy complex, a determination to stick by Douglas, a stand for gay rights, a misplaced confidence in his verbal dexterity, and a blow against the English oppressors by one keen on the cause of Irish Home Rule. That we shall probably never know whether it was one, all or none of the above only adds to the perennial fascination of Wilde as a biographical subject.

Wilde's downfall launched the twentieth century with a violent reaction against sexual immorality in general and homosexuality in particular. He had given a public face – languid, effete, ironic, ultra-aesthetic – to homo-sexuality. Taken in conjunction with new thought of the type advocated by Havelock Ellis, who argued in *Sexual Inversion* (1897) that 'inverts' had a medical condition, this encouraged the view that all homosexuals were 'naturally' like Wilde. Here, in a sense, is another 'invented tradition' from the Victorian age: for it is still widely assumed, in gay culture as well as straight, that Wilde represents some 'essence' of homosexuality.

'Camp' has long been assimilated as a legitimate weapon within sexual politics; but, where oppression is concerned, it is ironic that the first adjective that usually gets invoked is 'Victorian'.[35] Wilde, ever sensitive to the protean quality of human character, would surely have been one step ahead of such inconsistent thinking. One imagines that he would have been charmed but fundamentally suspicious of the way that many of the surface traits of his public manner – conveniently described as 'camp' – have been allowed to define the homosexual. The famous passage from *De Profundis* springs to mind about most people being other people, their thoughts belonging to someone else and their passions a quotation. How far have we been quoting Wilde's prosecutors on Wilde since those grim days in 1895?

One of the consequences of such historical ventriloquism was, for many years, the virtual eradication of any rival traditions of homosexual depiction. In Wilde's own time, however, there was a strong movement to integrate same-sex relationships with the new drive towards masculine robustness. The great prophet here was Edward Carpenter, a remarkable character who had been born into a comfortable family in 1844, taken holy orders and a Cambridge fellowship, and given it all up to lead a back-to-nature lifestyle with his working-class partner George Merrill.[36] Carpenter was a disciple of Walt Whitman and a distinguished poet in his own right, melding these principles with a belief in Platonic thought and socialism. 'He went on to try,' writes Gregory Woods, 'in his lifestyle and in his writing alike, to show that Whitman's democratic ideals could operate to beneficial effect even in the Britain of empire and Victoria.'[37] This places him in something like the tradition of public duty that has been identified elsewhere in this book as one of the great legacies of Victorianism. Carpenter published his view of a tolerant and progressive society in *Homogenic Love and its Place in a Free Society* just months before Wilde's demise. Almost inevitably, it was swept away in the deluge, and thereafter he experienced more trouble than ever in finding publishers.[38]

Carpenter lived on until 1929, but his name was marginalised amongst commentators on sexuality. It was only in the pages of E. M. Forster's *Maurice* (1914), inspired by a visit to Carpenter and Merrill, that the vision lingered; even then, Forster did not allow the novel to be published during his lifetime.[39] *Maurice* offers a telling vantage-point on the perception of homosexuality in Britain at the end of the Edwardian years. A less Wildean character than Forster, the man who habitually looked for all the world like a down-at-heel suburban clerk, it would be difficult to imagine. His novel of same-sex passion ends with a Carpenteresque escape into the greenwood, but not before the eponymous hero has experienced the panic of being 'an unspeakable of the Oscar Wilde sort'.[40] (The clever-talking character Risley, incidentally, expanded for the Merchant Ivory film, was based on Lytton Strachey.) And indeed, 'Oscar Wilde' had become by then a byword for moral and medical perversity. Robert Roberts recalled that in working-class Edwardian Salford there was prurient fascination with the aftermath of Wilde's trials. 'As late as the First World War', he writes, 'the ribald cry heard in the factories, "Watch out for oscarwile!" mystified raw young apprentices.'[41] Although a complete (or nearly complete) edition of Wilde's works appeared in 1908, he was a subject also to be glossed over in polite society. When the young Angus Wilson asked his father what Wilde did, he received the reply: 'Oh, he messed about – with – little girls.' [42] T. E. Lawrence's mother would not allow Wilde's name to be mentioned in front of young ladies.[43] The political establishment remained equally hostile: Charles Brookfield, the examiner of plays for the Lord Chamberlain after 1911, had a profound and personal hatred of Wilde.[44]

One of the plays that continued to be banned, on grounds of its depiction of biblical scenes and general immorality, was Wilde's *Salomé*. This play was to provoke a remarkable scandal during the First World War, a time of great moral fervour and suspicion of anything vaguely foreign. (The Continent was widely deemed to be awash with decadence: that *Salomé* had been written in French and performed in Paris did not surprise the authorities in the least.) Noel Pemberton Billing, the independent MP for East Hertfordshire and editor of the *Imperialist*, claimed in January 1918 that the Germans had a 'black book' of 47,000 British deviants who could be leant upon for espionage. Some of these names belonged to people involved in a private production of *Salomé*, and the actress in the lead role sued for libel. Once again, the forces of morality were ranged heavily against Wilde: even Lord Alfred Douglas, of all people, acted as a character witness in Billing's favour. Justice Darling, the presiding judge, magnanimously overlooked the fact that his name had been revealed to be one of the 47,000 in order to focus upon the real enemy. 'Well, gentlemen,' he summed up for the jury, 'it is possible to regard [Wilde] as a great artiste, but he certainly was a great beast; there is no doubt about that.' [45]

Grotesquely comic as such an incident may seem, the stifling pall of gloom and guilt associated with Wilde hung heavily over society. Those of the 'Oscar Wilde sort' were not the only ones to suffer. Wilde's estranged wife Constance, broken in spirit, was unable to cope with various physical ailments and died in 1898. Their young sons paid an equally heavy price. After Wilde's demise they were whisked away to a succession of places in Europe, never again to see their father. Nor were they allowed to keep his name: in 1895 Cyril and Vyvyan Wilde had their surname changed to 'Holland', a name with the reassuring obscurity of dating back to the eleventh century on their mother's side. The younger son, Vyvyan, did not really know what all the fuss was about, but Cyril did. Vyvyan in his autobiography describes an appalling panic when his brother found a name-badge in part of his school uniform still bearing the legend 'Wilde'. 'I can see my brother now,' he wrote, 'in the comparative seclusion of the washing-place, frantically hacking away at the tapes with his pocket-knife.' [46] Cyril sadly internalised the prevailing attitudes to his father, and was determined to set the record straight, if only before God's eyes. 'All these years my great incentive has been to wipe that stain away', he wrote to Vyvyan in June 1914. 'I must be a *man* ... I ask nothing better than to end in honourable battle for my King and Country.'[47] He was killed by a German sniper in May 1915.

Moral opprobrium hung scarcely less heavy after the war. John Betjeman, who included a poem called 'The Arrest of Oscar Wilde at the Cadogan Hotel' in his 1937 collection *Continual Dew*, began exchanging literary letters with Lord Alfred Douglas in the 1920s. He was soon given a stern reprimand by his father. 'He's a bugger', Betjeman *père* fulminated, 'You're not to write another letter to that man.'[48] There was, of course, something of a camp following for Wilde amongst Oxford undergraduates of Betjeman's generation: Harold Acton and Brian Howard, two of the leading lights, had already emulated Wilde at Eton. Both there and at Oxford, however, they were few in number, and looked upon with suspicion by their peers.[49] Nancy Mitford, in her 1945 novel *The Pursuit of Love*, would gently mock the awkward conversations brought about by several generations of inquisitive children:

> Linda and I were very much preoccupied with sin, and our great hero was Oscar Wilde.
>
> 'But what did he *do?*'
>
> 'I asked [Uncle Matthew] once and he roared at me – goodness, it was terrifying. He said: "If you mention that sewer's name again in this house I'll thrash you, do you hear, damn you?" So I asked Sadie and she looked awfully vague and said "Oh, duck, I never really quite knew, but whatever it was was worse than murder, fearfully bad. And, darling, don't talk about him at meals, will you?"'

Eventually finding out what Wilde's crime was, it became 'no longer a mystery' and therefore seemed 'dull, unromantic, and incomprehensible'.[50] So much for preserving the ears of vulnerable young people.

Even as Mitford was writing her squib, the plays of Wilde had long been doing a healthy trade across the world. In the financial year 1934–35, for example, the Wilde estate had accumulated over £73 in gross royalties. (The living Sir Edward Elgar, to put this in perspective, had only been paid £75 for the fifth *Pomp and Circumstance* march in 1930.) The BBC was always keen to broadcast extracts from the plays (though it had second thoughts about *Salomé*, dropped 'on policy grounds' in 1942), and in 1938 one of the first television broadcasts was a complete performance of *The Importance of Being Earnest*. Extracts from *Lady Windermere's Fan* were broadcast in 1946 for a programme on 'etiquette'. This must have rankled amongst those who felt – like Uncle Matthew – that Wilde the man was a 'sewer'.[51]

After the Second World War, the enduring stigmatisation of Wilde's name had indeed become something of a joke amongst anyone who took a sensible attitude to such matters. Lord Alfred Douglas, who spent thirty years after Wilde's death trying to distance himself from their association and libelling a string of high-profile figures, had died in 1945. His last years, marked by Catholic faith and a mellower attitude to the world, had seen him write some constructive and even affectionate pages on Wilde.[52] Hesketh Pearson's shrewd life of Wilde was published in 1946. In 1948 Montgomery Hyde published a transcript of the Wilde trials, and an edition of the complete works appeared. The following year an almost complete version of *De Profundis* was published. In 1954, the centenary of Wilde's birth, Vyvyan Holland published his *Son of Oscar Wilde*; and, as Merlin Holland (his own son) has commented, it was the war years and Vyvyan's happy marriage that enabled him to relax his previously very guarded attitude towards family history. It is striking, though, that Merlin was not given a copy of the book – a work of almost miraculous understatement and good taste – until 1961, when he was fifteen. (Vyvyan touchingly kept the copy in trust, so to speak, inscribing it 'For Merlin with fondest love from his Daddy' on the day of publication: an echo, surely, of the rupture that had been forced upon Vyvyan and his own father.)[53]

Still, the late 1940s and 1950s were undoubtedly marked by a traditional outlook on sexual morality on the part of the political establishment. As we have seen, there was widespread anxiety on the part of the establishment about standards of conduct after the war. Homosexuality, having been widely viewed since the inter-war years as a product of arrested development, was stigmatised more than ever before. Even Montgomery Hyde, a sympathetic and neutral observer, launched his account of the trials with the bald statement: 'Wilde must now be considered as a pathological case study.'[54] Part of the transcripts were held back in 1948 because they were deemed to infringe the Obscene Publications Act, and they did not appear until the 1962 edition. Merlin Holland recalls how, as a toddler, other children were steered away from him in the park after Hyde's book appeared.[55] The ghost of Wilde still haunted most images of sexual depravity. 'There is perhaps', scowled St John Irvine in his *Oscar Wilde: A Present Time Appraisal* (1951), 'too much tendency to-day to make light of sodomy, too great a tendency to condemn harshly and without attempt at understanding, those who were most ferocious in their denunciation of Wilde's offence.'[56] (That this seems not to have been Wilde's offence was, to such commentators, quite beside the point.)

The government, almost exactly a century after Wilde's birth, wanted to toughen laws against prostitution and homosexuality. In this respect their initiatives were, without question, more consciously homophobic than those of Labouchère in 1885. But what they got, in the Wolfenden Report of 1957, was a recommendation to decriminalise the activities of consenting men in private. In some respects the committee chaired by Sir John Wolfenden was in the best tradition of Victorian public duty, accentuating the belief that private conduct was no part of the law's business so long as it did not impinge upon public order. Despite having a glamorously homosexual son at Oxford (and which college could it have been other than Magdalen, Wilde's *alma mater*?), Wolfenden himself was antipathetic to same-sex relationships. 'His suggestion that homosexuality be decriminalised', reflects Sebastian Faulks, 'was a victory for intellectual process over personal distaste; it was a vindication of the disinterested mental disciplines of Oxford PPE [Politics, Philosophy and Economics].' [57] Wolfenden was supported by other advocates of traditional public duty, like Noël Annan and the elderly Clement Attlee, but most of his peers were not so gracious. Amidst shrill cries of the sort that 'incest is a much more natural act than homosexuality', criminal reform was shelved for another decade and another climate.[58]

That criminal reform did eventually take place in 1967 owed itself, in part, to the prominence of Wilde in the eyes of the younger post-war generation. (That reform took as long as it did might also, paradoxically, be attributed to the lasting resonance of the Wilde scandal.) The efforts of the previous fifteen or so years continued, with complete publication of *De Profundis* in 1960 and the important collection of letters edited by Rupert Hart-Davis two years later. In 1966 came the full version of the *Complete Works*. But perhaps most significant here were the two films about Wilde's demise (based on Hyde's trial transcripts) that appeared in 1960: one with Robert Morley and the other with Peter Finch. Wilde was depicted in these films as a hero, however flawed and tragic: for *Oscar Wilde* (Morley) and *The Trials of Oscar Wilde* (Finch) not only monopolised growing interest in the man but must be seen in the context of the debate over legal reform. Reviews in *The Times* did not play upon the topical nature of the films, but they did alight on the films' shared emphasis on Wilde as a victim, both of himself and of Douglas.[59] Advertising posters, by contrast, drove the historical point home vividly: 'Theirs was a relationship', they announced dramatically, 'the world could not, *would* not tolerate.' [60]

Seven years later, at least in the eyes of the law, such relationships were tolerated. Vyvyan Holland, happily, lived to see it happen. Born a year after the law that would destroy his father, and dying a few months after its repeal in 1967, the son of Oscar Wilde had lived almost entirely under the shadow of the past. That he bore the burden as graciously as he did also meant that Wildean values were kept alive well into the twentieth century. 'I have no quarrels with fate,' he wrote in 1966, 'which has almost overwhelmed me at times, but which has, in the end, left me, as it were, washed up on the shores of time in the warm sunlight.'[61] This is a passage one can imagine his father having penned.

Since the 1960s Wilde has inevitably, and as we have seen sometimes problematically, retained his status as an icon of martyred sexuality. But it is also noteworthy that his life and work have increasingly been interpreted from other perspectives, and these shed some illuminating light on how we have chosen to use the Victorian past. Wilde's putative anti-Victorianism was, for a long while, downplayed amongst observers. His old reputation as a satirist had been overlaid, after 1895, with an even more subversive resonance. But the glow soon dimmed, and with a certain intellectual reaction against Victorianism in the early years of the twentieth century, Wilde himself came to be seen as a dated figure. 'The wit of his "Golden lads and girls" in those superb comedies may soon fall a little faint and thin upon our ears', wrote one critic in 1916. 'To the next generation it may seem as faded and old-fashioned as the wit of Congreve or Sheridan.'[62] It was, of course, the very datedness that appealed to the Oxford aesthetes. However, for Vincent O'Sullivan, writing in 1936, Wilde seemed more remote than ever to the younger generation: 'There is no doubt that many young men and women feel themselves as remote from Wilde as from (say!) Matthew Arnold.'[63] Wilde had never, admittedly, been celebrated for his modernity. Instead he revelled in subverting most of the principles of modern aesthetics – modernity of form, for instance, he rubbished as 'a huge price to pay for a very poor result'.[64] 'The one duty we owe to history is to re-write it', he commented in 1891, and for many observers that was exactly what Wilde had done in his collection of poems published ten years before, a work where the thin line between pastiche and plagiarism had been repeatedly and cheerfully crossed.[65] Viewed as an original artist, Wilde for much of the twentieth century seemed to accord with his own saying that he had put his genius into his life and only his talent into his work.

It is precisely the life – epigrammatic, ironic, posed, protean – that has come to resonate so powerfully since the 1980s. In the age of post-modernism, sensitive to the way in which reality can be 'constructed' by language, Wilde appeared as a figure of almost visionary significance.[66] The three key essays in *Intentions* (1891) – 'The Decay of Lying', 'The Critic as Artist' and 'The Truth of Masks' – came in for renewed attention as tracts years ahead of their time. Is it not true that 'Life imitates Art far more than Art imitates Life', that the artist (always Wilde's supreme individual) can draw our attention to things that we would otherwise miss in banal reality? Should not real art-criticism be an act of imaginative (re)creation in its own right? Do not people only reveal the truth when they speak from behind a mask or pose? Phrases such as the following, from *The Picture of Dorian Gray*, have come to assume new significance: 'It is the spectator, and not life, that art really mirrors.' [67]

If we have accepted that biography is an art, then the same is true of books and films about Wilde: we find in him what we choose to look for. As Merlin Holland has commented, Wilde the man is a superb subject for such treatment on account of the manifold contradictions of his life: the Irishman who supported Home Rule but revelled in English high society; the Protestant with Catholic leanings; the married homosexual; the dedicated writer constantly impatient to put down his pen; the satirist of high society who was a snob; the acute observer of human nature who could not sense peril when it was blindingly obvious. 'It is simply not a life which can tolerate an either/or approach with logical conclusions,' Holland reflects, 'but demands the flexibility of a both/and treatment, often raising questions for which there are no answers.' [68] Small wonder, then, that shrewd writers like Peter Ackroyd have sought to elucidate Wilde by letting him do the talking in *The Last Testament of Oscar Wilde* (1983). Others, like Neil Bartlett, have loosely combined cultural analysis with personal comments addressed to Wilde, leaving readers to make as much (or as little) sense of the subject as they see fit.[69] 'His style does not translate easily into a more concise or lucid form', Thomas Wright has observed. 'Like his personality it seems to resist summary: it can only be repeated or, in some way, reperformed.' It is difficult, he adds, to say 'anything about Wilde better than he said it himself'.[70]

Richard Ellmann's biography of 1987 managed, nevertheless, to say a good deal about Wilde in a way that made few intellectual compromises but paid affectionate and discriminating tribute to its subject. Completed under the shadow of serious illness, Wilde lives irrepressibly within its pages and must have been a most agreeable companion on especially dark days. Not, of course, that Ellmann was an uncritical commentator on Wilde: as the lucid biographer of Yeats and Joyce, he brought to his work a clear-eyed perspective that noted his subject's inconsistencies and frailties. Perhaps, though, in addition to the sharply-honed scholarly sense, it is the unjudgemental quality of the biography that shines through: all the more so when, as we have seen, there was such a long history of pompous moralising about Wilde. It is tempting to add that Ellmann reached such a state of discerning empathy by paying heed to the 'essence' of Wilde. On the topic of Wilde's health (and especially death) he is questionable; on the topic of Wilde's sexuality he is impartial if evidently distanced; but on the topic of Wilde's intellectual significance – the really important issue – he is superbly illuminating. 'The object of life is not to simplify it', Ellmann writes, summarising Wilde's view of the world by the time that he left Oxford. 'As our conflicting impulses coincide, as our repressed feelings vie with our expressed ones, as our solid views disclose unexpected striations, we are all secret dramatists. In this light Wilde's works become exercises in self-criticism as well as pleas for tolerance.'[71]

Such indeterminacy may not help biographers less accomplished than Ellmann who are intent on painting a comprehensive portrait of Wilde, but it has reinvigorated attitudes to his place within history. Partly, perhaps, with the resurgence of unrest in Northern Ireland since the 1970s, we have become acquainted with a Wilde whose arch reversals of sober English morality could be interpreted as a blow for the nationalist cause. His mother, Lady 'Speranza' Wilde, was a prominent Irish nationalist. She told Wilde in 1895 that as long as he stood trial, whatever the outcome might be, her affection for him would remain undimmed. 'Oscar is an Irish gentleman,' his brother Willie explained, 'and he will face the music.'[72] Wilde had once written to Gladstone, the great advocate of Home Rule, that he and his fellow countrymen had 'deep admiration ... for the one English statesman who has understood us [and] will lead us to the grandest and justest political victory of this age'.[73] In his final delirium, laid out in exile on a bed in a Parisian hotel, he apparently thought he was returning home – to Ireland.[74] The most influential interpretation that pursued this theme was Terry Eagleton's play *Saint Oscar* (1989). Subtitled 'an irreverent musical biography', it was, as most intelligent recent readings have been, Wildean to the core. Stephen Rea literally unpeeled layer after layer of clothes to reveal a new Wilde each time: a purple velvet suit gave way to an outfit with a green carnation, which gave way to a prison uniform and then to rags *à la* Saint Sebastian. Same-sex practices, rife in England ('Homosexual behaviour', Rea proclaimed, 'is as English as Morris dancing, if somewhat less tedious'), were yet deemed dangerous in an Irishman.[75] Anachronistic and political it may have been: but that was Eagleton's point, and it was the kind of extravagantly artificial depiction that Wilde in all probability would have enjoyed. It is the duty of Wildeans always to be slightly improbable.

Performance is the key: Wilde's persona and use of language, constantly challenging expectations and subverting conventional definitions, has been seen as a strategy to discuss issues close to his heart. These issues, Wilde knew, did not give themselves easily to debate of a ponderously analytical nature. 'Art is the only serious thing in the world', he wrote in 1894. 'And the artist is the only person who is never serious.'[76] Possibly it is because Wilde was so helplessly embroiled in the society of his time – a recognisably 'modern' society – that many of his fundamentally chaste and serious observations were wrapped up in a form that we still find compelling.

Regenia Gagnier has reminded us that Wilde the accumulative Victorian gentleman was also Wilde the post-modernist: a man who saw the dangers, for himself as well as society in general, of being imprisoned within mindless conformity and ugly materialism.[77] That perhaps helps to explain some of Wilde's idiosyncratic socialism, his insistence on beauty, his belief in individuality. There were too many morals and messages in late Victorian society, he felt; rather than burdening people with more, and probably being ignored for his efforts, Wilde decided to show the importance of being less than earnest. That, at least, would be a reading that does not take account of arguments that Wilde was in reality only a shallow poser. Both readings would, of course, have delighted Wilde. After all, there is only one thing in the world worse than being talked about, and that is not being talked about.[78]

The depiction of Wilde that is probably most familiar to a wide audience today is that of Stephen Fry in Brian Gilbert's 1997 film *Wilde*. Based upon Richard Ellmann's biography, it shared much of the humanity and wisdom of that book, and managed to convey some of the more recent approaches considered above. The delightfully inventive opening scene, for example, is set in a mine in Colorado. Wilde's ultimate destiny is foreshadowed in his Dante-like descent into the earth, but so too is his redeeming belief in beautiful craftsmanship with a mini-lecture on Benvenuto Cellini to an audience of enthralled miners. The film succeeds in no small part on account of the excellent cast. Stephen Fry not only bears a striking resemblance to Wilde and delivers the epigrams with wonderful aplomb, but brings to the part a characteristic gentleness and urbanity. And Jude Law as Lord Alfred Douglas, blessed with the sort of looks as to make the original Bosie seem almost plain, launches superbly into the part with trademark absorption and edge. Both contribute powerfully to an already compelling scenario which plays up Wilde's underrated status as a loving family man: 'The Selfish Giant', his quasi-religious children's story about individual sacrifice, is used as a motif throughout. So, too, is the Irish dimension brought out, with a memorable scene between Lady Wilde (Vanessa Redgrave) and her son in which the nationalist challenge is fully emphasised. Lady Wilde is given the line about her son being an Irish gentleman, to which he replies: 'Of course I am your son, Madre. Which is why – even if I lose – the English will never forget me.' [79]

One's only reservations about this depiction – and of course, a film must conform to cinematic demands – relate to an emphasis, shared with the Ellmann biography, that Wilde was in some modern sense always 'homosexual'.[80] This seems a rather reductive and anachronistic reading, sitting oddly alongside the laudable decision to portray Wilde as a devoted husband and father. Here the film comes closest to importing modern notions about sexual identity into the Victorian age. Odd also is the ending which suggests, with the barest hint of ambivalence on screen (though the screenplay is more explicit: '[Wilde] moves slowly towards his doom'), that Wilde was happily reunited with Douglas after his release from prison. The truth – as Wilde had put it, rarely pure and never simple – was that they soon separated again. Wilde eked out his last years, disgraced and impoverished, in a succession of lodgings in France. The quips were still there, but not with as much frequency, and rarely committed to paper. He died, two months before Queen Victoria, in a modest hotel room in Paris, having taken violent exception to the flowery wallpaper. It would be, he said, a struggle to the death.

# Notes

## Notes to Preface

1. For an account of the tribunal see M. Holroyd, *Lytton Strachey* (revised edn, London, 1994), pp. 348–49.
2. L. Strachey, 'Carlyle' (1928), in M. Holroyd and P. Levy (eds), *The Shorter Strachey* (London, 1989), pp. 104–5.

## Notes to Chapter 1: The Victorians

1. *OED Supplement*, p. 1158.
2. *OED Supplement*, p. 1158: 'Perhaps the Annean authors, though inferior to the Elizabethans, are, on a general summation of merits, no less superior to the latter-Georgian and Victorian.' (*Athenaeum*, 2 November 1839.)
3. The librettist William Plomer sent Britten a copy of J. E. Neale's biography of Elizabeth I as a corrective to Strachey. But Britten was keen on pursuing the Elizabeth-Essex relationship, and in both characters created outsider/victim figures archetypical in his operas. It has also been commented that Britten was a little like Elizabeth in his court at Aldeburgh, habitually casting aside former favourites. H. Carpenter, *Benjamin Britten: A Biography* (London, 1992), pp. 307, 321, 323–24.
4. A. Andrews, *Kings and Queens of England and Scotland* (London, 1983), p. 153.
5. J. B. Bullen, 'Introduction', in idem (ed.), *Writing and Victorianism* (London, 1997), p. 1.
6. L. Strachey, *Queen Victoria* (London, 1921), pp. 141–42.
7. A. Briggs, 'The 1890s: Past, Present and Future in Headlines', in A. Briggs and D. Snowman (eds), *Fins de Siècle: How Centuries End, 1400–2000* (New Haven and London, 1996), p. 159; *The Times*, 23 January 1901.
8. J. Brewer, *The Pleasures of the Imagination: English Culture in the Eighteenth Century* (London, 1997).
9. R. C. K. Ensor, *England, 1870–1914* (Oxford, 1936), p. 137.
10. G. Eliot, *Middlemarch* (1872; Oxford, 1998), p. 822.
11. H. McLeod, *Religion and Society in England, 1850–1914* (Basingstoke, 1996), pp. 12–13.
12. L. Colley, *Britons: Forging the Nation, 1707–1837* (London, 1994), pp. 329–32.

13. F. Engels, *The Condition of the Working Class in England* (1845; Harmondsworth, 1987), p. 125.

14. G. M. Young, *Portrait of an Age: Victorian England* (2nd edn, Oxford, 1953), p. 131.

15. J. F. C. Harrison, *Early Victorian Britain, 1832–51* (London, 1988), p. 15; C. Matthew, 'Introduction', in idem (ed.), *Nineteenth-Century Britain* (Oxford, 2000), p. 1.

16. C. Dickens, *A Christmas Carol* (1843; Harmondsworth, 1986), p. 51.

17. D. Cannadine, *Class in Britain* (New Haven and London, 1998), ch. 3.

18. D. Newsome, *The Victorian World Picture: Perceptions and Introspections in an Age of Change* (London, 1997), p. 73.

19. D. J. Taylor, *Thackeray* (London, 2000), p. 19.

20. F. Thompson, *Lark Rise to Candleford* (1945; Harmondsworth, 1973), p. 18.

21. Newsome, *Victorian World Picture*, pp. 146–47.

22. A. Briggs, *Victorian Cities* (Harmondsworth, 1990), pp. 89, 101.

23. R. Samuel, 'Workshop of the World: Steam Power and Hand Technology in Mid-Victorian Britain', *History Workshop Journal*, 3 (1977), pp. 6–72; R. McKibbin, 'Why Was There No Marxism in Great Britain?', *English Historical Review*, 99 (1984), pp. 297–331.

24. The electorate, and electoral reform, was different in Scotland and Ireland. In accordance with the generally Anglocentric tone of Victorian politics, they tended to lag behind England where voting rights were concerned. In both countries only 13 per cent of men had the vote in the early 1860s, whereas 18 per cent of men did in England. By the early 1890s, 62 per cent of Englishmen had the vote, but only 56 per cent of Scotsmen and 58 per cent of Irishmen. Still, these figures were important in supplying the Liberals with a Celtic fringe of support. K. T. Hoppen, *The Mid-Victorian Generation, 1846–1886* (Oxford, 1998), pp. 239, 266.

25. E. J. Evans, *The Forging of the Modern State: Early Industrial England, 1783–1870* (2nd edn, London, 1996), pp. 220, 223.

26. A. Briggs, *Victorian People: A Reassessment of Persons and Themes, 1851–67* (Harmondsworth, 1990), p. 259.

27. See Maurice Hindle's introduction to the Penguin edition of *Frankenstein* (1818; Harmondsworth, 1992), pp. xxxviii–xl.

28. J. Ruskin, *Sesame and Lilies* (1865; London, 1909), p. 73.

29. C. Dickens, *Dombey and Son* (1848; Oxford, 1987), p. 63.

*Notes to Chapter 2: Anti-Victorianism*

1. L. Strachey, *Eminent Victorians* (1918; Harmondsworth, 1986), p. 266.

2. On the First World War and modernity see P. Fussell, *The Great War and Modern Memory* (Oxford, 1975); M. Eksteins, *Rites of Spring: The Great War and the Birth of the Modern Age* (London, 1989); S. Hynes, *A War Imagined: The First World War and English Culture* (London, 1990).

3. Henry James to Edward Emerson, 4 August 1914, in P. Horne (ed.), *Henry James: A Life in Letters* (Harmondsworth, 2000), p. 542.

4. Henry James to Edward Marsh, 6 June 1915, in Horne, *Henry James*, p. 547.

5. Hynes, *War Imagined*, p. 246.

6. Hynes, *War Imagined*, p. 249.

7. E. Gosse, 'The Agony of the Victorian Age' (1918), in *Some Diversions of a Man of Letters* (London, 1919), p. 313.

8. The scene is a famous one, caught on canvas by both A. C. Gow and John Charlton.

9. J. F. C. Harrison, *Late Victorian Britain, 1875–1901* (London, 1990), pp. 70–72.

10. See D. Cannadine, 'The Present and the Past in the English Industrial Revolution, 1880–1980', *Past and Present*, 116 (1987), pp. 169–91.

11. R. Kipling, *Something of Myself* (1936; Harmondsworth, 1992), p. 120.

12. P. J. Bowler, *Reconciling Science and Religion: The Debate in Early Twentieth-Century Britain* (Chicago, 2001).

13. A useful guide to the topic of declining church attendance is H. McLeod, *Religion and Society in England, 1850–1914* (Basingstoke, 1996).

14. See M. Bradbury and J. McFarlane (eds), *Modernism: A Guide to European Literature, 1890–1930* (new edn, Harmondsworth, 1991).

15. G. Kitson Clark, *The Making of Victorian England* (London, 1965), pp. 28–29, 287; P. Keating, *The Haunted Study: A Social History of the English Novel, 1875–1914* (London, 1989), pp. 102–3; M. Mason, *The Making of Victorian Sexuality* (Oxford, 1994), pp. 8–20. Mason is particularly keen on the idea of 'historical slippage' within anti-Victorianism, writing: 'By the end of the Great War the stigma of prudish moralism, which had passed from the early nineteenth century, to the early and then mid-Victorian years, comes to rest on the whole Victorian era – and there it has remained until the present' (p. 18). Still, specificity of reference can be found in many early-twentieth century writings. Robert Graves in his memoir *Goodbye to All That* (1929; Harmondsworth, 1960), for example, writes of public school 'romance of a conventional early Victorian type' and of 'heavy early Victorian jewellery' (pp. 39, 46).

16. H. H. Asquith, *Some Aspects of the Victorian Age* (Oxford, 1918), p. 4.

17. G. M. Young, *Portrait of an Age: Victorian England* (2nd edn, Oxford, 1953), p. 100.

18. M. Hovell, *The Chartist Movement* (Manchester, 1918); J. West, *A History of the Chartist Movement* (London, 1920).

19. H. Gaitskell, *Chartism: An Introductory Essay* (London, 1929). Ironically the Chartists had only petitioned for male, not universal, suffrage.

20. S. A. Dutt, *When England Arose: The Centenary of the People's Charter* (London, 1938), pp. 64, 5–6.

21. J. H. Clapham, 'The Study of Economic History', in N. B. Harte (ed.), *The Study of Economic History: Collected Inaugural Lectures, 1893–1970* (London, 1971), p. 59.

22. M. Holroyd, *Lytton Strachey* (revised edn, London, 1994), p. 428.

23. R. W. Seton-Watson, *Disraeli, Gladstone and the Eastern Question: A Study in Diplomacy and Party Politics* (London, 1935), p. ix.

24. T. H. White, *Farewell Victoria* (1933; London, 1993), p. 98.

25. S. Hynes, *The Edwardian Turn of Mind* (London, 1991), p. 329.

26. Holroyd, *Strachey*, p. 171.

27. V. Woolf, 'Mr Bennett and Mrs Brown', in *Collected Essays*, i (London, 1980), p. 320.

28. Hynes, *Edwardian Turn*, p. 344.

29. Kitson Clark, *Making*, p. 28.

30. H. G. Wells, *Ann Veronica* (London, 1909), p. 203.

31. E. Jepson, *Memories of a Victorian* (London, 1933), pp. 9, 83.

32. E. F. Benson, *As We Were: A Victorian Peep-Show* (London, 1930), p. 23.

33. B. Shaw, *A Mid-Victorian Trifle: A One-Act Comedy for Five Women* (London, 1940), p. 20.

34. See P. Mandler, *The Fall and Rise of the Stately Home* (New Haven and London, 1997), pp. 278–95.

35. M. Sweet, *Inventing the Victorians* (London, 2001), pp. 125–26.

36. W. Collins, *Basil* (1852; Oxford, 1990), p. 61.

37. C. Dickens, *Our Mutual Friend* (1865; Harmondsworth, 1997), p. 17.

38. A. Paul Oppé, 'Art', in G. M. Young (ed.), *Early Victorian England, 1830–1865*, ii (Oxford, 1934), p. 140.

39. L. Strachey, 'A Victorian Critic' (1914), in *Characters and Commentaries* (London, 1933), p. 187.

40. D. H. Lawrence, *Lady Chatterley's Lover* (1928; Harmondsworth, 1994), p. 147.

41. Mandler, *Fall and Rise*, pp. 283–85.

42. H. Carpenter, *The Brideshead Generation: Evelyn Waugh and his Friends* (London, 1989), p. 211.

43. R. Dixon and S. Muthesius, *Victorian Architecture* (2nd edn, London, 1985), p. 204.

44. N. Jones, *Rupert Brooke: Life, Death and Myth* (London, 1999), p. 36.

45. P. G. Wodehouse, *Summer Moonshine* (1937; Harmondsworth, 1996), p. 17.

46. A. E. Richardson, 'Architecture', in Young, *Early Victorian England*, ii, p. 235.

47. V. Woolf, *Orlando* (1928; Harmondsworth, 1993), p. 158.

48. D. Bush, 'The Victorians, God Bless Them!', *The Bookman*, 74 (1932), pp. 589–90.

49. D. Cecil, *Early Victorian Novelists: Essays in Revaluation* (1934; London, 1943), pp. 68, 255.

50. Woolf, 'Mr Bennett'.

51. See C. Ricks (ed.), *The New Oxford Book of Victorian Verse* (Oxford, 1987), pp. xxiii–xxv.

52. See J. Stuart Roberts, *Siegfried Sassoon* (London, 1999), pp. 102, 131–32, 160, 170, 183–84, 218–19; H. Ricketts, *The Unforgiving Minute: A Life of Rudyard Kipling* (London, 1999), pp. 354–57.

53. A. Wright, *Foreign Country: The Life of L. P. Hartley* (London, 1996), p. 179.

54. S. Butler, *The Way of All Flesh* (1903; Oxford, 1993), p. 185. Cf. M. Proust, *Swann's Way*, trans. C. K. Scott Moncrieff (1913; Harmondsworth, 1957), p. 37:

'That hateful staircase, up which I always passed with such dismay, gave out a smell of varnish which had to some extent absorbed, made definite and fixed the special quality of sorrow that I felt each evening, and made it perhaps even more cruel to my sensibility because, when it assumed this olfactory guise, my intellect was powerless to resist it.' The unhappy childhood memory of varnish was evidently not restricted to these shores.

55. E. Gosse, *Father and Son* (1907; Harmondsworth, 1989), pp. 251, 249.

56. Nigel Nicolson offers sensible comments on the character of the Bloomsbury Group in *Virginia Woolf* (London, 2000), pp. 28–31.

57. J. Brown, *Spirits of Place: Five Famous Lives in their English Landscape* (London, 2001), pp. 21–22.

58. H. Lee, *Virginia Woolf* (London, 1996), p. 481.

59. Holroyd, *Strachey*, pp. 5, 13.

60. L. Strachey, 'Lancaster Gate' (1922), in M. Holroyd (ed.), *Lytton Strachey by Himself: A Self-Portrait* (London, 1971), p. 20.

61. E. M. Forster, *Where Angels Fear to Tread* (1905; Harmondsworth, 1976), p. 125.

62. E. M. Forster, *A Room with a View* (1908; Harmondsworth, 1990), p. 144.

63. H. James, *The Wings of the Dove* (1902; Oxford, 1984), pp. 55–56

## Notes to Chapter 3: Survivals

1. N. Annan, *Our Age: The Generation that Made Post-War Britain* (London, 1990), p. 65.

2. V. Woolf, 'The Art of Biography' (1939), in *The Crowded Dance of Modern Life* (Harmondsworth, 1993), pp. 144–51.

3. M. Holroyd, *Lytton Strachey* (revised edn, London, 1994), pp. 562–63; British Library, Additional MS 60721 (Strachey Papers), fos 90–91.

4. M. Bradbury, *The Modern British Novel* (Harmondsworth, 1994), p. 115; N. Beauman, *Morgan: A Biography of E. M. Forster* (London, 1993), photograph between pp. 36–37.

5. E. M. Forster, *The Longest Journey* (1907; Harmondsworth, 1989), p. 171.

6. L. Strachey, 'Lancaster Gate' (1922), in M. Holroyd (ed.), *Lytton Strachey by Himself: A Self-Portrait* (London, 1971), p. 17.

7. Strachey, 'Lancaster', pp. 20–21.

8. J. Brown, *Spirits of Place: Five Famous Lives in their English Landscape* (London, 2001), p. 187.

9. Quoted in F. Spalding, *Duncan Grant: A Biography* (London, 1998), p. 457. Holroyd describes the reception of the biography in the 'Double Preface' to the 1994 edition (cited above).

10. V. Woolf, *Night and Day* (1919; Harmondsworth, 1992), p. 29.

11. D. Leader, *Why Do Women Write More Letters Than They Post?* (London, 1997), p. 67.

12. R. Graves and A. Hodge, *The Long Weekend: A Social History of Britain, 1918–1939* (London, 1940), pp. 15–16.

13. W. L. Burn, *The Age of Equipoise: A Study of the Mid-Victorian Generation* (London, 1964), p. 24.
14. R. Hoggart, *A Local Habitation: Life and Times, 1918–1940* (London, 1988), p. 11.
15. A. Calder and D. Sheridan (eds), *Speak for Yourself: A Mass-Observation Anthology, 1937–49* (London, 1984), pp. 159–60, 49; J. Richards and D. Sheridan (eds), *Mass-Observation at the Movies* (London, 1987), pp. 39–40.
16. A. Briggs, 'Victorian Images of Gladstone', in P. J. Jagger (ed.), *Gladstone* (London, 1998), pp. 33–49.
17. J. Drummond, *Tainted by Experience: A Life in the Arts* (London, 2000), p. 11.
18. *The Times*, 3 December 1936. On the afterlife of the Great Exhibition see J. A. Auerbach, *The Great Exhibition of 1851: A Nation on Display* (New Haven and London, 1999), ch. 8.
19. J. Rose, *The Intellectual Life of the British Working Classes* (New Haven and London, 2001), pp. 245–46.
20. Rose, *Intellectual Life*, pp. 139–40.
21. Rose, *Intellectual Life*, p. 138.
22. R. Hoggart, 'Memoir for our Grandchildren', in *Between Two Worlds: Essays* (London, 2001), p. 235.
23. Rose, *Intellectual Life*, p. 422.
24. W. Murdoch, *The Victorian Era: Its Strengths and Weakness* (Sydney, 1938), p. 2.
25. D. Montefiore, *From a Victorian to a Modern* (London, 1927).
26. M. Hughes, *A London Family, 1870–1900* (Oxford, 1991), p. 2. This edition brings together Hughes's *A London Child of the Seventies* (1934), *A London Girl of the Eighties* (1936) and *A London Home in the Nineties* (1937).
27. W. Kent, *The Testament of a Victorian Youth* (London, 1938).
28. J. Thorpe, *Happy Days: Recollections of an Unrepentant Victorian* (London, 1933), p. 303.
29. A. A. Baumann, *The Last Victorians* (London, 1927), p. 16.
30. A. Bott, *Our Fathers, 1870–1900* (London, 1931), p. 4.
31. The first use of the term 'mid-Victorian' is difficult to trace, though it seems probable that it dates from the last decade or so of Queen Victoria's reign. Arnold Bennett writes of the death of John Baines in *The Old Wives' Tale* (1908; Harmondsworth, 1990), p. 112: 'John Baines had belonged to the past, to the age when men really did think of their souls, when orators by phrases could move crowds to fury or to pity, when no one had learnt to hurry, when Demos was only turning in his sleep, when the sole beauty of life resided in its inflexible and slow dignity, when hell really had no bottom, and a gilt-clasped Bible really was the secret of England's greatness. Mid-Victorian England lay on the mahogany table. Ideals had passed away with John Baines.'
32. E. Hopkinson, *The Story of a Mid-Victorian Girl* (Cambridge, 1928), p. 3.
33. M. Betham-Edwards, *Mid-Victorian Memories* (London, 1919), p. xlviii.
34. Betham-Edwards, *Mid-Victorian Memories*, p. 118.
35. R. E. Francillon, *Mid-Victorian Memories* (London, 1914), p. 3.

36. As a socialist it is not surprising that Belfort Bax had mixed feelings about the nineteenth century, though, as Duncan Tanner has observed in *Political Change and the Labour Party, 1900–1918* (Cambridge, 1990), p. 33, he also 'recognised the strength of the past' in his thinking. It is difficult not to see some connection between this ambivalence and the feelings about his childhood. See also R. Arch, *Ernest Belfort Bax: Thinker and Pioneer* (London, 1927).

37. E. Belfort Bax, *Reminiscences and Reflexions of a Mid and Late Victorian* (London, 1918), pp. 12–13. Did growing into a 'late Victorian' lessen the taint of being born a 'mid-Victorian'?

38. Belfort Bax, *Reminiscences*, p. 20.

39. On the Victorianism of political figures in the early twentieth century, particularly as measured by their lingering religiosity, see also P. Clarke, *Hope and Glory: Britain, 1900–1990* (London, 1996), pp. 159–60.

40. A. J. P. Taylor, *English History, 1914–1945* (Oxford, 1965), p. 398.

41. D. Cannadine, 'The Context, Performance and Meaning of Ritual: The British Monarchy and the "Invention of Tradition", *c.* 1820–1977', in E. Hobsbawm and T. Ranger (eds), *The Invention of Tradition* (Cambridge, 1983), pp. 142, 151–52; P. Brendon, *The Dark Valley: A Panorama of the 1930s* (London, 2001), pp. 356–59.

42. K. Rose, *King George V* (London, 1983), p. xiii.

43. S. Bradford, *King George VI* (London, 1989), p. 4.

44. D. Cannadine, 'Constitutional Monarchy', in *History in Our Time* (New Haven and London, 1998), p. 19.

45. G. M. Young, 'The Greatest Victorian' (1938), in *Victorian Essays* (Oxford, 1962), pp. 123–28.

46. *The Times*, 11 May 1937.

47. H. Bolitho, *George VI* (London, 1937), pp. 17–18.

48. Admittedly, and perhaps not surprisingly, some commentators in 1937 were rather sceptical about this attempt to (re)invent tradition. At least two historians saw little historical sense in celebrating a given day or even year for the sake of it, especially in the light of how unpopular the monarchy was in 1837. See G. M. Young, '1837–1937: Centenary of Queen Victoria's Accession', *The Times*, 11 May 1937, reprinted in his *Victorian Essays* (Oxford, 1962), pp. 13–35; C. K. Webster, 'The Accession of Queen Victoria', *History*, 22 (1937–38), pp. 14–33.

49. Brendon, *Dark Valley*, p. 353.

50. D. Cannadine, *The Decline and Fall of the British Aristocracy* (London, 1996), pp. 246–47.

51. P. Hennessy, *Whitehall* (London: revised edn, 2001), pp. 31–32, 36–43.

52. Martin Pugh in J. Cannon (ed.), *The Oxford Companion to British History* (Oxford, 1997), p. 563.

53. See K. Robbins, *Appeasement* (2nd edn, London, 1997).

54. See P. Williamson, 'The Doctrinal Policies of Stanley Baldwin', in M. Bentley (ed.), *Public and Private Doctrine: Essays in British History Presented to Maurice*

Cowling (Cambridge, 1993), pp. 181–208; idem, *Stanley Baldwin: Conservative Leadership and National Values* (Cambridge, 1999); D. Marquand, *Ramsay MacDonald* (London, 1977).

55. M. J. Wiener, *English Culture and the Decline of the Industrial Spirit, 1850–1980* (Cambridge, 1981), pp. 100, 73.
56. See S. Collini, *Public Moralists: Political Thought and Intellectual Life in Britain, 1850–1930* (Oxford, 1991).
57. 'The Intellectual Aristocracy' is reprinted in Annan's *The Dons: Mentors, Eccentrics and Geniuses* (London, 1999), pp. 304–41.
58. D. Cannadine, 'The First Hundred Years', in H. Newby (ed.), *The National Trust: The Next Hundred Years* (London, 1995), pp. 16–17.
59. J. C. W. Reith, *Broadcast Over Britain* (London, 1925), p. 34.
60. See A. Briggs, *The Birth of Broadcasting* (Oxford, 1961) and *The Golden Age of Wireless* (Oxford, 1965); D. LeMahieu, *A Culture for Democracy: Mass Communication and the Cultivated Mind in Britain between the Wars* (Oxford, 1988).
61. See C. Baldick, *The Social Mission of English Criticism, 1848–1932* (Oxford, 1983).
62. T. Steele, *The Emergence of Cultural Studies, 1945–65: Cultural Politics, Adult Education and the 'English' Question* (London, 1997), pp. 86–87.
63. See S. Pedersen and P. Mandler (eds), *After the Victorians: Private Conscience and Public Duty in Modern Britain. Essays in Memory of John Clive* (London, 1994).
64. Quoted in R. Skidelsky, *John Maynard Keynes: The Economist as Saviour, 1920–1937* (London, 1994), p. xx.
65. *The Victorian Age, by A Later Victorian* (London, 1921), pp. viii, 79–80.
66. On Inge's view of the world see P. J. Bowler, *Reconciling Science and Religion: The Debate in Early Twentieth-Century Britain* (Chicago, 2001), pp. 270–77.
67. W. R. Inge, *The Victorian Age* (Cambridge, 1922), p. 42.
68. A. H. Jackson, *A Victorian Childhood* (London, 1932), p. 2.
69. Baumann, *Last Victorians*, p. 17.
70. G. M. Young, *Portrait of an Age: Victorian England* (1936; 2nd edn, Oxford, 1953), p. 164.
71. G. M. Young, 'The Greatest Victorian' (1938), in *Victorian Essays* (Oxford, 1962), p. 126.
72. On Peel's changing reputation see B. Hilton, 'Peel: A Reappraisal', *Historical Journal*, 22 (1979), pp. 585–614; D. Read, *Peel and the Victorians* (Oxford, 1987). Works published at the time include A. A. W. Ramsay, *Sir Robert Peel* (London, 1928); H. W. C. Davis, *The Age of Grey and Peel* (Oxford, 1929); R. L. Hill, *Toryism and the People, 1832–1846* (London, 1929); G. Kitson Clark, *Peel and the Conservative Party: A Study in Party Politics, 1832–1841* (London, 1929).
73. Clarke, *Hope*, p. 198.
74. H. Coote, *While I Remember* (London, 1937), p. 102.
75. J. A. Bridges, *Victorian Recollections* (London, 1919), p. 15; M. E. Perugini, *Victorian Days and Ways* (London, 1932), p. 46; E. Hamilton, *The Halcyon Era:*

*A Rambling Reveries of Now and Then* (London, 1933), pp. 8–9; N. Mitford, *The Pursuit of Love* (1945; Harmondsworth, 1949), p. 23.

76. *OED Supplement,* p. 1159.

77. The 'Royal Albert Society' was founded during the war at Osborne House, which had temporarily been turned into a military convalescent hospital. Robert Graves and fourteen others were members; one of the 'now popular burlesques of Victorianism', he wrote in *Goodbye to All That* (1929; Harmondsworth, 1960), p. 208, 'its pretended aim [was] to revive interest in the life and times of the Prince Consort'.

78. H. Carpenter, *The Brideshead Generation: Evelyn Waugh and his Friends* (London, 1989), p. 41. See also pp. 35–42, 72, 76, 78–79.

79. F. Partridge, *Memories* (London, 1981), p. 156.

80. M. Green, *Children of the Sun: A Narrative of 'Decadence' in England after 1918* (London, 1977), p. 189.

81. E. Waugh, *Vile Bodies* (1930; Harmondsworth, 1996), p. 104.

82. M. Ignatieff, *Isaiah Berlin: A Life* (London, 1998), p. 47.

83. S. Heffer, *Vaughan Williams* (London, 2001), pp. 92–93.

84. S. Sassoon, *The Complete Memoirs of George Sherston* (1937; London, 1972), p. 56.

85. S. Sassoon, *The Old Century and Seven More Years* (1938; London, 1968), p. 24.

86. G. Orwell, *Coming Up For Air* (1939; Harmondsworth, 1990), pp. 37, 110.

*Notes to Chapter 4: War*

1. G. Orwell, *The Lion and the Unicorn: Socialism and the English Genius* (1941; Harmondsworth, 1982), pp. 35, 53–54.

2. P. Hennessy, *Never Again: Britain, 1945–1951* (London, 1992); P. Addison, *The Road to 1945: British Politics and the Second World War* (revised edn, London, 1994).

3. J. Charmley, *Churchill: The End of Glory* (London, 1993), pp. 17, 251.

4. I. Berlin, 'Winston Churchill in 1940', in *The Proper Study of Mankind: An Anthology of Essays* (London, 1997), p. 608.

5. J. Stevenson and C. Cook, *Britain in the Depression: Society and Politics 1929–1939* (2nd edn, London, 1994), p. 79.

6. P. Hennessy, *The Prime Minister: The Office and its Holders since 1945* (revised edn, Harmondsworth, 2001), p. 172.

7. On Attlee and Morris see F. MacCarthy, *William Morris: A Life for Our Time* (London, 1994), pp. xvii–xviii.

8. P. Clarke, *A Question of Leadership, from Gladstone to Blair* (2nd edn, Harmondsworth, 1999), p. 43.

9. A Sked and C. Cook, *Post-War Britain: A Political History* (4th edn, Harmondsworth, 1993), p. 88.

10. R. Hewison, *Culture and Consensus: England, Art and Politics since 1940* (revised edn, London, 1997), pp. 29–49.

11. H. Carpenter, *The Envy of the World: Fifty Years of the BBC Third Programme and Radio 3* (London, 1996), pp. 7, 9.
12. Carpenter, *Envy*, pp. 10–11, 77–78.
13. Material from the series was subsequently published as *Ideas and Beliefs of the Victorians: An Historic Revaluation of the Victorian Age* (London, 1949).
14. Carpenter, *Envy*, p. 73.
15. Carpenter, *Envy*, p. 80
16. Carpenter, *Envy*, pp. 108–9.
17. R. Quinault, 'Britain 1950', *History Today*, 51 (April 2001), p. 19.
18. M. Forster, *Precious Lives* (London, 1998), pp. 8–9.
19. L. Sage, *Bad Blood* (London, 2000), pp. 18, 5, 178.
20. K. Chorley, *Manchester Made Them* (London, 1950); G. Raverat, *Period Piece: A Cambridge Childhood* (London, 1952).
21. J. Rose, *The Intellectual Life of the British Working Classes* (New Haven and London, 2001), p. 232; A. Calder, *The People's War* (London, 1969), p. 164.
22. F. R. Leavis, *The Great Tradition* (1948; Harmondsworth, 1983), p. 9; C. Ricks (ed.), *The New Oxford Book of Victorian Verse* (Oxford, 1987), pp. xxx–xxxi.
23. Carpenter, *Envy*, pp. 48, 109.
24. Carpenter, *Envy*, p. 115.
25. J. A. Auerbach, *The Great Exhibition of 1851: A Nation on Display* (New Haven and London, 1999), p. 214.
26. Patrick Wright, 'The Festival of Britain', BBC Radio 3 documentary, 3 May 2001.
27. Needless to say, many divisions within society remained ineradicable. Angus Calder has written of some of the realities behind the 'people's war' both in his book of that title (see note 21 above) and in *The Myth of the Blitz* (London, 1991).
28. A. Calder and D. Sheridan (eds), *Speak for Yourself: A Mass-Observation Anthology, 1937–49* (London, 1984), p. 103.
29. P. Ziegler, *London at War, 1939–1945* (London, 1995), pp. 156–57.
30. Ziegler, *London at War*, p. 304.
31. See G. E. Cherry, *Town Planning in Britain since 1900: The Rise and Fall of the Planning Ideal* (London, 1996), chs 5–6.
32. J. B. Cullingworth and V. Nadin, *Town and Country Planning in Britain* (11th edn, London, 1994), p. 8.
33. P. Mandler, *The Fall and Rise of the Stately Home* (New Haven and London, 1997), pp. 323, 365.
34. R. Samuel, *Theatres of Memory*, i, *Past and Present in Contemporary Culture* (London, 1994), pp. 51, 79.
35. K. Frampton, *Modern Architecture: A Critical History* (3rd edn, London, 1992), p. 263.
36. C. Frayling, 'The Crafts', in B. Ford (ed.), *The Cambridge Cultural History of Britain*, ix: *Modern Britain* (Cambridge, 1992), p. 175.
37. A. Marwick, *British Society since 1945* (3rd edn, Harmondsworth, 1996), p. 383.

38. A. Briggs, *Victorian Cities* (1963; Harmondsworth, 1990), p. 54.

39. Briggs, *Victorian Cities*, p. 18. Peter Hennessy adds a sort of regretful postscript in *Never Again*, p. 165: 'As Mayor of Birmingham, Joseph Chamberlain used [local authority] legislation to clear the centre of his city for the building of a Victorian glory which lasted until the 1960s development mania flattened it.'

40. H. J. Dyos and M. Wolff (eds), *The Victorian City: Images and Realities* (London, 1973).

41. F. Kermode, 'Grandeur and Filth', in *The Uses of Error* (London, 1991), p. 187.

42. Quoted in Samuel, *Theatres*, i, p. 79.

43. *Festival of Britain Guide* (1951), pp. 69, 72.

44. See Hennessy, *Never Again*, ch. 11.

45. R. Blake, *The Conservative Party: from Peel to Major* (London, 1997), p. 275.

46. See, for example, P. Hennessy, 'Never Again', in B. Brivati and H. Jones, *What Difference Did the War Make?* (London, 1993), p. 14; D. Cannadine, *Ornamentalism: How the British Saw Their Empire* (London, 2001), p. 187.

47. P. Vansittart, *In the Fifties* (London, 1995), p. 201.

48. L. James, *Raj: The Making and Unmaking of British India* (London, 1997), p. 613.

49. See D. Cannadine, 'The Present and the Past in the English Industrial Revolution', *Past and Present*, 103 (1984), pp. 152–58.

50. P. N. Furbank, *E. M. Forster: A Life* (London, 1988), ii, p. 308.

51. J. Winston, 'Queen Victoria in the *Funnyhouse*: Adrienne Kennedy and the Rituals of Colonial Possession', in M. Homans and A. Munich (eds), *Remaking Queen Victoria* (Cambridge, 1997), pp. 235–57.

52. J. Rhys, *Wide Sargasso Sea* (1966; Harmondsworth, 1997), p. xvii.

53. Both phrases belong to Richard Hoggart.

54. Rose, *Intellectual Life*, pp. 295–96, 437, 134.

55. See T. Steele, *The Emergence of Cultural Studies, 1945–65: Cultural Politics, Adult Education and the English Question* (London, 1997).

56. Q. D. Leavis had written about newspapers and popular journals in *Fiction and the Reading Public* (1932). It was a work which influenced Hoggart, for one; but he also felt that she did not relate it properly to the reality of working-class lives.

57. E. P. Thompson, *William Morris: Romantic to Revolutionary* (London, 1955).

58. MacCarthy, *Morris*, pp. 679–80.

59. Steele, *Emergence*, p. 163.

60. R. Hoggart, *The Uses of Literacy: Aspects of Working-Class Life with Special Reference to Publications and Entertainments* (1957; Harmondsworth, 1992), p. 174. Hoggart's original title, significantly enough, had been *The Abuses of Literacy*.

61. See J. Stapleton, 'Political Thought, Elites, and the State in Modern Britain', *Historical Journal*, 42 (1999), pp. 251–68. Many of these themes are also explored in Hewison, *Culture*.

62. Roy and Gwen Shaw, 'The Cultural and Social Setting', in Ford, *Cambridge Cultural History*, p. 12.

63. Samuel, *Theatres*, i, p. 161.

*Notes to Chapter 5: Youth*

1. The early lifetime of *Lady Chatterley's Lover* is dealt with by Michael Squires in the Penguin edition (Harmondsworth, 1994), pp. xiii–xvi. This edition also includes Lawrence's 1929 essay 'A Propos of "Lady Chatterley's Lover"'.

2. C. H. Rolph, *The Trial of Lady Chatterley: Regina v. Penguin Books Limited* (Harmondsworth, 1961), pp. 12–13. See also idem, *Books in the Dock* (London, 1969).

3. R. McKibbin, *Classes and Cultures: England, 1918–1951* (Oxford, 1998), pp. 303, 301.

4. H. David, *On Queer Street: A Social History of British Homosexuality, 1895–1995* (London, 1997), p. 154.

5. B. S. Rowntree and G. R. Lavers, *English Life and Leisure: A Social Study* (London, 1952), p. 215.

6. Rolph, *Trial*, p. 16.

7. As John Sutherland writes in *Offensive Literature: Decensorship in Britain, 1960–1982* (London, 1982), p. 1: 'Part of the motivation of the Mayflower-*Fanny Hill* trial [1963] was that John Cleland's chaste (linguistically) erotic picaresque fiction had the temerity to appear in a 3s. 6d. version.' The blurb on the back of the Penguin paperback about the trial (used here), also priced 3s. 6d., reads: 'it was not just a legal tussle, but a conflict of generation and class'.

8. Rolph, *Trial*, p. 17.

9. Rolph, *Trial*, p. 34.

10. R. Hoggart, '*Lady Chatterley* and the Censors', in *Between Two Worlds: Essays* (London, 2001), pp. 85–97; Rolph, *Trial*, p. 112.

11. B. Harrison, 'Underneath the Victorians', *Victorian Studies*, 10 (1967), pp. 239–62.

12. See esp. M. Mason, *The Making of Victorian Sexuality* and *The Making of Victorian Sexual Attitudes* (Oxford, 1994). More recently see I. Gibson, *The Erotomaniac: The Secret Life of Henry Spencer Ashbee* (London, 2001), and R. Christiansen, *The Voice of Victorian Sex: Arthur H. Clough, 1819–1861* (London, 2001).

13. S. Marcus, *The Other Victorians: A Study of Sexuality and Pornography in Mid-Nineteenth-Century England* (London, 1966), p. 265.

14. Sutherland, *Offensive Literature*, pp. 88–95.

15. M. Bradbury, *The Modern British Novel* (Harmondsworth, 1994), pp. 357–60. Some of Angus Wilson's novels written around this time played with a similar approach, including *As If By Magic* (1973), which opens with deliberate mock-Dickens.

16. J. Fowles, *The French Lieutenant's Woman* (1969; London, 1971), pp. 262, 172.

17. N. de Jongh, *Politics, Prudery and Perversions: The Censorship of the English*

*Stage, 1901–1968* (London, 2000); S. Hynes, *The Edwardian Turn of Mind* (London, 1991), ch. 7.

18. J. Orton, *Loot*, in *The Plays of the Sixties* (London, 1985), p. 556.
19. De Jongh, *Politics*, pp. 1–4, 231–37.
20. A. Marwick, *British Society since 1945* (3rd edn, Harmondsworth, 1996), p. 141.
21. A. Marwick, *The Sixties: Cultural Revolution in Britain, France, Italy, and the United States, c. 1958-c. 1974* (Oxford, 1998), p. 148.
22. S. Jones, 'Attic Attitudes: Leighton and Aesthetic Philosophy', in G. Marsden (ed.), *Victorian Values: Personalities and Perspectives in Nineteenth-Century Society* (2nd edn, London, 1998), p. 232; A. Huxley, *The Doors of Perception* (London, 1954); R. Hewison, *Too Much: Art and Society in the Sixties, 1960–75* (London, 1986), pp. 112–14.
23. R. Samuel, *Theatres of Memory*, i, *Past and Present in Contemporary Culture* (London, 1994), pp. 96–97.
24. J. Obelkevich reviewing Marwick's *The Sixties* in *Twentieth-Century British History*, 11 (2000), p. 335.
25. J. R. Gillis, *Youth and History: Tradition and Continuity in European Age Relations, 1770-Present* (revised edn, London, 1981), ch. 5; A. H. Halsey, *Change In British Society* (4th edn, Oxford, 1995), esp. ch. 5.
26. M. Holroyd, *Lytton Strachey* (revised edn, London, 1994), pp. 279–80, 723.
27. Introduction to the Penguin edition of *Eminent Victorians* (Harmondsworth, 1986), p. xii.
28. F. Partridge, entry for 6 March 1967, in *Good Company: Diaries, 1967–1970* (London, 1999), p. 12.
29. R. Marler, *Bloomsbury Pie: The Story of the Bloomsbury Revival* (London, 1997), pp. 37, 100–1.
30. S. Philips and I. Haywood, *Brave New Causes: Women in British Post-War Fictions* (London, 1998).
31. J. Richards, 'National Identity Post-War', in *Films and British National Identity, from Dickens to Dad's Army* (Manchester, 1997), p. 132.
32. Marwick, *Sixties*, p. 94.
33. A. Holdsworth, *Out of the Doll's House: The Story of Women in the Twentieth Century* (London, 1990), pp. 197–98; Marwick, *Sixties*, pp. 689–90.
34. B. Caine, *English Feminism, 1780–1980* (Oxford, 1997), p. 259.
35. P. Branca, *Silent Sisterhood: Middle-Class Women in the Victorian Home* (London, 1975); J. Liddington and J. Norris, *One Hand Tied Behind Us: The Rise of the Women's Suffrage Movement* (London, 1978).
36. L. Miller, *The Brontë Myth* (London, 2001), p. 163.
37. K. Amis, *Lucky Jim* (1954; Harmondsworth, 1992), pp. 8–10.
38. R. Samuel, 'North and South', in *Theatres of Memory*, ii, *Island Stories* (London, 1998), p. 165.
39. A. Sillitoe, *Life Without Armour: An Autobiography* (London, 1995), p. 235.
40. S. Callow, 'A Personal View of the British Theatre, 1954–1996', in *Snowdon on Stage* (London, 1996), p. 8.

41. Hewison, *Too Much*, p. 28.
42. Hewison, *Too Much*, p. 50.
43. Marwick, *Sixties*, p. 187.
44. Marwick, *Sixties*, p. 192.
45. L. Jackson, *The Sixties: Decade of Design Revolution* (London, 1998), p. 207.

## Notes to Chapter 6: Heritage

1. P. Hennessy, *The Prime Minister: The Office and its Holders since 1945* (revised edn, Harmondsworth, 2001), caption to illustration 49.
2. 'The Good Old Days', *Evening Standard*, 15 April 1983.
3. K. Flint, 'Plotting the Victorians: Narrative, Postmodernism, and Contemporary Fiction', in J. B. Bullen (ed.), *Writing and Victorianism* (London, 1997), pp. 289–94.
4. R. Samuel, 'Mrs Thatcher's Return to Victorian Values', in T. C. Smout (ed.), *Victorian Values* (Oxford 1992), pp. 9–29; S. Evans, 'Thatcher and the Victorians: A Suitable Case for Comparison?', *History*, 82 (1997), pp. 601–20; A. Jarvis, *Samuel Smiles and the Construction of Victorian Values* (Stroud, 1997); S. Collini, 'Victorian Values: From the Clapham Sect to the Clapham Omnibus', in *English Pasts: Essays in History and Culture* (Oxford, 1999), pp. 103–15.
5. Particularly notable was a series of articles by leading scholars in *History Today*, subsequently republished as G. Marsden (ed.), *Victorian Values: Personalities and Perspectives in Nineteenth-Century Society* (2nd edn, London, 1998). See also J. Walvin, *Victorian Values* (London, 1987); A. N. Wilson, *Eminent Victorians* (London, 1989).
6. Gareth Stedman Jones, quoted in Samuel, 'Thatcher's Return', p. 20.
7. M. J. Wiener, *English Culture and the Decline of the Industrial Spirit, 1850–1980* (Cambridge, 1981). For a critique see W. D. Rubinstein, *Capitalism, Culture and Decline in Britain, 1750–1990* (London, 1993).
8. Evans, 'Thatcher and Victorians'.
9. Samuel, 'Thatcher's Return', p. 24.
10. G. Himmelfarb, *The De-Moralization of Society: From Victorian Virtues to Modern Values* (London, 1995). It is also noteworthy that many of the screen adaptations considered below sold extremely well in the USA (and elsewhere), making the British costume drama one of the great industries at the end of the twentieth century.
11. D. Cannadine, 'The Past in the Present', in L. M. Smith (ed.), *The Making of Britain: Echoes of Greatness* (London, 1988), p. 16.
12. In English lettering: 'nostos' and 'algos'. D. Lowenthal, *The Past is a Foreign Country* (Cambridge, 1985), pp. 10–11.
13. D. Lowenthal, *The Heritage Crusade and the Spoils of History* (Cambridge, 1998), p. x.
14. R. Samuel, *Theatres of Memory*, i, *Past and Present in Contemporary Culture* (London, 1994), pp. 86–87, 98.

15. Samuel, *Theatres*, i, part 5; J. Green-Lewis, 'At Home in the Nineteenth Century: Photography, Nostalgia, and the Will to Authenticity', in J. Kucich and D. F. Sadoff (eds), *Victorian Afterlife: Postmodern Culture Rewrites the Nineteenth Century* (Minneapolis, 2000), pp. 29–48. For an example of contemporary fascination with Victorian photographs see P. Ziegler, *Britain Then and Now: The Francis Frith Collection* (London, 1999).

16. Morris and Company, fabric and paint brochures, 2001.

17. On Shaw and Ruskin see M. Holroyd, *Bernard Shaw* (London, 1997), pp. 83–84.

18. T. Hilton, *John Ruskin*, i, *The Early Years 1819–1859* (New Haven and London, 1985); ii, *The Later Years* (New Haven and London, 2000).

19. F. O'Gorman, *John Ruskin* (Stroud, 1999), pp. 76–77.

20. Lowenthal, *Heritage Crusade*, pp. 102–4, 121.

21. R. Giddings and K. Selby, *The Classic Serial on Television and Radio* (Basingstoke, 2001), p. 123.

22. P. Wright, *On Living in an Old Country: The National Past in Contemporary Britain* (London, 1985); R. Hewison, *The Heritage Industry: Britain in a Climate of Decline* (London, 1987).

23. J. M. Cameron, *Victorian Photographs of Famous Men and Fair Women* (London, 1926), p. 10.

24. A. Briggs, *Victorian Things* (Harmondsworth, 1990), p. 12.

25. J. Laver, *Victorian Vista* (London, 1954), p. 7.

26. A. Briggs, *The Age of Improvement, 1783–1867* (1959; revised edn, London, 1979), p. 471.

27. J. Miller (ed.), *Miller's Antiques Encyclopedia* (London, 1998), p. 10.

28. Miller, *Encyclopedia*, pp. 271, 214, 306, 368.

29. D. Cannadine, 'The First Hundred Years', in H. Newby (ed.), *The National Trust: The Next Hundred Years* (London, 1995), pp. 19–23; P. Mandler, *The Fall and Rise of the Stately Home* (New Haven and London, 1997), chs 8–9.

30. B. Hillier, *Young Betjeman* (London, 1988), p. 364.

31. N. Pevsner, *Pioneers of Modern Design: From William Morris to Walter Gropius* (1936 and subsequent revisions; Harmondsworth, 1991), pp. 22–23.

32. N. Pevsner, *The Englishness of English Art* (1956; Harmondsworth, 1993), p. 206.

33. Samuel, *Theatres*, pp. 125–27.

34. Giddings and Selby, *Classic Serial*, p. 10.

35. M. Sweet, *Inventing the Victorians* (London, 2001), p. 35.

36. Sweet, *Inventing*, pp. 31–34.

37. Giddings and Selby, *Classic Serial*, p. 21.

38. Obituary of Nyree Dawn Porter, *Daily Telegraph*, 12 April 2001.

39. Giddings and Selby, *Classic Serial*, pp. 41–3.

40. J. Drummond, *Tainted by Experience: A Life in the Arts* (London, 2000), p. 186.

41. Entry for 9 June 1970, in R. Strong, *The Roy Strong Diaries, 1967–1987* (London, 1998), p. 69.

42. Sweet, *Inventing*, p. 33.

43. R. E. Long, *The Films of Merchant Ivory* (London, 1992), p. 151.

44. This dilemma is aptly dramatised in contrasting reviews of Merchant Ivory's *The Golden Bowl*. See A. O'Hagan, 'A Study in Stupid Elegance', *Daily Telegraph*, 3 November 2000; D. Lodge, 'In the Home of Eternal Unrest', *Times Literary Supplement*, 10 November 2000.
45. *Daily Telegraph*, 23 November 1996.
46. Thackeray's 1848 novel is, of course, set during the Regency period; perhaps BBC producers felt that it would present another slant on years made phenomenally popular by recent Austen adaptations. In any case, *Vanity Fair* has been treated here as a 'Victorian' novel.
47. See *The Times*, 1 November 2001; *Radio Times*, 10–16 November 2001.
48. For a more authentic probing of the parallels between past and present see J. Taylor, 'Greed: The Way They Lived Then', *BBC History Magazine*, 2 (December 2001), pp. 40–42.
49. L. Miller, *The Brontë Myth* (London, 2001), p. 79.
50. Miller, *Brontë Myth*, pp. 98–108.
51. Flint, 'Plotting the Victorians', pp. 286, 296.
52. J. M. MacKenzie (ed.), *The Victorian Vision: Inventing New Britain* (London, 2001), p. 7.

*Notes to Chapter 7: History*

1. L. Strachey to G. M. Trevelyan, 16 December 1913. British Library, Additional Manuscript 60732 (Strachey Papers), fol. 193.
2. D. Cannadine, *G. M. Trevelyan: A Life in History* (London, 1992), pp. 214–15.
3. See L. Woodward, 'The Rise of the Professorial Historian in England', in K. Bourne and D. C. Watt (eds), *Studies in International History* (London, 1967), pp. 16–34; H. Butterfield, 'Some Early Trends in Scholarship, 1868–1968, in the Field of Modern History', *Transactions of the Royal Historical Society*, 19 (1969), pp. 159–84; D. Goldstein, 'The Organizational Development of the British Historical Profession, 1884–1921', *Bulletin of the Institute of Historical Research*, 55 (1982), pp. 180–93.
4. R. J. Evans, *In Defence of History* (London, 1997), pp. 16–23.
5. J. W. Burrow, 'Victorian Historians and the Royal Historical Society', *Transactions of the Royal Historical Society*, 39 (1989), pp. 125–40.
6. J. L. Altholz, 'Lord Acton and the Plan of *The Cambridge Modern History*', *Historical Journal*, 39 (1996), pp. 723–36.
7. K. Robbins, '*History*, The Historical Association and the "National Past"', *History*, 66 (1981), pp. 413–25.
8. S. Hynes, *A War Imagined: the First World War and English Culture* (London, 1990), pp. 67–74; N. Ferguson, *The Pity of War* (London, 1998), pp. 233–34.
9. M. Bentley, 'Approaches to Modernity: Western Historiography since the Enlightenment', in M. Bentley (ed.), *Companion to Historiography* (London, 1997), pp. 442–49; Burrow, 'Victorian Historians', pp. 138–40.
10. L. Strachey, *Eminent Victorians* (1918; Harmondsworth, 1986), p. 9.

11. L. Strachey, 'Six English Historians', in *Portraits in Miniature* (London, 1931), pp. 141–218.

12. Strachey, 'Creighton', in 'Six English Historians', pp. 208–9.

13. H. Butterfield, *The Whig Interpretation of History* (1931; London, 1965), p. 102.

14. D. C. Somervell, in *History*, 17 (1932–33), p. 86. See also the reviews in *English Historical Journal*, 48 (1933), pp. 174–75, and *Journal of Modern History*, 4 (1932), pp. 278–79. For a later critique see G. R. Elton, 'Herbert Butterfield and the Study of History', *Historical Journal*, 27 (1984), pp. 729–43.

15. R. N. Soffer, 'The Conservative Historical Imagination in the Twentieth Century', *Albion*, 28 (1996), pp. 1–17.

16. L. Parker, *The English Historical Tradition since 1850* (Edinburgh, 1980), pp. 119–21.

17. V. E. Chancellor, *History for their Masters: Opinion in the English History Textbook, 1800–1914* (London, 1970); S. Heathorn, '"Let Us Remember that We, Too, are English": Constructions of Citizenship and National Identity in English Elementary School Reading Books, 1880–1914', *Victorian Studies*, 38 (1995), pp. 395–427.

18. P. Brindle, 'Past Histories: History and the Elementary School Classroom in Early Twentieth-Century England', unpublished Ph.D. thesis, University of Cambridge, 1998.

19. E. W. Green, *A School History of England* (London, 1937).

20. J. Rose, *The Intellectual Life of the British Working Classes* (New Haven and London, 2001), p. 194.

21. G. H. Blore, *Victorian Worthies* (Oxford, 1920), p. v.

22. J. M. D. and M. J. C. Meiklejohn, *A School History of England and Great Britain* (London, 1939), p. 447.

23. R. N. Soffer, 'The Modern University and National Values, 1850–1930', *Bulletin of the Institute of Historical Research*, 60 (1987), p. 172.

24. R. Jann, 'From Amateur to Professional: The Case of the Oxbridge Historians', *Journal of British Studies*, 22 (1983), pp. 122–47.

25. Woodward, 'Rise', pp. 29–30; Burrow, 'Victorian Historians', pp. 138–39; Kenyon, *History Men*, pp. 170–71.

26. Soffer, 'Modern University', p. 175.

27. File on recommended reading and related correspondence 1933–40 in the archives of the Seeley Historical Library, Cambridge. It appears that reading lists for before 1933 have not been preserved.

28. P. E. Roberts, in *The Cambridge Modern History*, xii, *The Latest Age* (Cambridge, 1910), pp. 498–99.

29. Parker, *English Historical Tradition*, p. 132.

30. J. H. Buckley, *The Victorian Temper: A Study in Literary Culture* (London, 1952); A. Briggs, *Victorian People: A Reassessment of Persons and Themes, 1851–67* (1954; Harmondsworth, 1990); idem, *Victorian Cities* (1963; Harmondsworth, 1990); W. E. Houghton, *The Victorian Frame of Mind, 1830–1870* (New Haven and London, 1957); W. L. Burn, *The Age of Equipoise: A Study of the Mid-Victorian Generation* (London, 1964).

31. D. Cannadine, 'Welfare State History', in *The Pleasures of the Past* (Harmondsworth, 1997), p. 182.

32. G. M. Young, *Portrait of an Age: Victorian England* (2nd edn, Oxford, 1953), p. vi.

33. Buckley, *Victorian Temper*, pp. vii, 5.

34. Houghton, *Victorian Frame*, p. xiii.

35. Briggs, *Victorian People*, p. 9.

36. A. Briggs, 'History that Improves with Age', *Times Higher Education Supplement*, 25 February 2000.

37. Houghton, *Victorian Frame*, p. xiii; Briggs, *Victorian People*, p. 15; G. Kitson Clark, *The Making of Victorian England* (London, 1962), p. 29. See also H. R. Trevor-Roper, 'Lytton Strachey as Historian', in *Historical Essays* (London, 1957), pp. 279–84.

38. J. Clive, 'More or Less Eminent Victorians' (1958), in *Not by Fact Alone: Essays on the Writing and Reading of History* (London, 1989), p. 231.

39. R. D. Altick, 'Eminent Victorianism: What Lytton Strachey Hath Wrought', *American Scholar*, 64 (1995), p. 86.

40. Examples from the current (2001–2) MA in Victorian Studies at the University of Leicester.

41. H. Perkin, *The Origins of Modern English Society, 1780–1880* (London, 1963).

42. E. Hobsbawm, *Labouring Men: Studies in the History of Labour* (London, 1964).

43. H. J. Hanham, *Elections and Party Management: Politics in the Time of Disraeli and Gladstone* (London, 1959); J. Vincent, *The Formation of the Liberal Party, 1857–1868* (London, 1965); R. Blake, *Disraeli* (London, 1966); M. Cowling, *1867: Disraeli, Gladstone and Revolution. The Passing of the Second Reform Bill* (Cambridge, 1967).

44. J. Schumpeter, *Imperialism and the Social Classes* (Oxford, 1951).

45. R. Robinson and J. Gallagher (with A. Denny), *Africa and the Victorians: The Official Mind of Imperialism* (London, 1965).

46. See for example K. T. Hoppen, *The Mid-Victorian Generation, 1846–1886* (Oxford, 1998); D. Cannadine, *Class in Britain* (New Haven and London, 1998).

47. J. Parry, *The Rise and Fall of Liberal Government in Victorian Britain* (New Haven and London, 1993); E. H. H. Green, *The Crisis of Conservatism: The Politics, Economics and Ideology of the British Conservative Party, 1880–1914* (London, 1995).

48. G. Stedman Jones, *Languages of Class: Studies in English Working-Class History* (Cambridge, 1983).

49. J. M. MacKenzie (ed.), *Propaganda and Empire: The Manipulation of British Public Opinion, 1880–1960* (Manchester, 1984); idem (ed.), *Imperialism and Popular Culture* (Manchester, 1986).

50. L. Davidoff and C. Hall, *Family Fortunes: Men and Women of the English Middle Class, 1780–1850* (London, 1987).

51. J. Tosh, *A Man's Place: Masculinity and the Middle-Class Home in Victorian England* (New Haven and London, 1999).

52. J. Walkowitz, *City of Dreadful Delight: Narratives of Sexual Danger in Late-Victorian London* (London, 1992).

53. *Exposed: The Victorian Nude*, exhibition guide. See also L. Nead, 'Nudes Fit to Print', *BBC History Magazine*, 2 (November 2001), pp. 26–28; J. Edwards, 'Edmund Gosse and the Victorian Nude', *History Today*, 51 (November 2001), pp. 29–35.

54. R. Colls and P. Dodd (eds), *Englishness: Politics and Culture, 1880–1920* (Beckenham, 1986); K. Robbins, *Nineteenth-Century Britain: Integration and Diversity* (Oxford, 1988); R. Samuel (ed.), *Patriotism: The Making and Unmaking of British National Identity* (London, 1989); A. Grant and K. Stringer (eds), *Uniting the Kingdom? The Making of British History* (London, 1995).

55. H. Cunningham, 'The Language of Patriotism, 1750–1914', *History Workshop Journal*, 12 (1981), pp. 8–33.

56. These figures do not include writings on Ireland or the British Empire. In 1997, there were 713 publications (books, articles, chapters and so on) for Britain between 1714 and 1815, and 1075 publications for Britain since 1914. Figures quoted by Miles Taylor in his internet review of Hoppen's *Mid-Victorian Generation*.

57. S. Rothblatt, 'G. M. Young: England's Historian of Culture', *Victorian Studies*, 22 (1978–79), p. 415.

58. R. Samuel, *Theatres of Memory*, ii, *Island Stories* (London, 1998), part 3.

59. History guidelines, in *The National Curriculum* (London, 1995).

60. J. Shuter and A. Hook, *Victorian Britain* (Oxford, 1992), p. 60.

61. T. Deary and M. Brown, *The Vile Victorians* (London, 1994).

62. M. Roberts, 'Proper History and Sixth-Form History', *History Today*, 51 (November 2001), p. 37. Cf. Jan Milsom's equally disenchanted account of returning to teach history in schools in 'Backwards, in All Directions', *Daily Telegraph*, 29 August 2001.

## Notes to Chapter 8: Biography

1. M. Forster, *Hidden Lives: A Family Memoir* (London, 1995) and *Precious Lives* (London, 1998); L. Sage, *Bad Blood* (London, 2000); M. Amis, *Experience* (London, 2000).

2. P. R. Backscheider, *Reflections on Biography* (Oxford, 1999), esp. ch. 7.

3. R. Holmes, *Footsteps: Adventures of a Romantic Biographer* (London, 1995), esp. pp. 65–69, 119–20, 135–36, 173–75.

4. Backscheider, *Reflections*, p. 30.

5. G. Dyer, *Out of Sheer Rage: In The Shadow of D. H. Lawrence* (London, 1997).

6. P. Clarke, *Hope and Glory: Britain, 1900–1990* (London, 1996), p. 166.

7. Works which have been taken to include Harold Nicolson's *Tennyson* (1923), Philip Guedalla's *Palmerston* (1926), André Maurois' *Disraeli* (1927) and Hugh Kingsmill's *Matthew Arnold* (1928). The last, Kingsmill subsequently admitted, was 'written, it may be, too much in the spirit of a young man chasing his

great-grandfather round the garden with a pitchfork'. M. Holroyd, *Hugh Kingsmill: A Critical Biography* (London, 1964), p. 143.

8. A. S. Byatt, *The Biographer's Tale* (London, 2001), p. 236.

9. L. Edel, *Literary Biography* (Bloomington, 1973), p. 157.

10. L. Strachey, *Eminent Victorians* (London, 1918), pp. viii–ix.

11. Strachey, *Eminent Victorians*, p. viii; British Library, Additional Manuscript 54219 (*Eminent Victorians*), fol. 103.

12. A. O. J. Cockshut, *Truth to Life: The Art of Biography in the Nineteenth Century* (London, 1974).

13. C. R. Sanders, 'Lytton Strachey's Conception of Biography', *PMLA*, 66 (1951), p. 302 n. 25.

14. S. Johnson, *The Rambler*, no. 60, 13 October 1750, in W. J. Bate and A. B. Strauss (eds), *The Yale Edition of the Works of Samuel Johnson* (New Haven and London), iii, pp. 318–23.

15. Strachey, *Eminent Victorians*, p. vii.

16. Strachey, *Eminent Victorians*, p. vii.

17. L. Strachey to D. Carrington, n.d. (early 1924?), British Library, Additional MS 60721 (Strachey Papers), fol. 112.

18. L. Strachey, 'A Russian Humorist', in M. Holroyd and P. Levy (eds), *The Shorter Strachey* (London, 1989), pp. 183–87.

19. V. Woolf, 'The Art of Biography' (1939), in *The Crowded Dance of Modern Life* (Harmondsworth, 1993), pp. 144–51.

20. H. Nicolson, *The Development of English Biography* (London, 1927). Cf. Cockshut's suggestion that there was a 'moral parabola' to Victorian biography in which prudery and servility were at their worst between 1840 and 1875.

21. Strachey, *Eminent Victorians*, p. viii.

22. M. Holroyd, *Lytton Strachey* (revised edn, London, 1994), pp. 89–92.

23. G. E. Moore, *Principia Ethica* (1903, revised edn, 1922; Cambridge, 1993), pp. 237–38.

24. L. Strachey to J. C. Squire, 3 August 1918. British Library, Additional MS 60721, fol. 12. On the Lansdowne affair see K. Robbins, *The Abolition of War: The 'Peace Movement' in Britain, 1914–1919* (Cardiff, 1976), pp. 149–53; D. Cannadine, *The Decline and Fall of the British Aristocracy* (London, 1996), pp. 77–78.

25. C. R. Sanders, 'Lytton Strachey's "Point of View"', *PMLA*, 68 (1953), p. 76.

26. J. Russell, 'Lytton Strachey', *Horizon*, 15 (1947), p. 91.

27. E. M. Forster, 'What I Believe' (1939), in *Two Cheers for Democracy* (1951; San Diego and New York, 1979), p. 68; L. Strachey, *Elizabeth and Essex: A Tragic History* (1928; Harmondsworth, 2000), pp. 244–45.

28. L. Strachey, *Eminent Victorians*, pp. 188–89.

29. A. C. Ward, *The Nineteen-Twenties: Literature and Ideas in the Post-War Decade* (London, 1930), pp. 169–70.

30. Holroyd, *Strachey*, p. 269. On Strachey's admiration for some Victorians see C. R. Sanders, 'Lytton Strachey and the Victorians', *Modern Language Quarterly*, 15 (1954), pp. 329–30.

31. Strachey, *Elizabeth*, p. 9.
32. *Nation*, 1 June 1918; *Times Literary Supplement*, 16 May 1918.
33. H. H. Asquith, *Some Aspects of the Victorian Age* (Oxford, 1918), p. 7.
34. G. M. Trevelyan to L. Strachey, 12 August 1918. British Library, Additional MS 60732 (Strachey Papers), fol. 195. It has been suggested that Trevelyan subsequently changed his mind in the wake of the 'cheap ... nasty ... absurd one-volume biographies' that followed Strachey. D. Cannadine, *G. M. Trevelyan: A Life in History* (London, 1992), p. 44.
35. Holroyd, *Strachey*, p. 427.
36. G. M. Young, 'Victorian History', in *Selected Modern English Essays* (Oxford, 1932), p. 276.
37. D. S. Freeman, quoted in Sanders, 'Strachey's Conception', p. 310.
38. G. Boas, *Lytton Strachey* (Oxford, 1935); Woolf, 'Art'; M. Beerbohm, *Lytton Strachey* (Cambridge, 1943).
39. Holroyd's introduction to *Eminent Victorians* (Harmondsworth, 1986), p. xii.
40. J. Clive, 'More or Less Eminent Victorians' (1958), in *Not By Fact Alone: Essays on the Writing and Reading of History* (London, 1989), p. 231.
41. V. Woolf, *Orlando* (1928; Harmondsworth, 1993), p. 211.
42. R. D Altick, 'Eminent Victorianism: What Lytton Strachey Hath Wrought', *American Scholar*, 64 (1995), p. 86.
43. A. Easson, 'Letters of Dickens', in P. Schlicke (ed.), *Oxford Reader's Companion to Dickens* (Oxford, 2000), p. 337.
44. D. J. Taylor, *Thackeray* (London, 2000), pp. 6–7.
45. Maud Ellmann's introduction to the 'World's Classics' edition of *Dracula* (Oxford, 1996), p. xii.
46. L. Miller, *The Brontë Myth* (London, 2001), p. 58.
47. Miller, *Brontë Myth*, p. 100.
48. Miller, *Brontë Myth*, p. 167. The other key work identified by Miller is Lyndall Gordon's *Charlotte Brontë: A Passionate Life* (1994).
49. R. Marler, *Bloomsbury Pie: The Story of the Bloomsbury Revival* (London, 1997), p. 263.
50. The footnote appears in R. Ellmann, *Oscar Wilde* (Harmondsworth, 1988), at p. 88; on this and the photograph see M. Holland, 'Biography and the Art of Lying', in P. Raby (ed.), *The Cambridge Companion to Oscar Wilde* (Cambridge, 1997), pp. 10–14.
51. A. Sinfield, *The Wilde Century: Effeminacy, Oscar Wilde and the Queer Moment* (New York, 1994), p. 6.
52. Backscheider, *Reflections*, p. 187.
53. R. Letwin, *The Gentleman in Trollope: Individuality and Moral Conduct* (London, 1982); D. Thompson, *Queen Victoria: Gender and Power* (London, 2001); D. Read, *Peel and the Victorians* (Oxford, 1987); G. Beer, *Darwin's Plots: Evolutionary Thought in Darwin, George Eliot and Nineteenth-Century Fiction* (London, 1983).
54. Taylor, *Thackeray*, p. 13.

55. Taylor, *Thackeray*, p. 180.
56. V. Glendinning, *Jonathan Swift* (London, 1999), p. 276.
57. Backscheider, *Reflections*, p. 187.
58. P. Ackroyd, *Dickens* (London, 1990), p. 754. On some of the implications of this approach see M. Andrews, 'Charles Dickens, *Dickens* and Peter Ackroyd', in D. Ellis (ed.), *Imitating Art: Essays in Biography* (London, 1993), pp. 174–86.
59. 'On the Web: Charles Dickens', *Guardian*, 20 February 2001.
60. Strachey, *Eminent Victorians*, p. viii.

*Notes to Chapter 9: Victoria*

1. H. Lee, *Virginia Woolf* (London, 1996), pp. 97–98.
2. E. Longford, *Victoria R.I.* (London, 1964), p. 401.
3. *Daily Telegraph*, 22 January 2001.
4. V. Bogdanor, 'An Exceptional Monarch Who Cast a Mighty Shadow', *Daily Telegraph*, 22 January 2001.
5. R. Shannon, *Gladstone: Heroic Minister, 1865–1898* (Harmondsworth, 2000), p. 564.
6. B. Pimlott, *The Queen: A Biography of Elizabeth II* (London, 1996), p. 309.
7. Pimlott, *The Queen*, p. 540.
8. L. Valentine, *The Queen: Her Early Life and Reign* (London, 1887).
9. W. T. Stead, *Her Majesty the Queen: Studies of the Sovereign and the Reign* (London, 1897), p. 2.
10. D. Campbell, *Victoria, Queen and Empress* (Edinburgh, 1901), p. 52.
11. J. Campbell, 9th Duke of Argyll, *V. R. I.: Queen Victoria. Her Life and Reign* (New York, 1901), p. 53.
12. Valentine, *The Queen*, pp. 33, 71–72.
13. Campbell, *Victoria*, p. 232.
14. D. Cannadine, 'The Context, Performance and Meaning of Ritual: The British Monarchy and the "Invention of Tradition", *c.* 1820–1977', in E. Hobsbawm and T. Ranger (eds), *The Invention of Tradition* (Cambridge, 1983), p. 119; Argyll, *V. R. I.*, p. 273.
15. G. M. Young, *Portrait of an Age: Victorian England* (2nd edn, Oxford, 1953), p. 161.
16. A. Bennett, *The Journal of Arnold Bennett* (New York, 1933), p. 112.
17. A. C. Benson and Viscount Esher (eds), *Letters of Queen Victoria*, first series, *1837–61* (London, 1907).
18. P. Guedalla, *The Queen and Mr Gladstone* (London, 1933), i, p. 4.
19. L. Strachey, *Queen Victoria* (London, 1921), p. 218.
20. G. E. Buckle (ed.), *Letters of Queen Victoria*, second series, *1862–85* (London, 1926–28); idem (ed.), *Letters of Queen Victoria*, third series, *1886–1901* (London, 1930–32).
21. F. Ponsonby, *Sidelights on Queen Victoria* (London, 1930); F. Hardie, *The Political Influence of Queen Victoria, 1861–1901* (2nd edn, London, 1938).

22. L. Housman, *Victoria Regina: A Dramatic Biography* (1934; London, 1949), pp. 11–12.

23. Housman, *Victoria Regina*, p. 470.

24. Cf. the off-stage death of Queen Victoria in Noël Coward's 1931 *Cavalcade*: it was this 'of the many incidents of public affairs portrayed … which seemed most to touch the chords of memory of older members of the audience'. Hardie, *Political Influence*, p. 219.

25. C. K. Webster, 'The Accession of Queen Victoria', *History*, 22 (1937–38), p. 14.

26. *The Times*, 22 June 1937.

27. *Dictionary of National Biography, 1951–1960*, p. 514.

28. S. Weintraub, *Victoria* (revised edn, London, 1996), p. 3.

29. M. Holroyd, *Lytton Strachey* (revised edn, London, 1994), p. 495.

30. L. Strachey to the Society of Authors, 22 September 1921. British Library, Additional MS 63334 (Society of Authors Papers), fol. 17.

31. M. Green, *Children of the Sun: A Narrative of 'Decadence' in England after 1918* (London, 1977), p. 190.

32. Holroyd, *Strachey*, p. 490.

33. Holroyd, *Strachey*, p. 495. My reading of *Queen Victoria* is heavily indebted to Holroyd's discussion.

34. Strachey, *Victoria*, p. 281.

35. Strachey, *Victoria*, p. 130.

36. Strachey, *Victoria*, p. 208.

37. *Times Literary Supplement*, 7 April 1921.

38. *The Times*, 21 June 1937.

39. Full details (and use) of these volumes can be found in various biographical studies, such as J. M. Packard, *Victoria's Daughters* (Stroud, 1999).

40. Packard, *Victoria's Daughters*, p. 228.

41. Longford, *Victoria*, p. 398.

42. Longford, *Victoria*, p. 401.

43. Longford, *Victoria*, p. 143.

44. Longford, *Victoria*, p. 575.

45. Weintraub, *Victoria*, p. x. Contemporary fascination with medical matters was not restricted to Queen Victoria; in these years there was even greater interest in subjects like the cause of George III's 'madness'.

46. D. Cannadine, 'Prince Albert', in *The Pleasures of the Past* (Harmondsworth, 1997), p. 15.

47. Longford, *Victoria*, p. 576; Weintraub, *Victoria*, p. 643.

48. For a reading of the Queen Caroline affair attuned to the feminist perspective see R. McWilliam, *Popular Politics in Nineteenth-Century England* (London, 1998), ch. 1.

49. J. F. C. Harrison, *Late Victorian Britain, 1875–1901* (London, 1990), p. 178.

50. See for example D. Thompson, *Queen Victoria: Gender and Power* (London, 2001).

51. See L. Langbauer, 'Queen Victoria and Me', in J. Kucich and D. F. Sadoff,

*Victorian Afterlife: Postmodern Culture Rewrites the Nineteenth Century* (Minneapolis, 2000), pp. 211–33.

52. M. Loeffelholz, 'Crossing the Atlantic with Victoria: American Receptions, 1837–1901', in Homans and Munich, *Remaking*, p. 33.

53. L. Vallone, *Becoming Victoria* (New Haven and London, 2001). See also M. Charlot, *Victoria: The Young Queen* (Oxford, 1991).

54. Homans and Munich, 'Introduction', p. 2. See also M. Homans, *Royal Representations: Queen Victoria and British Culture, 1837–1876* (Chicago, 1998); A. Munich, *Queen Victoria's Secrets* (New York, 1996).

55. T. Aronson, *Heart of a Queen: Queen Victoria's Romantic Attachments* (London, 1991), p. xi.

56. An accompanying BBC documentary, *Empire of the Nude*, was broadcast in October 2001. It emphasised the point even further by showing the locked cabinet in Prince Albert's bathroom in which more select items were stored.

57. Thompson, *Victoria*, ch. 4.

58. Coming in 1938, the film also touched on affairs outside Britain. Robert Vansittart of the Foreign Office, a leading opponent of appeasement, carefully vetted the screenplay. And as if Strachey had never debunked General Gordon, his martyrdom at Khartoum, and the Queen's subsequent wrath at her ministers' pusillanimity, were fully emphasised. S. Harper, *Picturing the Past: The Rise and Fall of the British Costume Film* (London, 1994), pp. 53–55; J. Richards, *The Age of the Dream Palace: Cinema and Society in Britain, 1930–1939* (London, 1984), pp. 264–69.

59. E. J. Dickson, 'When Love Reigned', *Radio Times*, 25–31 August 2001.

## Notes to Chapter 10: Dickens

1. G. Marsden (ed.), *Victorian Values: Personalities and Perspectives in Nineteenth-Century Society* (2nd edn, London, 1998), p. 49.

2. A similar effect was achieved on the cover of Peter Ackroyd's *Dickens* (London, 1990). See M. Andrews, 'Charles Dickens, *Dickens* and Peter Ackroyd', in D. Ellis (ed.), *Imitating Art: Essays in Biography* (London, 1993), pp. 175–76.

3. N. Bradbury, 'Dickens and the Form of the Novel', in J. O. Jordan (ed.), *The Cambridge Companion to Charles Dickens* (Cambridge, 2001), p. 152.

4. F. Kaplan, *Dickens: A Biography* (London, 1988), p. 124.

5. A. Huxley, 'Vulgarity in Literature' (1930), in *Music at Night* (London, 1994), p. 228.

6. M. Slater, *An Intelligent Person's Guide to Dickens* (London, 1999), p. 30.

7. Ackroyd, *Dickens*, pp. 301–5.

8. R. Samuel, *Theatres of Memory*, i, *Past and Present in Contemporary Culture* (London, 1994), pp. 51, 382.

9. Obituary in the *Daily Telegraph*, 12 December 1996.

10. W. W. Crotch, *The Secret of Dickens* (London, 1919), p. xv.

11. M. Slater, 'Dickens, 1870–1970; 1920–1940: "Superior Folk" and Scandalmongers', *Dickensian*, 66 (1970), p. 132.
12. P. Davis, *The Lives and Times of Ebenezer Scrooge* (New Haven and London, 1990), p. 136.
13. Davis, *Lives*, p. 143.
14. J. Marsh, 'Dickens and Film', in Jordan, *Cambridge Companion*, p. 219.
15. J. Richards, 'Dickens – Our Contemporary', in *Films and British National Identity: From Dickens to Dad's Army* (Manchester, 1997), p. 334.
16. Slater, 'Dickens', p. 125.
17. J. Rose, *The Intellectual Life of the British Working Classes* (New Haven and London, 2001), p. 114.
18. Slater, 'Dickens', pp. 128–29.
19. C. Dickens, *A Christmas Carol* (1843; Harmondsworth, 1986), p. 108.
20. I am grateful to Richard Carter for showing me this review, and for sharing his enthusiastic memories of the production.
21. G. K. Chesterton, *Charles Dickens* (1906; London, 1960), pp. 125–27.
22. A. Maurois, 'The Philosophy of Dickens' (1927), in M. Hollington (ed.), *Charles Dickens: Critical Assessments*, i (Mountfield, 1995), p. 683
23. C. Dickens, *Our Mutual Friend* (1865; Harmondsworth, 1997), p. 135.
24. Samuel, *Theatres*, p. 247.
25. Samuel had characteristic misgivings: see *Theatres*, pp. 413–16.
26. F. Muir (ed.), *The Oxford Book of Humorous Prose* (Oxford, 1990), p. xxx.
27. F. Muir, *A Kentish Lad* (London, 1998), p. 308.
28. There was a renovation of the centre in the mid-1990s, but the layout described here is broadly the same. Quotations are taken from the visitor's guide, *c.* 1990.
29. A notable recent collection that approaches Dickens mostly from this perspective is Jordan, *Cambridge Companion*.
30. Ackroyd, *Dickens*, p. 966.
31. J. Carey, *The Violent Effigy: A Study of Dickens' Imagination* (2nd edn, London, 1991), p. 207.
32. M. Andrews, *Dickens on England and the English* (Hassocks, 1979), pp. 195–96.
33. R. Giddings and K. Selby, *The Classic Serial on Television and Radio* (Basingstoke, 2001), p. 178.
34. Interestingly enough, the Miss Havisham of Giannetti's ballet version, featured on promotional material and on the over of the CD (NPC021), is made even more alluring. Adrian Edwards, writing in *Gramophone*, 78, July 2000, p. 61, notes that she is 'a voluptuous creature swathed in white over clinging satin'. She rather looks as if she is executing a catwalk turn amongst the flames of Satis House.
35. BBC Video 6783.
36. S. Hastings, *Evelyn Waugh: A Biography* (London, 1994), pp. 13, 278–79, 316–17.
37. See Richard Jacobs's introduction to the Penguin edition (1957; Harmondsworth, 1998), pp. xxix–xxxi.

38. C. Waters, 'Gender, Family, and Domestic Ideology', in Jordan, *Cambridge Companion*, p. 120.

39. E. Wilson, 'Dickens: The Two Scrooges' (1940), in *The Wound and the Bow* (Boston, 1941), pp. 1–93.

40. G. H. Lewes, 'Dickens in Relation to Criticism' (1872), in Hollington, *Critical Assessments*, p. 461.

41. Ackroyd, *Dickens*, p. 720.

42. E. M. Forster, *Aspects of the Novel* (1927; Harmondsworth, 1990), pp. 33–34.

43. Q. D. Leavis, *Fiction and the Reading Public* (1932; London, 1965), pp. 156–58.

44. I. MacKillop, *F. R. Leavis: A Life in Criticism* (London, 1995), p. 31.

45. F. R. Leavis, *The Great Tradition* (1948; Harmondsworth, 1983), p. 30. I have not been able to trace when Leavis changed his mind, but the note appears to have been added sometime in the 1960s.

46. G. Orwell, 'Charles Dickens' (1940), in Hollington, *Critical Assessments*, pp. 722, 728.

47. See for example Grahame Smith, 'The Life and Times of Charles Dickens', in Jordan, *Cambridge Companion*, pp. 1–15.

48. Good coverage of Dickensian scandal is offered by Slater, 'Dickens', pp. 133–40.

49. M. Holroyd, *Hugh Kingsmill: A Critical Biography* (London, 1964), p. 149.

50. K. Brownlow, *David Lean: A Biography* (London, 1996), p. 211.

51. Samuel, *Theatres*, p. 420.

## Notes to Chapter 11: Gladstone

1. C. W. White, '*The Strange Death of Liberal England* in its Time', *Albion*, 17 (1985), pp. 425–47.

2. *Times Literary Supplement*, 29 February 1936.

3. *Manchester Guardian*, 3 July 1936. Dangerfield responded in person to Ensor's review, acknowledging his points. G. Dangerfield to R. C. K. Ensor (via Constable), 5 August 1936. Ensor Papers, Bodleian Library.

4. See for example G. R. Searle, *The Liberal Party: Triumph and Disintegration, 1910–1929* (Basingstoke, 1992).

5. P. Magnus, *Gladstone* (1954; Harmondsworth, 2001), p. xii.

6. Magnus, *Gladstone*, pp. 18–19.

7. On Gladstone's intellectual influences see E. F. Biagini, *Gladstone* (Basingstoke, 2000), ch. 1.

8. G. M. Young, *Portrait of an Age: Victorian England* (2nd edn, Oxford, 1953), p. 82. On the subject of just how intellectual Gladstone was, Roy Jenkins is characteristically sensible and delicate, observing that he was 'perhaps a powerful rather than a subtle scholar'. R. Jenkins, *Gladstone* (London, 1996), pp. xvi, 401–2.

9. Magnus, *Gladstone*, p. 5.

10. P. Clarke, *A Question of Leadership, from Gladstone to Blair* (2nd edn, Harmondsworth, 1999), p. 28.

11. R. W. Seton-Watson, *Disraeli, Gladstone and the Eastern Question: A Study in Diplomacy and Party Politics* (London, 1935), p. ix.
12. P. Brendon, *The Dark Valley: A Panorama of the 1930s* (London, 2001), p. 269.
13. H. Gladstone, *After Thirty Years* (London, 1928), p. 108.
14. H. R. Williamson, *Mr Gladstone: A Play in Three Acts* (London, 1937), p. 81.
15. J. A. Spender, *Mr Gladstone* (London, 1937), p. 25.
16. Clarke, *Question*, p. 122.
17. G. Best, *Churchill: A Study in Greatness* (London, 2001), pp. 283–84.
18. H. C. G. Matthew, *Gladstone, 1809–1898* (Oxford, 1997), p. 436.
19. Best, *Churchill*, p. 100.
20. F. Birrell, *Gladstone* (London, 1933), p. 118.
21. J. L. Hammond, *Gladstone and the Irish Nation* (London, 1938), pp. 721, 716.
22. H. C. G. Matthew, 'Disraeli, Gladstone and the Politics of Mid-Victorian Budgets', *Historical Journal*, 22 (1979), pp. 615–43; idem, 'Gladstonian Finance', in G. Marsden (ed.), *Victorian Values: Personalities and Perspectives in Nineteenth-Century Society* (2nd edn, London, 1998), pp. 127–37.
23. See also above, Chapter 7.
24. See Biagini, *Gladstone*, pp. 55–56.
25. In this chapter I have made use of '*Diaries*' to indicate the fourteen-volume published set, and 'diaries' to indicate the source material in a more general way.
26. M. Bentley, *The Climax of Liberal Politics: British Liberalism in Theory and Practice, 1868–1918* (London, 1987), pp. 132–33.
27. R. Kelley, 'Midlothian: A Study in Politics and Ideas', *Victorian Studies*, 4 (1960), pp. 118–40.
28. Clarke, *Question*, p. 344.
29. B. Hilton, 'Gladstone's Theological Politics', in M. Bentley and J. Stevenson (eds), *High and Low Politics in Victorian Britain* (Oxford, 1983), pp. 28–57.
30. R. Shannon, *Gladstone: Heroic Minister, 1865–1898* (Harmondsworth, 2000), p. 228.
31. J. Parry, *The Rise and Fall of Liberal Government in Victorian Britain* (New Haven and London, 1993), pp. 256–57.
32. Biagini, *Gladstone*, pp. 70–71.
33. P. Hennessy, *The Prime Minister: The Office and its Holders since 1945* (revised edn, Harmondsworth, 2001), pp. 536–37. See also Clarke, *Question*, ch. 14; Biagini, *Gladstone*, epilogue. The cover of Clarke's *Question*, incidentally, features a clever illustration by Peter Brookes of Gladstone evolving (via Thatcher) into Blair.
34. L. Strachey, *Eminent Victorians* (London, 1918), p. 272.
35. A. Roberts, *Salisbury: Victorian Titan* (London, 2000), p. 236; Clarke, *Question*, p. 29.
36. D. A. Hamer, 'Gladstone: The Making of a Political Myth', *Victorian Studies*, 22 (1978–79), pp. 28–50; Matthew, *Gladstone*, pp. 287, 295–301, 550–57.
37. They are discussed in Hamer, 'Making', pp. 30–36.

38. M. R. D. Foot, 'Morley's Gladstone: A Reappraisal', *Bulletin of the John Rylands Library*, 51 (1969), pp. 368–80; A. O. J. Cockshut, *Truth to Life: The Art of Biography in the Nineteenth Century* (London, 1974), ch. 10; D. M. Schreuder, 'The Making of Mr Gladstone's Posthumous Career: The Role of Morley and Knaplund as "Monumental Masons", 1903–27', in B. L. Kinzer (ed.), *The Gladstonian Turn of Mind: Essays Presented to J. B. Conacher* (Toronto, 1985), pp. 197–243; G. M. Ditchfield, '"Between Boswell and Strachey": Morley's *Life of Gladstone*', in D. Ellis (ed.), *Imitating Art: Essays in Biography* (London, 1993), pp. 36–52.

39. See I. Thomas, *Gladstone of Hawarden: A Memoir of Henry Neville, Lord Gladstone of Hawarden* (London, 1936); C. Mallet, *Herbert Gladstone: A Memoir* (London, 1932), and *Dictionary of National Biography, 1921–1930*, pp. 336–39. For a fuller account of their efforts to protect and promote their father's memory in the inter-war years see J. P. Gardiner, 'Gladstone, Gossip and the Post-War Generation', *Historical Research*, 74 (2001), pp. 409–24.

40. P. E. Wright, *Portraits and Criticisms* (London, 1925), pp. 152–53.

41. See *The Times*, 28–29 January and 2–4 February 1927; H. J. Gladstone, *After Thirty Years* (London, 1928), pp. 435–36; Mallet, *Gladstone*, pp. 299–302; Jenkins, *Gladstone*, pp. 105–6, 115; Matthew, *Gladstone*, p. 630.

42. A. Douglas to Herbert Gladstone, 28 July 1925. Lambeth Palace Library, Additional MS 2771 (Gladstone Papers), fol. 183.

43. W. H. Fox to P. Wright, 28 July 1925. Lambeth Palace Library, Additional MS 2771, fol. 176. In preparing for the possible use of such 'evidence', the brothers secured a statement in May 1926 from a former policeman whose job it was in the 1880s to trail their father and observe any conversations he had with women on the street. He wrote: 'The reputation that Mr Gladstone had with the Police Force at Scotland Yard was of the highest character, and although this eccentric conduct of his was well known it was never misinterpreted or misjudged.' Lambeth Palace Library, Additional MS 2759 (Gladstone Papers), fol. 82. Of course this nevertheless testifies to the renowned nature of Gladstone's 'rescue work', and to the establishment's anxiety about it.

44. Letter of support from T. Cuthbert, 27 July 1925. Lambeth Palace Library, Additional MS 2771, fol. 162.

45. Letter of support from J. Brechin, 28 July 1925. Lambeth Palace Library, Additional MS 2771, fos 196, 194.

46. Letter dated 29 July 1925. Lambeth Palace Library, Additional MS 2771, fol. 249.

47. *The Times*, 4 February 1927.

48. Thomas, *Gladstone*, p. 243.

49. Lambeth Palace Library, Additional MS 2771, fos 62–105.

50. The declaration is reproduced in Matthew, *Gladstone*, p. 629.

51. Herbert to Henry Gladstone, 21 January 1927. Lambeth Palace Library, Additional MS 2759, fol. 7.

52. Herbert Gladstone to C. Russell, 24 January 1927; Henry to Herbert Gladstone 25 January 1927. Lambeth Palace Library, Additional MS 2759, fos 10, 17.

53. This version of the diaries ran to 3000 typed pages and left intact what Herbert felt to be important political and family matters. Details of many letters and interviews were left out, as was much of Gladstone's commentary on his reading. The most significant omission, however, were details of Gladstone's 'rescue work'. This was partly because, as Herbert later coyly admitted, he was 'dictating to a girl typist'; but it also suggests that he hoped in 1919 that it might be written out of what was considered important in the family history. Lambeth Palace Library, Additional MS 2759, fos 49–54.
54. Herbert to Henry Gladstone, 9 December 1926. Lambeth Palace Library, Additional MS 2773 (Gladstone Papers), fos 183–5.
55. R. Craemer to Herbert Gladstone, 17 December 1928. British Library, Additional MS 46086 (Gladstone Papers), fol. 172.
56. M. R. D. Foot and H. C. G. Matthew (eds), *The Gladstone Diaries with Cabinet Minutes and Prime-Ministerial Correspondence* (Oxford, 1968–94), i, p. xxxv.
57. *Gladstone Diaries*, i, pp. xxxiv–xxxv.
58. C. Lang to Henry Gladstone, 17 May 1927. Lambeth Palace Library, Additional MS 2773, fol. 277.
59. Henry and Herbert Gladstone to R. Davidson, 24 February 1928. Lambeth Palace Library, Additional MS 2774 (Gladstone Papers), fos 33–34.
60. See, however, J. Vincent, *Disraeli* (Oxford, 1990), and P. Smith, *Disraeli: A Brief Life* (Cambridge, 1996).
61. An illuminating and moving notice by Peter Ghosh in the *Guardian*, 2 November 1999.
62. Matthew, *Gladstone*, pp. 99–100.
63. Matthew, *Gladstone*, epilogue.
64. Jenkins, *Gladstone*, p. 100.
65. Jenkins, *Gladstone*, p. 52.
66. Magnus, *Gladstone*, p. 8. Magnus's attitude towards Gladstone's 'rescue work' – 'a priestly office which he could fulfil as a layman' (p. 107) – clearly derives itself from his sense of the worldly versus religious tension in Gladstone's life, but is tactful to the point of naivety. Perhaps we should remember that the 1950s, when this biography appeared, was a distinctly 'Victorian' decade.
67. J. Morley, *The Life of William Ewart Gladstone* (London, 1903), i, p. 6.
68. T. L. Crosby, *The Two Mr Gladstones: A Study in Psychology and History* (New Haven and London, 1997), p. 4.
69. Biagini, *Gladstone*, p. 65.
70. Matthew, *Gladstone*, p. 6.
71. R. Shannon, *Gladstone: Peel's Inheritor, 1809–1865* (1982; Harmondsworth, 1999), p. 96.
72. Shannon, *Heroic Minister*, pp. 643–44.
73. Biagini, *Gladstone*, p. 62.

*Notes to Chapter 12: Wilde*

1. F. Harris, *Oscar Wilde: His Life and Confessions* (1916; London, 1997), pp. 140–42; R. Ellmann, *Oscar Wilde* (Harmondsworth, 1988), pp. 428–29.
2. O. Wilde, *De Profundis* (1897; Harmondsworth, 1986), p. 151.
3. M. S. Foldy, *The Trials of Oscar Wilde: Deviance, Morality, and Late-Victorian Society* (New Haven and London, 1997), pp. 52–53.
4. O. Wilde, 'The Soul of Man under Socialism' (1891), in *Complete Works of Oscar Wilde* (revised edn, London, 1994), p. 1188.
5. O. Wilde to A. and E. Leverson, 9 April 1895. M. Holland and R. Hart-Davis (eds), *The Complete Letters of Oscar Wilde* (London, 2000), pp. 641–42.
6. O. Wilde to A. Leverson, 23 April 1895. Holland and Hart-Davis, *Complete Letters*, p. 645.
7. Significantly enough, Rosebery was to experience bouts of debilitating insomnia that coincided almost exactly with Wilde's trials. The Crown's notable determination to secure a conviction against Wilde may have had something to do with a sense of the wider damage Queensberry could do. See Foldy, *Trials*, pp. 21–30.
8. H. M. Hyde, *The Trials of Oscar Wilde* (revised edn, New York, 1962), p. 14.
9. Hyde, *Trials*, p. 134.
10. Hyde, *Trials*, p. 201.
11. Hyde, *Trials*, p. 272.
12. Hyde, *Trials*, p. 273.
13. Ellmann, *Wilde*, p. 465.
14. Wilde, *De Profundis*, pp. 175, 185.
15. Wilde, *De Profundis*, p. 181.
16. O. Wilde to the Home Secretary, 2 July 1896; O. Wilde to the editor of the *Daily Chronicle*, 27 May 1897. Holland and Hart-Davis, *Complete Letters*, pp. 660, 847–55.
17. O. Wilde, 'Phrases and Philosophies for the Use of the Young', in *Complete Works*, p. 1244.
18. Hyde, *Trials*, p. 53.
19. The matter can be followed up in Hyde, *Trials*, p. 60. Most biographers, inhibited by a 'Victorian' reticence, tended not to go into such things; important, in a way, as they were to an understanding of what the Wilde trials meant in cultural history. The noble Richard Ellmann has only a brief but telling digression on Wilde's preferred sexual arrangements.
20. S. Fry, 'Playing Oscar', in A. Rolfe (ed.), *Nothing ... Except My Genius* (Harmondsworth, 1997), p. xix.
21. M. Sweet, *Inventing the Victorians* (London, 2001), p. 223.
22. T. Stoppard, *The Invention of Love* (London, 1997), p. 96.
23. Foldy, *Trials*, p. 80.
24. P. Ackroyd, Introduction to *The Picture of Dorian Gray* (1891; Harmondsworth, 1985), p. vii.

25. J. Weeks, *Sex, Politics and Society: The Regulation of Sexuality since 1800* (London, 1981), p. 101.

26. Sweet, *Inventing*, ch. 4.

27. See for example Weeks, *Sex, Politics and Society.*

28. Foldy, *Trials*, pp. 87–88.

29. A. Sinfield, *The Wilde Century: Effeminacy, Oscar Wilde and the Queer Moment* (New York, 1994), p. 93.

30. O. Wilde to Mrs George Lewis, *c.* 20 March 1882. Holland and Hart-Davis, *Complete Letters*, p. 154.

31. Holland and Hart-Davis, *Complete Letters*, p. 788n.

32. This is the line most convincingly taken by Sinfield, *Wilde Century.*

33. Hyde, *Trials*, p. 127.

34. Foldy, *Trials*, p. 20; Ellmann, *Wilde*, p. 430.

35. The *OED Supplement*, significantly enough, cites the first use of 'camp' as from 1909: both post-Wilde and at a time when the reaction against Victorianism was gathering momentum in intellectual circles.

36. See S. Hynes, *The Edwardian Turn of Mind* (London, 1991), ch. 5.

37. G. Woods, *A History of Gay Literature: The Male Tradition* (New Haven and London, 1998), pp. 178–79.

38. Hynes, *Edwardian Turn*, pp. 261–62.

39. See Forster's 1960 'Terminal Note' to *Maurice* (1914; Harmondsworth, 1972), pp. 217–22.

40. Forster, *Maurice*, p. 139.

41. Sinfield, *Wilde Century*, p. 146.

42. M. Drabble, *Angus Wilson: A Biography* (London, 1996), p. 70.

43. Sinfield, *Wilde Century*, p. 125.

44. J. B. Priestley, *The Edwardians* (Harmondsworth, 2000), p. 169.

45. S. Hynes, *A War Imagined: The First World War and English Culture* (London, 1990), p. 228. For a full account of the incident see P. Hoare, *Wilde's Last Stand: Decadence, Conspiracy and the First World War* (London, 1997).

46. V. Holland, *Son of Oscar Wilde* (1954; revised edn, London, 1999), p. 94.

47. Holland, *Son*, p. 140.

48. D. Murray, *Bosie: A Biography of Lord Alfred Douglas* (London, 2000), pp. 256–57.

49. H. Carpenter, *The Brideshead Generation: Evelyn Waugh and his Friends* (London, 1989), pp. 8, 19, 28.

50. N. Mitford, *The Pursuit of Love* (1945; Harmondsworth, 1949), pp. 7, 36.

51. British Library, Additional MS 56861 (Society of Authors Papers), fos 113–16, 280, 176–78, 403.

52. The tale of internecine warfare amongst Wilde's former intimates is an unhappy one. The principal rift existed between Lord Alfred Douglas and Robert Ross, Wilde's old friend and literary executor. For Douglas's shameful attack on Wilde (mitigated only on account of having been largely ghostwritten by the journalist T. W. H. Crosland) see A. Douglas, *Oscar Wilde and Myself* (London,

1914). A far more mature and generous account can be found in idem, *Oscar Wilde: A Summing-Up* (London, 1940), in which Douglas retracts some of his more unreasonable comments and accusations. On Douglas generally see Murray, *Bosie*.

53. See Merlin Holland's foreword to Holland, *Son*.

54. Hyde, *Trials*, p. 50.

55. C. FitzHerbert, 'A Refusal to Let the Name Die', *Daily Telegraph*, 4 November 2000.

56. S. Irvine, *Oscar Wilde: A Present Time Appraisal* (London, 1951), p. 35.

57. S. Faulks, *The Fatal Englishman: Three Short Lives* (London, 1997), p. 243.

58. H. David, *On Queer Street: A Social History of British Homosexuality, 1895–1995* (London, 1997), pp. 188–89.

59. *The Times*, 20 and 24 May 1960. Both reviews are reproduced in J. Goodman (ed.), *The Oscar Wilde File* (London, 1988).

60. R. Tanitch, *Oscar Wilde on Stage and Screen* (London, 1999), p. 28.

61. Holland, *Son*, p. 6.

62. John Cowper Powys in K. Beckson (ed.), *Oscar Wilde: The Critical Heritage* (London, 1970), p. 365.

63. V. O'Sullivan, *Aspects of Wilde* (London, 1936), p. 228.

64. O. Wilde, 'The Decay of Lying' (1891), in *Complete Works*, p. 1077.

65. O. Wilde, 'The Critic as Artist' (1891), in *Complete Works*, p. 1121.

66. For an example of this reassessment see L. Danson, 'Wilde as Critic and Theorist', in Raby, *Cambridge Companion*, pp. 80–95.

67. Wilde, *Dorian Gray*, p. 4.

68. M. Holland, 'Biography and the Art of Lying', in P. Raby (ed.), *The Cambridge Companion to Oscar Wilde* (Cambridge, 1997), p. 4.

69. N. Bartlett, *Who Was That Man? A Present for Mr Oscar Wilde* (London, 1988).

70. T. Wright, 'In the Mouth of Fame', *Times Literary Supplement*, 9 February 2001, p. 3.

71. Ellmann, *Wilde*, p. 96.

72. Ellmann, *Wilde*, p. 439.

73. O. Wilde to W. E. Gladstone, 2 November 1888. British Library, Additional MS 44505 (Gladstone Papers), fol. 88. Also in Holland and Hart-Davis, *Complete Letters*, p. 369.

74. Ellmann, *Wilde*, p. 548.

75. See Tanitch, *Wilde on Stage*, pp. 54–56.

76. O. Wilde, 'A Few Maxims for the Instruction of the Over-Educated', in *Complete Works*, p. 1242.

77. R. A. Gagnier, *Idylls of the Marketplace: Oscar Wilde and the Victorian Public* (Stanford, 1986).

78. The guide to the centenary exhibition 'The Wilde Years' at the Barbican, 2000–2001, played upon this very ambiguity. 'Oscar Wilde: Professor of Aesthetics or the First Doctor of Spin?', it asked.

79. J. Mitchell, *Wilde: The Screenplay* (London, 1997), p. 177.

80. This reservation is taken up at greater length by Shelton Waldrep, in 'The Uses and Misuses of Oscar Wilde', in J. Kucich and D. F. Sadoff (eds), *Victorian Afterlife: Postmodern Culture Rewrites the Nineteenth Century* (Minneapolis, 2000), pp. 49–63.

# Bibliography

## Manuscript Sources

*Bodleian Library, Oxford*

Ensor Papers

*British Library, London*

Additional MS 44505 (Gladstone Papers)
Additional MS 46086 (Gladstone Papers)
Additional MS 54219 (*Eminent Victorians*)
Additional MS 56861 (Society of Authors Papers)
Additional MS 60721 (Strachey Papers)
Additional MS 60732 (Strachey Papers)
Additional MS 63334 (Society of Authors Papers)

*Lambeth Palace Library, London*

Additional MS 2759 (Gladstone Papers)
Additional MS 2771 (Gladstone Papers)
Additional MS 2773 (Gladstone Papers)
Additional MS 2774 (Gladstone Papers)

*Seeley Historical Library, Cambridge*

File on recommended tripos reading and related correspondence, 1933–40

## Secondary Sources

Ackroyd, P., *Dickens* (London, 1990)

Acton, J. (ed.), *The Cambridge Modern History*, xii, *The Latest Age* (Cambridge, 1910)

Addison, P., *The Road to 1945: British Politics and the Second World War* (revised edn, London, 1994)

Altholz, J. L., 'Lord Acton and the Plan of the *Cambridge Modern History*', *Historical Journal*, 39 (1996), pp. 723–36

Altick, R. D., 'Eminent Victorianism: What Lytton Strachey Hath Wrought', *American Scholar*, 64 (1995), pp. 81–89

Amis, K., *Lucky Jim* (1954; Harmondsworth, 1992)

Amis, M., *Experience* (London, 2000)

Andrews, A., *Kings and Queens of England and Scotland* (London, 1983)

Andrews, M., 'Charles Dickens, *Dickens* and Peter Ackroyd', in D. Ellis (ed.), *Imitating Art: Essays in Biography* (London, 1993), pp. 174–86

—, *Dickens on England and the English* (Hassocks, 1979)

Annan, N., *Our Age: The Generation that Made Post-War Britain* (London, 1990)

—, *The Dons: Mentors, Eccentrics and Geniuses* (London, 1999)

Anon., *The Victorian Age, by a Later Victorian* (London, 1921)

Arch, R., *Ernest Belfort Bax: Thinker and Pioneer* (London, 1927)

Aronson, T., *Heart of a Queen: Queen Victoria's Romantic Attachments* (London, 1991)

Asquith, H. H., *Some Aspects of the Victorian Age* (Oxford, 1918)

Auerbach, J. A., *The Great Exhibition of 1851: A Nation on Display* (New Haven and London, 1999)

Backscheider, P. R., *Reflections on Biography* (Oxford, 1999)

Baldick, C., *The Social Mission of English Criticism, 1848–1932* (Oxford, 1983)

Bartlett, N., *Who Was That Man? A Present for Mr Oscar Wilde* (London, 1988)

Baumann, A. A., *The Last Victorians* (London, 1927)

Beauman, N., *Morgan: A Biography of E. M. Forster* (London, 1993)

Beckson, K. (ed.), *Oscar Wilde: The Critical Heritage* (London, 1970)

Beer, G., *Darwin's Plots: Evolutionary Thought in Darwin, George Eliot and Nineteenth-Century Fiction* (London, 1983)

Beerbohm, M., *Lytton Strachey* (Cambridge, 1943)

Belfort Bax, E., *Reminiscences and Reflexions of a Mid and Late Victorian* (London, 1918)

Bennett, A., *The Journal of Arnold Bennett* (New York, 1933)

—, *The Old Wives' Tale* (1908; Harmondsworth, 1990)

Benson, A. C. and Esher, R. (eds), *Letters of Queen Victoria*, first series, *1837–61* (London, 1907)

Benson, E. F., *As We Were: A Victorian Peep-Show* (London, 1930)

Bentley, M., 'Approaches to Modernity: Western Historiography since the Enlightenment', in idem (ed.), *Companion to Historiography* (London, 1997), pp. 395–506

—, *The Climax of Liberal Politics: British Liberalism in Theory and Practice, 1868–1918* (London, 1987)

Berlin, I., 'Winston Churchill in 1940', in *The Proper Study of Mankind: An Anthology of Essays* (London, 1997), pp. 605–27

Best, G., *Churchill: A Study in Greatness* (London, 2001)

Betham-Edwards, M., *Mid-Victorian Memories* (London, 1919)

Biagini, E. F., *Gladstone* (Basingstoke, 2000)

Birrell, F., *Gladstone* (London, 1933)

Blake, R., *Disraeli* (London, 1966)

—, *The Conservative Party: from Peel to Major* (London, 1997)

Blore, G. H., *Victorian Worthies* (Oxford, 1920)

Boas, G., *Lytton Strachey* (Oxford, 1935)

Bogdanor, V., 'An Exceptional Monarch who Cast a Mighty Shadow', *Daily Telegraph*, 22 January 2001

Bolitho, H., *George VI* (London, 1937)

Bott, A., *Our Fathers, 1870–1900* (London, 1931)

Bowler, P. J., *Reconciling Science and Religion: The Debate in Early Twentieth-Century Britain* (Chicago, 2001)

Bradbury, M. and McFarlane, J. (eds), *Modernism: A Guide to European Literature, 1890–1930* (new edn, Harmondsworth, 1991)

Bradbury, M., *The Modern British Novel* (Harmondsworth, 1994)

Bradbury, N., 'Charles Dickens and the Form of the Novel', in J. O. Jordan (ed.), *The Cambridge Companion to Charles Dickens* (Cambridge, 2001), pp. 152–66

Bradford, S., *King George VI* (London, 1989)

Branca, P., *Silent Sisterhood: Middle Class Women in the Victorian Home* (London, 1975)

Brendon, P., *The Dark Valley: A Panorama of the 1930s* (London, 2001)

Brewer, J., *The Pleasures of the Imagination: English Culture in the Eighteenth Century* (London, 1997)

Bridges, J. A., *Victorian Recollections* (London, 1919)

Briggs, A., 'History that Improves with Age', *Times Higher Education Supplement*, 25 February 2000

—, 'The 1890s: Past, Present and Future in Headlines', in A. Briggs and D. Snowman (eds), *Fins de Siècle: How Centuries End, 1400–2000* (New Haven and London, 1996), pp. 156–95

—, *The Age of Improvement, 1783–1867* (revised edn, London, 1979)

—, *The Birth of Broadcasting* (Oxford, 1961)

—, *The Golden Age of Wireless* (Oxford, 1965)

—, *Victorian Cities* (Harmondsworth, 1990)

—, 'Victorian Images of Gladstone', in P. J. Jagger (ed.), *Gladstone* (London, 1998), pp. 33–49

—, *Victorian People: A Reassessment of Persons and Themes, 1851–67* (Harmondsworth, 1990)

—, *Victorian Things* (Harmondsworth, 1990)

Brindle, P., 'Past Histories: History and the Elementary School Classroom in Early Twentieth-Century England', unpublished Ph.D. thesis, University of Cambridge, 1998

Brown, J., *Spirits of Place: Five Famous Lives in their English Landscape* (London, 2001)

Brownlow, K., *David Lean: A Biography* (London, 1996)

Buckle, G. E. (ed.), *Letters of Queen Victoria*, second series, *1862–85* (London, 1926–28); third series, *1886–1901* (London, 1930–32)

Buckley, J. H., *The Victorian Temper: A Study in Literary Culture* (London, 1952)

Bullen, J. B. (ed.), *Writing and Victorianism* (London, 1997)

Burn, W. L., *The Age of Equipoise: A Study of the Mid-Victorian Generation* (London, 1964)

Burrow, J. W., 'Victorian Historians and the Royal Historical Society', *Transactions of the Royal Historical Society*, 39 (1989), pp. 125–40

Bush, D., 'The Victorians, God Bless Them!', *The Bookman*, 74 (1932), pp. 589–90

Butler, S., *The Way of All Flesh* (1903; Oxford, 1993)

Butterfield, H., 'Some Early Trends in Scholarship, 1868–1968, in the Field of Modern History', *Transactions of the Royal Historical Society*, 9 (1969), pp. 159–84

—, *The Whig Interpretation of History* (1931; London, 1965)

Byatt, A. S., *The Biographer's Tale* (London, 2001)

Caine, B., *English Feminism, 1780–1980* (Oxford, 1997)

Calder, A., *The Myth of the Blitz* (London, 1991)

—, *The People's War* (London, 1969)

Calder, A. and Sheridan, D. (eds), *Speak for Yourself: A Mass-Observation Anthology, 1937–49* (London, 1984)

Cameron, J., *Victorian Photographs of Famous Men and Fair Women* (London, 1926)

Campbell, D., *Victoria, Queen and Empress* (Edinburgh, 1901)

Campbell, J., *V. R. I. Queen Victoria: Her Life and Reign* (New York, 1901)

Cannadine, D., *Class in Britain* (New Haven and London, 1998)

—, 'Constitutional Monarchy', in *History in Our Time* (New Haven and London, 1998), pp. 19–24

—, *G. M. Trevelyan: A Life In History* (London, 1992)

—, *Ornamentalism: How the British Saw their Empire* (London, 2001)

—, 'Prince Albert' and 'Welfare State History', in *The Pleasures of the Past* (Harmondsworth, 1997), pp. 12–22, 172–183

—, 'The Context, Performance and Meaning of Ritual: The British Monarchy and the "Invention of Tradition", c. 1820–1977', in E. Hobsbawm and T. Ranger (eds), *The Invention of Tradition* (Cambridge, 1983), pp. 101–64

—, *The Decline and Fall of the British Aristocracy* (London, 1996)

—, 'The First Hundred Years', in H. Newby (ed.), *The National Trust: The Next Hundred Years* (London, 1995), pp. 11–31

—, 'The Past and the Present', in L. M. Smith (ed.), *The Making of Britain: Echoes of Greatness* (London, 1988), pp. 9–20

—, 'The Present and the Past in the English Industrial Revolution, 1880–1980', *Past and Present*, 116 (1987), pp. 169–91

Cannon, J. (ed.), *The Oxford Companion to British History* (Oxford, 1997)

Carey, J., *The Violent Effigy: A Study of Dickens' Imagination* (2nd ed, London, 1991)

Carpenter, H., *Benjamin Britten: A Biography* (London, 1992)

—, *The Brideshead Generation: Evelyn Waugh and his Friends* (London, 1989)

—, *The Envy of the World: Fifty Years of the BBC Third Programme and Radio 3* (London, 1996)

Cecil, D., *Early Victorian Novelists: Essays in Revaluation* (London, 1943)

Chancellor, V. E., *History for their Masters: Opinion in the English History Textbook, 1800–1914* (London, 1970)

Charlot, M., *Victoria; The Young Queen* (Oxford, 1991)

Charmley, J., *Churchill: The End of Glory* (London, 1993)

Cherry, G. E., *Town Planning in Britain since 1900: The Rise and Fall of the Planning Ideal* (London, 1996)

Chesterton, G. K., *Charles Dickens* (1906; London, 1960)

Chorley, K., *Manchester Made Them* (London, 1950)

Christiansen, R., *The Voice of Victorian Sex: Arthur H. Clough, 1819–1861* (London, 2001)

Clapham, J. H., 'The Study of Economic History', in N. B. Harte (ed.), *The Study of Economic History: Collected Inaugural Lectures, 1893–1970* (London, 1971), pp. 55–70

Clarke, P., *A Question of Leadership, from Gladstone to Blair* (2nd edn, Harmondsworth, 1999)

—, *Hope and Glory: Britain, 1900–1990* (London, 1996)

Clive, J., 'More or Less Eminent Victorians', in *Not By Fact Alone: Essays on the Writing and Reading of History* (London, 1989), pp. 228–50

Cockshut, A. O. J., *Truth to Life: The Art of Biography in the Nineteenth Century* (London, 1974)

Colley, L., *Britons: Forging the Nation, 1707–1837* (London, 1994)

Collini, S., *Public Moralists: Political Thought and Intellectual Life in Britain, 1850–1930* (Oxford, 1991)

—, 'Victorian Values: From the Clapham Sect to the Clapham Omnibus', in *English Pasts: Essays in History and Culture* (Oxford, 1999), pp. 103–15

Collins, W., *Basil* (1852; Oxford, 1990)

Colls, R .and Dodd, P. (eds), *Englishness: Politics and Culture, 1880–1920* (Beckenham, 1986)

Coote, H., *While I Remember* (London, 1937)

Cowling, M., *1867: Disraeli, Gladstone and Revolution. The Passing of the Second Reform Bill* (Cambridge, 1967)

Crosby, T. L., *The Two Mr Gladstones: A Study in Psychology and History* (New Haven and London, 1997)

Crotch, W. W., *The Secret of Dickens* (London, 1919)

Cullingworth, J. B. and Nadin, V., *Town and Country Planning in Britain* (11th edn, London, 1994)

Cunningham, H., 'The Language of Patriotism, 1750–1914', *History Workshop Journal*, 12 (1981), pp. 8–33

Danson, L., 'Wilde as Critic and Theorist', in P. Raby (ed.), *The Cambridge Companion to Oscar Wilde* (Cambridge, 1997), pp. 80–95

David, H., *On Queer Street: A Social History of British Homosexuality, 1895–1995* (London, 1997)

Davidoff, L. and Hall, C., *Family Fortunes: Men and Women of the English Middle Class, 1780–1850* (London, 1987)

Davis, H. W. C., *The Age of Grey and Peel* (Oxford, 1929)

Davis, P., *The Lives and Times of Ebenezer Scrooge* (New Haven and London, 1990)

De Jongh, N., *Politics, Prudery and Perversions: The Censorship of the English Stage, 1901–1968* (London, 2000)

Deary, T. and Brown, M., *The Vile Victorians* (London, 1994)

Dickens, C., *A Christmas Carol* (1843; Harmondsworth, 1986)

—, *Dombey and Son* (1848; Oxford, 1987)

—, *Our Mutual Friend* (1865; Harmondsworth, 1997)

Dickson, E. J., 'When Love Reigned', *Radio Times*, 25–31 August 2001

Ditchfield, G. M., '"Between Boswell and Strachey": Morley's *Life of Gladstone*', in D. Ellis (ed.), *Imitating Art: Essays in Biography* (London, 1993), pp. 36–52

Dixon, R. and Muthesius, S., *Victorian Architecture* (2nd edn, London, 1985)

Douglas, A., *Oscar Wilde and Myself* (London, 1914)

—, *Oscar Wilde: A Summing-Up* (London, 1940)

Drabble, M., *Angus Wilson: A Biography* (London, 1996)

Drummond, J., *Tainted by Experience: A Life in the Arts* (London, 2000)

Dutt, S. A., *When England Arose: The Centenary of the People's Charter* (London, 1938)

Dyer, G., *Out of Sheer Rage: In the Shadow of D. H. Lawrence* (London, 1997)

Dyos, H. J. and Wolff, M. (eds), *The Victorian City: Images and Realities* (London, 1973)

Edel, L., *Literary Biography* (Bloomington, 1973)

Edwards, J., 'Edmund Gosse and the Victorian Nude', *History Today*, 51 (November 2001), pp. 29–35

Eksteins, M., *Rites of Spring: The Great War and the Birth of the Modern Age* (London, 1989)

Eliot, G., *Middlemarch* (1872; Oxford, 1998)

Ellmann, R., *Oscar Wilde* (Harmondsworth, 1988)

Elton, G. R., 'Herbert Butterfield and the Study of History', *Historical Journal*, 27 (1984), pp. 729–43

Engels, F., *The Condition of the Working Class in England* (1845; Harmondsworth, 1987)

Ensor, R. C. K., *England, 1970–1914* (Oxford, 1936)

Evans, E. J., *The Forging of the Modern State: Early Industrial England, 1783–1870* (2nd edn, London, 1996)

Evans, R. J., *In Defence of History* (London, 1997)

Evans, S., 'Thatcher and the Victorians: A Suitable Case for Comparison?', *History*, 82 (1997), pp. 601–20

Faulks, S., *The Fatal Englishman: Three Short Lives* (London, 1997)

Ferguson, N., *The Pity of War* (London, 1998)

FitzHerbert, C., 'A Refusal to Let the Name Die', *Daily Telegraph*, 4 November 2000

Flint, K., 'Plotting the Victorians: Narrative, Postmodernism, and Contemporary Fiction', in J. B. Bullen (ed.), *Writing and Victorianism* (London, 1997), pp. 286–305

Foldy, M. S., *The Trials of Oscar Wilde: Deviance, Morality and Late Victorian Society* (New Haven and London, 1997)

Foot, M. R. D., 'Morley's Gladstone: A Reappraisal', *Bulletin of the John Rylands Library*, 51 (1969), pp. 368–80

Foot, M. R. D. and Matthew, H. C. G. (eds), *The Gladstone Diaries with Cabinet Minutes and Prime-Ministerial Correspondence* (Oxford, 1968–94)

Forster, E. M., *A Room with a View* (1908; Harmondsworth, 1990)

—, *Aspects of the Novel* (1927; Harmondsworth, 1990)

—, *Maurice* (1914; Harmondsworth, 1972)

—, *The Longest Journey* (1907; Harmondsworth, 1989)

—, *Where Angels Fear to Tread* (1905; Harmondsworth, 1976)

—, 'What I Believe' (1939), in *Two Cheers for Democracy* (1951; San Diego and New York, 1979), pp. 67–76

Forster, M., *Hidden Lives: A Family Memoir* (London, 1995)

—, *Precious Lives* (London, 1998)

Fowles, J., *The French Lieutenant's Woman* (1969; London, 1971)

Frampton, K., *Modern Architecture: A Critical History* (3rd edn, London, 1992)

Francillon, R. E., *Mid-Victorian Memories* (London, 1914)

Frayling, C., 'Crafts', in B. Ford (ed.), *The Cambridge Cultural History of Britain*, ix, *Modern Britain* (Cambridge, 1992), pp. 168–95

Fry, S., 'Playing Oscar', in A. Rolfe (ed.), *Nothing ... Except My Genius* (Harmondsworth, 1997), pp. vii–xxv

Furbank, P. N., *E. M. Forster: A Life* (London, 1988)

Fussell, P., *The Great War and Modern Memory* (Oxford, 1975)

Gagnier, R., *Idylls of the Marketplace: Oscar Wilde and the Victorian Public* (Stanford, 1986)

Gaitskell, H., *Chartism: An Introductory Essay* (London, 1929)

Gardiner, J. P., 'Gladstone, Gossip and the Postwar Generation', *Historical Research*, 74 (2001), pp. 409–24

Gibson, I., *The Erotomaniac: The Secret Life of Henry Spencer Ashbee* (London, 2001)

Giddings, R. and Selby, K., *The Classic Serial on Television and Radio* (Basingstoke, 2001)

Gillis, J. R., *Youth and History: Tradition and Continuity in European Age-Relations, 1770-Present* (revised edn, London, 1981)

Gladstone, H., *After Thirty Years* (London, 1928)

Glendinning, V., *Jonathan Swift* (London, 1999)

Goldstein, D., 'The Organizational Development of the British Historical Profession, 1884–1921', *Bulletin of the Institute of Historical Research*, 55 (1982), pp. 180–93

Goodman, J. (ed.), *The Oscar Wilde File* (London, 1988)

Gosse, E., *Father and Son* (1907; Harmondsworth, 1989)

—, 'The Agony of the Victorian Age' (1918), in *Some Diversions of a Man of Letters* (London, 1919), pp. 313–37

Grant, A. and Stringer, K. (eds), *Uniting the Kingdom? The Making of British History* (London, 1995)

Graves, R., *Goodbye to All That* (1929; Harmondsworth, 1960)

Graves, R. and Hodge, A., *The Long Weekend: A Social History of Britain, 1918–1939* (London, 1940)

Green, E. H. H., *The Crisis of Conservatism: The Politics, Economics and Ideology of the British Conservative Party, 1880–1914* (London, 1995)

Green, E. W., *A School History of England* (London, 1937)

Green, M., *Children of the Sun: A Narrative of 'Decadence' in England after 1918* (London, 1977)

Green-Lewis, J., 'At Home in the Nineteenth Century: Photography, Nostalgia and the Will to Authenticity', in J. Kucich and D. F. Sadoff (eds), *Victorian Afterlife: Postmodern Culture Rewrites the Nineteenth Century* (Minneapolis, 2000), pp. 29–48

Guedalla, P., *The Queen and Mr Gladstone* (London, 1933)

Halsey, A. H., *Change in British Society* (4th edn, Oxford, 1995)

Hamer, D. A., 'Gladstone: The Making of a Political Myth', *Victorian Studies*, 22 (1978–79), pp. 28–50

Hamilton, E., *The Halcyon Era: A Rambling Reverie of Now and Then* (London, 1933)

Hammond, J. L., *Gladstone and the Irish Nation* (London, 1938)

Hanham, H. J., *Elections and Party Management: Politics in the Time of Disraeli and Gladstone* (London, 1959)

Hardie, F., *The Political Influence of Queen Victoria, 1861–1901* (2nd edn, London, 1938)

Harper, S., *Picturing the Past: The Rise and Fall of the British Costume Film* (London, 1994)

Harris, F., *Oscar Wilde: His Life and Confessions* (1916; London, 1997)

Harrison, B., 'Underneath the Victorians' *Victorian Studies*, 10 (1967), pp. 239–62

Harrison, J. F. C., *Early Victorian Britain, 1832–51* (London, 1988)

—, *Late Victorian Britain, 1875–1901* (London, 1990)

Hastings, S., *Evelyn Waugh: A Biography* (London, 1994)

Heathorn, '"Let Us Remember that We, Too, are English": Constructions of Citizenship and National Identity in English Elementary School Reading Books, 1880–1914', *Victorian Studies*, 38 (1995), pp. 395–427

Heffer, S., *Vaughan Williams* (London, 2001)

Hennessy, P., *Never Again: Britain, 1945–1951* (London, 1992)

—, 'Never Again', in B. Brivati and H. Jones (eds), *What Difference did the War Make?* (London, 1993)

—, *The Prime Minister: The Office and its Holders since 1945* (revised edn, Harmondsworth, 2001)

—, *Whitehall* (revised edn, London, 2001)

Hewison, R., *Culture and Consensus: England, Art and Politics since 1940* (revised edn, London, 1997)

—, *The Heritage Industry: Britain in a Climate of Decline* (London, 1987)

—, *Too Much: Art and Society in the Sixties, 1960–75* (London, 1986)

Hill, R. L., *Toryism and the People, 1832–1846* (London, 1929)

Hillier, B., *Young Betjeman* (London, 1988)

Hilton, B., 'Gladstone's Theological Politics', in M. Bentley and J. Stevenson (eds), *High and Low Politics in Victorian Britain* (Oxford, 1983), pp. 28–57

—, 'Peel: A Reappraisal', *Historical Journal*, 22 (1979), pp. 585–614

Hilton, T., *John Ruskin*, i, *The Early Years, 1819–1859* (New Haven and London, 1985); ii, *The Later Years* (New Haven and London, 2000)

Himmelfarb, G., *The De-Moralization of Society: From Victorian Virtues to Modern Values* (London, 1995)

Hoare, P., *Wilde's Last Stand: Decadence, Conspiracy and the First World War* (London, 1997)

Hobsbawm, E., *Labouring Men: Studies in the History of Labour* (London, 1964)

Hoggart, R., *A Local Habitation: Life and Times, 1918–1940* (London, 1988)

—, 'Lady Chatterley and the Censors' and 'Memoir for Our Grandchildren', in *Between Two Worlds: Essays* (London, 2001), pp. 85–97, 211–43

—, *The Uses of Literacy: Aspects of Working-Class Life with Special Reference to Publications and Entertainments* (1957; Harmondsworth, 1992)

Holdsworth, A., *Out of the Doll's House: The Story of Women in the Twentieth Century* (London, 1990)

Holland, M., 'Biography and the Art of Lying', in P. Raby (ed.), *The Cambridge Companion to Oscar Wilde* (Cambridge, 1997), pp. 3–17

Holland, M. and Hart-Davis, R. (eds), *The Complete Letters of Oscar Wilde* (London, 2000)

Holland, V., *Son of Oscar Wilde* (1954; revised edn, London, 1999)

Holroyd, M., *Bernard Shaw* (London, 1997)

—, *Hugh Kingsmill: A Critical Biography* (London, 1964)

—, *Lytton Strachey* (revised edn, London, 1994)

Homans, M., *Queen Victoria and British Culture, 1837–1876* (Chicago, 1998)

Homans, M. and Munich, A. (eds), *Remaking Queen Victoria* (Cambridge, 1997)

Hopkinson, E., *The Story of a Mid-Victorian Girl* (Cambridge, 1928)

Hoppen, K. T., *The Mid-Victorian Generation, 1846–1886* (Oxford, 1998)

Horne, P. (ed), *Henry James: A Life in Letters* (Harmondsworth, 2000)

Houghton, W. E., *The Victorian Frame of Mind, 1830–1870* (New Haven and London, 1957)

Housman, L., *Victoria Regina: A Dramatic Biography* (1934; London, 1949)

Hovell, M., *The Chartist Movement* (Manchester, 1918)

Hughes, M., *A London Family, 1870–1900* (1934–37; Oxford, 1991)

Huxley, A., *The Doors of Perception* (London, 1954)

—, 'Vulgarity in Literature' (1930) in *Music at Night* (London, 1994), pp. 183–228

Hyde, H. M., *The Trials of Oscar Wilde* (revised edn, New York, 1962)

Hynes, S., *A War Imagined: The First World War and English Culture* (London, 1990)

—, *The Edwardian Turn of Mind* (London, 1991)

*Ideas and Beliefs of the Victorians: An Historic Revaluation of the Victorian Age* (London, 1949)

Ignatieff, M., *Isaiah Berlin: A Life* (London, 1998)

Inge, W. R., *The Victorian Age* (Cambridge, 1922)

Irvine, S., *Oscar Wilde: A Present Time Appraisal* (London, 1951)

Jackson, A. H., *A Victorian Childhood* (London, 1932)

Jackson, L., *The Sixties: Decade of Design Revolution* (London, 1998)

James, H., *The Wings of the Dove* (1902; Oxford, 1984)

James, L., *Raj: The Making and Unmaking of British India* (London, 1997)

Jann, R., 'From Amateur to Professional: The Case of the Oxbridge Historians', *Journal of British Studies*, 22 (1983), pp. 122–47

Jarvis, A., *Samuel Smiles and the Construction of Victorian Values* (Stroud, 1997)

Jenkins, R., *Gladstone* (London, 1996)

Jepson, E., *Memories of a Victorian* (London, 1933)

Johnson, S., *The Rambler*, no. 60, in W. J. Bate and A. B. Strauss (eds), *The Yale Edition of the Works of Samuel Johnson* (New Haven and London), iii, pp. 318–23

Jones, N., *Rupert Brooke: Life, Death and Myth* (London, 1999)

Jones, S., 'Attic Attitudes: Leighton and the Aesthetic Philosophy', in G. Marsden (ed.), *Victorian Values: Personalities and Perspectives in Nineteenth-Century Society* (2nd edn, London, 1998), pp. 231–41

Kaplan, F., *Dickens: A Biography* (London, 1988)

Keating, P., *The Haunted Study. A Social History of the English Novel, 1875–1914* (London, 1989)

Kelley, R., 'Midlothian: A Study in Politics and Ideas', *Victorian Studies*, 4 (1960), pp. 118–40

Kent, W., *The Testament of a Victorian Youth* (London, 1938)

Kermode, F., 'Grandeur and Filth', in *The Uses of Error* (London, 1991), pp. 183–99

Kipling, R., *Something of Myself* (1936; Harmondsworth, 1992)

Kitson Clark, G., *Peel and the Conservative Party: A Study in Party Politics, 1832–1841* (London, 1929)

—, *The Making of Victorian England* (London, 1965)

Langbauer, L., 'Queen Victoria and Me', in J. Kucich and D. F. Sadoff (eds), *Victorian Afterlife: Postmodern Culture Rewrites the Nineteenth Century* (Minneapolis, 2000), pp. 211–33

Laver, J., *Victorian Vista* (London, 1954)

Lawrence, D. H., *Lady Chatterley's Lover* (1928; Harmondsworth, 1994)

Leader, D., *Why Do Women Write More Letters Than They Post?* (London, 1997)

Leavis, F. R., *The Great Tradition* (1948; Harmondsworth, 1983)

Leavis, Q. D., *Fiction and the Reading Public* (1932; London, 1965)

Lee, H., *Virginia Woolf* (London, 1996)

LeMahieu, D., *A Culture for Democracy: Mass Communication and the Cultivated Mind in Britain between the Wars* (Oxford, 1988)

Letwin, R., *The Gentleman in Trollope: Individuality and Moral Conduct* (London, 1982)

Lewes, G. H., 'Dickens in Relation to Criticism' (1872), in M. Hollington (ed.), *Charles Dickens: Critical Assessments,* i (Mountfield, 1995), pp. 454–67

Liddington, J. and Norris, J., *One Hand Tied Behind Us: The Rise of the Women's Suffrage Movement* (London, 1978)

Lodge, D., 'In the Home of Eternal Unrest', *Times Literary Supplement,* 10 November 2000

Loeffelholz, 'Crossing the Atlantic with Victoria: American Receptions, 1837–1901', in M. Homans and A. Munich (eds), *Remaking Queen Victoria* (Cambridge, 1997), pp. 33–56

Long, R. E., *The Films of Merchant Ivory* (London, 1992)

Longford, E., *Victoria R.I.* (London, 1964)

Lowenthal, D., *The Past is a Foreign Country* (Cambridge, 1985)

—, *The Heritage Crusade and the Spoils of History* (Cambridge, 1998)

MacCarthy, F., *William Morris: A Life for Our Time* (London, 1994)

MacKenzie, J. M. (ed.), *Imperialism and Popular Culture* (Manchester, 1986)

—, (ed.), *Propaganda and Empire: The Manipulation of British Public Opinion, 1880–1960* (Manchester, 1984)

—, (ed.), *The Victorian Vision: Inventing New Britain* (London, 2001)

MacKillop, I., *F. R. Leavis: A Life in Criticism* (London, 1995)

Magnus, P., *Gladstone* (1954; Harmondsworth, 2001)

Mallet, C., *Herbert Gladstone: A Memoir* (London, 1932)

Mandler, P., *The Fall and Rise of the Stately Home* (New Haven and London, 1997)

Marcus, S., *The Other Victorians: A Study of Sexuality and Pornography in Mid-Nineteenth-Century England* (London, 1966)

Marler, R., *Bloomsbury Pie: The Story of the Bloomsbury Revival* (London, 1997)

Marquand, D., *Ramsay MacDonald* (London, 1977)

Marsden, G. (ed.), *Victorian Values: Personalities and Perspectives in Nineteenth-Century Society* (2nd edn, London, 1998)

Marsh, J., 'Dickens and Film', in J. O. Jordan (ed.), *The Cambridge Companion to Charles Dickens* (Cambridge, 2001), pp. 204–23

Marwick, A., *British Society since 1945* (3rd edn, Harmondsworth, 1996)

—, *The Sixties: Cultural Revolution in Britain, France, Italy, and the United States, c. 1958 – c. 1974* (Oxford, 1998)

Mason, M., *The Making of Victorian Sexual Attitudes* (Oxford, 1994)

—, *The Making of Victorian Sexuality* (Oxford, 1994)

Matthew, H. C. G., 'Disraeli, Gladstone and the Politics of Mid-Victorian Budgets', *Historical Journal,* 22 (1979), pp. 615–43

—, *Gladstone, 1809–1898* (Oxford, 1997)

—, 'Gladstonian Finance', in G. Marsden (ed.), *Victorian Values: Personalities and Perspectives in Nineteenth-Century Society* (2nd edn, London, 1998), pp. 127–37

—, (ed.), *Nineteenth-Century Britain* (Oxford, 2000)

Maurois, A., 'The Philosophy of Dickens' (1927), in M. Hollington (ed.), *Charles Dickens: Critical Assessments*, i (Mountfield, 1995), pp. 678–91

McKibbin, R., *Classes and Cultures: England, 1918–1951* (Oxford, 1998)

—, 'Why Was There No Marxism in Great Britain?', *English Historical Review*, 99 (1984), pp. 297–331

McLeod, H., *Religion and Society in England, 1850–1914* (Basingstoke, 1996)

McWilliam, R., *Popular Politics in Nineteenth-Century England* (London, 1998)

Meiklejohn, J. M. D. and M. J. C., *A School History of England and Great Britain* (London, 1939)

Miller, J. (ed.), *Miller's Antiques Encyclopedia* (London, 1998)

Miller, L., *The Brontë Myth* (London, 2001)

Milsom, J., 'Backwards, in All Directions', *Daily Telegraph*, 29 August 2001

Mitchell, J., *Wilde: The Screenplay* (London, 1997)

Mitford, N., *The Pursuit of Love* (1945; Harmondsworth, 1949)

Montefiore, D., *From a Victorian to a Modern* (London, 1927)

Moore, G. E., *Principia Ethica* (1903, revised edn, 1922; Cambridge, 1993)

Morley, J., *The Life of William Ewart Gladstone* (London, 1903)

Muir, F., *A Kentish Lad* (London, 1998)

—, (ed.), *The Oxford Book of Humorous Prose* (Oxford, 1990)

Munich, A., *Queen Victoria's Secrets* (New York, 1996)

Murdoch, W., *The Victorian Era: Its Strengths and Weakness* (Sydney, 1938)

Murray, D., *Bosie: A Biography of Lord Alfred Douglas* (London, 2000)

Nead, L., 'Nudes Fit to Print', *BBC History Magazine*, 2 (November 2001), pp. 26–28

Newsome, D., *The Victorian World Picture: Perceptions and Introspections in an Age of Change* (London, 1997)

Nicolson, H., *The Development of English Biography* (London, 1927)

Nicolson, N., *Virginia Woolf* (London, 2000)

O'Gorman, F., *John Ruskin* (Stroud, 1999)

O'Hagan, A., 'A Study in Stupid Elegance', *Daily Telegraph*, 3 November 2000

O'Sullivan, V., Aspects of Wilde (London, 1936)

Orwell, G., 'Charles Dickens' (1940), in M. Hollington (ed.), *Charles Dickens: Critical Assessments*, i (Mountfield, 1995), pp. 717–55

—, *Coming Up For Air* (1939; Harmondsworth, 1990)

—, *The Lion and the Unicorn: Socialism and the English Genius* (1941; Harmondsworth, 1982)

Packard, J. M., *Victoria's Daughters* (Stroud, 1999)

Parker, L., *The English Historical Tradition since 1850* (Edinburgh, 1980)

Parry, J., *The Rise and Fall of Liberal Government in Victorian Britain* (New Haven and London, 1993)

Partridge, F., *Good Company: Diaries, 1967–1970* (London, 1999)

—, *Memories* (London, 1981)

Paul Oppé, A., 'Art', in G. M. Young (ed.), *Early Victorian England, 1830–1865* (Oxford, 1934), ii, pp. 99–176

Pedersen, S. and Mandler, P. (eds), *After the Victorians: Private Conscience and Public Duty in Modern Britain. Essays in Memory of John Clive* (London, 1994)

Perkin, H., *The Origins of Modern English Society, 1780–1880* (London, 1963)

Perugini, M. E., *Victorian Days and Ways* (London, 1932)

Pevsner, N., *Pioneers of Modern Design: From William Morris to Walter Gropius* (1936 and subsequent revisions; Harmondsworth, 1991)

—, *The Englishness of English Art* (1956; Harmondsworth, 1993)

Philips, S. and Haywood, I., *Brave New Causes: Women in British Post-War Fictions* (London, 1998)

Pimlott, B., *The Queen: A Biography of Elizabeth II* (London, 1996)

*Plays of the Sixties* (London, 1985)

Ponsonby, F., *Sidelights on Queen Victoria* (London, 1930)

Priestley, J. B., *The Edwardians* (Harmondsworth, 2000)

Proust, M., *Swann's Way* (trans. C. K. Scott-Moncrieff; Harmondsworth, 1957)

Quinault, R, 'Britain 1950', *History Today*, 51 (April 2001), pp. 14–21

Ramsay, A. A. W., *Sir Robert Peel* (London, 1928)

Raverat, G., *Period Piece: A Cambridge Childhood* (London, 1952)

Read, D., *Peel and the Victorians* (Oxford, 1987)

Reith, J. C. W., *Broadcast Over Britain* (London, 1925)

Rhys, J., *Wide Sargasso Sea* (1966; Harmondsworth, 1997)

Richards, J., 'National Identity Post-War' and 'Dickens – Our Contemporary', in *Films and British National Identity, from Dickens to Dad's Army* (Manchester, 1997), pp. 128–46, 326–50

—, *The Age of the Dream Palace: Cinema and Society in Britain, 1930–1939* (London, 1984)

Richards, J. and Sheridan, D. (eds), *Mass-Observation at the Movies* (London, 1987)

Richardson, A. E., 'Architecture', in G. M. Young (ed.), *Early Victorian England, 1830–1865* (Oxford, 1934), ii, pp. 179–247

Ricketts, H., *The Unforgiving Minute: A Life of Rudyard Kipling* (London, 1999)

Ricks, C. (ed.), *The New Oxford Book of Victorian Verse* (Oxford, 1987)

Robbins, K., *Appeasement* (2nd edn, London, 1997)

—, 'History, the Historical Association and the "National Past"', *History*, 66 (1981), pp. 413–25.

—, *Nineteenth-Century Britain: Integration and Diversity* (Oxford, 1988)

—, *The Abolition of War: The 'Peace Movement' in Britain, 1914–1919* (Cardiff, 1976)

Roberts, A., *Salisbury: Victorian Titan* (London, 2000)

Roberts, M., 'Proper History and Sixth-Form History', *History Today*, 51 (November 2001), pp. 36–37

Robinson, R. and Gallagher, J., *Africa and the Victorians: The Official Mind of Imperialism* (London, 1965)

Rolph, C. H., *Books in the Dock* (London, 1969)

—, *The Trial of Lady Chatterley: Regina v. Penguin Books Limited* (Harmondsworth, 1961)

Rose, J., *The Intellectual Life of the British Working Classes* (New Haven and London, 2001)

Rose, K., *King George V* (London, 1983)

Rothblatt, S., 'G. M. Young: England's Historian of Culture', *Victorian Studies*, 22 (1978–79), pp. 413–29

Rowntree, B. S. and Lavers, G. R., *English Life and Leisure: A Social Study* (London, 1952)

Rubinstein, W. D., *Capitalism, Culture and Decline in Britain, 1750–1990* (London, 1993)

Ruskin, J., *Sesame and Lilies* (1865; London, 1909)

Russell, J., 'Lytton Strachey', *Horizon*, 15 (1947), pp. 91–116

Sage, L., *Bad Blood* (London, 2000)

Samuel, R., 'Mrs Thatcher's Return to Victorian Values', in T. C. Smout (ed.), *Victorian Values* (Oxford, 1992), pp. 9–29

—, (ed.), *Patriotism: The Making and Unmaking of British National Identity* (London, 1989)

—, *Theatres of Memory*, i, *Past and Present in Contemporary Culture* (London, 1994); ii, *Island Stories* (London, 1999)

—, 'The Workshop of the World: Steam Power and Hand Technology in Mid-Victorian Britain', *History Workshop Journal*, 3 (1977), pp. 6–72

Sanders, C. R., 'Lytton Strachey and the Victorians', *Modern Language Quarterly*, 15 (1954), pp. 326–42

—, 'Lytton Strachey's Conception of Biography', *PMLA*, 66 (1951), pp. 295–315

—, 'Lytton Strachey's "Point of View"', *PMLA*, 68 (1953), pp. 75–94

Sassoon, S., *The Complete Memoirs of George Sherston* (1937; London, 1972)

—, *The Old Century and Seven More Years* (1938; London, 1968)

Schlicke, P. (ed.), *Oxford Reader's Companion to Dickens* (Oxford, 2000)

Schreuder, D. M., 'The Making of Mr Gladstone's Posthumous Career: The Role of Morley and Knaplund as "Monumental Masons", 1903–27', in B. L. Kinzer (ed.), *The Gladstonian Turn of Mind: Essays Presented to J. B. Conacher* (Toronto, 1985), pp. 197–243

Schumpeter, J., *Imperialism and the Social Classes* (Oxford, 1951)

Searle, G. R., *The Liberal Party: Triumph and Disintegration, 1910–1929* (Basingstoke, 1992)

Seton-Watson, R. W., *Disraeli, Gladstone and the Eastern Question: A Study in Diplomacy and Party Politics* (London, 1935)

Shannon, R., *Gladstone*, i, *Peel's Inheritor, 1809–1865* (Harmondsworth, 1999); ii, *Heroic Minister, 1865–1898* (Harmondsworth, 2000)

Shaw, B., *A Mid-Victorian Trifle: A One-Act Comedy for Five Women* (London, 1940)

Shaw, R. and G., 'The Cultural and Social Setting', in B. Ford (ed.), *The Cambridge Cultural History of Britain*, ix, *Modern Britain* (Cambridge, 1992), pp. 1–44

Shelley, M., *Frankenstein* (1818; Harmondsworth, 1992)

Shuter, J. and Hook, A., *Victorian Britain* (Oxford, 1992)

Sillitoe, A., *Life Without Armour: An Autobiography* (London, 1995)

Sinfield, A., *The Wilde Century: Effeminacy, Oscar Wilde and the Queer Moment* (New York, 1994)

Sked, A. and Cook, C., *Post-War Britain: A Political History* (4th edn, Harmondsworth, 1993)

Skidelsky, R., *John Maynard Keynes: The Economist as Saviour, 1920–1937* (London, 1994)

Slater, M., *An Intelligent Person's Guide to Dickens* (London, 1999)

—, 'Dickens, 1870–1970; 1920–1940: "Superior Folk" and Scandalmongers', *The Dickensian*, 66 (1970), pp. 121–42

Smith, G., 'The Life and Times of Charles Dickens', in J. O. Jordan (ed.), *The Cambridge Companion to Charles Dickens* (Cambridge, 2001), pp. 1–15

Smith, P., *Disraeli: A Brief Life* (Cambridge, 1996)

Snowdon, *Snowdon on Stage* (London, 1996)

Soffer, R. N., 'The Conservative Historical Imagination in the Twentieth Century', *Albion*, 28 (1996), pp. 1–17

—, 'The Modern University and National Values, 1850–1930', *Bulletin of the Institute of Historical Research*, 60 (1987), pp. 166–87

Spalding, F., *Duncan Grant: A Biography* (London, 1998)

Spender, J. A., *Mr Gladstone* (London, 1937)

Stapleton, J., 'Political Thought, Elites, and the State in Modern Britain', *Historical Journal*, 42 (1999), pp. 251–68

Stead, W. T., *Her Majesty the Queen: Studies of the Sovereign and the Reign* (London, 1897)

Stedman Jones, G., *Languages of Class: Studies in English Working-Class History* (Cambridge, 1983)

Steele, T., *The Emergence of Cultural Studies, 1945–65: Cultural Politics, Adult Education and the 'English' Question* (London, 1997)

Stevenson, J. and Cook, C., *Britain in the Depression: Society and Politics, 1929–1939* (2nd edn, London, 1994)

Stoker, B., *Dracula* (1897; Oxford, 1996)

Stoppard, T., *The Invention of Love* (London, 1997)

Strachey, L., 'A Victorian Critic', in *Characters and Commentaries* (London, 1933), pp. 187–94

—, 'Carlyle' and 'A Russian Humorist', in M. Holroyd and P. Levy (eds), *The Shorter Strachey* (London, 1989), pp. 99–105, 183–87

—, *Elizabeth and Essex: A Tragic History* (1928; Harmondsworth, 2000)

—, *Eminent Victorians* (London, 1918) and (Harmondsworth, 1986)

—, 'Lancaster Gate' (1922), in M. Holroyd (ed.), *Lytton Strachey by Himself: A Self-Portrait* (London, 1971), pp. 16–28

—, *Queen Victoria* (London, 1921)

—, 'Six English Historians', in *Portraits in Miniature* (London, 1931), pp. 141–218

Strong, R., *The Roy Strong Diaries, 1967–1987* (London, 1998)

Stuart Roberts, J., *Siegfried Sassoon* (London, 1999)

Sutherland, J., *Offensive Literature: Decensorship in Britain, 1960–1982* (London, 1982)

Sweet, M., *Inventing the Victorians* (London, 2001)

Tanitch, R., *Oscar Wilde on Stage and Screen* (London, 1999)

Tanner, D., *Political Change and the Labour Party, 1900–1918* (Cambridge, 1990)

Taylor, A. J. P., *English History, 1914–1945* (Oxford, 1965)

Taylor, D. J., *Thackeray* (London, 2000)

Taylor, J., 'Greed: The Way They Lived Then', *BBC History Magazine*, 2 (December 2001), pp. 40–42

Thomas, I., *Gladstone of Hawarden: A Memoir of Henry Neville, Lord Gladstone of Hawarden* (London, 1936)

Thompson, D., *Queen Victoria: Gender and Power* (London, 2001)

Thompson, E. P., *William Morris: Romantic to Revolutionary* (London, 1955)

Thompson, F., *Lark Rise to Candleford* (1945; Harmondsworth, 1973)

Thorpe, J., *Happy Days: Recollections of an Unrepentant Victorian* (London, 1933)

Tosh, J., *A Man's Place: Masculinity and the Middle-Class Home in Victorian England* (New Haven and London, 1999)

Trevor-Roper, H. R., 'Lytton Strachey as Historian', in *Historical Essays* (London, 1957), pp. 279–84

Valentine, L., *The Queen: Her Early Life and Reign* (London, 1887)

Vallone, L., *Becoming Victoria* (New Haven and London, 2001)

Vansittart, P., *In the Fifties* (London, 1995)

Vincent, J., *Disraeli* (Oxford, 1990)

—, *The Formation of the Liberal Party, 1857–1868* (London, 1965)

Waldrep, S., 'The Uses and Misuses of Oscar Wilde', in J. Kucich and D. F. Sadoff (eds), *Victorian Afterlife: Postmodern Culture Rewrites the Nineteenth Century* (Minneapolis, 2000), pp. 49–63

Walkowitz, J., *City of Dreadful Delight: Narratives of Sexual Danger in Late Victorian London* (London, 1992)

Walvin, J., *Victorian Values* (London, 1987)

Ward, A. C., *The Nineteen-Twenties: Literature and Ideas in the Post-War Decade* (London, 1930)

Waters, C., 'Gender, Family, and Domestic Ideology', in J. O. Jordan (ed.), *The Cambridge Companion to Charles Dickens* (Cambridge, 2001), pp. 120–35

Waugh, E., *The Ordeal of Gilbert Pinfold* (1957; Harmondsworth, 1998)

—, *Vile Bodies* (1930; Harmondsworth, 1996)

Webster, C. K., 'The Accession of Queen Victoria', *History*, 22 (1937–38), pp. 14–33

Weeks, J., *Sex, Politics and Society: The Regulation of Sexuality since 1800* (London, 1981)

Weintraub, S., *Victoria* (revised edn, London, 1996)

Wells, H. G., *Ann Veronica* (London, 1909)

West, J., *A History of the Chartist Movement* (London, 1920)

White, C. W., 'The Strange Death of Liberal England in its Time', *Albion*, 17 (1985), pp. 425–47

White, T. H., *Farewell Victoria* (1933; London, 1993)

Wiener, M. J., *English Culture and the Decline of the Industrial Spirit, 1850–1980* (Cambridge, 1981)

Wilde, O., *Complete Works of Oscar Wilde* (revised edn, London, 1994)

—, *De Profundis* (1897; Harmondsworth, 1986)

—, *The Picture of Dorian Gray* (1891; Harmondsworth, 1985)

Williamson, H. R., *Mr Gladstone: A Play in Three Acts* (London, 1937)

Williamson, P., 'The Doctrinal Policies of Stanley Baldwin', in M. Bentley (ed.), *Public and Private Doctrine: Essays Presented to Maurice Cowling* (Cambridge, 1993), pp. 181–208

—, *Stanley Baldwin: Conservative Leadership and National Values* (Cambridge, 1999)

Wilson, A. N., *Eminent Victorians* (London, 1989)

Wilson, E., 'Dickens: The Two Scrooges' (1940), in *The Wound and the Bow* (Boston, 1941), pp. 1–93

Winston, J., 'Queen Victoria in the *Funnyhouse*: Adrienne Kennedy and the Rituals of Colonial Possession', in M. Homans and A. Munich (eds), *Remaking Queen Victoria* (Cambridge, 1997), pp. 235–57

Wodehouse, P. G., *Summer Moonshine* (1937; Harmondsworth, 1996)

Woods, G., *A History of Gay Literature: The Male Tradition* (New Haven and London, 1998)

Woodward, L., 'The Rise of the Professorial Historian in England', in K. Bourne and D. C. Watt (eds), *Studies in International History* (London, 1967), pp. 16–34

Woolf, V., 'Mr Bennett and Mrs Brown' (1924), in *Collected Essays*, i (London, 1980), pp. 319–37

—, *Night and Day* (1919; Harmondsworth, 1992)

—, *Orlando* (1928; Harmondsworth, 1993)

—, 'The Art of Biography' (1939), in *The Crowded Dance of Modern Life* (Harmondsworth, 1993), pp. 144–51

—, *To the Lighthouse* (1927; Oxford, 1992)

Wright, A., *Foreign Country: The Life of L. P. Hartley* (London, 1996)

Wright, P., *On Living in an Old Country: The National Past in Contemporary Britain* (London, 1985)

Wright, P. E., *Portraits and Criticisms* (London, 1925)

Wright, T., 'In the Mouth of Fame', *Times Literary Supplement*, 9 February 2001

Young, G. M., '1837–1937: Centenary of Queen Victoria's Accession' (1937) and 'The Greatest Victorian' (1938), in *Victorian Essays* (Oxford, 1962), pp. 13–35, 123–28

—, *Portrait of an Age: Victorian England* (2nd edn, Oxford, 1953)

—, 'Victorian History' (1932), in *Selected Modern English Essays* (Oxford, 1932), pp. 261–77

Ziegler, P., *Britain Then and Now: The Francis Frith Collection* (London, 1999)

—, *London at War, 1939–1945* (London, 1995)

# Index

*Titles have been omitted except where original names might be confusing*